Where to Live in London

SARA McCONNELL

SIMON & SCHUSTER

London . New York . Sydney . Tokyo . Singapore . Toronto . Dublin

A VIACOM COMPANY

Published in Great Britain by Simon & Schuster UK Ltd
A Viacom Company

First published 1999
Second edition 2000
Third edition 2001

1 3 5 7 9 10 8 6 4 2

Simon & Schuster UK Ltd
Africa House
64-78 Kingsway
London WC2B 6AH

Text design: Rachel Hardman Carter
Typeset by Textype
Printed and bound in Italy

A CIP catalogue record for this book is available from the British Library

ISBN 0 743 4 1531 0
(ISBN 0 671 0 3333 6 1st edition)
(ISBN 0 743 4 0919 1 2nd edition)

Also published in this series:
The London Pub & Bar Guide
Children's London
Where to Get the Look: Shopping for the home in London
Weekend Breaks

All information was checked and correct at press time. London is a constantly
changing city however so some of the information may change over time.

CONTENTS

MAP 5

Havering

Barking &
Dagenham

Bexley

INTRODUCTION

How do you make sense of London? It's one of the world's largest cities, teeming with 7 million people, stretching over more than 600 square miles of the south east of England. But it's incoherent, haphazard and almost totally unplanned. Most Londoners live in homes flung up by generations of speculative builders on any piece of spare land they could find. The capital's outward sprawl, unchecked for most of its history, has sucked up any settlement lying in its path and covered fields and woods with bricks and mortar. Expensive houses sit cheek by jowl with council blocks, respectable suburbs are just a couple of stops on the bus away from industrial estates, factories and warehouses. And to confuse things further, London's social landscape is constantly changing as new areas become fashionable and injections of government cash resuscitate areas left derelict by the disappearance of traditional industries.

All this makes the decision of where to live in London a daunting one. If you don't know London, where do you start? If you know your own bit of it but want or need to move elsewhere, what are your options?

This book will help you to answer these vital questions. It's not solely a property guide although it does of course contain information about the cost of buying and renting and the types of property in each area. Its main aim is to paint a physical, social and economic portrait of all the main areas of Greater London. What do places look like? Who lives there? Where's cheap and where's expensive? Are they fashionable, up-and-coming, rich, poor, suburban or cutting-edge trendy? What are the shops and schools like? How quickly can you get to the centre of town? How much greenery is there and what is there to do in your spare time? How easy is it to park and how much does it cost? What are the crime levels? And how efficient (and expensive) is the council? It makes no apology for being opinionated but opinions are backed by a range of factual information and statistics.

HOW THE BOOK WORKS

The book is based on London's 32 boroughs plus the City of London, with a chapter devoted to each borough. The borough you live in can have a dramatic impact on the amount of council tax you pay as well as the standards of local schools and other amenities. But despite their importance to the daily lives of millions, the boroughs are seen as distant bureaucracies with arbitrarily drawn boundaries which slice through more familiar local areas. So each borough has been broken down into five or six main areas, which provide the main focus for the chapter. Consult the at-a-glance list of areas with their boroughs on pages 10 and 11 to locate the places you're interested in. If an area straddles a borough boundary (Highgate for example falls into more than one borough), it will be dealt with under the borough responsible for its largest part. If an area falls equally into two boroughs (Blackheath and Thamesmead for example), it will be mentioned under both boroughs with cross references where necessary.

THE CHAPTERS

Each chapter tells you where the borough is, the areas contained within its boundaries and what sort of people live there, as well as information on the borough's ethnic makeup, unemployment rates, plans for regeneration and investment and local issues.

PROPERTY AND ARCHITECTURE

This isn't intended to be an exhaustive street-by-street guide but rather a pen portrait of the main types of property, broken down into areas, along with prices for buying and renting. These are only meant to give you an idea: London prices change constantly and these are a snapshot of the market in the last months of 2000. Buying prices fell slightly in London over the latter part of 2000 but estate agents were predicting that they would start to rise again in 2001. Rentals are quoted weekly which is common practice in central and inner London although many agents in outer London will quote per calendar month. The section shows which places are good for flats, which for houses, which places are favoured by families, which by first-time buyers or professional couples without children. If certain types of property (studios for example) aren't mentioned, this is because they either don't exist in the area or are very rare. Consult the at-a-glance guide on pages 12 and 13 to help you locate areas suitable for you. Remember that factors such as transport links have a big impact on prices, which is why the arrival of new links such as the Jubilee Line extension, the Docklands Light Railway extension and the Croydon Tramlink are dealt with at some length and proposed links like the East London Line extension are mentioned frequently. This section also lists conservation areas, which look attractive but which can be tricky if you want to alter your property.

POSTCODES

There's big postcode snobbery in some parts of London which can bump up or reduce prices by thousands of pounds. Each chapter has a pecking order of the best postcodes in the borough.

BOROUGH AMENITIES

Graded with a star system, with * being the lowest and *****
the highest and best. The grades are based on evidence which is both objective or semi-objective (performance statistics, league tables, extent of provision) and subjective (evidence of the author's own eyes, opinions of residents).

SCHOOLS

League tables may be controversial but they're all parents have to compare one school and one borough with another. The top three state primaries and the top three state secondaries in each borough in the latest (2000) league tables are listed. There is also an overall league table performance ranking for each borough's primary and secondary schools. This shows how each borough's schools have performed collectively compared to other local education authorities in England. There are 150 local primary education authorities and 149 local secondary education authorities. In the collective league tables, 1 is best and 149 or 150 worst. Private prep and secondary schools are listed, as are the numbers of state and private nurseries and playgroups and the proportion of under-fives in state nurseries. Boroughs are working toward offering all four year-olds a nursery place.

TRANSPORT

Includes details of public transport (trains, tubes, Docklands Light Railway) with cost and speed of direct journeys to central London from the main areas of each borough, using an annual Travelcard. Train journey times are measured to the nearest London terminus, while tube journey times are measured to a convenient central point reachable without changing lines. The section also lists main bus routes to town, traffic troublespots, and the cost and location of controlled parking zones where you have to buy a resident's parking permit. Other parking costs (car parks, meters) aren't included. Controlled parking zones are spreading like wildfire so you're likely to end up paying for the privilege of parking outside your own front door.

LEISURE FACILITIES

Lists theatres, concert halls, cinemas, museums, art galleries, local authority-run sports facilities and libraries. But this doesn't claim to be a listings book so clubs and some smaller theatres and temporary arts events (festivals or one-off performances) have been excluded as have private gyms and health clubs. Consult the Evening Standard's Hot Tickets Supplement for weekly listings.

GREEN SPACE

A run-down of the general state and nature of the parks, woods and greenery in each borough with personally tested recommendations for visits. But borough boundaries are strictly observed and nothing outside the greater London limit is included.

SHOPS & RESTAURANTS

A description of the main shopping centres and streets of each borough, including their physical appearance, the types of shops on offer and a (not exhaustive) list of the main superstores. As elsewhere, London's shopping is becoming depressingly uniform as major chains take over. The restaurant section indicates, places where restaurants are plentiful or otherwise but doesn't list or test individual restaurants.

THE COUNCIL

Includes each borough's political affiliation and its plus and minus points (general efficiency at administration, rubbish collection, street-sweeping, recycling, turnaround and charges for property searches, collection of council tax), and a complete list of council tax charges for 2000-2001. By law, all councils now have to publish an annual performance report to their council tax payers, showing how they compare with other London boroughs on a wide range of performance indicators, from how quickly they answer the telephone to how many rubbish collections they miss. These reports, which you can find in your local library, at the town hall or on your council's website (see useful addresses at the end of this book), provide a wealth of useful information, although some boroughs make more effort to communicate clearly with residents than others.

SOME STATISTICAL EXPLANATIONS

See page 7 for explanations of school league tables. The average proportion of under-fives in state nurseries in London is 59%. The average number of library visits is 6.96 per head of population. Library-use league tables don't include the City of London because figures are distorted by the large daytime population. In the rankings, 1st is best and 32 worst. In the Metropolitan Police crime statistics tables, 1 is worst and 32 best. Again, the figures don't include the City of London because the City has its own police force and isn't under the jurisdiction of the Metropolitan Police.

This is the third edition of this book. The original book was the result of six months of walking the streets of every London borough, from the grandest streets of Belgravia or Mayfair to the bleak Victorian terraces and tower blocks of Erith or Edmonton. For this edition, I revisited the main areas of every borough, on foot and using public transport. It says a lot for London that I have only once felt fearful for my own safety. And London's public transport system may not be perfect but it's got me there, to every corner.

SOURCES

Employment figures: London Research Centre

Deprivation index: Department of the Environment, Transport and the Regions 1998

Ethnic minorities: Census figures 1991, London Research Centre

Performance statistics: Proportion of under-fives in state nursery education, library use, turnaround of property searches, standard search fees, council tax collected: Audit Commission: local authorities' performance indicators 1998-99 (latest audited figures available at time of going to press)

Pre-school provision: individual London boroughs and What School 1998–1999, On Course Publications

School League Tables: Secondary Schools, Department for Education and Science Listings 2000, Primary Schools DfEE listings 2000

Private Prep and Secondary Schools: The Independent Schools Information Service (ISIS)

Train and Tube information: local transport guides. London Transport 1999-2000

Residents' parking costs, council tax rates, regeneration initiatives: individual London boroughs

Crime figures: Metropolitan Police, 2000

Maps: Nicholson, Greater London 5 sheet series, 1995; Nicholson Greater London Street Atlas 1997; Collins London Street Plan 1998

ACKNOWLEDGEMENTS

I would like to thank the many people who have given up their time to answer questions and share their knowledge of London, including hundreds of estate agents, the staff of all the London Boroughs and the City, and individual residents, especially Dee Mitchell. Special thanks go to Peter Haler, Jenny Bloom, John Nicholson and Suresh Karthigesu who gave up valuable time to drive me round their home boroughs for the first edition of this book, and to Emily who has put up with more months of maps, notebooks and walking boots for this latest edition and provided constant support and encouragement.

LONDON AREAS AT A GLANCE

AREA	BOROUGH	AREA	BOROUGH
Abbey Wood	Greenwich	East Dulwich	Southwark
Acton	Ealing	East Greenwich	Greenwich
Addiscombe	Croydon	East Ham	Newham
Anerley	Bromley	East Sheen	Richmond upon Thames
		Edgware	Barnet
Balham	Wandsworth	Edmonton	Enfield
Barbican	City of London	Elephant & Castle	Southwark
Barking	Barking & Dagenham	Eltham	Greenwich
Barnes	Richmond upon Thames	Enfield Town	Enfield
Barnet	Barnet	Erith	Bexley
Barons Court	Hammersmith & Fulham		
Battersea	Wandsworth	Farnborough	Bromley
Bayswater	Westminster	Feltham	Hounslow
Beckenham	Bromley	Finchley	Barnet
Beckton	Newham	Finsbury	Islington
Becontree	Barking & Dagenham	Finsbury Park	Haringey, Camden,
Beddington	Sutton		Islington
Bedford Park	Hounslow, Ealing	Fleet Street	City of London
Belgravia	Westminster	Forest Gate	Newham
Belsize Park	Camden	Forest Hill	Lewisham
Belvedere	Bexley	Fulham	Hammersmith & Fulham
Bermondsey	Southwark		
Bethnal Green	Tower Hamlets	Gants Hill	Redbridge
Bexley	Bexley	Gidea Park	Havering
Bexleyheath	Bexley	Gipsy Hill	Lambeth
Blackfen	Bexley	Golders Green	Barnet
Blackheath	Lewisham, Greenwich	Goodmayes	Redbridge
Bloomsbury	Camden	Greenford	Ealing
Borough	Southwark	Grove Park	Lewisham
Bow	Tower Hamlets	Gunnersbury	Hounslow
Brentford	Hounslow		
Brixton	Lambeth	Hackney	Hackney
Brockley	Lewisham	Hadley Wood	Enfield
Bromley	Bromley	Hainault	Redbridge
Brondesbury	Brent	Ham	Richmond upon Thames
		Hammersmith	Hammersmith & Fulham
Camberwell	Southwark	Hampstead	Camden
Camden Town	Camden	Hampstead Garden	
Carshalton Beeches	Sutton	Suburb	Barnet
Carshalton Village	Sutton	Hanwell	Ealing
Catford	Lewisham	Hanworth	Hounslow
Chadwell Heath	Barking & Dagenham	Harold Hill	Havering
Charlton	Greenwich	Harrow	Harrow
Cheam	Sutton	Harrow-on-the Hill	Harrow
Chelsea	Kensington & Chelsea	Hatch End	Harrow
Chelsea Harbour	Hammersmith & Fulham	Havering atte Bower	Havering
Chessington	Kingston	Hayes (Kent)	Bromley
Chingford	Waltham Forest	Hayes (Middlesex)	Hillingdon
Chislehurst	Bromley	Hendon	Barnet
Chiswick	Hounslow	Highams Park	Waltham Forest
Clapham	Lambeth	Highbury	Islington
Clapton	Hackney	Highgate	Haringey, Camden
Clayhall	Redbridge	Hillingdon	Hillingdon
Clerkenwell	Islington	Hither Green	Lewisham
Colliers Wood	Merton	Holborn	Camden
Coombe	Kingston	Holland Park	Kensington & Chelsea
Coulsdon	Croydon	Hornchurch	Havering
Covent Garden	Westminster	Hornsey	Haringey
Cricklewood	Brent	Hounslow	Hounslow
Crouch End	Haringey	Hoxton	Hackney
Dagenham	Barking & Dagenham	Ickenham	Hillingdon
Dalston	Hackney	Ilford	Redbridge
Dartmouth Park	Camden	Isle of Dogs	Tower Hamlets
De Beauvoir Town	Hackney	Isleworth	Hounslow
Deptford	Lewisham	Islington	Islington
Dollis Hill	Brent		
Dulwich	Southwark	Kennington	Lambeth
		Kensington	Kensington & Chelsea
Ealing	Ealing	Kentish Town	Camden, Islington
Earls Court	Kensington & Chelsea	Kenton	Brent
Earlsfield	Wandsworth	Keston	Bromley
Eastcote	Hillingdon	Kew	Richmond upon Thames
East Croydon	Croydon	Kidbrooke	Greenwich

AREA	BOROUGH
Kilburn	Brent
Kingsbury	Brent
Kings Cross	Camden
Kingston	Kingston
Knightsbridge	Westminster
Lee	Lewisham
Lewisham	Lewisham
Leyton	Waltham Forest
Leytonstone	Waltham Forest
Limehouse	Tower Hamlets
London Fields	Hackney
Maida Vale	Westminster
Manor Park	Newham
Marylebone	Westminster
Mayfair	Westminster
Mill Hill	Barnet
Mitcham	Merton
Morden	Merton
Mortlake	Richmond upon Thames
Muswell Hill	Haringey
Neasden	Brent
New Cross	Lewisham
New Eltham	Greenwich
New Malden	Kingston
Norbury	Croydon
Northolt	Ealing
North Ealing	Ealing
North Cheam	Sutton
North Kensington	Kensington & Chelsea
Northwood	Hillingdon
Notting Hill	Kensington & Chelsea
Nunhead	Southwark
Orpington	Bromley
Osterley	Hounslow
Paddington	Westminster
Palmers Green	Enfield
Parsons Green	Hammersmith & Fulham
Peckham	Southwark
Penge	Bromley
Petersham	Richmond upon Thames
Petts Wood	Bromley
Pimlico	Westminster
Pinner	Harrow
Plaistow	Newham
Plumstead	Greenwich
Ponders End	Enfield
Primrose Hill	Camden
Purley	Croydon
Putney	Wandsworth
Queens Park	Brent
Ravenscourt Park	Hammersmith & Fulham
Raynes Park	Merton
Richmond	Richmond upon Thames
Roehampton	Wandsworth
Romford	Havering
Rotherhithe	Southwark
Ruislip	Hillingdon
St Helier	Sutton
St John's Wood	Westminster
St Margarets	Richmond upon Thames
St Paul's	City of London
St Paul's Cray	Bromley
Selsdon	Croydon
Seven Kings	Redbridge
Shepherds Bush	Hammersmith & Fulham
Shirley	Croydon
Shoreditch	Hackney
Sidcup	Bexley
Silvertown	Newham
Soho	Westminster
Southall	Ealing
South Croydon	Croydon
Southfields	Wandsworth
Southgate	Enfield
South Kensington	Kensington & Chelsea
South Norwood	Croydon
South Wimbledon	Merton
South Woodford	Redbridge
Spitalfields	Tower Hamlets
Stamford Hill	Hackney
Stanmore	Harrow
Stockwell	Lambeth
Stoke Newington	Hackney
Stratford	Newham
Strawberry Hill	Richmond upon Thames
Streatham	Lambeth
Surbiton	Kingston
Sutton	Sutton
Sydenham	Lewisham
Teddington	Richmond upon Thames
The Hamptons	Richmond upon Thames
Thamesmead	Bexley, Greenwich
Thornton Heath	Croydon
Tolworth	Kingston
Tooting	Wandsworth
Tottenham	Haringey
Totteridge	Barnet
Tufnell Park	Islington
Twickenham	Richmond upon Thames
Upminster	Havering
Upper Holloway	Islington
Upper Norwood	Croydon
Upton	Newham
Uxbridge	Hillingdon
Victoria Park	Hackney
Wallington	Sutton
Walthamstow	Waltham Forest
Wandsworth	Wandsworth
Wanstead	Redbridge
Wapping	Tower Hamlets
Waterloo	Lambeth
Wealdstone	Harrow
Welling	Bexley
Wembley	Brent
West Chelsea	Kensington & Chelsea
West Ealing	Ealing
West Greenwich	Greenwich
West Ham	Newham
West Hampstead	Camden
West Kensington	Hammersmith & Fulham
West Kilburn	Westminster
West Norwood	Lambeth
West Wickham	Bromley
Whitechapel	Tower Hamlets
Whitton	Richmond upon Thames
Willesden	Brent
Willesden Green	Brent
Wimbledon	Merton
Wimbledon Village	Merton
Winchmore Hill	Enfield
Wood Green	Haringey
Woodside	Croydon
Woolwich	Greenwich

WHERE TO LIVE
AT A GLANCE

FIRST-TIME BUYERS & RENTERS

- Anerley
- Brockley
- Camberwell
- Catford
- Charlton
- Cricklewood
- Dalston
- Deptford
- East Dulwich
- East Greenwich
- East Ham
- Elephant & Castle
- Forest Gate
- Forest Hill
- Grove Park
- Ham
- Hayes (Middlesex)
- Hither Green
- Kilburn
- Leyton & Leytonstone
- Lewisham
- Manor Park
- New Cross
- Peckham
- Penge
- Plumstead
- Shepherds Bush
- Stratford
- South Norwood
- South Wimbledon
- Upton
- Upper Holloway
- Upper Norwood
- Walthamstow
- West Ealing
- West Norwood
- West Kilburn
- Willesden
- Woolwich

YOUNG PROFESSIONALS

- Acton
- Battersea
- Balham
- Bayswater
- Barbican
- Beckenham
- Belsize Park
- Bermondsey
- Bethnal Green
- Blackheath
- Bloomsbury
- Brentford
- Brixton
- Bromley
- Brondesbury
- Bow
- Camberwell
- Camden Town
- Chelsea Harbour
- Chiswick
- Clapham
- Clerkenwell
- Covent Garden
- Crouch End
- De Beauvoir Town
- Earls Court
- East Dulwich
- East Greenwich
- Fleet Street
- Finchley

- Finsbury Park
- Fulham
- Hackney
- Hammersmith
- Harrow on the Hill
- Highbury
- Holborn
- Hornsey
- Kennington
- Kensington
- Isleworth
- Isle of Dogs
- Islington
- Kew
- Kilburn
- Lee
- Limehouse
- London Fields
- Maida Vale
- Muswell Hill
- North Kensington
- Notting Hill
- Paddington
- Pimlico
- Queens Park
- Richmond
- Rotherhithe
- St Pauls
- Shepherds Bush
- Soho
- South Kensington
- Stockwell
- Stoke Newington
- Stratford
- Strawberry Hill
- Streatham
- Tooting
- Tufnell Park
- Twickenham
- Walthamstow
- Wapping
- Waterloo
- Wandsworth
- West Greenwich
- West Kensington
- West Kilburn
- Willesden Green
- Wimbledon

OVERSEAS RESIDENTS

- Acton (Japanese)
- Barnes (Swedish)
- Finchley (Japanese)
- Holland Park (international)
- Kensington (international)
- Knightsbridge (Europeans)
- Maida Vale (international)
- Mayfair (Americans, Greeks, Asians, Arabs)
- New Malden (Koreans)
- Richmond (Germans)
- Soho (Europeans)
- St John's Wood (Americans)
- South Kensington (Europeans, particularly French)
- Wimbledon (Norwegians)

FAMILIES

- Balham
- Barnes
- Barnet
- Beckenham
- Bexley
- Blackheath
- Bromley
- Brondesbury
- De Beauvoir Town
- Carshalton
- Chingford
- Chiswick
- Clapham
- Coulsdon
- Dulwich
- East Sheen
- Ealing
- Earlsfield
- Eltham
- Enfield
- Forest Hill
- Fulham
- Gidea Park
- Hammersmith
- Hampstead
- Hanwell
- Harrow
- Havering Atte Bower
- Hendon
- Highams Park
- Highgate
- Holland Park
- Hornchurch
- Ilford
- Kentish Town
- Kingsbury
- Kingston
- Kensington
- Kew
- Lee
- Mill Hill
- Mortlake
- Muswell Hill
- New Eltham
- New Malden
- North Ealing
- North Kensington
- Palmers Green
- Petersham
- Primrose Hill
- Purley
- Putney
- Richmond
- St John's Wood
- St Margarets
- Sidcup
- Southfields
- Southgate
- South Kensington
- South Woodford
- Stamford Hill
- Stanmore
- Stoke Newington
- Strawberry Hill
- Sutton
- Sydenham
- Teddington
- The Hamptons
- Tooting
- Tufnell Park
- Twickenham
- Teddington
- Upminster
- Victoria Park

Wallington
Wandsworth
Wanstead
Wembley
West Greenwich
West Hampstead
Wimbledon
Winchmore Hill
Woodford

GLITTERATI & NEW MONEY

Chislehurst
East Sheen
Hadley Wood
Hampstead Garden
  Suburb
Knightsbridge
Petersham
Totteridge
Winchmore Hill

ARTY-MEDIA-INTELLECTUAL TYPES

Barnes
Bermondsey
Blackheath
Borough
Brixton
Camberwell
Camden Town
Chelsea
Clerkenwell
Covent Garden
Greenwich
Hackney
Highbury
Hampstead
Hoxton
Islington
Kew
Notting Hill
Rotherhithe
Shoreditch
Soho
Spitalfields
Whitechapel

STOCKBROKERS, BANKERS & CAPTAINS OF INDUSTRY

Belgravia
Carshalton Beeches
Chelsea
Hampstead
Holland Park
Kensington
Knightsbridge
Marylebone
Mayfair
Northwood
St John's Wood

COMMUTER BELT

Beckenham
Bexley
Bromley
Carshalton Beeches
Cheam & North Cheam
Chislehurst
Eastcote
Croydon
Eltham
Gidea Park
Hayes (Kent)

Ickenham
New Eltham
Petts Wood
Pinner
Purley
Ruislip
Shirley
Sidcup
Surbiton
Orpington
Wallington

JEWISH

Clapton
Edgware
Gants Hill
Golders Green
Hampstead
Hampstead Garden
  Suburb
Hendon
Kingsbury
Mill Hill
St John's Wood
Stamford Hill
Stanmore
West Hampstead

ASIAN

East Ham
Forest Gate
Kenton
Ilford
Manor Park
Neasden
St John's Wood
Seven Kings
Southall
Stanmore
Upton
Wealdstone
Wembley

AFRO-CARIBBEAN

Brixton
Brockley
Camberwell
Catford
Deptford
Hither Green
Kilburn
Lewisham
New Cross
Plaistow
Tottenham
West Ham
West Kilburn

TURKISH & GREEK

Hornsey
Lewisham
Stoke Newington
Wood Green

PIEDS-A-TERRE

Borough
Chelsea
Covent Garden
Knightsbridge
Marylebone
Notting Hill
Soho
South Kensington
Stratford

BARGAIN BASEMENT

Becontree
Belvedere
Dagenham
Edmonton
Erith
Feltham
Goodmayes
Hainault
Hanworth
Harold Hill
Hayes (Middlesex)
Mitcham
Plumstead
Ponders End
St Helier
Seven Kings
Southall
Thamesmead
Thornton Heath
Whitechapel
Woolwich

AFFORDABLE HOUSES
(4-bedroom house under £200,000)

Abbey Wood
Bexleyheath
Catford
Chadwell Heath
Colliers Wood
East Ham
Erith
Forest Gate
Greenford
Grove Park
Harrow
Hither Green
Ilford
Leytonstone
Morden
Neasden
New Cross
Norbury
Northolt
Nunhead
Peckham
Plumstead
Romford
Southall
South Norwood
Thamesmead
Thornton Heath
Uxbridge
Welling
Woolwich
West Norwood

EXPENSIVE

Barnes
Belgravia
Chelsea
Hampstead
Highgate
Holland Park
Kensington
Knightsbridge
Islington
Mayfair
Notting Hill
Petersham
Richmond
South Kensington

BARKING AND DAGENHAM

Most of Barking and Dagenham is a vast sprawling council estate. Not 1960s concrete tower blocks and deck-access flats but miles of low, functional red brick terraces built by the London County Council on its Becontree estate between 1920 and 1938 to house workers, many from slums in the East End. Even on a sunny day, the estate, which covers a large part of the borough's central area, is bleak, despite the hedged small gardens and curving streets. With more recent council estates spreading up to the borough's northern tip and only a smattering of privately built property, the borough can boast no salubrious suburbs. It's mostly flat (this was marshland), its parks are municipal, its shops unexciting.

But if you want a cheap house on a fairly reliable tube or train line, Barking and Dagenham's a contender as one of the cheapest areas of London. Many of the houses were sold to their tenants under the right-to-buy scheme (the clues are in the new double-glazed windows, elaborate front doors and porches installed to proclaim their separateness from their council tenant neighbours). From Barking, the borough's main shopping and administrative centre in the west, the Becontree estate stretches in a rough square as far east as Dagenham and nearly as far north as the 1930s semis of Chadwell Heath. As a glance at the A-Z will tell you, this doesn't leave much else.

There are plans for 4,500 new homes, some privately owned and some earmarked for social housing, at Barking Reach by the river. By 2010 what is now mostly a stretch of derelict marshland is expected to be home to about 15,000 people.

Barking and Dagenham is mostly working class and mostly white. Only 7% of its population is from an ethnic minority, with Indians the largest single group. Unemployment is high compared with neighbouring outer London boroughs at 4.8% (although half that of Newham to the west) and the borough is the 15th most deprived in the country. Here people tuck into pie and mash not because it's trendy but because it's cheap, nourishing and filling. But although many residents originally came from the East End, they like to stress that Barking is Essex, nearly the country.

Like other eastern riverside boroughs, Barking's riverfront and tributaries were left decimated and contaminated by the death of London's traditional riverside industries. But money is pouring into regenerating riverfront sites along the River Roding west of Barking town centre and a total of £9 million is being invested in the Artscape Project, an ambitious public art and landscaping project for the main A13 trunk road running through the borough. Last year plans were announced to invest a massive £468 million over the next seven years to boost job opportunities and training and revamp the dreary environment round the Ford motor plant at Dagenham. But Ford's announcement that it wants to wind down operations at Dagenham have put the future of the area in doubt.

PROPERTY AND ARCHITECTURE

BARKING

A mixture of small Victorian terraces near the centre and larger Edwardian and inter-war houses in roads between the town centre and Mayesbrook Park. Some of the houses still have their original decorative iron porches and front doors but others have suffered from pebble-dashing, double-glazing, louvred windows and other unsightly alterations. The best roads are in the series of crescents west of Mayesbrook Park, on the Leftley estate, with slightly cheaper houses in the grids off Longbridge Road. Despite being main roads, Longbridge Road and Upney Lane are both popular for their large houses. New property built on Barking Reach is starting to come back onto the market and several big name developers are active in the area. There's lots of ex-council property alongside the privately built houses and property at the lower end of the price ranges given is mostly ex-council.

ATTRACTS *First-time buyers; loyal locals; investors* • **CONSERVATION AREAS** *Barking Abbey and Town Centre; Abbey Road riverside* • **AVERAGE PRICES** *Flats: studio £45,000-£50,000; 1-bed £40,000+; 2-bed £75,000+ Houses: 2-bed £70,000-£120,000; 3-bed £80,0000-£200,000; 4-bed £200,000+* • **AVERAGE RENTS (WEEKLY)** *Flats: 1-bed £105; 2-bed £115-£150 Houses: 2-bed £130-£150; 3-bed £160-£200; 4-bed £250-£300.*

BECONTREE & DAGENHAM

The long low red brick terraces of the Becontree estate, mostly two- and three-bedroom houses, predominate. The older ones towards Goodmayes and the border with Redbridge are built in a more cottagey style with deep eaves and small-paned windows. The later ones towards the centre and east are more functional and brutal. Some are set back from the roads around small squares and cul-de-sacs and the uniformity is broken by brick front door arches and passages to back gardens but the overall effect is still dreary. Some modern blocks in Dagenham mixed with 1930s speculatively-built terraces and semis.

ATTRACTS *Loyal locals; bargain hunters; first-time buyers* • **CONSERVATION AREA** *Dagenham Village* • **AVERAGE PRICES** *Flats: 1-bed £50,000-£55,000; 2-bed £65,000+ Houses: 2-bed £65,000-£110,000; 3-bed £85,000+* • **AVERAGE RENTS (WEEKLY)** *Flats: 1-bed £110; 2-bed £120-£125 Houses: 2-bed £130; 3-bed £145-£150.*

CHADWELL HEATH

"If you live in Dagenham, you think Chadwell Heath's posh," says one longstanding resident. Possibly. A fairly dreary collection of 1930s semis and terraces with some new blocks by the station. The main reason it's more up-market than Dagenham is because it has a certain snob value as

an area where many of the houses were originally privately built.
ATTRACTS *Loyal locals; local first-time buyers* ● **CONSERVATION AREA**
Chadwell Heath anti-aircraft gun site ● **AVERAGE PRICES** *Flats: studio
£45,000-£50,000; 1-bed £55,000-£60,000; 2-bed £70,000-£75,000
Houses: 2-bed £85,000-£90,000; 3-bed £115,000-£160,000;
4-bed £170,000-£190,000* ● **AVERAGE RENTS (WEEKLY)** *Flats:
studio £90-£95; 1-bed £115+; 2-bed £130+ Houses: 2-bed £130-£140;
3-bed £155-£160; 4-bed £180-£200.*

BEST POSTCODES
Irrelevant. Barking has Essex postcodes.

AMENITIES

SCHOOLS**

Not spectacular but improving at both primary and secondary level. No
single-sex secondary schools. The third most generous state provision for
under-fives in London. No private prep or secondary schools.
PRE-SCHOOL PROVISION *4 state day nurseries, 34 nursery classes in state
primary and church schools, 41 private and community day nurseries and
playgroups. Proportion of under-fives in state nurseries: 74%* ● **STATE
PRIMARY SCHOOLS** *Overall league table position: 75th out of 150. Top
scorers: St Theresa RC (with nursery unit), Dagenham; William Ford C of E,
Dagenham; St Margaret's CE (with nursery unit) Barking* ● **STATE
SECONDARY SCHOOLS** *Overall league table position: 117th out of 149. Top
scorers: Barking Abbey (mixed), Barking; All Saints Catholic School and
Technology College (mixed), Dagenham; The Warren (mixed), Chadwell
Heath*

TRANSPORT***

Pretty good in most parts of the borough, with District Line tubes and trains
running west to east. Lines peter out a bit further up though, with only trains
linking Chadwell Heath and central London.
TRAINS *Chadwell Heath Zone 5. Cost of annual season ticket £1332;
average journey time to Liverpool Street 23 minutes* ● **TUBES** *Barking
(District, Hammersmith & City) Zone 4. Cost of annual season ticket
£1104; average journey time to Liverpool Street 22 minutes, Baker Street
36 minutes. Dagenham Heathway (District) Zone 5. Average journey time
to Tower Hill 29 minutes, Embankment 37 minutes* ● **BUSES** *Vital if you want
to travel north to south within the borough, as all trains and tubes run east
to west. Generally efficient connections between Barking and Dagenham
and other nearby shopping centres like Romford. Not many buses into
town. Night bus services include the N25 from Trafalgar Square to
Chadwell Heath and the N15 from Trafalgar Square to Barking and
Becontree Heath* ● **TRAFFIC TROUBLESPOTS** *The A13: Trafficky at the best of
times since it's the main road into London from Essex and now even worse
while being upgraded. Heathway: The main north/south drag to
Dagenham shopping centre is cluttered with buses and delivery vans,
especially at rush-hour. Barking: The pedestrianised centre of Barking
around East Street pushes traffic out onto surrounding roads, causing traffic
back-ups around the nearby north circular which marks the borough's
western boundary* ● **PARKING** *There are controlled parking zones in*

Barking Town Centre and around tube stations in Upney, Becontree, Dagenham Heathway, Dagenham East and Chadwell Heath to stop unofficial park and riding. Cost of annual resident's permit: £15.

LEISURE FACILITIES * * *

THEATRES & CONCERT HALLS *The Broadway theatre in Barking has mostly local and family shows, golden oldie pop stars and amateur shows. Otherwise it's an out-of-borough trip to town or further out into Essex. Range of arts activities also at Eastbury Manor House, a National Trust-owned Elizabethan merchant's house in Barking* ● **CINEMAS** *Well endowed for a small borough although not a good bet if your idea of fun is a black and white French art movie. The six-screen Odeon opposite the station is an impressive newly painted modernist building showing mainstream films. More of the same at the Warner Village multiplex on the A13 in Dagenham* ● **MUSEUMS & GALLERIES** *Only one museum, Valence House, an attractive manor house dating in part from the 14th century with panelled rooms and a sweeping staircase. The local history museum is here although it's disappointingly small, particularly given the social interest of the development of the Becontree estate on its doorstep. A couple of moderately interesting mock-up rooms of typical Becontree estate homes of the 1930s. Collection of portraits and temporary exhibitions in the O'Leary Gallery. New gallery in Barking central library created as part of the A13 Artscape project* ● **SPORTS FACILITIES** *Plentiful. Three leisure centres, one at Barking and two at Dagenham. Pools at Dagenham and Barking, gyms and fitness centres at all three venues. Boating lake at Mayesbrook Park. Fishing at Eastbrookend Country Park. Tennis, football and other sports in parks across the borough* ● **LIBRARIES** *Handsome central library in Barking with helpful staff and reasonable opening hours in larger branch libraries throughout the borough. But some smaller branches are closed more than they're open, a classic sign of a borough strapped for cash. 4.17 library visits per head, although the Audit Commission expressed doubts about the borough's information collecting methods. Position in library use league table: 28th out of 32.*

OPEN SPACES * *

On paper there's reasonable open space, but in practice most of it's flat and drab, its lack of natural interest not enhanced by litter, graffiti and uncared-for park furniture. Mayesbrook Park is particularly bad in this respect, with piles of old litter by the boating lake and burnt-out benches. Not recommended as a pleasant place to sit.

WIDE OPEN SPACE *Eastbrookend Country Park. Created just five years ago from derelict land used first to provide gravel for the rebuilding of the Becontree estate after the estate was bombed during the blitz and then used as a dumping ground in the 60s and 70s. Now the borough's largest open space, with fishing lakes, wildlife and flat grasslands with big skies. The large Swedish-style building is the Millennium Centre for environmental education. Good if you want to get away from it all but can be slightly intimidating if you're alone.* ● **RIVER WALKS** *Watch out for continuing improvements and access to the River Roding.*

SHOPS * *

BARKING *A pleasant surprise. The borough's main shopping area has a recently built shopping centre, Vicarage Fields, in an elegant red brick* *building which unusually for such buildings looks as good from the back as it does from the front. Inside it has distinctive shopfronts, not just plate glass and some interesting shops, including jewellers, perfume shops and bookshops, although some of these seem to open and close again pretty swiftly. Indoor market on the ground floor. More down-market shops in the pedestrianised shopping streets around selling cheap clothes and 'fancy goods' with a number of boarded-up shops and to let signs. This whole town square area is set for a big revamp. Somerfields in the shopping centre ● CHADWELL HEATH The main 1930s shopping parade in the High Road could be quite distinguished if it was better maintained. Mostly local shops (cheap clothes, discount stores, furniture) mixed with the usual take-aways and banks. Big Sainsbury's ● DAGENHAM Pretty much the pits. A dreary parade of discount shops, gift shops and sewing shops (often seen in poorer areas) around Heathway Station and a strictly functional shopping mall (low ceilings, harsh lighting, lots of stubbed-out cigarette ends on the floor). Cheap chain stores with Poundstretcher and Poundstore dominating. Sainsbury's. Safeway at Beacontree Heath. A noticeable lack of ethnic stores.*

RESTAURANTS*

A culinary desert.

CRIME RATES***

Position in Metropolitan Police league table: 17th out of 32 (where 1 is worst and 32 best).

THE COUNCIL***

POLITICAL AFFILIATION *Labour* ● **MINUS POINTS** *Litter collection and street sweeping can be poor although rubbish collections are getting more efficient and are well rated by residents. Park maintenance poor. Slow turnaround of property searches* ● **PLUS POINTS** *Energetic participant in regeneration initiatives. High level of nursery provision. Door-to-door recycling being piloted in 22,000 homes, currently newspapers only but set to expand into other items* ● **PROPERTY SEARCHES CARRIED OUT IN 10 WORKING DAYS** *88.8%* ● **STANDARD SEARCH FEE** *£105.60* ● **COUNCIL TAX COLLECTED** *95.3%*

● **COUNCIL TAX 2000-2001**

BAND	PROPERTY VALUE	CHARGE	BAND	PROPERTY VALUE	CHARGE
A	up to £40,000	£523	E	£88,001-£120,000	£959
B	£40,001-£52,000	£610	F	£120,001-£160,000	£1,133
C	£52,001-£68,000	£697	G	£160,001-£320,000	£1,307
D	£68,001-£88,000	£784	H	over £320,000	£1,569

BARNET

Barnet is sleek and prosperous. Its schools are good, its green spaces plentiful, its crime low and many of its residents wealthy. The inner city stops well to the south of its borders, contained on the other side of the railway tracks in Brent and the other side of Hampstead Heath in Camden. Its northern boundaries merge smoothly into Hertfordshire. All safely middle class. But it manages to have more bite than the average commuter suburb, thanks mainly to its many distinctive ethnic and religious communities. Nearly a fifth of the population is from an ethnic minority. Barnet has one of the largest and most established Jewish communities in London as well as the largest Gujerati population, bringing a satisfyingly cosmopolitan feel to its suburban streets.

The borough is large. At its narrowest point in the south is the seriously wealthy Hampstead Garden Suburb and the slightly (but only slightly) more restrained areas of Hendon, Mill Hill and Golders Green, full of large detached 1930s houses with neat gardens. East of Mill Hill is the popular mostly Victorian suburb of Finchley. Further north, a large tract of fields and green space separates the council estates of Burnt Oak and the middling 1930s semis of Edgware from the expensive detached houses of Totteridge and the Georgian survivors of the suburban onslaught in Barnet and Hadley.

Most of Barnet grew up around the Northern Line tube which stretched out into Edgware and High Barnet in the early years of this century, turning fields and villages into roads and houses. It has little of the post-industrial legacy of unemployment that has devastated some parts of inner London, with unemployment standing at just 3.2%. This is the home of managers and middle managers, a solid family area, increasingly leavened by young professionals who favour the large Victorian properties of Finchley, and growing numbers of entrepreneurs. (Barnet claims to have more self-employed people within its borders than any other part of Greater London.)

The borough has the doubtful privilege of being home to the start of the M1 motorway, the first and still one of the busiest, and like other outer London boroughs parts of Barnet are carved up by dual carriageways carrying fast traffic. But this doesn't put residents off car ownership – rather the opposite, as most households have at least one car and use it frequently, if the traffic's anything to go by.

Walking as a means of getting from A to B comes into its own on the Jewish Sabbath when Orthodox Jews are forbidden to drive their cars and Golders Green Road is a flurry of furs, high heels and black Homberg hats after the end of synagogue services. But the Jewish community has met with fierce opposition in its attempts to create an *eruv*, an area in which Sabbath laws can be relaxed. The sticking point has been that the area's boundaries would be designated by tall poles linked with thin wire high above street level, which opponents say would be unsightly and dangerous. The council has approved the *eruv* but lawyers are still dotting the i's and crossing the t's.

PROPERTY AND ARCHITECTURE

HAMPSTEAD GARDEN SUBURB

This area just north of Hampstead Heath proper was created as a social experiment in the early years of the century by energetic social reformer Henrietta Barnett. The original idea was to have rich and poor living and working side by side in healthy and morally uplifting (no pubs) surroundings. But nowadays even the more modest cottagey properties around Denman Drive north of Big Wood are way beyond the reach of the poor and the large, gloomy houses round the Central Square are seriously expensive. The Suburb (as it's known locally) also has one of London's millionaire's rows, Bishops Avenue, home to princes, film stars and others with more money than taste. Lots of Dallas-style iron gates and porticoed, colonnaded porches but the overall effect is soulless. Few flats, mostly houses, partly because planners won't allow flat conversions in such a tightly controlled conservation area. A slightly self-conscious community, which was furious when it was portrayed on television as being obsessed with making sure residents didn't make any changes to their properties.
ATTRACTS *The wealthy and aristocratic; the Jewish community; families*
• **CONSERVATION AREAS** *Hampstead Garden Suburb: Hampstead Village (Spaniards End); Hampstead Village (Heath Passage)* • **AVERAGE PRICES** *Flats: 1-bed £135,000+; 2-bed £175,000-£300,000 Houses: 2-bed £250,000-£300,000; 3-bed £350,000+; 4-bed £450,000+* • **AVERAGE RENTS (WEEKLY)** *Flats: 1-bed £200+; 2-bed £250+ Houses: 2-bed £325+; 3-bed £375-£500; 4-bed £450-£800.*

GOLDERS GREEN

Home to many of Barnet's Jewish community. Lots of large detached and semi-detached Edwardian and between-the-wars houses and less overwhelming than Hampstead Garden Suburb. A varying choice of styles from arts and crafts red brick with leaded windows to 1930s up-market surburban with half-timbered gables. Some of the houses have been converted into synagogues. A good choice of flats in modern blocks, many on wide main roads. The cheaper parts are near the Brent Cross shopping centre and prices rise sharply the nearer you are to Hampstead Garden Suburb.
ATTRACTS *Members of the Jewish community; families* • **CONSERVATION AREAS** *none* • **AVERAGE PRICES** *Flats: 1-bed £115,000+; 2-bed £150,000+ Houses: 2-bed £160,000+; 3-bed £200,000+; 4-bed £250,000+*
• **AVERAGE RENTS (WEEKLY)** *Flats: studio £160+; 1-bed £180+; 2-bed £250+; Houses: 2-bed £270+; 3-bed £300+; 4-bed £400+.*

HENDON & MILL HILL

Both areas are cruelly carved up by roads (Mill Hill has the M1 at the end of its main shopping street) and the semis on the main roads are generally uninspiring. But large and handsome detached houses in large gardens take over as soon as you turn off. The roads are quiet and tree-lined and the cars in the drives expensive. Good views from roads round Church Road and The Burroughs in Hendon, which still have a handful of cottages and old buildings as a reminder of Hendon's beginnings as farmland. Mostly houses, with flats in modern blocks. Hendon tends to be a bit more expensive than Mill Hill because the transport links are better. But Mill Hill is considered more rural and has some good private schools. The most sought after parts of Mill Hill are in the grid of streets known as Poets Corner just off The Ridgeway.

ATTRACTS *Families; members of the Jewish community; young professionals (Hendon)* • **CONSERVATION AREAS** *Mill Hill; The Burroughs; Church End* • **AVERAGE PRICES** *Flats: studio £70,000-£90,000; 1-bed £80,000-£130,000; 2-bed £130,000-£260,000 Houses: 2-bed £180,000+; 3-bed £200,000-£400,000; 4-bed £280,000-£500,000* • **AVERAGE RENTS (WEEKLY)** *Flats: studio £120-£130; 1-bed £140-£180; 2-bed £230-£250 Houses: 3-bed £250-£350; 4-bed £300+.*

FINCHLEY

A sprawling area of Victorian and Edwardian terraces and villas, and the part of the borough of Barnet which feels most like London rather than suburbia or the Home Counties. A good place to look for conversions as many of the large red brick four-storey terraces have been divided up into flats. Central Finchley is the most consistently attractive part, with solid Victorian and Edwardian terraces. The nearer you go to Hampstead Garden Suburb in East Finchley, the more expensive it is. North Finchley is more suburban than East Finchley which has more of an inner city feel. The cheaper parts, including council property, are nearest the North Circular.

ATTRACTS *First-time buyers; young professionals; families; people who can't afford Highgate (East Finchley); Japanese who established themselves here when there was a Japanese school* • **CONSERVATION AREAS** *Church End; Finchley Garden Village; Moss Hall* • **AVERAGE PRICES** *Flats: studio £65,000-£85,000; 1-bed £90,000+; 2-bed £120,000+ Houses: 2-bed £170,000+; 3-bed £220,000+; 4-bed £250,000-£300,000* • **AVERAGE RENTS (WEEKLY)** *Flats: 1-bed £160-£170; 2-bed £180-£190 Houses: 3-bed £220-£230; 4-bed £250+.*

TOTTERIDGE

Totteridge's main road is called Totteridge Village but don't be misled. There's nothing villagey about it and no village centre, just a trafficky road lined with detached houses which get larger and grander as built-up areas give way to fields. The open space is the main attraction, tempting a fair smattering of pop stars, footballers and other celebrities to buy houses here. Few flats or small houses. The flats that do exist tend to be luxury rather than ordinary.

ATTRACTS *Families; minor celebrities* • **CONSERVATION AREAS** *Totteridge* • **AVERAGE PRICES** *Flats: 2-bed £300,000+ Houses: 2-bed £250,000+; 3-bed £300,000; 4-bed £500,000* • **AVERAGE RENTS (WEEKLY)** *Flats: 2-bed £300 Houses 3-bed £400+; 4-bed £1000+.*

EDGWARE

A mixture of middling 1930s semis, larger detached red brick houses in tree-lined roads and some newly built townhouses and apartment blocks.

Solid and unexciting. It never takes long to get to a major main road from almost anywhere in Edgware but the up side of this is that you can escape fairly effortlessly to the countryside. One of the cheaper areas of Barnet and a good place to look for family homes. Some good value homes in Burnt Oak on the council estate built by the LCC at the beginning of the century – you can pick up a three-bedroom house here for around £120,000.

ATTRACTS *Families; members of the Jewish community; investors*
• **CONSERVATION AREAS** *none* • **AVERAGE PRICES** *Flats: studio £65,000-£75,000; 1-bed £80,000-£90,000+; 2-bed £120,000+ Houses: 2-bed £145,000; 3-bed £170,000-£350,000; 4-bed £250,000+* • **AVERAGE RENTS (WEEKLY)** *Flats: studio £120; 1-bed £145+; 2-bed £170+ Houses: 3-bed £200+; 4-bed £350+.*

BARNET

Doesn't really feel like London at all but more like the market town it once was, with a curving main street of small shop buildings and a church looking out onto a green. Some large Victorian houses and smaller terraces off Wood Street near the centre of Barnet itself. Early 20th-century houses in roads west of Barnet Hill and a jumble of everything from large Victorian villas to modern blocks on the east towards New Barnet. The grandest houses in Barnet (and some of the loveliest in the borough) are Georgian townhouses facing onto Hadley Common on the way to Monken Hadley, which definitely feels villagey, with small white plastered and red brick cottages. High Barnet, round the high street and the tube station, is more expensive than New Barnet or Friern Barnet.

ATTRACTS *Families; members of the Jewish community* • **CONSERVATION AREAS** *Monken Hadley; Wood Street* • **AVERAGE PRICES** *Flats: studio £65,000-£70,000; 1-bed £85,000-£110,000; 2-bed £95,000-£150,000 Houses: 2-bed £150,000-£200,000; 3-bed £180,000-£350,000; 4-bed £250,000+* • **AVERAGE RENTS (WEEKLY)** *Flats: studio £100+; 1-bed £150+; 2-bed £180+ Houses: 2-bed £200+; 3-bed £250+; 4-bed £350+.*

BEST POSTCODES

The poshest postcode is Golders Green NW11 which includes Hampstead Garden Suburb. After this things get a bit more complicated because the postcode areas are mixed but Finchley N3, East Finchley N2, Hendon NW4 and Whetstone N20, which includes Totteridge, are all highly rated. Proximity to a tube line affects prices more than postcodes.

AMENITIES

SCHOOLS * * * *

Excellent in most respects. Very good league table performance from both primary and secondary schools with some chart-topping (and oversubscribed) state schools. A good selection of private schools. A wide choice of private nurseries. The proportion of under-fives with state nursery places is only average but still better than that of several surrounding boroughs.

PRE-SCHOOL PROVISION *4 state nursery schools; 38 state, Church and Jewish primary schools with nursery units; 89 private day nurseries and playgroups. Proportion of under-fives in state nurseries: 58%* • **STATE PRIMARY SCHOOLS** *Overall league table position: 7th out of 150. Top* scorers: Mathilda Marks-Kennedy, Hendon; St Paul's CE, Mill Hill; St Theresa's RC, Finchley • **STATE SECONDARY SCHOOLS** Overall league table position: 13th out of 149. Top scorers: (all selective); St Michael's Catholic Grammar (girls), Finchley; Henrietta Barnett (girls), Hampstead Garden Suburb; Queen Elizabeth's School for Boys, Barnet • **PRIVATE PREP SCHOOLS** Hendon Prep (mixed from 2), Hendon; Belmont (Mill Hill Junior, mixed), Mill Hill • **PRIVATE SECONDARY SCHOOLS** Mill Hill (mixed), Mill Hill; Mount (girls), Mill Hill; King Alfred School (mixed from 4), Golders Green; Beth Jacob Grammar School (girls), Golders Green; Menorah Grammar (boys), Golders Green; Pardes House (Jewish, top scorer, boys), Finchley.

TRANSPORT***

People can be lulled into thinking that the furthest flung parts of the borough are nearer than they are because they're on the Northern Line but the journey to High Barnet, Edgware or Mill Hill on the branch line is slow and tedious. The Northern Line has improved but still suffers from delays and overcrowding at rush hour. Some parts of the borough, notably Hampstead Garden Suburb, are a brisk walk from the tube (plans for a station here were scuppered by Henrietta Barnett who feared a rash of speculative building and bought up the land), but many of the wealthy residents probably don't feel the lack too deeply.

TRAINS Mill Hill Broadway Zone 4. Cost of annual season ticket £1104. Average journey time to Kings Cross (Thameslink) 18 minutes • **TUBES** Golders Green (Northern) Zone 3. Cost of annual season ticket £896. Average journey time to Euston 14 minutes. Edgware (Northern) Zone 5. Cost of annual season ticket £1332. Average journey time to Euston 27 minutes. Finchley Central (Northern) Zone 4. Average journey time to Euston 18 minutes. High Barnet Zone 6. Cost of annual season ticket £1456. Average journey time to Euston 27 minutes • **BUSES** Bus journeys to town can be slow, travelling up trafficky main roads, but unlike some outer London boroughs the services do at least go all the way to the centre. The southern parts, particularly Finchley, Mill Hill and Golders Green, are the best served. Crossing from one side of the borough to another is a frustrating experience as few buses venture across the open space in the middle. Services to town include the 113 from Edgware via Mill Hill and Hendon to Oxford Circus, the 82 from North Finchley via Golders Green to Victoria and the 43 from Friern Barnet to London Bridge • **TRAFFIC TROUBLESPOTS** Brent Cross: A surreal tangle of concrete bridges, flyovers, underpasses, roundabouts, pedestrian bridges and subways separates Brent Cross shopping centre from the rest of civilisation. Getting there on foot is a challenge but it's worse by car, particularly in the Saturday afternoon shopping crowds. Barnet: An otherwise attractive shopping street is blighted by long queues of traffic coming from the north straight down Barnet High Street. Hendon: Sliced into pieces by a dual carriageway, which forces pedestrians into subways. Long tail-backs particularly at the junction with the North Circular and the joining roads to the M1 • **PARKING** Six controlled parking zones in the borough in Golders Green, Edgware, High Barnet, Mill Hill, West Hendon and around the Brent Cross shopping centre. Further residents' parking zones in East Finchley and central Finchley are under consideration. Cost of annual resident's permit: £20 per vehicle.

LEISURE FACILITIES***

THEATRES & CONCERT HALLS *The Bull, housed in a small building with a recently revamped café in Barnet High Street, has plays, dance, stand-up comedy, an art gallery and children's shows. Lots of new plays and one man shows. Live music and classical concerts also at The Bull. There are plans for a new £11.4 million arts centre at Tally Ho Corner, North Finchley, which should massively improve Barnet's relatively low theatre provision, although the design of the building has proved controversial* • **CINEMAS** *The Phoenix Cinema in East Finchley has a mixture of mainstream West End hits and more rarefied repertory films on Sunday afternoons. Predictable programmes of blockbusters at UGC, Staples Corner, Warner Village, Finchley and the Edgware Cinemax* • **MUSEUMS & GALLERIES** *A small, fun, varied collection of specialist museums. The Museum of Jewish Life in Finchley has exhibitions of documents, photographs and oral history telling the social history of Jewish London. The Stephens Collection, the original house of Henry Stephens, of ink fame, has exhibitions of writing materials. If you crave more excitement, try flying a Tornado at the Royal Air Force Museum in Hendon. Local history in Barnet and at Church Farmhouse in Hendon, a mellow 17th-century reminder of Hendon's rural days. Mock-ups of 19th-century rooms including kitchen with very realistic-looking food* • **SPORTS FACILITIES** *Five leisure centres in Hendon (two including the youth sports centre), Barnet, Southgate (on Enfield borders, see Enfield) and North Finchley. Finchley has a lido with saunas, jacuzzis and fitness classes. Tennis and other outdoor sports in open spaces throughout the borough. Sailing, canoeing and windsurfing on Welsh Harp Reservoir (see also Brent)* • **LIBRARIES** *Well visited and well spaced throughout the borough. Opening hours are reasonable although there's some lunchtime closing in smaller branch libraries. Monday is not a good day. Sunday afternoon opening at Golders Green and Hendon. 8.8 library visits per head. Position in library use league table: 5th out of 32 (where 1 is best and 32 worst).*

OPEN SPACES****

Excellent and well documented. Barnet council is an enthusiastic promoter of green walks and woodland trails and was one of the first to complete its section of the huge circular London Loop walk round the outskirts of London.

HEATHLAND *The Hampstead Heath extension. The less frequented part of the heath by Hampstead Garden Suburb, saved from development by Henrietta Barnett. More open and less wooded than other nearby parts of the heath* • **TRAILS** *You can walk all the way from Hampstead Heath to Woodside Park without walking on a main road (an amazing feat) by following the Dollis Valley Greenwalk along the Dollis and Mutton Brooks. Peaceful grassy banks and clear water within earshot of the roar of traffic* • **WOODS** *Monken Hadley Common, once part of the Royal hunting ground of Enfield Chase and now a fitting backdrop to the grand houses opposite.*

SHOPS****

GOLDERS GREEN *Almost every other shop in Golders Green Road is Jewish, with kosher butchers and restaurants, bakeries and a bookshop with a window display of barmitzvah gifts. In vivid contrast to Brent Cross, just a skip and a jump across a concrete bridge over the M1, the streets are deserted on Saturday morning while the owners and customers of the* shops are at synagogue. Brent Cross, which from the outside looks like a series of enlarged nuclear bunkers, was one of the first out-of-town shopping malls and now its size and choice of shops are nothing special as other places have caught up • **FINCHLEY** Ballards Lane has mostly chain stores, including a couple of interior design shops and junk shops by Finchley Central station. Estate agents abound, including a couple of Japanese operators to cater for the Japanese community in Finchley. Tesco in Ballards Lane. More lively shops in East Finchley, with delis, brasseries, a fireplace shop and a real fishmonger • **HENDON & MILL HILL** Generally uninspiring local shops in Hendon around a series of dual carriageways crossed by litter-filled subways and lots of shops to let (the council's trying to reverse this trend). Mill Hill is much better, with long-established individual shops lining the Broadway. Large M&S with carpark. Sainsbury's in West Hendon and London's only Eastern shopping mall, Oriental City, a cornucopia of Japanese, Vietnamese and Korean indoor market stalls, food court, bookshop and public massage service • **EDGWARE** The Broadwalk, in the main shopping street, a neo-Georgian 1930s red brick parade of tidy local shops and discount shops, is a middle-sized, middle-of-the-road but clean and pleasant mall. A clutch of kosher bakeries and butchers' shops for the large Jewish population and travel agents advertising trips to Israel • **BARNET** Attractive looking, up-market shops particularly in the Spires shopping centre, cleverly converted from an old church. An eclectic collection of shops at the far end of the high street towards Hadley Common, including a tatooist and a cobbler.

RESTAURANTS***

GOLDERS GREEN & HENDON This is the place to come for Jewish food. Both places have a range of recommended bakeries and grander restaurants. A couple of Indian, Indonesian, Middle Eastern and Japanese restaurants also worth visiting • **ELSEWHERE** East Finchley rings the changes with a Hungarian brasserie. Otherwise mostly pizza and pasta chains, take-aways and local restaurants.

CRIME RATES*****

Position in Metropolitan Police crime table: 25th out of 32 (where 1 is worst and 32 best).

THE COUNCIL****

POLITICAL AFFILIATION Labour and Liberal Democrat coalition • **MINUS POINTS** Has had big problems with rubbish contractors but seems to have sorted out the worst of it • **PLUS POINTS** Fortnightly door-to-door recycling collections of waste paper. Generally praised by residents as efficient and effective. Excellent schools. Good at sweeping the streets and has introduced daily street sweeping of town centres and a graffiti hit squad.
PROPERTY SEARCHES CARRIED OUT IN 10 WORKING DAYS 98.6% • **STANDARD SEARCH FEE** £120.60 • **COUNCIL TAX COLLECTED** 95.3%
• **COUNCIL TAX 2000-2001**

BAND	PROPERTY VALUE	CHARGE	BAND	PROPERTY VALUE	CHARGE
A	up to £40,000	£543	E	£88,001-£120,000	£996
B	£40,001-£52,000	£634	F	£120,001-£160,000	£1,177
C	£52,001-£68,000	£642	G	£160,001-£320,000	£1,358
D	£68,001-£88,000	£815	H	£320,000+	£1,630

BEXLEY

For motorists on their way up from the Channel Ports, the eastern border of Bexley is where London starts (give or take a few yards through neighbouring Bromley). The dreary 1930s semis lining the main A20 Sidcup bypass manage to be both smug and down-at-heel, prompting people to put their foot down and escape as quickly as they can.

There's no getting away from it; Bexley is suburban, criss-crossed by main roads, with miles of streets of undistinguished semis flung up during the building booms of the 1920s and 1930s. But among the dross there are some beautiful properties, miles of rivers, meadows and woods, some excellent, sought-after state schools and as an antidote to the residential south, an industrial riverfront set for a face-lift.

Bexley stretches from the smart family homes of Sidcup, one of the best areas once you're off the main roads, to the Victorian village streets of Old Bexley with its river and mill (now a restaurant). Further north and west at Bexleyheath and Welling semi-detached suburbia takes over again, getting gradually shabbier towards Belvedere and the Victorian workmens' terraces of Erith on Bexley's northern shore. On the flat marshland of the northernmost tip are the new houses of Thamesmead North.

Riverside regeneration is on nowhere near the scale of that in next door Greenwich. But government grants and private sector investment totalling more than £11 million have been poured into regenerating Erith's former industrial riverside with a new riverside walk. Parts of the town centre have been pedestrianised, there are tasteful new benches and signposts and the grim concrete shopping precinct and multistorey carpark which ripped the heart out of Erith in the 1960s is set to be replaced or refurbished (whichever makes most economic sense to private developers, although residents want to see it replaced).

Like many of its outer London neighbours, Bexley generally has low unemployment at 2.5%, and low crime rates. It has its fair share of the affluent middle classes as well as upwardly mobile working classes. But life can be uncomfortable for non-whites in what is mostly a white area. Just 6% of the population is from an ethnic minority, mostly concentrated in the poorest, northern parts of the borough. The National Front bookshop in Welling has been a flashpoint for racial unrest and there have been a number of race-related murders in Thamesmead.

PROPERTY AND ARCHITECTURE

SIDCUP & BLACKFEN

Sidcup is considered one of the best parts of the borough. Mostly houses with some purpose-built blocks of flats. Large Victorian and Edwardian detached and semi-detached family homes and smart semi-detached houses with steep roofs and big gardens in roads off Main Road and the High Street. Some of the best roads are around Christchurch Road and Priestlands Park Road. Smaller semi-detached mostly 1920s and 1930s houses in streets nearer the A20. Victorian cottages in Halfway Street. Blackfen, in between Sidcup and Eltham, is around 10 per cent cheaper than Sidcup because it's further from a station. Mostly 1920s and 1930s with the best roads around Hollyoak Wood Park.

ATTRACTS *Affluent commuter families; people moving up from Welling or Bexleyheath or out from yuppified areas of south-east London like Rotherhithe; loyal locals; first time buyers* ● **CONSERVATION AREAS** *The Hollies; Halfway Street; Old Forge Way; Christ Church; The Green; Longlands Road; North Cray Village; the Oval; Willersley Avenue and Braundton Avenue* ● **AVERAGE PRICES** *Flats: studio £45,000-£50,000; 1-bed £60,000+; 2-bed £90,000+ Houses: 2-bed £120,000+; 3-bed £145,000-£180,000; 4-bed £200,000-£300,000* ● **AVERAGE RENTS (WEEKLY)** *Flats: studio £85+; 1-bed £105+; 2-bed £130+ Houses: 3-bed £160-£210; 4-bed £270+.*

BEXLEY

Bexley is pretty and villagey, with Victorian cottages and shop fronts in the high street alongside larger Victorian and Edwardian terraces near the River Cray. Mostly houses rather than flats. A mixture of large modern and 1930s semis and detached houses in roads off Parkhill Road and Bexley High Street.

ATTRACTS *Families wanting green space, good schools; commuters; some first-time buyers* ● **CONSERVATION AREAS** *Old Bexley; Parkhurst* ● **AVERAGE PRICES** *Flats: 1-bed £65,000-£85,000; 2-bed £85,000-£140,000 Houses: 2-bed £115,000-£125,000; 3-bed £115,000-£230,000; 4-bed £150,000-£280,000* ● **AVERAGE RENTS (WEEKLY)** *Flats: 1-bed £105-£120; 2-bed £115-£145 Houses: 2-bed £135-£155; 3-bed £150-£205; 4-bed £175-£325.*

WELLING & BEXLEYHEATH

Welling is almost entirely a 1930s creation, with private housing development following council house building in the 1920s. Mostly fairly dull, bleak roads of two-, three- and four-bedroom suburban terraces and semis with the best near Danson Park and on what estate agents call the scientists' estate, where the roads are named after famous scientists. Some larger houses in slightly more up-market Bexleyheath but mostly inter-war terraces and semis like Welling, with some flats above shops and in purpose-built blocks.

ATTRACTS *First-time buyers; loyal locals; people who can't afford Sidcup or Bexley; people moving out of newly trendified areas of south London to get more for their money; families wanting to be near good schools*

• **CONSERVATION AREAS** Red House, Bexleyheath • **AVERAGE PRICES** Flats:
1-bed £60,000-£75,000; 2-bed £85,000-£95,000+ Houses: 2-bed
£100,000+; 3-bed £135,000-£165,000; 4-bed £165,000-£200,000
• **AVERAGE RENTS (WEEKLY)** Flats: 1-bed £105+; 2-bed £125-£135
Houses: 2-bed £135+; 3-bed £150+; 4-bed £175.

ERITH, BELVEDERE & THAMESMEAD

Roads of Victorian munition workers' terraces in industrial Erith, many
'improved' with ugly new windows, doors or pebbledash. But this is a
good hunting ground for cheap houses. The best properties in Erith are on
the Lesney estate north of the sports centre where there are large four- and
five-bed family houses. A series of tower blocks dominates the town centre
and some of these are privately owned. Modern blocks mixed with 1930s
semis and bungalows in the anonymous areas of Northumberland Heath
and Barnehurst just south of Erith. More messed-about Victorian terraces in
lower Belvedere with some pleasant family houses in upper Belvedere, the
poshest bit of the area. Developers have been frantically busy in
Thamesmead (see also Greenwich) over the past few years, hoovering up
some of the last remaining riverside sites in London and the results in north
Thamesmead include a mix of traditionally built starter homes, apartments
and townhouses. Riverside townhouses are fetching (for Thamesmead) high
prices – you can pay £100,000 for a one-bed flat with river view and
£140,000 for a two-bed. South Thamesmead is a different matter, a grim
estate of tower blocks and deck access flats built by the GLC in the 1960s
on reclaimed marshland. Thamesmead itself is half in Bexley and half in
the borough of Greenwich. Properties in Bexley are more sought after
because council tax is much lower than Greenwich.

ATTRACTS First-time buyers; families wanting new or cheap houses;
members of the Asian community (Belvedere) • **CONSERVATION AREAS** Erith
Riverside; Woolwich Road, Belvedere; Crossness Pumping Station,
Thamesmead • **AVERAGE PRICES** Flats: studio £40,000+; 1-bed £47,000+;
2-bed £50,000-£140,000 Houses: 2-bed £75,000-£130,000; 3-bed
£65,000-£170,000; 4-bed £85,000-£225,000 • **AVERAGE RENTS**
(WEEKLY) Flats: studio £80-£95; 1-bed £92-£115; 2-bed £125-£175
Houses: 2-bed £125-£175; 3-bed £140-£195; 4-bed £195+.

BEST POSTCODES

Only a small section of the north of the borough has London postcodes
with Abbey Wood SE2 and Thamesmead SE28 ranking as among the
least smart postcodes in the whole of London. Postcodes are almost
irrelevant elsewhere as London codes give way to Kent.

AMENITIES

SCHOOLS ****

Several excellent, league-topping selective state secondary schools with hot
competition for places, not least from middle-class parents in the
neighbouring inner London boroughs of Lewisham and Greenwich where
state schools are poor. No private secondary schools. Both primary and
secondary schools perform well overall in national league tables without
being stunning. A good selection of pre-school provision, both state and
private.

PRE-SCHOOL PROVISION *45 nursery classes attached to state and church primary and infant schools; 1 state nursery; 73 private and voluntary day nurseries and playgroups. Proportion of under-fives in state nursery schools: 66%* ● **STATE PRIMARY SCHOOLS** *Overall league table position: 55th out of 150. Top scorers: St Paulinus C of E, Dartford; St Peter Chanel RC, Sidcup; Birkbeck (with nursery unit), Sidcup* ● **STATE SECONDARY SCHOOLS** *Overall league table position: 52nd out of 150. Top scorers (all selective): Townley Grammar (girls), Bexleyheath; Bexley Grammar (mixed), Welling; Chislehurst and Sidcup Grammar (mixed), Sidcup* ● **PRIVATE PREP SCHOOL** *Harenc School (boys), Sidcup.*

TRANSPORT**

Only trains throughout the borough with provision particularly poor in Thamesmead where there's no station nearer than Abbey Wood. Stations fairly evenly spread throughout the borough but services slacken off outside rush hours and buses are a better bet for short journeys.

TRAINS *Sidcup Zone 5. Cost of annual season ticket £1332. Average journey time to London Bridge 26 minutes; to Charing Cross 31 minutes. Bexley Zone 6. Cost of annual season ticket £1456; Average journey time to London Bridge 29 minutes; to Charing Cross 37 minutes. Welling Zone 4. Cost of annual season ticket £1104. Average journey time to London Bridge 22 minutes; to Charing Cross 32 minutes; to Victoria 34 minutes. Erith Zone 6. Average journey time to London Bridge 35 minutes; to Charing Cross 43 minutes* ● **BUSES** *Strictly suburban services during the day time. Links to town improve radically at night with a choice of three night buses from Trafalgar Square – the N21 to Sidcup, the N53 to Erith and the N81 to Welling and Bexleyheath* ● **TRAFFIC TROUBLESPOTS** *Sidcup: Roads around the narrow, curved high street can get jammed with cars, delivery lorries and buses and there can be long delays at the junction with Station Road. The busy A20 usually flows, if not freely then at least slowly, but traffic is constant. Bexley & Bexleyheath: Trafficky in the narrow streets of Old Bexley, particularly at the confluence of three roads at the roundabout at the top of the high street. Bexleyheath is crossed by the main A2 to Dover which is too narrow for the pressure of traffic here* ● **PARKING** *Getting more difficult as the borough tries to discourage unofficial park-and-ride by commuters. There are controlled parking zones in Bexleyheath, Crayford, Sidcup, Welling, New Eltham, Falconwood, Abbey Wood and Albany Park. Cost of annual resident's permit: £50 a year in Bexleyheath town centre, £40 a year in Hamilton Road and Stanhope Road (near Bexleyheath Station), £20 elsewhere.*

LEISURE FACILITIES****

THEATRES & CONCERT HALLS *Well provided for. Theatres include the Geoffrey Whitworth Theatre, Crayford; the Playhouse Theatre, Erith; the Edward Alderton Theatre, Bexleyheath; the Old Barn Theatre and the Theatre in the Round, Rose Bruford College, Sidcup with performances by students of the college. Concerts at Hall Place (see below)* ● **CINEMAS** *Nine screen Cineworld in a 1930s wireless-style building at Bexleyheath* ● **MUSEUMS & GALLERIES** *Surprisingly interesting and varied choice including a number of gracious country houses saved from the building onslaughts of the 1920s and 1930s. The list includes Hall Place, a Tudor mansion set in formal gardens with rooms open to the public (although the grand effect from the front is slightly spoilt by its position on a busy main* road); Lesnes Abbey, the remains of a 12th-century abbey in quiet gardens framed by woods, and the Red House, built in 1860 for William Morris, the designer and writer, containing some of the original furnishings. The local history musuem at Erith is housed in a listed library building. And if you're into industrial architecture, a visit (by appointment only) to the Crossness Engine and Pumping Station on the river at Thamesmead is a must, as the massive beam engines built as part of London's 19th-century sewage system are restored to their original glory • **SPORTS FACILITIES** Erith, Bexleyheath and Sidcup all have leisure centres and pools. There are plans to update facilities and develop state of the art sports centres on existing sites. Watersports in the beautiful setting of Danson Park with sailing, canoeing and windsurfing, and tennis, golf, football and cricket at Danson Park and other parks throughout the borough • **LIBRARIES** Well-used and helpful. Reasonable opening hours (although no late evenings) at the central library in Bexleyheath but truncated hours in some smaller branch libraries including all day closing on Wednesday or Thursday. Sunday opening at Bexleyheath. Local history centre at Hall Place. 7.3 library visits per head. Position in library-use league table: 13th out of 32 (where 1 is best and 32 worst).

OPEN SPACES****

Excellent variety of open space from formal parks to river walks, meadows and woods with the Thames in the north of the borough. Bexley is hilly, with good views over neighbouring wooded hills towards Kent from various vantage points and even from Bexleyheath shopping centre. Green spaces from Thamesmead to the ruined Lesnes Abbey and Lesnes Abbey Woods are part of the 40-mile network of trails on the Green Chain Walk through south-east London to Crystal Palace and Chislehurst (see also Bromley, Greenwich and Lewisham) • **RIVER WALKS** The Cray Riverway Walk along the River Cray from Footscray Meadows to the Thames. A quiet walk through meadow and marshland except where brutally interrupted by the A2. Also worth checking out is the riverside at Erith, where new walks are being created from the remains of a once-thriving industrial riverside • **WIDE OPEN SPACES** Footscray Meadows with mature trees and views over distant hills • **FORMAL PARKS** Danson Park, landscaped by the 18th-century landscaper Capability Brown, with lake, mature trees and the Danson Mansion with stable block renovated as a restaurant.

SHOPS**

SIDCUP A once pleasant high street which has gone downhill in the last couple of years. Residents blame high rents and the pre-eminence of Bexleyheath up the road for the appearance of more and more To Let signs and charity shops (usually a sign that somewhere is on the down). Heavy traffic doesn't help. Mainly chains and local shops. Somerfields in the High Street; Tesco by the A20 • **BEXLEY & BEXLEYHEATH** Self-consciously villagey shops in Old Bexley including a choice of delis and bakeries, children's clothes and antique shops. The centre of Bexleyheath is dominated by a pleasant pedestrianised shopping street with a large Edwardian clocktower and the Broadway indoor shopping centre. Good if predictable choice of clothes and other chains including a large M&S. The shopping centre is now expanding still further to combat competition from the massive

Bluewater shopping centre near Dartford, and the new development will include a Sainsburys • **WELLING** *Undistinguished high street. Roads off the high street are lined with chains, local shops and cheap discount shops. A huge choice of DIY and double glazing shops, which may account for the appalling 'improvements' made to most of the properties in Welling. Co-op superstore* • **ERITH** *A sad concrete 1960s shopping centre with a horrible multistorey car park above. The high street has been partly pedestrianised which has improved things a bit but until the shopping centre is revamped, residents will have to put up with a couple of rows of pathetic shops whose owners haven't even got the will to mount window displays. Many of them are there on short leases pending refurbishment, which may explain why the whole precinct has such a temporary feel. Twice-weekly clothes and food market. Large Morrison's superstore recently built on former industrial riverside site* • **THAMESMEAD** *New shopping centre built in answer to complaints that there were no shops nearer than Woolwich. Handsome Safeway but otherwise small unremarkable shops.*

RESTAURANTS*

Generally a bit of a culinary desert. Old Bexley has a couple of brasseries and tavernas. Elsewhere it's the usual choice of variable high street Indian, Chinese, take-aways and other local restaurants.

CRIME RATES****

Position in Metropolitan Police league table: 26th out of 32 (where 1 is worst and 32 best).

THE COUNCIL****

POLITICAL AFFILIATION *Conservative* • **MINUS POINTS** *Has been upbraided by residents for not repairing roads and pavements quickly enough and has pledged to spend an extra £400,000 on this* • **PLUS POINTS** *Good schools. Three quarters of residents in the last survey thought the council was doing a good job. Efficient at rubbish collections and street sweeping. One of the most efficient boroughs in London at turning round property searches quickly. Fortnightly door-to-door recycling collections and a scheme for recycling householders' garden compost* • **PROPERTY SEARCHES CARRIED OUT IN 10 WORKING DAYS** *100%* • **STANDARD SEARCH FEE** *£123* • **COUNCIL TAX COLLECTED** *94.2%*
• **COUNCIL TAX 2000-2001**

BAND	PROPERTY VALUE	CHARGE	BAND	PROPERTY VALUE	CHARGE
A	up to £40,000	£535	E	£88,001-£120,000	£981
B	£40,001-£52,000	£624	F	£120,001-£160,000	£1,159
C	£52,001-£68,000	£713	G	£160,001-£320,000	£1,337
D	£68,001-£88,000	£802	H	over £320,000	£1,605

BRENT

Brent is a bit schizophrenic. It's technically outer London but its eastern half is as inner city as anywhere, a melting pot of races living in a jumble of Victorian terraces and council blocks criss-crossed by tube and train tracks and busy, polluted roads. By contrast, its western half is suburban, not super-smart but mostly respectable.

In the 1980s Brent had the dubious distinction of being the only 'loony left' outer London borough, with high council tax and administrative and political chaos much more characteristic of the uncontrolled inner city than polite suburbia. The borough's wild reputation put off many who might otherwise have moved there and until recently, it was often a last resort for people who couldn't afford smarter areas like Notting Hill, Maida Vale or West Hampstead or even the better suburbs of Barnet or Harrow. Now council tax has fallen, the council's getting better, even if it's still struggling financially and more people are moving to areas like Kilburn and Queen's Park by choice, attracted by their good transport links and plentiful supply of period property.

Brent starts in the east with the Victorian terraces of Kilburn, long colonised by the Irish and more recently by West Indians. The borough is one of the most multiracial with nearly half the population from an ethnic minority, including large Indian and Jewish communities as well as Irish and Afro-Caribbeans. To the west are the larger Victorian houses of Brondesbury and Willesden Green before the miles of red suburban roofs of Neasden and Dollis Hill take over to the north and west. Beyond the North Circular lies Wembley, with its large and colourful Indian community, and the council blocks of Stonebridge. On the hills beyond Neasden is the respectable 1930s suburb of Kingsbury.

The borough is nowhere near as poor as many inner London boroughs but is on the cusp between inner city and suburb, coming near the top of the deprivation leagues for outer London. Unemployment is the second highest in outer London at 6.7% and it's the 20th most deprived area in England. There's widespread poverty and poor housing, particularly in Harlesden in the south. However large sums of public and private money are being spent on training and job creation as well as environmental improvements and crime reduction in busy shopping areas like Kilburn High Road.

One of the chief beneficiaries of regeneration funds will be Wembley, whose drab High Road and graffiti-covered stations are set to benefit from the building of a new £600 million national sports stadium and the upgrading of surrounding areas with shops, leisure facilities and better parking. More than £100 million will be spent in Wembley Park, with £70 million going on rebuilding Wembley Park Station. Residents whose lives are regularly disrupted by up to 80,000 visitors arriving for events (and trying to park) are desperate to see improvements.

PROPERTY AND ARCHITECTURE

KILBURN & QUEENS PARK

Lots of Victorian terraces of varying sizes off Kilburn High Road and in the grids around Willesden Lane cemetery. Kilburn is still a bit shabby and many of the larger houses have been sliced up into flats but this is a classic example of an area ripe for gentrification (close to the centre, good transport links, expensive and established residential areas nearby). Queens Park is posher than Kilburn, with three- and four-storey Victorian and Edwardian houses around the park and a growing colony of middle-class families who can't afford houses in Notting Hill or North Kensington. Queens Park is increasingly a first choice for those who want a good choice of period homes and a well-kept park nearby. The neighbouring areas of Kensal Green and Kensal Rise have benefited from an influx of buyers priced out of North Kensington or Notting Hill and are now almost as expensive as Queens Park (for West Kilburn, see Westminster).

ATTRACTS First-time buyers; young professionals; people priced out of neighbouring more expensive areas; families; people moving from Maida Vale or Ladbroke Grove to get more space for their money
• **CONSERVATION AREAS** Queens Park; Paddington Cemetery; North Kilburn; Kilburn • **AVERAGE PRICES** Flats: studio £80,000-£100,000; 1-bed £120,000-£190,000; 2-bed £150,000-£300,000 Houses: 3-bed £300,000-£500,000; 4-bed £450,000-£600,000 • **AVERAGE RENTS (WEEKLY)** Flats: studio £100-£120; 1-bed £170-£200; 2-bed £200-£240 Houses: 3-bed £350-£400; 4-bed £370-£450.

WILLESDEN, WILLESDEN GREEN & BRONDESBURY

Brondesbury was the first of these areas to gentrify, as buyers who couldn't afford West Hampstead crossed the rubicon of the Kilburn High Road and discovered a plentiful supply of period property in tree lined streets which were still in the vital West Hampstead NW6 postcode area. Now the ripple is spreading to Willesden Green, much of which is early 20th-century with a more suburban feel. Willesden Green is generally cheaper than Brondesbury except for the jewel in its crown, the Mapesbury conservation area around Mapesbury Road, with huge Victorian piles converted into well proportioned flats. On the other side of Willesden Lane, large houses around Aylestone Avenue are popular with diplomats whose countries can't afford St. John's Wood. Incongruous among the modern apartment blocks and inter-war semis and detached houses in Willesden Lane is the Shree Swaminavaga Temple, sprouting cupolas, minarets, domes and trellises. Willesden is shabbier and cheaper than Willesden Green or Brondesbury with smaller Victorian terraces.

ATTRACTS First-time buyers; flat-hunters; people who can't afford West Hampstead or Maida Vale; families • **CONSERVATION AREAS** Mapesbury; Willesden; Brondesbury • **AVERAGE PRICES** Flats: studio £85,000+; 1-bed £95,000+; 2-bed £150,000+ Houses: 3-bed £170,000-£250,000;

4-bed £300,000+ • **AVERAGE RENTS (WEEKLY)** *Flats: studio £140+; 1-bed £190+; 2-bed £250+ Houses: 3-bed £300+; 4-bed £375+.*

NEASDEN & DOLLIS HILL

Neasden's been the butt of more scornful metropolitan jokes than almost any other part of London. Yes, it's suburban and not very exciting, but it's set on gentle hills leading up to its centrepiece at Gladstone Park and has some good views to relieve the monotony. It also has the largest Hindu temple outside India, the Shree Swaminarayan Mandir, carved from 2000 tons of marble and 3000 tons of limestone by volunteer craftsmen. Neasden's vernacular architecture by contrast is mainly 1930s semis with few conversions. More up-market Dollis Hill also has good views and enclaves of Edwardian property around Gladstone Park as well as 1930s semis and modern blocks with a good choice of flats.

ATTRACTS *Families; members of the Asian community; people who can't afford Willesden* • **CONSERVATION AREAS** *Homestead Park; Neasden Village; St Andrews* • **AVERAGE PRICES** *Flats: studio £65,000-£70,000; 1-bed £75,000-£80,000; 2-bed £100,000-£115,000 Houses: 3-bed £130,000-£165,000; 4-bed £180,000-£270,000* • **AVERAGE RENTS (WEEKLY)** *Flats: studio £120; 1-bed £150; 2-bed £180 Houses: 3-bed £240+; 4-bed £250-£350.*

WEMBLEY

The largest commercial and retail area of Brent, with Wembley Stadium to the east. A large stretch of middling 1930s semis sprawling up and down hills, with the occasional stone lion or wrought iron gate to assert individuality and superiority. Deep eaves, half-timbering and large curved bays – they're all here. North Wembley is the poshest part of Wembley with the Sudbury Court estate around East Lane and Watford Road one of the most sought-after parts. Roads round Wembley Park station have improved a lot, and prices are rising as the last blocks of the grim Chalkhill Estate come down to be replaced by low-rise housing and Wembley Park station and surroundings get an upgrade as part of the national stadium improvements. The best properties, large detached family homes, are in the Barn Hill conservation area near Fryent Country Park.

ATTRACTS *Families; members of the Asian and Afro-Caribbean communities* • **CONSERVATION AREAS** *Barn Hill; Preston Park; Lawns Court; Wembley Hill Garden Suburb* • **AVERAGE PRICES** *Flats: studio £65,000+; 1-bed £75,000+; 2-bed £85,000+ Houses: 3-bed £150,000+; 4-bed £260,000+* • **AVERAGE RENTS (WEEKLY)** *Flats: studio £115-£120; 1-bed £140-£150; 2-bed £175+ Houses: 2-bed £195-£205; 3-bed £230-£275; 4-bed £300-£345.*

KINGSBURY & KENTON

Parts of Kingsbury are some of the nearest things Brent has to smart suburbia. Some handsome detached houses in tree-lined roads with leaded light windows and large gardens by the wonderful open space of Fryent Country Park. Around Roe Green there are some quirky thatched houses with authentic looking Tudor beams, actually built in the 1920s by Ernest Trobridge. Elsewhere mostly fairly standard 1930s semis and some small neo-Georgian town houses on Fryent Way. Middling semis in Kenton.

ATTRACTS *Families; members of the Jewish community (Kingsbury); members of the Asian community (Kenton)* • **CONSERVATION AREAS** *Roe Green;*

Slough Lane; Buck Lane; Manor Close ● **AVERAGE PRICES** *Flats: studio
£65,000; 1-bed £85,000-£100,000; 2-bed £90,000-£130,000 Houses:
2-bed £125,000-£140,000; 3-bed £160,000-£180,000; 4-bed
£210,000-£300,000* ● **AVERAGE RENTS (WEEKLY)** *Flats: studio £115-£120;
1-bed £140-£150; 2-bed £175+ Houses: 2-bed £175+; 3-bed £195-
£275; 4-bed £255+.*

BEST POSTCODES

The part of West Hampstead NW6 which is in Brondesbury Park is
undoubtedly the best postcode, appreciated by residents who can quite
truthfully say they live in West Hampstead. Cricklewood NW2 includes the
Mapesbury Estate and Dollis Hill and is smarter than Willesden NW10,
which is improving rapidly but includes the council estates of Harlesden.

AMENITIES

SCHOOLS***

Not as bad as you might expect given the borough's unfortunate image.
State primary and secondary schools are far from scraping the bottom.
Good level of pre-school provision for under-fours in both state and private
nurseries. Two private Asian schools.

PRE-SCHOOL PROVISION *90 private and voluntary nurseries; 4 state nursery
schools; 47 state primary, church and Jewish schools with nursery places.
Proportion of under-fives in state nurseries: 74%* ● **STATE PRIMARY SCHOOLS**
*Overall league table position: 59th out of 150. Top scorers: Kilburn Park
Foundation, Kilburn; Christ Church CE (with nursery unit), Brondesbury; St
Margaret Clitherow (with nursery unit), Neasden* ● **STATE SECONDARY
SCHOOLS** *Overall league table position: 73rd out of 149. Top scorers:
Claremont High (mixed), Kenton; Preston Manor High (mixed), Wembley;
Kingsbury High (mixed), Kingsbury* ● **PRIVATE SCHOOLS** *Swaminarayan
(mixed from 2); Islamia Girls High (from 11).*

TRANSPORT****

An even spread of tubes and trains throughout the borough. Brent has long
stretches of the generally efficient Jubilee and Bakerloo lines for quick
journeys to the centre of town and Wembley is particularly well served by
both tubes and trains.

TRAINS *Willesden Junction Zone 2. Cost of annual season ticket: £756.
Average journey time to Euston 16 minutes; to Highbury and Islington
24 minutes. Wembley Stadium Zone 4. Cost of annual season ticket
£1104. Average journey time to Marylebone 11 minutes* ● **TUBES**
*Kilburn (Jubilee) Zone 2. Average journey time to Charing Cross 18
minutes. Willesden Junction (Bakerloo) Zone 2. Average journey time to
Oxford Circus 20 minutes. Wembley Park (Jubilee and Metropolitan)
Zone 4. Average journey time to Baker Street 18 minutes* ● **BUSES** *A good
choice to town although journeys can be slow, particularly at rush hour
along the borough's many main roads. Services include the 16 via
Kilburn High Road and Brondesbury to Victoria, the 18 via Wembley
and Harlesden to Euston and the 52 from Willesden to Victoria*
● **TRAFFIC TROUBLESPOTS** *Kilburn: The high road is often blocked with
delivery vans, buses and people trying to do U turns in a road that's too
narrow. Neasden: The horrible spaghetti junction of dual carriageways*

around the North circular is always busy, which begs the urgent question of why the borough has seen fit to put its local history museum in the middle of one of the largest roundabouts on this road system. Harrow Road: Particularly bad (and that's saying something) round the junctions with the North Circular Road ● **PARKING** *Until recently Brent was one of only two London boroughs not charging for residents' parking permits unless they have more than one car. But it's started charging, to curb car use and to protect residents from cross-border sorties from motorists in neighbouring Camden and Westminster looking for free parking. There are controlled parking zones in the centre of Wembley, Harlesden, around the Hindu temple in Neasden, Queens Park, Kilburn, Willesden and Kenton Road. Cost of permit: £50 for the first car, £75 for a second car, £100 for a third car.*

LEISURE FACILITIES***

THEATRES & CONCERT HALLS *One repertory theatre, the Tricycle in Kilburn High Road, which has recovered from a devastating fire and filled a large gap in provision of theatres in this part of north-west London. New and off-the-wall plays (often exploring multiracial themes) and theatre for children in a clean modern building (look up at the ceiling in the entrance hall to see the intriguing moving arrangement of tricycle wheels and chains), a complete contrast to the grubby Kilburn High Road. Live music at Wembley Arena and at the Mean Fiddler in Harlesden. Classical concerts at the Stables Gallery and Arts Centre in Gladstone Park, Dollis Hill* ● **CINEMAS** *The Tricycle cinema, which had a struggle to raise enough cash for a new auditorium and visual arts studio, specialises in art films. More mainstream films at Willesden Green Belle Vue, part of a recently-built complex with café, bookshop and the borough's flagship library around a spacious atrium. A new multiplex cinema is being planned for Wembley* ● **MUSEUMS & GALLERIES** *Not a huge choice. The Stables Gallery and Arts Centre at Dollis Hill has exhibitions of paintings, sculpture and pottery. The Grange Museum of Community History (the one marooned on a traffic roundabout) is well worth a look for exhibitions about the development of Brent, with lots of fascinating old photographs and displays. Tours of Wembley Stadium at Wembley* ● **SPORTS FACILITIES** *Three sports centres at Wembley, Willesden and Kilburn. All have recently been refurbished and the council has put in a bid for lottery funds to revamp tired changing rooms at Wembley. Pools at Wembley and Willesden. Sailing at the Welsh Harp Reservoir (see also Barnet). Athletics stadium at Willesden Green. International football (watching not playing) at Wembley Stadium. Tennis courts and other sports in parks across the borough* ● **LIBRARIES** *Above average use but opening hours have been slashed even at the flagship Willesden Green centre because of budget cuts and libraries are generally under-resourced. But some long evening openings on days when libraries are open. Sunday opening at Willesden Green. 7.1 library visits per head. Position in library-use league table: 17th out of 32 (where 1 is best and 32 worst).*

OPEN SPACES***

Brent doesn't have great swathes of greenbelt land but it's well-endowed with green space particularly in the north, as well as a section of the Grand Union Canal (although this flows almost unremittingly through dreary warehouses and industrial parks). Parks in the south tend to be small and a bit municipal although Queens Park (run by the Corporation of London rather than Brent Council) is well kept and popular with local residents. Ironically, given that the borough takes its name from the river running through it, the river Brent in Brent is silted up and generally in poor condition although there are plans to improve it.

WIDE OPEN SPACES *Fryent Country Park. A wonderful surprise in the midst of suburbia with rolling fields, framed by wooded hills in the distance. It's rural enough for the locals to harvest hay here in summer* ● **RIVERS & WATER** *The Welsh Harp Reservoir and surrounding open space. The reservoir was formed in 1835 from damming the River Brent to provide a source for the Grand Union Canal and it's now a sailing and wildlife haven. The rural effect of the water itself is marred by the gantries of the North Circular Road visible in the distance but it doesn't take long to lose yourself in the grass and woodland around.*

SHOPS***

KILBURN & HARLESDEN *Kilburn High Road has the same collection of chains, cheap high fashion clothes shops, discount stores, electrical goods, wholesalers and ethnic supermarkets as many inner London high streets, although a couple of more trendy shops have opened up recently and there are some interesting individual shops including a musical instrument shop and a local bookstore. But there are a number of boarded-up shops and 'to let' signs. Afro hairdressers and Jamaican and Irish newspapers displayed prominently are reminders of the area's multiracial makeup. Sainsbury's. Mostly local shops in Harlesden with big Afro-Caribbean influence (bakers, hairdressers and supermarkets)* ● **WILLESDEN & BRONDESBURY** *Mostly local shops, wholesalers and Halal butchers in Willesden High Road, another of London's Victorian shopping streets turned into a traffic jam. But cleaner and more litter-free than Kilburn High Road. Suffers from being within easy reach of Brent Cross (see Barnet)* ● **NEASDEN** *Dreary parades of small shops around Neasden Lane and Blackbird Hill. Large Tesco at Brent Park* ● **WEMBLEY** *The borough's main shopping centre, set for a badly needed face-lift as part of the revamp of Wembley Stadium and surroundings. Currently the high road has medium-size cheap chain stores, everything-for-£1 shops and a handful of depressing outlets in a 1960s outdoor shopping precinct near Wembley Central Station. There are plans to redevelop this area with a cinema and 'other leisure facilities'. Ealing Road just off the high road is by contrast a riot of colour and interest, with Indian sari and wedding shops, jewellers, Asian supermarkets and sweet shops selling delectable sweets and cakes full of coconut and nuts* ● **KINGSBURY** *Busy roads around the roundabout at Kingsbury Circus lined with half-timbered and brick 1930s parades. Lots of discount and charity shops, Halal butchers and an Aldi superstore.*

RESTAURANTS***

KILBURN, WILLESDEN & HARLESDEN *A couple of good Indian restaurants and a recommended Japanese and Spanish restaurant in Willesden. Thai restaurant in Harlesden* ● **WEMBLEY** *The place to go in Brent for a good choice of Indian restaurants* ● **ELSEWHERE** *Nothing of note. Huge range of ethnic restaurants of varying quality.*

CRIME RATES***

Position in Metropolitan Police league table: 15th out of 32 (where 1 is worst and 32 best).

THE COUNCIL***

POLITICAL AFFILIATION *Labour* ● **MINUS POINTS** *Often sloppy at street-sweeping and litter collection (lots of old litter in main streets); budget cuts have meant slashes in services including libraries* ● **PLUS POINTS** *Trying to extricate itself from the adminstrative and political chaos of past years. Band D council tax for 2000–2001 is one of the lowest in London rather than one of the highest although levels may yet rise because of the council's financial problems. Door-to-door recycling of almost anything, including newspapers, textiles, glass, cans, shoes and engine oil*
● **PROPERTY SEARCHES CARRIED OUT IN 10 WORKING DAYS** *99.1%*
● **STANDARD SEARCH FEE** *£120* ● **COUNCIL TAX COLLECTED** *91.4%*
● **COUNCIL TAX 2000-2001**

BAND	PROPERTY VALUE	CHARGE	BAND	PROPERTY VALUE	CHARGE
A	up to £40,000	£493	E	£88,001-£120,000	£904
B	£40,001-£52,000	£575	F	£120,001-£160,000	£1,069
C	£52,001-£68,000	£658	G	£160,001-£320,000	£1,233
D	£68,001-£88,000	£740	H	over £320,000	£1,480

BROMLEY

Bromley has never really wanted to be part of London. Successive local councils have made that much clear ever since they resisted pressure to re-house poor people from inner London in the 1960s and then took the Greater London Council to court in the 1980s over the GLC's attempts to cut tube fares using ratepayers' money. With half its area designated as greenbelt land, Bromley's affluent residents in their detached commuter belt homes like to think they live in Kent rather than south-east London.

But Bromley has its fair share of Victorian suburbia as well as 1930s developments and Kentish villages. The largest borough in London, it stretches from Crystal Palace Park and the once fashionable Victorian villas and terraces of Anerley and Penge at its north-west tip, down through the detached 1930s houses with gardens further east on the outskirts of Bromley and Beckenham. These give way again to the handsome Victorian houses and stockbroker-belt mock-Tudor of sought-after Chislehurst. Further south, roads of well-kept semi-detached and detached houses mixed with salubrious modern developments radiate from the stations and shopping centres of Hayes, Petts Wood and Orpington and tempting paths disappear through woods and commons to the villages of Keston and Farnborough.

Much of the borough is affluent commuterland, built up during the housing booms of the first three decades of the century. Given the daily flows of workers to town and back, it's not surprising that unemployment is low, even by outer London standards, at 2.4%.

Residents are mostly white (only 5% of the borough is from an ethnic minority), from middle-class families seduced by the prospect of good schools, large gardens, lots of green space and well stocked, if undramatic, shops.

But the north-west corner around Crystal Palace feels as if it belongs more to neighbouring inner-city Lewisham or Lambeth than Bromley, with boarded-up and down-at-heel shops and Victorian houses which have seen better days. It's here, in Penge, Anerley and around Crystal Palace Park, that £150 million is being invested by the council, central government and the private sector to regenerate town centres, provide employment and training and improve public transport. The triangle of roads next to Crystal Palace Park, known as the Upper Norwood or Westow triangle (see Lambeth and Croydon), has already seen a dramatic improvement over the past few years, thanks more to an influx of young affluent professionals priced out of neighbouring areas by the property boom than to any council regeneration initiative. Ironically, despite its growing popularity, Crystal Palace technically doesn't exist as an area. You're either in Upper Norwood (see Croydon), West Norwood/Gipsy Hill (Lambeth) or Penge (Bromley).

Bromley's ambitious plans for a £58 million leisure centre on the site of the old Crystal Palace are still being bitterly opposed by many local residents, who argue that the proposed centre (with multiplex cinema, sports facilities and restaurant) will create huge amounts of extra traffic and congestion. The plans are now set to go ahead following an overwhelming vote in favour by Bromley council, which argues the development is key to regeneration plans. For a time, groups of residents formed an unlikely alliance with a band of eco-warriors, many veterans of past road and building-site battles, who set up camp around the Crystal Palace TV mast and held on for a year before being evicted.

PROPERTY AND ARCHITECTURE

ANERLEY & PENGE

Both areas are mainly slightly down-at-heel Victorian with some roads of terraces of varying sizes and some of Victorian cottages. Some large villas still survive in roads around Crystal Palace Park, reminders of the days when Crystal Palace was one of the wonders of London, and in Anerley off the Croydon Road. But most of the large houses have been converted into flats. There are smaller detached and semi-detached Victorian houses mixed with 1930s houses off Lennard Road. A mixture of Edwardian and 1930s terraces and council blocks can be found around the shopping parades of Elmers End further south. The big draw of Anerley and Penge is that they're in Bromley, with low council tax and good schools. If and when the East London tube line is extended southwards, there could be stations at Anerley and Penge West, pushing up the value of property here significantly.
ATTRACTS First-time buyers; people who can't afford Beckenham or

Streatham; those wanting lots of space for their money • **CONSERVATION AREAS** *Crystal Palace Park; Penge High Street; Cator Road* • **AVERAGE PRICES** *Flats: 1-bed £60,000-£85,000; 2-bed £80,000-£105,000 Houses: 2-bed £125,000+; 3-bed £130,000-£145,000+; 4-bed £165,000+* • **AVERAGE RENTS (WEEKLY)** *Flats: 1-bed £115+; 2-bed £140-£160 Houses: 2-bed £155+; 3-bed £205+; 4-bed £250+.*

BECKENHAM & BROMLEY

Several steps up from Anerley or Penge. Despite its current image as 20th-century suburbia par excellence Bromley was a thriving market town by the 19th century. So there's a lot of Victoriana near the centre of Bromley, with everything from cottages to large Victorian and turn-of-the-century family homes. Further out there are 1920s and 1930s detached and semi-detached houses of all shapes and sizes with lots of Tudor beams, wood fronts, deep sloping roofs and well mown front gardens. Shortlands, just west of Bromley, was aptly once home to Enid Blyton, who doubtless relished its pleasant suburban atmosphere. Flats are mostly in purpose-built blocks. Beckenham is also Victorian in the middle with some large detached houses on the main Beckenham Road, now mostly flats, and roads of Victorian terraces. Its smartest area is Park Langley with roads of large detached 1920s and 1930s homes.

ATTRACTS *Families wanting good schools and gardens; City workers wanting good transport links; some first-time buyers* • **CONSERVATION AREAS** *Beckenham St George's; Beckenham Kelsey Square; Chancery Lane; Manor Way Beckenham; Park Langley; Bromley Town Centre; Bromley Common; Shortlands; Garden Road; Durham Avenue; Garden Road; Sundridge Avenue* • **AVERAGE PRICES** *Flats: 1-bed £75,000+; 2-bed £100,000+ Houses: 2-bed £130,000+; 3-bed £140,000+; 4-bed £220,000+* • **AVERAGE RENTS (WEEKLY)** *Flats: 1-bed £125-£160; 2-bed £175-£275 Houses: 2-bed £175+; 3-bed £205; 4-bed: £300+.*

CHISLEHURST & PETTS WOOD

Some of the best parts of the borough, surrounded by commons and green space on all sides. Chislehurst is slightly grander and has more of a buzz than Petts Wood. A mixture of cottages and larger Victorian houses round Chislehurst Common, with 1980s neo-Georgian 'executive homes' and stockbroker houses with mock Tudor and leaded lights in roads around. Some pleasant estates of 1970s detached houses in Bickley to the south mixed in with 1930s half-timbered houses. The best parts of Petts Wood are east of the railway line where there's lots of mock Tudor and neat lawns. West of the railway line is considered less smart, with smaller more recently built homes. Mostly houses rather than flats, especially in Petts Wood and the flats that do exist are in purpose-built blocks.

ATTRACTS *Families looking for good schools (roads in Petts Wood in the Bullers Wood school catchment area are much sought after); City workers; professional couples moving out from south-east London areas like Lewisham for more space* • **CONSERVATION AREAS** *Chislehurst; The Chenies, Petts Wood; Station Square, Petts Wood; Chislehurst Road, Petts Wood* • **AVERAGE PRICES** *Flats: 2-bed £100,000+ Houses: 2-bed £170,000+; 3-bed £175,000-£250,000; 4-bed £250,000-£300,000+* • **AVERAGE RENTS (WEEKLY)** *Flats: 1-bed £120; 2-bed £140+ Houses: 2-bed £160+; 3-bed £195+; 4-bed £230+.*

ORPINGTON & ST PAUL'S CRAY

More detached houses around Orpington with some of the best in roads off Crofton Road. Some roads of smaller Victorian terraces and cottage-style houses in roads off the main shopping streets around the old priory, now the local museum and library. A lot of St Paul's Cray is ex-council bought by tenants under the right-to-buy scheme and now back on the market but there are bargains to be had. Local advice is to stay well north of the railway line and west of the A224.

ATTRACTS *Families wanting to get children into sought-after schools (Orpington); first-time buyers (St. Paul's Cray)* • **CONSERVATION AREAS** *Broomhill; Orpington Priory; St Paul's Cray; St Mary Cray* • **AVERAGE PRICES** *Flats: 1-bed £70,000+; 2-bed £85,000+ Houses: 2-bed £95,000-£155,000; 3-bed £105,000-£165,000+; 4-bed £225,000+* • **AVERAGE RENTS (WEEKLY)** *Flats: 1-bed £110+; 2-bed £125+ Houses: 2-bed £145+; 3-bed £175+; 4-bed £220+.*

WEST WICKHAM & HAYES

A step up from Beckenham or Bromley. More roads of large early 20th-century detached and semi-detached houses built as London spilled out into the fields of Kent round the new commuter stations. Every style known to builders from mock Tudor to brick and some satisfyingly crunchy gravel drives. Some of the best roads are near the wooded Hayes Common in Hayes and Spring Park in West Wickham. Flats are mostly in purpose-built blocks. Hayes used to be more sought after than West Wickham but the latter is catching up. Mostly houses – if you want a flat here, West Wickham's a better bet than Hayes.

ATTRACTS *Families wanting to be near good schools; professionals; people moving out from south-east London* • **CONSERVATION AREAS** *Hayes Village; Nash* • **AVERAGE PRICES** *Flats: 1-bed £60,000+; 2-bed £90,000+ Houses: 3-bed £165,000-£275,000; 4-bed £270,000+* • **AVERAGE RENTS (WEEKLY)** *Flats: 1-bed £125+; 2-bed £160+ Houses: 3-bed £205-£230; 4-bed £275.*

KESTON & FARNBOROUGH

These Kentish villages feel as if they've been included in London by mistake. Keston is surrounded on three sides by wooded commons (one of the most attractive features of the area) and centres on a pub and village green, overlooked by some attractive and well-maintained Victorian semi-detached cottages. There's a mixture of everything from Victorian to modern in other roads, although few flats. Farnborough has flat-fronted Victorian cottages around a village green with some low-key modern estates of small brick houses spreading out in roads around. The biggest houses are in the private estates of Keston Park and Farnborough Park. You'll get little change from £700,000 but for the price of a flat in Notting Hill you can buy a detached 1930s house with secluded wooded garden, wrought iron gates and a couple of garages for the Rolls. Again, few flats.

ATTRACTS *Families; City workers* • **CONSERVATION AREAS** *Keston Park; Keston Village; Farnborough Village; Farnborough Park* • **AVERAGE PRICES** *Flats: 1-bed £85,000+; 2-bed £110,000+ Houses: 2-bed £130,000+; 3-bed: £170,000-£250,000; 4-bed £265,000-£650,000+* • **AVERAGE RENTS (WEEKLY)** *Flats: 2-bed £130+ Houses: 3-bed £195+; 4-bed £345+.*

BEST POSTCODES

Not a major issue. Most of the borough has out-of-London postcodes with only the not-very-smart postcodes of Upper Norwood SE19 and Anerley SE20 in London. The borough boundary is more important, as people are prepared to pay thousands of pounds more for the privilege of living in low-cost, efficient Bromley rather than in Lewisham, Lambeth or Southwark, where schools are poor and council tax higher.

AMENITIES

SCHOOLS★★★★

State schools' performance is excellent in league tables and they are widely praised by parents. They are coveted by the less fortunate in neighbouring boroughs and almost all heavily over-subscribed, particularly at secondary level. In true Tory spirit, just one of Bromley's secondary schools is run by the local authority, with the other comprehensives being foundation or voluntary aided. Two, Newstead Woods and St Olave's, are selective. Some other schools used to reserve up to 25% of their places for the children who did best in academic tests but this has changed, under pressure from parents. Little state provision for children under-five so expect to pay for pre-school. A good selection of private prep and secondary schools.

PRE-SCHOOL PROVISION *10 primary schools with part-time nursery classes, 152 private day nurseries and playgroups. Proportion of under-fives in state nurseries: 34%* • **STATE PRIMARY SCHOOLS** *Overall league table position: 20th out of 150. Top scorers: St Mary's RC, Beckenham; St James' RC, Orpington; Perry Hall, Orpington* • **STATE SECONDARY SCHOOLS** *Overall league table position: 9th out of 149. Top scorers: Newstead Woods (girls), Orpington; St Olave's and St Saviour's (boys), Orpington; Bullers Wood (girls), Chislehurst (operates tight catchment area)* • **PRIVATE PREP SCHOOLS** *Bishop Challoner (mixed to 18), Shortlands; St David's College (mixed), West Wickham; Baston (girls to 18), Hayes; Bickley Park Prep (boys), Bickley; Holy Trinity College (mixed to 5, girls to 18), Bromley; Babington House (boys to 7, girls to 16), Chislehurst; Farringtons and Stratford House (girls to 18), Chislehurst* • **PRIVATE SECONDARY SCHOOLS** *Chart-toppers Bromley High (girls), Bromley; Eltham College (boys from 7, girls in 6th), Mottingham.*

TRANSPORT★★★

Trains only throughout the borough. Stations are fairly evenly spread out but commuter services to the east, particular to Orpington, which is on two different lines, are the most frequent.

TRAINS *Anerley Zone 4. Cost of annual season ticket £1104. Average journey time to London Bridge 21 minutes. Beckenham Junction Zone 4. Average journey time to London Bridge 30 minutes; to Victoria 20 minutes. Bromley South Zone 5. Cost of annual season ticket £1332. Average journey time to Victoria 17 minutes. Chislehurst Zone 5. Average journey time to London Bridge 20 minutes; to Charing Cross 28 minutes. Petts Wood Zone 5. Average journey time to London Bridge 23 minutes; to Charing Cross 30 minutes. Hayes Zone 5. Average journey time to London Bridge 33 minutes; to Charing Cross 41 minutes* • **BUSES** *Quite a lot of them – especially in Bromley and Crystal Palace – but they're almost all suburban with few going anywhere more central than Lewisham. The exception is the*

176 from Penge to Oxford Circus. Only at night can you get back from town directly by bus. Night buses include the N3 to Crystal Palace and Penge from Trafalgar Square, the N21 to Chislehurst from Trafalgar Square and the N47 from Victoria to Orpington ● **TRAFFIC TROUBLESPOTS** Crystal Palace: Four roads converge at the end of Crystal Palace Parade by the Park with uncontrolled zebra crossings on each road. Long tail-backs frequent on Westow Hill, Crystal Palace Parade and Anerley Hill. Bromley: Busy around the entrances to car parks and roads around the Glades shopping centre where several main roads converge. Chislehurst: Trafficky in roads around the common and around the main shopping areas particularly on Saturdays with long queues to get into Sainsbury's car park. Orpington: The high street is often busy and traffic can build up around the mini-roundabout near the bottom of the street ● **PARKING** Not too bad in most parts of the borough because of wide roads and lots of space, although it can get sticky around Crystal Palace and in shopping centres on Saturdays. Currently only one controlled parking zone, in Bromley itself, with three zones: inner around the main shopping centre (cost of annual permit £30); north and south (cost of annual permit £15). Further zones in Orpington and West Wickham are being considered.

LEISURE FACILITIES***

THEATRES & CONCERT HALLS A good selection. The Churchill Theatre in Bromley town centre has an eclectic choice of touring West End shows, dance, music and amateur theatre productions. The Studio in Beckenham has workshops (including stand-up comedy and dance), live music, comedy and theatre. Open-air concerts now with a permanent stage at the Crystal Palace Bowl in Crystal Palace Park, with a mixture of nostalgic rock and pop and middle-of-the-road classical, with a backdrop of some of the best views in London ● **CINEMAS** Only two, the Odeon in Bromley and the ABC in Beckenham, both showing mainstream films. There are plans for a multiplex cinema in Crystal Palace Park ● **MUSEUMS & GALLERIES** A small but interesting choice. The Bromley Museum in Orpington is housed in an attractive 700-year-old mullion-windowed priory next to the library with a rather thin collection of local history (although the mock-up of a 1930s breakfast room is fun). You can see the beautiful house and gardens in Downe where Charles Darwin wrote The Origin of Species. Regular tours of Chislehurst Caves, used as an air raid shelter by thousands of Londoners during the Blitz. The Crofton Roman villa at Orpington ● **SPORTS FACILITIES** Well-resourced and used. Four leisure centres at Beckenham (recently refurbished), Orpington, Bromley and West Wickham. Pools at West Wickham. Also during evenings and weekends, use of school facilities at Orpington, Biggin Hill, Mottingham and Beckenham. Golf at High Elms Country Park, Farnborough, and Bromley. Athletics track and sports centre at Crystal Palace Park. ● **LIBRARIES** Good, particularly the central library in Bromley, housed in a spacious three-storey building overlooking the lake in Church House Gardens. Good long opening hours in libraries throughout the borough although all branch libraries close either Wednesday or Thursday and there's no Sunday opening. Surprisingly only just above-average library use at 7.39 visits per head. Position in library-use league table: 12th out of 32 (where 1 is best and 32 worst).

OPEN SPACES *****

A good variety of green space and lots of it. Almost half the borough is greenbelt land. The bits that aren't have some wonderful commons and woods as well as more formal parks of all sizes, and tree-lined streets and well-looked-after gardens add their own dash of colour. The borough's conservation department offers guided walks around conservation areas taking in listed buildings, and the borough has designed a series of waymarked walks in Bromley's greenbelt

VIEWS *Crystal Palace Park. Great views over London from the Crystal Palace site above the crumbling stone terraces and lions which are all that remains of the original glass palace, burnt down in 1936. There are plans to 'restore the park to its former glory' but many people prefer it as it is*

• **WOODS AND COMMONS** *Hayes and Keston Commons with mature oak trees, bracken undergrowth and nature trails. The river Ravensbourne which flows up to the Thames via Lewisham and Deptford rises on Keston Common. Elmstead Woods and nearby Chislehurst Common are part of the beautiful Green Chain Walk, with 40 miles of trails through south-east London's green spaces (see also Bexley, Greenwich and Lewisham)*

• **FAMILY ATTRACTIONS** *The frighteningly realistic Victorian model dinosaurs on the lake at Crystal Palace, the world's first theme park. Crystal Palace Zoo and mini-railway.*

SHOPS ****

PENGE & ANERLEY *Victorian parades of mostly unexciting local shops. But Penge High Street is improving thanks to an injection of government funds and now has newly landscaped town squares, hanging baskets and refurbished shop fronts. Sainsbury's in Penge High Street* • **ELMERS END & BECKENHAM** *Elmers End has a series of dull Tudorbethan local shopping parades around a busy roundabout, with the usual take-aways, newsagents and hardware stores. There's a pretty raised section of High Street at Beckenham by the church with pleasant branches of all the usual chain stores further along. Big Waitrose by Beckenham Junction Station. Safeway in the high street* • **BROMLEY** *Excellent variety of shopping, drawing in people from all over south-east London and Kent. The Glades shopping centre tolled the death knell for many smaller shopping centres when it opened in 1991. Its French château-style twin towers manage to merge skilfully (at least at the front – the back's a bit of a mess) with the pedestrianised high street and market square. Lots of hanging baskets and pavement cafés help to jolly shoppers along. Good branches of all chains, including more up-market ones like Habitat, and two department stores, the Army & Navy and Allders, as well as a large M&S and several bookshops. Waitrose* • **CHISLEHURST** *Mostly decorative rather than useful shops in attractive Royal Parade next to the common with antiques and designer clothes. Bank branches and Sainsbury's in the high street* • **PETTS WOOD & ORPINGTON** *Orpington's Walnut Shopping Centre is looking a bit tired, overshadowed by Bromley as well as more recent mega shopping centres like Bluewater. The high street is better if mostly predictable – small branches of chains, new and second hand bookshops and other individual shops. Weekly market in the Walnut shopping centre. Sainsbury's. Duller parade-style shopping at Petts Wood. Safeway.*

RESTAURANTS**

The culinary desert that is outer south-east London continues, with the honourable exception of Chislehurst, now something of an oasis for restaurant-goers. Maybe not top of the critics' list but a pleasant place for a stroll. Choice of restaurants includes Thai, Indian, Caffe Uno, Café Rouge and a range of pubs and brasseries. Belgian restaurant with extensive beer list among the usual Café Rouges and Starbucks in Bromley.

CRIME RATES****

Position in Metropolitan Police league table: 29th out of 32 (where 1 is worst and 32 best).

THE COUNCIL****

POLITICAL AFFILIATION Liberal Democrat/Labour • **MINUS POINTS** Poor state nursery provision for under-fours. The fourth slowest borough in outer London at carrying out property searches while charging a higher fee than most neighbouring boroughs • **PLUS POINTS** Excellent academic results in schools. Active programme of leisure and arts activities. Generally clean and tidy streets and efficient rubbish collection. Plans to introduce kerbside recycling collections of items other than paper and extend paper collections. Collects more council tax than any other London borough except the City of London • **PROPERTY SEARCHES CARRIED OUT IN 10 WORKING DAYS** 84% • **STANDARD SEARCH FEE** £120 • **COUNCIL TAX COLLECTED** 97%

• **COUNCIL TAX 2000-2001**

BAND	PROPERTY VALUE	CHARGE	BAND	PROPERTY VALUE	CHARGE
A	up to £40,000	£490	E	£88,001–£120,000	£899
B	£40,001–£52,000	£572	F	£120,001–£160,000	£1,063
C	£52,001–£68,000	£654	G	£160,001–£320,000	£1,226
D	£68,001–£88,000	£736	H	over £320,000	£1,471

CAMDEN

There's scarcely a corner of Camden which isn't up-and-coming, already trendy or seriously rich, if you believe everything you read in the press. Its blend of metropolitan sophistication, seething energy and in-your-face wealth cheek-by-jowl with poverty and deprivation have proved irresistible to London commentators. It does the borough's image no harm that it harbours large numbers of journalists, broadcasters and writers within its borders (encouraged by a council keen to attract media and communications companies away from their traditional Soho haunts), as well as scores of academics at London University.

At Camden's southern tip lie the Georgian terraces of Holborn and Bloomsbury, home of London's top lawyers and the University of London respectively. West of Bloomsbury and brash Tottenham Court Road is the small enclave of Georgian and Victorian streets known as Fitzrovia. Across the Euston Road, with the skyline dominated by the red Gothic spires of the restored St Pancras station, are the shabby flat-fronted Georgian terraces of Kings Cross. The council blocks of Somers Town contrast starkly with the

Nash terraces of Regent's Park and the grand Georgian terraces and Victorian crescents of west Camden Town. To the north west are the large white stucco and multicoloured Italianate villas of Primrose Hill and Belsize Park, giving way to more modest terraces and mansion blocks at West Hampstead and Kilburn (see Brent). High on Hampstead Heath, with majestic views over London, sit Hampstead and some of the most beautiful Georgian parts of Highgate (see Haringey). Victoriana takes over again to the east of Hampstead Heath beyond the council blocks of Gospel Oak, with the large terraces of Kentish Town and Dartmouth Park.

Camden has some of the wealthiest people in London but it's also the 17th most deprived borough in England. Unemployment is lower at 7.2% than that of any of its immediate inner London neighbours except Westminster but there are still significant pockets of poverty and joblessness particularly in the areas around Kings Cross, Euston and Somers Town. Race relations have been uneasy over the past few years, creating tensions for the fifth of the population which comes from an ethnic minority, although the significant African, Afro-Caribbean, Asian and Turkish communities, along with large numbers of Jewish and Irish residents, help make Camden one of the most cosmopolitan areas of central London.

One of the biggest question marks over Camden is still the future of Kings Cross, dogged by government stop-and-go over the Channel Tunnel rail link and blighted by uncertainty over funding. The target opening year for the London section of the tunnel is now 2007. There are some signs of progress – developers have now been chosen for the massive £1 billion regeneration of the area around Kings Cross and St Pancras stations, to be known as 'Kings Cross Central' with new shops, living space, offices, bars and restaurants. Meanwhile £253 million of public and private money is still earmarked for the area over seven years (2001 is the sixth year) and is already being used to improve housing, community health, job prospects and security, with better street-lighting and CCTV.

PROPERTY AND ARCHITECTURE

HOLBORN & BLOOMSBURY

Both areas have benefited hugely from Londoners' renewed enthusiasm for central London living, encouraged by a government under pressure to stop new housebuilding on greenfield sites. Houses are rare and usually change hands by word of mouth. Flats are either in converted office blocks or in the area's characteristic flat-fronted Georgian terraces around Grays Inn Road, the British Museum and London University. Lots of ex-council property. There are also flats above shops and restaurants or in former council blocks in Covent Garden (see Westminster) as well as the ever more buzzing enclave of Fitzrovia around Charlotte Street and Fitzroy Street.

ATTRACTS *Singles wanting to be at the centre of things; young professionals*

• **CONSERVATION AREAS** *Bloomsbury; Charlotte Street; Covent Garden; Kingsway* • **AVERAGE PRICES** *Flats: studio £90,000-£130,000; 1-bed £170,000-£215,000; 2-bed £280,000-£330,000 Houses 2/3 bed £500,000+; 4-bed £800,000+* • **AVERAGE RENTS (WEEKLY)** *Flats: studio £180-£240; 1-bed £250-£350; 2-bed £300-£425 Houses: 2/3-bed £500-£800; 4-bed £900+.*

KINGS CROSS

Traditionally known for sleazy bed and breakfast hotels, prostitution, drug-taking, pickpockets and drunks, none of which are a recommendation if you're looking for a place to live. The council and the police claim they've stamped out much of the worst drug-taking and some of the B&Bs in attractive Georgian terraces in streets round the station are gradually closing as tighter housing benefit rules for single people start to bite. The area has great potential if you don't mind living on the edge and not knowing exactly what the place's future is going to be but it's a long term punt (ten years minimum). A lot of ex-council property but houses are rare (most have been converted to flats). The borough has injected £40 million into the area round Argyll Street south of the Euston Road. Developers have moved in around the Regents Canal at Kings Cross basin and along York Road, and properties here sell to Islington people for Islington prices. Flats in the Ice Wharf development on the Regents Canal start at around £250,000 for a two-bed flat and fitted lofts in York Central can cost around £400,000. (This part of Kings Cross is technically in the borough of Islington but will be included here.)

ATTRACTS *Creative people (artists, photographers, architects and media types) who like a central location with a bit of bite; young professionals; single people* • **CONSERVATION AREAS** *Kings Cross and St Pancras* • **AVERAGE PRICES** *(excluding new developments) Flats: 1-bed £120,000-£140,000; 2-bed £130,000-£160,000 Houses: 3-bed £350,000+* • **AVERAGE RENTS (WEEKLY)** *Flats: 1-bed £160+; 2-bed £250+ Houses: 3 bed £400+.*

CAMDEN TOWN

Almost a victim of its own success as tourists mix with the grunge crowds and New Agers at the ever-expanding weekend market. A mixture of every type of property from smart Georgian terraces off Parkway and tucked away *rus in urbe* Nash villas at Park Village West and East to handsome Victorian houses in Gloucester Crescent, big semi-detached mid-Victorian houses and Victorian flat conversions in streets off Camden Road. A lot of council blocks round Mornington Crescent.

ATTRACTS *Young professionals; young singles; creative types; media people; families who can't afford or don't want to live in Hampstead* • **CONSERVATION AREAS** *Camden Town; Regents' Canal; Jeffrey's Street; Camden Square* • **AVERAGE PRICES** *Flats: studio £90,000+; 1-bed £135,000+; 2-bed £175,000+ Houses: 2-bed £300,000-£325,000; 3-bed £350,000; 4-bed £500,000+* • **AVERAGE RENTS (WEEKLY)** *Flats: studio £200+; 1-bed £250+; 2-bed £350+ Houses: 3-bed £450+; 4-bed £600+.*

PRIMROSE HILL & BELSIZE PARK

Lots of four- and five-storey white stucco Victorian houses in both areas although Primrose Hill's are better looked after and fewer are converted into flats. Pretty multicoloured houses around Chalcot Square in Primrose Hill, one of the area's best addresses. There are flats in mansion blocks and tall red brick Victorian terraces in Primrose Gardens, Belsize Park. There is white stucco around Belsize Avenue and some attractive mews cottages tucked away off Belsize Lane. Belsize Park is becoming an increasingly acceptable alternative to Hampstead.

ATTRACTS *Families; well-off couples; people who can't afford Hampstead Village* • **CONSERVATION AREAS** *Primrose Hill; Belsize Park; Eton* • **AVERAGE PRICES** *Flats 1-bed £225,000+; 2-bed £265,000+; 3 bed £350,000+ Houses: 4 bed £850,000+* • **AVERAGE RENTS (WEEKLY)** *Flats: 1-bed £185-£200; 2-bed £220+; 3-bed £325+ Houses: 4-bed £500+.*

WEST HAMPSTEAD

Hampstead's poor cousin, on the wrong side of the Finchley Road but popular with its many supporters who argue that it's less smug and self-satisfied and friendlier than Hampstead. Others go further and say it's set to be the next Notting Hill, with solid Victorian properties, good transport and shops. Streets of handsome red brick mansion blocks and houses divided into generously-sized flats and maisonettes just off the Finchley Road, some with beautiful hidden communal gardens at the back. Well-kept two- and three-storey Victorian terraces with small front gardens in roads off Fortune Green. Lots of conversion flats but beware the problem of short leases.

ATTRACTS *People who can't afford Hampstead; people who've come up in the world from Kilburn; young professionals; members of the Jewish community* • **CONSERVATION AREAS** *Swiss Cottage; West End Green and Parsifal Road* • **AVERAGE PRICES** *Flats: studio £90,000-£110,000; 1-bed £145,000+; 2-bed £185,000+ Houses: 3-bed £350,000+; 4-bed £425,000* • **AVERAGE RENTS (WEEKLY)** *Flats: studio £170+; 1-bed £220+; 2-bed £300+ Houses: 3-bed £450+; 4-bed £450+.*

HAMPSTEAD

One of the places in London where you live if you've arrived. Home of opinion-formers and chatterati of all sorts including actors, successful writers and artists, media magnates and editors as well as the seriously rich and simply well off. Active community organisations fiercely defend the village and heath from unwanted shops and developments (although they failed to halt McDonalds). There's a good mix of property, with everything from more modest Victorian terraces south of the heath, large Victorian houses converted into flats and mansion blocks overlooking the heath, and Georgian cottages and houses in winding lanes near the centre of the village. Beautiful individual early 19th-century houses in Downshire Road leading to the heath. Just a walk away across the heath to the east, a small but perfect slice of Highgate Village includes the Georgian red brick townhouses of the Grove and the wide tree-lined roads of the half-timbered Edwardian Holly Lodge Estate (see Haringey for the rest of Highgate).

ATTRACTS *The creative and those who like to think they're creative; wealthy families and young professionals; Americans; members of the Jewish community* • **CONSERVATION AREAS** *Hampstead Village; Fitzjohns and Netherhall; Redington and Frognal; South Hill Park; Mansfield; Holly Lodge Estate; Highgate Village* • **AVERAGE PRICES** *Flats: studio £130,000+; 1-bed £175,000+; 2-bed £225,000+ Houses: 2-bed £350,000; 3-bed £600,000+; 4-bed £900,000+* • **AVERAGE RENTS (WEEKLY)** *Flats: studio*

£200+; 1-bed £250+; 2-bed £350+; 3-bed £550+ Houses 4-bed
£1,200+.

KENTISH TOWN & DARTMOUTH PARK

More poor relations of Hampstead (but then, where isn't?) Kentish Town
has a slightly more raffish feel than Dartmouth Park, with main roads lined
with once handsome early Victorian terraces now crumbling. Much more
gentrified in roads off the main road with well looked after, carefully
restored two- and three-storey terraces in roads off Fortess Road. Mostly
grim council estates with tower blocks in Gospel Oak, west of Kentish
Town Road (although the council is set to spend £6 million regenerating
and possibly demolishing some of the worst examples). But even here there
are some surprises with small, pretty, flat-fronted and bay window
Victorian terraces in roads by Gospel Oak Station. Dartmouth Park is the
most expensive part of this area, an enclave of well looked after three- and
four-storey Victorian terraces.

ATTRACTS *Families wanting good schools (some good performers nearby);
people who can't afford Hampstead or Highgate* ● **CONSERVATION AREAS**
Dartmouth Park; Kentish Town; Kelly Street ● **AVERAGE PRICES** *Flats: studio
£80,000-£100,000+; 1-bed £120,000-£150,000+; 2-bed £180,000+
Houses: 2-bed £300,000; 3-bed £350,000+; 4-bed £400,000+*
● **AVERAGE RENTS (WEEKLY)** *Flats: studio £150+; 1-bed £190+; 2-bed
£210+ Houses: 2-bed £240+; 4-bed £400+.*

BEST POSTCODES

Hampstead NW3 is one of the prime postcodes of London, let alone
Camden, and people are prepared to pay significantly more for the
coveted code. Elsewhere areas are so mixed that it's difficult to rank codes.
Parts of Camden Town NW1 are smart but the code also includes the
council blocks of Kings Cross and Somers Town. Similarly, Kentish Town
NW5 is slightly better than West Hampstead NW6 because it includes
Dartmouth Park but it also includes the council blocks of Gospel Oak.

AMENITIES

SCHOOLS ****

Camden seems to have achieved what few other inner London boroughs have
managed – schools which attract middle-class parents rather than sending them
fleeing to the nearest outer London borough in search of a decent education for
their children. Good overall results, particularly at secondary level, and some
sought-after state schools including the upfront Camden School for Girls, which
has spawned writers, MPs and journalists. A good selection of private prep and
secondary schools as well as private nurseries. Expect to have to pay for
nursery schools for under-fives as provision is below average.

PRE-SCHOOL PROVISION *112 private or voluntary nurseries and
playgroups; nine state nursery schools; 30 nursery classes in state primary
and church schools. Proportion of under-fives in state nurseries: 51%*
● **STATE PRIMARY SCHOOLS** *Overall league table position: 98th out of
150. Top scorers: Hampstead Parochial CE, Hampstead; St Eugene de
Mazenod RC, West Hampstead; New End (with nursery unit), Hampstead*
● **STATE SECONDARY SCHOOLS** *Overall league table position: 42nd out
of 149. Top scorers: Jews Free School (mixed), Camden Town; La*

Sainte Union RC (girls), Dartmouth Park; Camden School for Girls, Camden Town • **PRIVATE PREP SCHOOLS** Devonshire House (mixed), Hampstead; The Hall (boys), Hampstead; Hereward House (boys), Hampstead; Lyndhurst House (boys), Hampstead; St Anthony's, (boys), Hampstead; St Christopher's (girls), Belsize Park; St Margaret's (girls to 16), Hampstead; St Mary's (mixed) Hampstead; Sarum Hall (girls), Hampstead; University College Junior (boys), Hampstead • **PRIVATE SECONDARY SCHOOLS** Chart-toppers South Hampstead High (girls from 4) and University College School (boys) Hampstead; also The Royal School (girls) Hampstead.

TRANSPORT * * * * *

Excellent connections to all parts of London, particularly in the south of the borough. Plentiful tubes, trains and buses.

TRAINS Gospel Oak Zone 2. Cost of annual season ticket £756. Average journey time to Blackhorse Road, Tottenham 16 minutes. West Hampstead Zone 2. Average journey time (Thameslink) to Kings Cross 9-11 minutes. Kentish Town Zone 2. Average journey time (Thameslink) to Kings Cross 5 minutes • **TUBES** Holborn (Central and Piccadilly), Russell Square (Piccadilly), Euston Square (Metropolitan, Circle), Warren Street (Northern, Victoria), Kings Cross (Victoria, Northern, Circle, Metropolitan, Hammersmith and City) Zone 1. Cost of annual season ticket £636. Camden Town Zone 2. Cost of annual season ticket £756. Average journey time to Charing Cross 10 minutes; to Kings Cross 6 minutes. Kentish Town Zone 2. Average journey time to Charing Cross 12 minutes; to Kings Cross 8 minutes. Hampstead Zone 2. Average journey time to Charing Cross 16 minutes; to Kings Cross 12 minutes. West Hampstead Zone 2. Average journey time to Charing Cross 16 minutes • **BUSES** Lots of buses into town and out to the suburbs with the biggest choice round Camden Town and Mornington Crescent. Services include the 24 from Hampstead to Pimlico via Camden Town, the 13 to Oxford Circus via Finchley Road and Swiss Cottage, the 113 to Oxford Circus via Finchley Road and Swiss Cottage and the 29 via Camden Town to Trafalgar Square • **TRAFFIC TROUBLESPOTS** Holborn and Bloomsbury: Central, so most streets are busy during the day. Long daytime queues along Southampton Row heading up towards Russell Square across Theobalds Road. Kings Cross and St Pancras: The Euston Road is a main west to east through-road and always clogged with several lanes of traffic each way. There are often jams at the junction of Pentonville Road, Caledonian Road and Euston Road. Camden: The one-way high street is often jammed up to the lights by Camden Town tube and at weekends pedestrians visiting the markets do their best to pretend that the high street and Chalk Farm Road are pedestrianised. Hampstead: The narrow high street often has long queues stretching back from the lights at the junction with Heath Street. Heath Street coming down to the tube is also busy • **PARKING** Difficult throughout the whole borough. Wardens are zealous and Camden is experimenting with the reduction or eradication of car parking spaces on new developments. Almost the whole borough is now in a controlled parking zone with residents having to pay to park outside their own front doors. Consultations are continuing over the introduction of another three zones in Swiss Cottage, Kilburn and West Hampstead, despite reservations from traders and residents. Cost of annual resident's permit: £82.

LEISURE FACILITIES * * * * *

THEATRES & CONCERT HALLS *With part of the West End within the borough boundaries there is an excellent choice, although it helps to like musicals or long-running murder mysteries. The Roundhouse at Camden Town (converted from an old railway engine turner) has off-West-End plays, repertory and ambitious plans to become a creative centre of studios and workshops. The Hampstead Theatre shows a lot of new works. Open-air concerts at Kenwood House on Hampstead Heath and concerts at Lauderdale House in Waterlow Park, Highgate. Good selection of other live music venues in pubs and clubs* ● **CINEMAS** *Nine cinemas including several in the West End, showing everything from mainstream to arty films. Also the eight-screen Odeon in Camden Town (replacing the much-lamented Parkway) and two repertory cinemas in Hampstead, the Everyman and Screen on the Hill. The latest owners of The Everyman are planning to invest £1 million to revamp the cinemas and foyers, add new bars and restaurants and install state of the art audiovisual techonology for a 'club-like ambiance'. Not all Hampstead residents are convinced.* ● **MUSEUMS & GALLERIES** *A huge range, from the famous (the British Museum) to the eclectic (the Jewish Museum, Camden Town, Freud's House in Hampstead, Dickens' House in Bloomsbury, the Sir John Soane collection in Lincoln's Inn Fields, the London Canal Musuem in Kings Cross in an old ice warehouse). Art collection at Kenwood House; Hampstead history museum at Burgh House, Hampstead* ● **SPORTS FACILITIES** *Four sports centres at Swiss Cottage, Covent Garden, Kentish Town and Mornington Crescent, Camden, run in partnership with Holmes Place and all recently refurbished. New sports hall at Somers Town. Outdoor heated pool at Covent Garden. Outdoor swimming on Hampstead Heath at Highgate Pond (men), Kenwood Pond (women), Hampstead Pond (mixed) and Parliament Hill lido. Tennis, bowls, athletics and other sports at parks across the borough. Discount card scheme in operation* ● **LIBRARIES** *£15 million has been invested over the past couple of years in repairs and technology. A huge and well-publicised protest over the proposed closure of three libraries forced Camden Council to backtrack and it has now introduced increased opening hours at a number of libraries as well as pushing ahead with plans for a revamp of the main Swiss Cottage library as part of a £49 million facelift for the dreary concrete blocks which now house the library and sports centre. But opening hours in smaller branch libraries are still patchy. Below-average use: 6.5 library visits per head. Place in library-use league table: 20th out of 32 (where 1 is best and 32 worst).*

OPEN SPACES * * * *

A built-up borough but it still manages to have an interesting and varied selection of open space from small hidden gardens to the wooded acres of Hampstead Heath (owned by the Corporation of London). Camden rises steeply to the north and there are some wonderful views of London.
TOWN SQUARES AND SPACES *Gray's Inn Gardens with long lawns overlooked by barristers' chambers – a haven away from the busy Theobalds Road (restricted opening hours); Bloomsbury Square, which is more intimate than the larger Russell Square* ● **VIEWS** *Kite-flying at Primrose Hill, an otherwise featureless grassy mound but excellent views over the West End and City; Parliament Hill Fields, Hampstead Heath, a wide open space framed with extensive woods; Waterlow Park, with lush lawns and ponds leading down to Highgate cemetery* ● **WOODS** *Hampstead Heath,*

easy to lose yourself and think you're nowhere near London ● **CEMETERIES**
*Highgate, the mother of all mysterious overgrown Victorian cemeteries,
with lots of trailing ivy and broken angels.*

SHOPS * * * * *

HOLBORN, BLOOMSBURY & WEST END *Everything from small arty shops and
New Age-type places in the cluster of shops around Seven Dials and
Covent Garden to the hi-fi, electronics and computer shops of Tottenham
Court Road where the furniture shops of Heal's and Habitat can also be
found. Hatton Garden, the jewellery quarter of London, and neighbouring
Leather Lane market have had a multimillion pound revamp. Mostly dull
chain stores along High Holborn. Big Safeway in Bloomsbury at the
Brunswick Shopping Centre which is also set for a facelift* ● **KINGS CROSS**
*Can only improve. Currently run-down shops along Pentonville and
Caledonian Road, many boarded up because of uncertainty over the
Channel Tunnel Rail Link. Lots of burger bars and discount stores and used
car dealers under the arches. But there are plans for new shops and a
superstore as part of developments around Kings Cross station.* ● **PRIMROSE
HILL & BELSIZE PARK** *An attractive villagey street of local shops in Primrose
Hill with delis, interior design shops including a minimalist bathroom shop,
clothes shops and a second-hand bookshop. More local shops in Englands
Lane, Belsize Park, including interior design shops and galleries, as well as
a clutch of shops around Belsize Crescent* ● **CAMDEN TOWN** *Has ballooned
in recent years as Camden Market spread along Regents Canal at
Camden Lock, and up Chalk Farm Road, closely followed by shops selling
Doc Martens, grunge clothes, leather jackets and records. Huge choice of
records, books, clothes, antiques and food and crowded with tourists as
well as locals at weekends. The south end of the high street has good
branches of Boots, Waterstones and other chains. Stables Market in Chalk
Farm Road which has clothes and bric-a-brac stalls is to become a 'media
village' with shops and leisure facilities in a £25 million development and
a further £80 million is going into a shopping and leisure development on
Parkway. Sainsbury's in bizarre metal building on Camden Road. Safeway
in Chalk Farm Road* ● **HAMPSTEAD** *A network of streets tumbling down the
hill from the tube station in Hampstead village. Lots of good patisseries and
delis, a big Waterstones, designer clothes shops, a real butchers and a
second-hand bookshop among the collection of interesting local shops.
Spoilt by traffic* ● **WEST HAMPSTEAD & FINCHLEY ROAD** *Massive
improvements here over the past few years as the middle classes ripple out
from Hampstead, although Finchley Road is the main road to the M1.
Several patisseries, popular meeting places for the area's East European
and Jewish communities, have disappeared. Habitat and large Waitrose.
Sainsbury's has recently opened as part of the O2 development with
multiscreen Warner village and leisure facilities. West End Lane is more
interesting than it used to be with a lot of furniture shops, a second-hand
bookshop and music shop among other local shops* ● **KENTISH TOWN** *Rather
run-down shops lining the busy Kentish Town Road with a lot of discount
shops, off-licences and ethnic supermarkets.*

RESTAURANTS * * * * *

BLOOMSBURY, HOLBORN & WEST END *A huge choice, particularly in Covent
Garden and Fitzrovia around Charlotte Street (Greek, Italian, Korean and
Japanese just for starters). Holborn's a bit dead in the evening but*

*Bloomsbury is more interesting, especially in the streets around the British Museum and around Great Ormond Street Hospital in the pedestrian Lambs Conduit Street ● **CAMDEN TOWN** Everything from brasseries to Scandinavian with Chinese, Indian, Vietnamese and Italian in between. The best selection is round Regents Park Road and Parkway just off Camden High Street. Very lively in the evening and if you live here there's no need to leave your own patch to have a good time ● **HAMPSTEAD & WEST HAMPSTEAD** Better choice in West Hampstead with wine bars, sushi bars, Italian and East European in West End Lane. Lots of pavement cafés and people braving the traffic for a wine or coffee after work. Brasseries, cafés and some modern European in Hampstead and a friendly branch of Café Rouge ● **ELSEWHERE** A couple of notable African restaurants and pubs in Kentish Town, as well as a Pizza Express and locally praised Italian.*

CRIME RATES*

Position in Metropolitan Police league table: 2nd out of 32 (where 1 is worst and 32 best). But the council argues that this figure is distorted by the huge daytime influx of population.

THE COUNCIL***

POLITICAL AFFILIATION Labour ● **MINUS POINTS** the highest Band D council tax in inner London. Residents complain that the planning department can be inconsistent and tricky to deal with. Camden is trying to deal with complaints that there is not enough ongoing supervision in playgrounds and that they are vulnerable to vandalism ● **PLUS POINTS** Litter collection and street-sweeping improved around Camden Town following complaints from residents, although still poor around Tottenham Court Road and in areas like Kentish Town. Much praised, efficient, twice weekly rubbish collection and fortnightly recycling collections for newspapers. Good secondary schools ● **PROPERTY SEARCHES CARRIED OUT IN 10 WORKING DAYS** 99.1% ● **STANDARD SEARCH FEE** £100 ● **COUNCIL TAX COLLECTED** 91.5%
● **COUNCIL TAX 2000-2001**

BAND	PROPERTY VALUE	CHARGE	BAND	PROPERTY VALUE	CHARGE
A	up to £40,000	£604	E	£88,001-£120,000	£1,108
B	£40,001-£52,000	£705	F	£120,001-£160,000	£1,309
C	£52,001-£68,000	£806	G	£160,001-£320,000	£1,511
D	£68,001-£88,000	£906	H	over £320,000	£1,813

CITY OF LONDON

This is where London began. From this small square mile on the north bank of the Thames, the capital grew in wealth and influence from Roman times onwards, stretching its tentacles ever further into the outlying countryside, halted only by the twin deterrents of Adolf Hitler and the greenbelt. For centuries, people lived as well as worked in the City, which was the centre of political, intellectual, economic and social life. But as the habit of travelling to work took off in the 18th century, the City's residential population dwindled to a few thousand, swollen by thousands more workers every weekday morning.

The City is still primarily commercial, a world centre of global banks and finance houses, blinking computer screens and plate glass office blocks rearing up on every side. From Monday to Friday, its pavements seethe with smart suits. At weekends, it's pretty dead, with shops, restaurants and pubs closed. Despite this it's seen a residential renaissance in the last few years as developers have responded to government pressure to build on previously used inner-city sites, converting office blocks and warehouses to smart new apartments. Most of the purchasers have been City workers who spend long hours in the office and don't want the hassle of a commute or investors buying to rent. This has swelled the City's resident population to around 7,000, with more to come as more residential developments are completed.

The City begins in the west at Temple and the attractive collegiate gardens and buildings of the Inns of Court, home of London's barristers. To the east are Fleet Street, once the home of the newspaper industry, and St Paul's, where the ugly 1960s office blocks surrounding the sublime cathedral buildings have finally been demolished after years of wrangling. North of St Paul's is the Barbican. The series of tower blocks which stabs the skyline like jagged teeth is the City's largest concentration of private housing. Travel along London Wall, the route of the City's old Roman wall, and cut south, and you reach the financial heart of the city around the Bank of England and Lloyd's of London. At its eastern boundary by the Tower of London and Aldgate, the wealth of the city starts to recede, giving way abruptly to the beginning of the East End.

Until recently, there was no challenge to the City's financial and economic pre-eminence. But the last decade hasn't altogether been a success story. For a start, Canary Wharf (see Tower Hamlets), which looked dead in the water at the beginning of the decade, revived with the last economic upturn and has taken some of the City's best corporate tenants. On top of this, there's been a lot of looking over shoulders at European pretenders to the City's financial throne. Physically the heart of the City has been twice devastated by bombs, leading to the creation of complex traffic systems to control movement round the City more tightly and reduce crime. The City's wealth has also aroused the anger of anti-capitalist groups who continue to threaten the square mile with violence and mayhem at regular intervals.

On the plus side for the City, it's managed to survive attempts to modernise London government. In return the City is putting in place radical reforms to its much criticised 'jobs for the boys' electoral system. It's also been an active player in regeneration initiatives across east London and a staunch keeper of some of London's most treasured green spaces.

PROPERTY AND ARCHITECTURE

FLEET STREET & ST PAUL'S

A number of luxury developments have sprung up, tucked away behind street facades along Fleet Street and Ludgate Hill up towards St Paul's. There are fabulous views of St Paul's now that the horrible blue railway bridge to Holborn Viaduct has been taken down. Almost all properties for sale or to rent here are flats.

ATTRACTS *People who want to be in the centre of things; City workers; investors; older people wanting a pied-à-terre* • **CONSERVATION AREAS** Dyers Buildings; Chancery Lane; Fleet Street; Temples; Whitefriars; Ludgate Hill • **AVERAGE PRICES** Flats: studio £120,000-£150,000; 1-bed £140,000+; 2-bed £270,000+ • **AVERAGE RENTS (WEEKLY)** Flats: studio £180-£225; 1-bed £220-£350; 2-bed £300+.

BARBICAN

Built in the 1970s on a site almost completely razed by bombing during the blitz and originally intended as council flats. Only 2% of residents are still council tenants and the Corporation of London, which is the freeholder, is selling flats off if they become free. You either love the Barbican or you hate it. It has all the worst architectural accoutrements of the 1970s – huge towers, walkways, dead walls and concrete that soaks in the rain. It's so confusing to find your way around that there's a yellow line painted on the pavement to mark the route. But once you penetrate the complex, the centre has gardens, fountains, flats with large windows and balconies. And of course, the Barbican Arts centre is right in the middle, along with the Guildhall School of Music and Drama and the City of London Girls School. Increasingly popular as the City livens up. Residents pay premiums for south- and west-facing flats or apartments on high floors of tower blocks and often buy after renting. Beware high service charges.

ATTRACTS *Singles; City workers; people wanting pieds-à-terre; empty nesters and, increasingly, families who want to be in the heart of London* • **CONSERVATION AREAS** Postman's Park; The Brewery, Chiswell Street • **AVERAGE PRICES** *Flats: studio £100,000+; 1-bed £150,000-£230,000; 2-bed £240,000+; 3-bed £370,000+; Penthouse: £625,000* • **AVERAGE RENTS (WEEKLY)** *Flats: studio:£180-£225; 1-bed £220-£350; 2-bed £300+ 3-bed: £400-£600.*

BEST POSTCODES

City postcode areas are so small that you hardly notice when you're walking from one to another. Fenchurch EC3 is primarily commercial, with most of the residential action in Queen Victoria Street EC4 and Moorgate EC2 which includes the Barbican. Postcodes have little snob value although some agents say it can be more difficult to sell properties in the heart of the city than a short distance further away in Clerkenwell for example. For Clerkenwell EC1, see Islington.

AMENITIES

SCHOOLS ★★★

The City counts several good private schools within its boundaries. No state secondary schools. One primary school, Sir John Cass's Foundation School, which performs well above average in league tables. Below-average proportion of under-fives in state nurseries.

PRE-SCHOOL PROVISION *1 state-run nursery (for residents only, not open to day time workers from outside the borough); 1 nursery class in a state primary school; 6 private or voluntary playgroups or day nurseries (more available in surrounding boroughs, for example Islington or Westminster). Proportion of under-fives in state nurseries: 40%* ● **STATE PRIMARY SCHOOLS** *Overall league table position: 14th out of 150* ● **PRIVATE PREP SCHOOLS** *St Paul's Cathedral School (boys)* ● **PRIVATE SECONDARY SCHOOLS** *City of London Girls (from 7), Barbican; City of London Boys, EC4.*

TRANSPORT ★★★★★

You can't get much more central. All Zone 1. Cost of annual season ticket £636. There are three main line stations within its boundaries (Liverpool Street, Fenchurch Street and Cannon Street), as well as 11 tube and Docklands Light Railway lines and countless buses. London Bridge station isn't in the City but thousands of commuters stream across London Bridge every weekday morning to the City and back across to head out to the southern suburbs in the evening.

TRAFFIC *After the IRA bomb which hit Bishopsgate in 1993, the whole City was encompassed by barriers and police checkpoints. The idea was to block off smaller streets and keep traffic flowing only through the City's main arteries. There was much grumbling at first as the restrictions caused huge jams, particularly when travelling east to west (to get across London Bridge from east of Tower Hill means elaborate detours round the Aldgate one-way system or south of the river), but the ring of plastic, as it quickly became known, reduced traffic and cut crime according to City police, and has now been made permanent* ● **TRAFFIC TROUBLESPOTS** *Aldgate: Several main roads converge, all carrying heavy traffic which then has to manoeuvre to change lanes to get onto other main roads. Upper Thames Street: The alternative to Aldgate to get out of the City going west. Once you're stuck in it there's no way out. Moorgate: Clogged with traffic going north to Islington. Particularly bad at the junction with London Wall* ● **PARKING** *Don't even think about parking on the streets unless you want to keep popping out to feed the meter. No resident's parking permits but you can get a concessionary rate in car parks: £170 for 12 weeks. Is it worth it? Developments with underground parking are understandably popular.*

LEISURE FACILITIES ★★★★

THEATRES & CONCERT HALLS *A wealth of venues and activity. The Barbican Centre has managed to shake off its initial image of being miles from anywhere with nothing much going on, although it's still a bit confusing to find your way around. Now the London home of the Royal Shakespeare Company but there's plenty besides Shakespeare, both in the more formal theatre and the more intimate Pit. There's also music of all sorts from classical and choral to jazz and rock and roll, as well as films and art galleries. Next door at the Guildhall School of Music and Drama there's a* steady flow of plays, opera and orchestral music. One of the City's other musical pleasures is the wide range of organ, piano and other recitals in the sublime setting of its churches • **CINEMAS** Two cinemas at the Barbican showing both the latest films and more arty films and classics • **MUSEUMS & GALLERIES** A large selection packed into a small area, including the excellent Museum of London, charting the history of London from Roman times to the present. Unprepossessing from the outside with no proper street entrance but worth it once you're in. Lots of small museums run by churches, livery companies and city firms, as well as the Bank of England (coins, banknotes and a peep behind the scenes of a modern bank). Dr Johnson's house is tucked away behind Fleet Street. Art galleries at the Barbican and the Guildhall, the 15th-century headquarters of the Corporation of London (worth visiting for the splendour of both its exterior and interior, despite the ugly modern office buildings of the Corporation overshadowing it) • **SPORTS FACILITIES** Just one publicly funded leisure centre at Golden Lane, with a swimming pool, badminton, tennis and classes. Other boroughs' facilities close by. Otherwise the City is choc-a-bloc with private gyms and pools for workaholic bankers who need to use up adrenalin • **LIBRARIES** Specialist reference collections open to the public as well as lending libraries. The City Business Library, Guildhall (great for London obsessives) and St Bride's Printing Library are some of the collections available. Good music collection as well as general library at the Barbican. Opening hours reflect City's tendency to close down at weekends, with the Barbican and Guildhall libraries the only ones to open on Saturday. Huge numbers of visits per head of population because of daily influx of workers. Not included in library-use league tables because its figures aren't comparable with other boroughs.

OPEN SPACES**(***)

A tricky area to judge, at least within the borough structure of this book, because the Corporation of London owns and cares for some of London's best known open spaces. But they're all outside the City boundary. Hence the three extra stars in brackets, for Hampstead Heath (Camden), Highgate Wood (Haringey), Queen's Park (Brent), West Ham Park (Newham), Epping Forest (Waltham Forest), West Wickham Common (Bromley), Coulsdon Common (Croydon) and Bunhill Fields, the dissenters' burial ground in Islington. The City itself is densely built up and populated. You don't live here for wide open space and this can be wearing, particularly in summer. At summer lunchtimes, green spaces are crowded with City workers. Most of Finsbury Circus, the City's largest public garden, is taken up with the bowling green, which looks lovely but cuts down sitting or walking room for everyone else. But there are some lovely small spaces. **CHURCHYARDS** St Paul's. One of the largest with lots of good places to sit and have a sandwich. Can be crowded in the summer though because St Paul's is such a tourist honeypot. The small churchyard of St Olave's, where Samuel Pepys is buried, is a welcome retreat from the city crowds, as are the churchyards of St Bride's Fleet Street and St Botolph's Bisphopsgate.

SHOPS***

Lots of shops are still closed at weekends and by early evening but during the week shopping is improving, as the upmarket chains realise the City is awash with people with lots of money to spend. **CHEAPSIDE, BISHOPSGATE,**

MOORGATE & FENCHURCH STREET *The main shopping drags of the City, with small branches of middle market and smarter chains and (inevitably) lots of sandwich bars, coffee houses and City menswear shops. All are trafficky with motorcycle couriers an ever-present hazard and more for desperate last minute rushes than a leisurely shop. Lunchtimes are hell. Tesco Metro in Cheapside, huge M&S in Moorgate and recently opened food M&S at St Mary Axe.* • **LEADENHALL & LIVERPOOL STREET** *Good and interesting shopping in the restored Victorian Leadenhall Arcade, several streets of pedestrianised covered shopping. Lots of restaurants and sandwich bars of course, but also a real fishmonger, hardware and independent leather goods shops as well as large Waterstones. The Liverpool Street arcade, until recently fairly sorry for itself, has been given a new lease of life with expensive designer clothes shops, cafés and restaurants* • **PETTICOAT LANE** *One of London's best-known markets, particularly for clothes and leather goods, on the City's eastern boundary, where it starts turning into the East End.*

RESTAURANTS***

During the week, a huge choice of wine bars and coffee bars as well as Thai, Chinese, Japanese, French, Italian, British and anything else you can think of. Many are stuffed to the gunnels at weekday lunchtimes, as are pubs. Don't believe all you read about the death of City lunches. But most restaurants are closed at weekends. The City also closes down early in the evening as workers stop for a quick drink after work and then move on elsewhere.

CRIME RATES

There are no comparable figures because the City has its own police force and isn't under the jurisdiction of the Metropolitan Police. The City police also handle different types of crime from the Met – white collar fraud is a big concern in the City, for example.

THE COUNCIL****

POLITICAL AFFILIATION *Independent. The City has its own electoral system, with annual elections where each ward returns representatives to the court of common council. All common councillors face elections every year. Each ward also has an alderman, who is currently elected for life but under reforms being proposed, will face regular elections. There's nothing to stop the court of common council from being elected on party lines but in practice it's been independent for some years. A bill currently going through parliament will give residents and businesses more electoral clout* • **MINUS POINTS** *Small or non-existent choice of state schools meaning children of secondary school age have to cross the borough boundary or go private. Low state nursery provision. Many services (e.g. libraries) only function during working hours. No door-to-door recycling collections* • **PLUS POINTS** *Generally clean streets and well maintained roads. The most efficient household rubbish collection in London. Collects a higher proportion of council tax owed than any other London borough. Well maintained green space. Low council tax* • **PROPERTY SEARCHES CARRIED OUT IN 10 WORKING DAYS** *96.4%* • **STANDARD SEARCH FEE** £*105.60* • **COUNCIL TAX COLLECTED** *97.4%*

● COUNCIL TAX 2000-2001

BAND	PROPERTY VALUE	CHARGE	BAND	PROPERTY VALUE	CHARGE
A	up to £40,000	£371	E	£88,001-£120,000	£681
B	£40,001-£52,000	£433	F	£120,001-£160,000	£804
C	£52,001-£68,000	£495	G	£160,001-£320,000	£928
D	£68,001-£88,000	£557	H	over £320,000	£1,114

CROYDON

It's easy to dismiss Croydon as at best, dull and at worst, a dump. Most people are more familiar with it as a series of railway stations en route to the south coast or Gatwick than as a place to live, and what passing travellers see looks dire. Ugly 1960s office slabs mixed with more recent red brick towers and blocks of every shape and size suddenly rise on all sides as trains pull into East Croydon station then just as quickly disappear, as the view from the window gives way to a sea of suburbia, tatty on the way into London and smarter on the way out.

But appearances can be deceptive. The tower blocks of Croydon itself hide some beautiful restored 19th-century public buildings. There's a vast choice of shops. And Croydon town centre is geographically a tiny part of Croydon borough, which stretches from the inner suburbs of South London down to the Surrey greenbelt. In the north, it touches four other boroughs (Bromley, Lambeth, Southwark and Lewisham) at Crystal Palace before plunging down the hill to Upper Norwood whose huge detached Victorian villas still manage to look gracious despite being mostly converted into flats. In next door South Norwood the houses show more signs of neglect, and shabby conversions mix with Edwardian semis and modern houses. To the east and north of Croydon town centre is the sea of late 19th- and early 20th-century suburbia which includes Woodside, Addiscombe and Thornton Heath and the 1930s semis of Norbury. To the east and south of Croydon and in parts of Purley things get grand, with detached stockbroker-belt houses set in large gardens with backdrops of wooded hills. Smaller detached and semi-detached houses from Edwardian to modern line the suburban crescents of Selsdon and Coulsdon.

Predictably the more suburban parts of Croydon are popular with families who want access to houses with gardens, good schools, good transport links and green space. But the borough is more cosmopolitan than neighbouring Bromley for example, with significant Asian and West Indian communities. Nearly a fifth of the population is from an ethnic minority. Just 3.9% of Croydon's citizens are unemployed, with large numbers of people working locally in white collar jobs (particularly financial services) or commuting to central London.

The borough is energetically marketing Croydon town centre as the dynamic, modern commercial centre for a huge swathe of south London and the south east, trying to rid the area of its reputation as a boring set of office blocks. As if there weren't already plenty of shops in Croydon there are multi-million pound plans to expand both the town's existing shopping centres. A ten-screen cinema and health club is taking shape behind the preserved Victorian façade of the former Grants department store and the long vacant site next to East Croydon station is designated for a 12,000 seat arena with supermarket, bars, restaurants and offices. And after three years of digging up roads and laying tracks, the Croydon Tramlink, London's first modern tram system, is up and running. Swish red and yellow trams link Croydon with the south west at Wimbledon and the south east at Beckenham, giving travellers access to a wide range of train services into London and even more importantly providing a fast link into Croydon for previously isolated parts of the borough.

PROPERTY AND ARCHITECTURE

UPPER NORWOOD

Grand, detached red brick Victorian villas with gables, wooden carved balconies and other lush original features in roads running down from Crystal Palace and Westow Hill into Upper Norwood. The most elevated corner of Upper Norwood, which most people prefer to think of as Crystal Palace, is bordered by Westow Hill, Church Road and Westow Street and is known as the Westow Hill or Upper Norwood Triangle. It has attracted an interesting mix of middle-class residents claiming village status for the area, artists, and New Agers (see also Bromley and Lambeth). Elsewhere there are roads of 1930s semi-detached and detached properties mixed with modern blocks and council property.

ATTRACTS *First-time buyers; flat-hunters of all descriptions; some families; people who can't afford Streatham, Tooting or Dulwich* • **CONSERVATION AREAS** *Harold Road; Upper Norwood Triangle; Church Road* • **AVERAGE PRICES** *Flats: studio £50,000-£55,000; 1-bed £70,000+; 2-bed £95,000+ Houses 3-bed £150,000+; 4-bed £200,000; 5-bed £250,000+* • **AVERAGE RENTS (WEEKLY)** *Flats: studio £95-£105; 1-bed £115-£140; 2-bed £160+ Houses: 3-bed £230+.*

SOUTH NORWOOD

More down-market than Upper Norwood. Some large detached Victorian houses in South Norwood, most of which have been converted into flats and seen better days, alongside roads of Edwardian semis, half-timbered 1930s semis and low-rise council houses. Depressing rows of pebble-dashed, louvre-windowed houses fronted with scrubby trees off Portland and Morland Roads in Woodside, relieved by the open space of Woodside Green lined with some handsome semi-detached Victorian villas. Woodside now has a Tramlink station which has dramatically improved its accessibility to Croydon and made it more popular with buyers who would previously have scorned it. Tubes on an extended East London line would also stop at Norwood Junction, which makes this area worth watching.

ATTRACTS *First-time buyers; local locals; families wanting a lot of space for their money* • **CONSERVATION AREAS** *South Norwood* • **AVERAGE PRICES**

Flats: studio £45,000+; 1-bed £55,000+; 2-bed £70,000+ Houses: 2-bed £100,000+; 3-bed £125,000+; 4-bed £160,000+ • **AVERAGE RENTS (WEEKLY)** *Flats: studio £95-£105; 1-bed £115-£125; 2-bed £150-£160 Houses: 2-bed £160+; 3-bed £175; 4-bed £205+.*

THORNTON HEATH & NORBURY

Mostly streets of two- and three-storey Victorian terraces and Edwardian or 1930s semis in Thornton Heath, many of which have been 'improved' by their owners with louvred windows and modern doors, to dreary effect. This is fruitful flat-hunting territory with flats in conversions or modern blocks. Norbury's slightly more up-market, with a lot of 1930s semis in roads off London Road. Some attractive individual 1930s and modern detached houses in Gibson's Hill, with beautiful views over London and Surrey.

ATTRACTS *First-time buyers; loyal locals; members of the Asian community* • **CONSERVATION AREAS** *None* • **AVERAGE PRICES** *Flats: studio £45,000; 1-bed £50,000+; 2-bed £65,000+ Houses: 2-bed £95,000; 3-bed £120,000+; 4-bed £170,000+* • **AVERAGE RENTS (WEEKLY)** *Flats: studio £95+; 1-bed £115+; 2-bed £150+ Houses 2-bed £160+; 3-bed £175+; 4-bed £195+.*

CROYDON

East Croydon is the town's best side, closely followed by South Croydon (where a lot of the most sought-after schools are). East Croydon's where commuter belt takes over from London sprawl and Croydon starts to feel part of Surrey. The grandest roads are on the Whitgift estate by Lloyd Park. Wide, handsome but slightly bleak roads of big 1930s detached houses with gardens, in every style from stockbroker Tudor to overgrown rustic cottage with exaggeratedly deep eaves. As a definite sign that the owners have arrived, houses have names not numbers. Spending half a million pounds upwards here isn't unusual. Shirley Hills, sandwiched between Addington Golf Course and Addington Hills, is another sought-after area, with private roads of large detached houses. More large detached and semi-detached houses in parts of South Croydon, especially round the Waldrons conservation area. West Croydon is the cheapest part of town, a mixture of small Victorian terraces and industrial estates. But it has a new Tramlink station and could be linked into the tube network via the East London line extension in a few years' time, so it could be one to watch. Addiscombe, on the other side of town, also has a new Tramlink station which has made its Victorian terraces and detached and semi-detached early 20th-century homes more attractive to potential buyers.

ATTRACTS *Commuters wanting to be near stations with good services to London, particularly East Croydon; families wanting good schools and green space* • **CONSERVATION AREAS** *The Waldrons; Parish Church; central Croydon* • **AVERAGE PRICES** *Flats: studio £45,000-£55,000; 1-bed £60,000-£100,000; 2-bed £70,000-£150,000 Houses: 2-bed £85,000-£150,000; 3-bed £90,000-£180,000; 4-bed £140,000+* • **AVERAGE RENTS (WEEKLY)** *Flats: studio £105-£125; 1-bed £150; 2-bed £165+ Houses: 2-bed £195; 3-bed £205-£220; 4-bed £230+.*

SELSDON

Much of Selsdon was built in the 1960s and 1970s on three estates, Forestdale, Ashendale and Selsdon Dale. Lots of small houses and blocks of flats in cul-de-sacs. This and neighbouring Addington Village, previously out on a limb for the carless, have seen prices rise following the arrival of the Tramlink, which whisks them to Croydon in under 20 minutes. Good territory for first time buyers and others on limited budgets who want decent space for their money, particularly if they work within striking distance of a Tramlink station.

ATTRACTS Commuters; families • **CONSERVATION AREA** Addington Village • **AVERAGE PRICES** Flats: 1-bed £65,000-£80,000; 2-bed £90,000-£140,000 Houses: 2-bed £120,000-£135,000; 3-bed £135,000+; 4-bed £200,000+ • **AVERAGE RENTS (WEEKLY)** Flats: 1-bed £125+; 2-bed £150+ Houses: 2-bed £160+; 3-bed £185+; 4-bed £220-£230.

PURLEY & COULSDON

Just like its reputation, Purley is safe and predictable, inhabited by regular commuters who catch the same train to town every day. More turn of the century and inter-war suburbia set in greenbelt land with a generous supply of golf courses. Pleasant but unremarkable residential streets. The grandest part of Purley is the Webb estate to the south west of Purley town centre. Here there are tree-lined private roads (with firm notices telling the hoi polloi to keep out), with huge detached houses, many behind high hedges or with elaborate entrance gates and money no object. The further away you are from the main Brighton Road in Coulsdon the better. Mainly 1930s semis and some Victorian terraces in Coulsdon itself, with larger semis and detached houses in grander West Coulsdon. Up the hill, Old Coulsdon has a more villagey atmosphere, helped by views over the surrounding Downs, a village green, shops and some good pubs.

ATTRACTS The wealthy; commuters of more modest means; families wanting good schools and green space • **CONSERVATION AREAS** Webb Estate and Upper Woodcote Village; Bradmore Green • **AVERAGE PRICES** Flats: 1-bed £95,000+; 2-bed £100,000+ Houses: 2-bed £130,000+; 3-bed £140,000-£225,000; 4-bed £200,000-£300,000+ • **AVERAGE RENTS (WEEKLY)** Flats: 1-bed £105; 2-bed £115-£195 Houses: 2-bed £115-£175; 3-bed £196-£220; 4-bed £255+.

BEST POSTCODES

Largely irrelevant as most of the area has Croydon rather than London postcodes. Of the two areas with London postcodes, Norwood SE19 and South Norwood SE25, neither is considered particularly smart, even by South London standards.

AMENITIES

SCHOOLS * * *

Some excellent and sought-after state schools at both primary and secondary level. Primary schools perform creditably in league tables but secondary schools are more disappointing despite some good schools. A good choice of private prep and secondary schools. State nursery provision has expanded significantly in the past year and there are a number of private nurseries in the borough.

PRE-SCHOOL PROVISION 4 state nursery schools; 41 nursery classes in state primary or church schools; 121 private and voluntary day nurseries.

Proportion of under-fives in state nurseries: 74% • **STATE PRIMARY SCHOOLS**
*Overall league table position: 86th out of 150. Top scorers: Coulsdon C of
E, Coulsdon; Margaret Roper RC, Purley; St Aidan's RC, Coulsdon;*
• **STATE SECONDARY SCHOOLS** *Overall league table position: 94th out of
149. Top scorers: Coloma Convent RC (girls), Croydon; Archbishop
Tenison's C of E (mixed), Croydon; St Andrew's CE (mixed), Croydon •*
PRIVATE PREP SCHOOLS *The Lodge (girls to 18), Purley; St David's (mixed),
Purley; West Dene (mixed), Purley; Sanderstead Junior (mixed),
Sanderstead; Croham Hurst (girls to 18), South Croydon; Croydon High
(girls to 18), South Croydon; Cumnor House (boys), South Croydon;
Elmhurst (boys), South Croydon; Old Palace (girls to 18), Croydon; Royal
Russell Prep (mixed), Croydon •* **PRIVATE SECONDARY SCHOOLS** *Royal Russell
(mixed) Croydon; Trinity (boys), Croydon; Whitgift (boys), South Croydon.*

TRANSPORT * * *

The arrival of the £200 million Tramlink provides much needed east–west
links and they're well used. (Unfortunately the open station platforms are
already covered in graffiti, particularly in more outlying areas.) Otherwise,
it's rail only throughout the borough. Connections from Croydon,
particularly East Croydon, are excellent, with fast trains to and from
London, Gatwick and the south coast often stopping only at East Croydon.
Trains from here go to Victoria and London Bridge, Blackfriars and Kings
Cross on the Thameslink, and an estimated 600 trains a day pass through
East Croydon. But services are more patchy to outlying parts of the
borough, particularly in the east where large tracts are nowhere near a
railway station.
TRAINS *Thornton Heath Zone 4. Cost of annual season ticket £1104.
Average journey time to Victoria 22 minutes; to London Bridge 31 minutes.
Norwood Junction Zone 4. Average journey time to London Bridge 24
minutes; to Victoria 29 minutes. East Croydon Zone 5. Cost of annual
season ticket £1332. Average journey time to London Bridge 14 minutes;
to Victoria 16 minutes; to Blackfriars 21 minutes. Purley Zone 6. Cost of
annual season ticket £1456. Average journey time to London Bridge 20
minutes; to Victoria; 35 minutes •* **TRAMLINK** *East Croydon. Average
journey time to Wimbledon 26 minutes; to Elmers End 11 minutes •* **BUSES**
*On the outer limits of the bus network. Good links to and from Croydon
and Purley to the rest of the borough but again buses are less frequent in
more far-flung areas. Routes out of the borough normally link suburbs in
neighbouring south London rather than going to the centre of town. Night
buses include the N68 from Coulsdon and Purley to Trafalgar Square and
the N159 from Trafalgar Square to Thornton Heath, Croydon and New
Addington •* **TRAFFIC TROUBLESPOTS** *Purley: The main A23 between
Croydon and Purley is trafficky all down the Purley Way culminating in tail-
backs at the junction where four main roads meet at Purley. Notorious for
trapping irate motorists desperate to get to the coast or Gatwick airport.
Residents claim traffic in Purley itself has got worse since the arrival of
Tesco. Croydon: generally trafficky in roads round the pedestrianised town
centre and around stations. South Norwood: Long tail-backs at the lights at
the junction of Portland Road and the high street •* **PARKING** *Not generally
a problem in the south of the borough where there's lots of space and wide
roads but can get tricky around shopping centres and stations. There are
controlled parking zones in Croydon, South Norwood, Thornton Heath,
Norbury, Selsdon, Purley, Coulsdon and Sanderstead. Cost of annual
resident's permit: £27.*

LEISURE FACILITIES****

THEATRES & CONCERT HALLS *Much improved since the arrival of the Croydon Clocktower arts centre, a stunning conversion of the town centre's clock tower and town hall into a light modern theatre, cinema and library behind a beautiful 19th-century facade. The Braithwaite Hall at the Clocktower has fringe theatre, jazz and live music and dance. The Clocktower has made Fairfield Halls, Croydon's main theatre and concert venue, look decidedly tired by comparison and the 40-year-old Halls could be in line for a facelift or even demolition. The Ashcroft Theatre at the Fairfield Halls shows musicals and plays by touring companies. New plays at the Warehouse Theatre. Classical, jazz and rock concerts at the Fairfield Halls, home of the London Mozart players. Community shows at Stanley Halls, South Norwood* • **CINEMAS** *Currently four film venues including the David Lean cinema at the Clocktower showing a mix of mainstream and more off-the-wall films; Fairfield Halls (mostly mainstream); the new eight screen Warner Village in Croydon and the three screen Safari Cinema. All this plus another ten screens at the new multiplex on the Grant department store site in central Croydon – how many cinemas does Croydon need to keep it happy?* • **MUSEUMS & GALLERIES** *A small selection. Lifetimes, an interactive local history museum, and galleries at the Clocktower. Croydon Old Palace (now a school but once the medieval home of the Archbishops of Canterbury) and Addington Palace (once the 18th-century home of the Archbishops of Canterbury and now a conference centre, restaurant and country club) are both open to visitors* • **LEISURE FACILITIES** *Sports and fitness centre at Selsdon. Newly refurbished pools at New Addington, Purley, South Norwood and Thornton Heath. Well provided with golf courses with two public ones at Addington and Coulsdon alongside the seven private ones. Boating and fishing on South Norwood Lake. Tennis, football and other outdoor sports in various parks. Crystal Palace football team has its ground at Selhurst Park* • **LIBRARIES** *Improving all the time. An impressive three-storey library at the Clocktower with active childrens library, music library and local history archive. Twelve branch libraries, 8.1 library visits per head. Position in library-use league table: 9th out of 32 (where 1 is best and 32 worst).*

OPEN SPACES****

A quarter of the borough's area is greenbelt land and there are plentiful parks, open spaces and woods, particularly in the south. But there are some unexpected treats in the north, including Norwood Grove, a white 17th-century mansion set in beautiful grounds with sloping lawns, flower gardens and wonderful views over south London and Surrey. A complete surprise in suburban Upper Norwood.

VIEWS *Addington Hills, rising south of the open space of Lloyd Park with views to Croydon and beyond to Windsor and Epping (on a good day) make a satisfying finish to the walk across Lloyd Park (see below)* • **RURAL SPACES** *Lloyd Park is one of many open spaces in Croydon with wild grass and heathland, framed by trees and a backdrop of hills that remove you instantly from built-up suburbia. If you're desperate to escape from the tower blocks of Croydon town centre, Lloyd Park is nearest* • **DOWNS** *The ring of open spaces around Coulsdon, Whyteleafe and Kenley including Happy Valley Park, Coulsdon Common and Riddlesdown are part of the Surrey Downs with lovely views and walks* • **WILDLIFE** *South Norwood Country Park. Not as rural as its name suggests (there are always views of suburban streets through the trees). But an interesting open space in an* *otherwise built-up area, with mature trees and wetlands area with wildlife, all developed from 120 acres of derelict land.*

SHOPS * * * *

CRYSTAL PALACE & UPPER NORWOOD *Don't be put off by boarded-up shops at the park end of Church Row. There are a couple of interesting shops including a second-hand bookshop further up. Interesting individual shops in Westow Street. Safeway in Westow Street (see also Lambeth)* • **SOUTH NORWOOD & THORNTON HEATH** *Typically inner London suburban high streets, with mostly local shops – newsagents, take-aways and discount shops are prominent. Depressing and a bit run-down on roads often clogged with traffic. Both have suffered from being too near Croydon, which dominates the borough, although the council is targeting both districts with grants for shop face-lifts as part of its regeneration. Safeway in South Norwood; Sainsbury's in Thornton Heath* • **CROYDON TOWN CENTRE** *Excellent shopping, if a bit predictable. There can't be a chain store that's not got a branch either in the pedestrianised North End or in the Whitgift or Drummond indoor shopping centres. Large branches of national chains, Allders department store and a definite American feel to the galleried malls with quietly moving escalators and glass ceiling. Like Bromley, probably its nearest competitor, new shopping centres are well-integrated with existing streets. The pedestrianised tree-lined shopping street of North End feels almost continental, with its Parisian style advertising pillars and trams crossing the street in the distance. The 16th-century Whitgift almshouses at the corner of North End are a poignant antidote to the consumerism raging on all sides. Fruit and veg market at Surrey Street, the less glitzy face of Croydon, with greasy spoon cafes and crumbling Victorian buildings* • **PURLEY** *Another town centre suffering from the spread of Croydon. Several streets of shops centring on a busy one-way system. Mostly banks, building societies, chainstores and charity shops. Purley Way, one of the main roads between Purley and Croydon, is now lined with out-of-town superstores, DIY, computer and white goods stores, causing big traffic jams on weekends and bank holidays. Big Tesco.*

RESTAURANTS * *

CRYSTAL PALACE & UPPER NORWOOD *Westow Street, one edge of the Westow Hill Triangle (see also Lambeth) is attracting a number of good restaurants, including Italian, American, Chinese, Thai and vegetarian. This area is an evening magnet for residents of less interesting parts of south London* • **CROYDON** *Struggling to get over its reputation as being dead in the evening. More pubs and restaurants are opening and it's becoming less of a joke among younger people to say they're going out on the town in Croydon. The usual pizza, pasta and other chains, and recommended Indonesian, Malaysian and vegetarian restaurants* • **ELSEWHERE** *A couple of restaurants in Purley popular with locals and good pubs in Old Coulsdon. The rest of the borough has nothing of note.*

CRIME RATES * * *

Position in Metropolitan Police league table: 21st out of 32 (where 1 is worst and 32 best).

THE COUNCIL ★★★

POLITICAL AFFILIATION *Labour* • **MINUS POINTS** *Has had an uneven record on rubbish collection which the council blamed on unreliable contractors. Central recycling bins aren't emptied often enough although there are plenty of them. Slowish on turning round property searches which it blames on the introduction of a new computer system* • **PLUS POINTS** *Enthusiastic promotion of a borough whose attractions aren't immediately obvious to outsiders. Introducing kerbside recycling for 30,000 properties. Energetic policy of bringing empty homes into use* • **PROPERTY SEARCHES CARRIED OUT IN 10 WORKING DAYS** *88.6%* • **STANDARD SEARCH FEE** *£118* • **COUNCIL TAX COLLECTED** *92.8%*

• COUNCIL TAX 2000-2001

BAND	PROPERTY VALUE	CHARGE	BAND	PROPERTY VALUE	CHARGE
A	up to £40,000	£538	E	£88,001-£120,000	£987
B	£40,001-£52,000	£628	F	£120,001-£160,000	£1,167
C	£52,001-£68,000	£718	G	£160,001-£320,000	£1,346
D	£68,001-£88,000	£808	H	over £320,000	£1,615

EALING

The title of Queen of the Suburbs is hotly contested, it seems, with Ealing and Surbiton (see Kingston) both laying claim to the accolade. Without any set criteria it's tricky to judge the real winner (maybe the government should get on to it) but if it means having a good mix of historically interesting suburban architecture, a variety of shops to suit all moods, excellent links to town and country and lots of parkland and rural green space, then Ealing wins hands down. Even if the contest is a bit David and Goliath with a whole borough pitted against a single area. Sorry, Surbiton.

A walk from east to west in Ealing is as good a lesson in the outward spread of London's development as you're likely to get. At the bottom eastern end is the exclusive enclave of Bedford Park (see Hounslow). Separated from Bedford Park only by a railway line is Victorian Acton. To the west is the grander Victoriana of Ealing and the more modest cottages and terraces of West Ealing and Hanwell. North Ealing, on the hills above Ealing itself, is Edwardian, with its own pioneering garden suburb at Brentham built in the heyday of such social experiments before the First World War. To the east of Brentham is up-market 1930s suburbia; to the west and north towards Southall and Greenford are the speculative 1930s terraces and semis chucked up hurriedly during the 1930s building boom.

Ealing is mostly middle class and white collar, popular with young professionals who value a quick trip to the City and more space for their money than they'd get in cramped and expensive Fulham or Hammersmith. But it also has London's largest Indian community and the largest Sikh community outside India, clustered in Southall on the borough's western border, as well as a large Afro-Caribbean community. Nearly a third of Ealing's population is from an ethnic minority, the fifth highest in London. Unemployment is middling for outer London at 4.1% although there are particular problems in poorer areas like South Acton and Southall.

Ealing itself has perked up considerably since its shopping centre was opened 15 years ago, but as is often the way, neighbouring areas have suffered. Acton High Street and neighbouring roads are still shabby despite the building of a small shopping mall but there are plans for a further revamp of the town centre as part of a larger regeneration scheme taking in the council estates of South Acton. In a bid to encourage owners to improve their town centre properties the council is also offering grants to pay for repairs of original features.

PROPERTY AND ARCHITECTURE

ACTON

Just a step to the west of Bedford Park but substantially cheaper. Historically, Acton is second best to Ealing, blighted by ugly council blocks around Acton Town station. But now people are starting to discover the area's large stock of Victorian houses and conversion flats and admitting that you live in Acton no longer means social death. The group of streets just off the high street known as Poets Corner (including Shakespeare, Milton and Cowper Roads) has hit the headlines recently as a hitherto undiscovered enclave of pretty Victorian terraces and large flat conversions. On the other side of the tracks around West Acton, it's all change architecturally, with distinctive half-timbered houses and flats disguised as Tudor houses on the Hanger Hill Garden Estate (known locally as the Tudor Estate).

ATTRACTS *Young professionals; people who can't afford Ealing, Hammersmith or Fulham; Japanese wanting to be near the Japanese school*
● **CONSERVATION AREAS** *Acton Town Centre; Acton Park; Creffield Road; Hanger Hill Garden Estate* ● **AVERAGE PRICES** *Flats: studio £70,000+; 1-bed £100,000-£150,000; 2-bed £150,000-£200,000 Houses: 2-bed £180,000+; 3-bed £200,000-£350,000; 4-bed £350,000-£550,000*
● **AVERAGE RENTS (WEEKLY)** *Flats: studio £140+; 1-bed £185+; 2-bed £205+ Houses: 2-bed £205+; 3-bed £230+; 4-bed £275+.*

EALING & NORTH EALING

A popular middle-class family area with a good range of solid Victorian and Edwardian property. Mostly medium and large Victorian terraces and semis with some roads of detached villas in roads round the attractive open space of Walpole Park. Victorian villas, some converted into flats, around Ealing Common. Larger and grander Victorian and Edwardian houses mixed with some modern blocks around Castlebar and Montpelier Park in North Ealing. Modernist 1930s houses on the Hanger Hill Haymills Estate. Brentham, north of Montpelier Park, part of what estate agents now call Pitshanger Village, was built to provide cottage homes for working people in the early years of this century. Now the whitewashed homes with small paned windows and neatly clipped hedges are home to the middle classes. A strong community atmosphere and sought after for good schools. The best choice of flats is in central Ealing.

ATTRACTS *Families* • **CONSERVATION AREAS** *Brentham Garden Estate; Grange and White Ledges; Ealing Green; Haven Green; Montpelier Park; Mount Park; Ealing Town Centre; Ealing Common; Hanger Lane (Haymills) Estate* • **AVERAGE PRICES** *Flats: studio £90,000+; 1-bed £100,000-£200,000; 2-bed £150,000-£250,000 Houses: 2-bed £190,000-£280,000; 3-bed £220,000-£400,000; 4-bed £350,000-£550,000+* • **AVERAGE RENTS (WEEKLY)** *Flats: studio £140+; 1-bed £205; 2-bed £230+ Houses: 2-bed £230+; 3-bed £310+; 4-bed £500+.*

WEST EALING & HANWELL

West Ealing is the cheapest part of Ealing, with grids of Victorian and Edwardian terraces, many pebble-dashed and 'improved' in stark contrast to the carefully preserved original features further north. But it's still more expensive than Hanwell, although it lacks Hanwell's attractive green space and larger family homes. Agents say this is partly due to postcode snobbery (West Ealing W13 is posher than Hanwell W7) and partly because it is nearer tubes. Hanwell is a mix of large Victorian houses around Golden Manor near the Brent Valley (the poshest bit), smaller terraces and cottages in roads round the station and later 1930s terraces, many with hideous modern windows and pebble-dashing. Two- and three-bed ex-council properties on the Cuckoo Estate around Cuckoo Avenue.

ATTRACTS *Families; people who can't afford Ealing; first-time buyers (especially West Ealing)* • **CONSERVATION AREAS** *Cuckoo Estate; Hanwell Clock Tower; Hanwell Village Green* • **AVERAGE PRICES** *Flats: studio £70,000+; 1-bed £90,000-£140,000; 2-bed £110,000-£160,000 Houses: 2-bed £120,000-£170,000; 3-bed £145,000-£180,000; 4-bed £190,000-£450,000* • **AVERAGE RENTS (WEEKLY)** *Flats: studio £140+; 1-bed £160+; 2-bed £195+ Houses: 2-bed £195+; 3-bed £230+; 4-bed £275+.*

GREENFORD & NORTHOLT

Mostly roads of 'improved' small and medium-sized 1930s semis with more modern estates of small houses and blocks of flats. Architecturally some of the dullest parts of Ealing, carved up by the busy A40, tube and train lines. The Westway Cross retail park has been built on the site of former factories around the Grand Union Canal. A good area for cheap family homes and fairly good transport links (especially Greenford). Northolt is cheaper than Greenford and there's a lot of ex-council property.

ATTRACTS *First-time buyers; bargain hunters; families; investors* • **CONSERVATION AREAS** *Northolt Village Green* • **AVERAGE PRICES** *Flats: studio £65,000+; 1-bed £70,000+; 2-bed £85,000-£115,000 Houses: 2-bed £120,000+; 3-bed £140,000+; 4-bed £180,000+* • **AVERAGE RENTS (WEEKLY)** *Flats: studio £140+; 1-bed £150+; 2-bed £175+ Houses: 2-bed £175+; 3-bed £220+; 4-bed £230+.*

SOUTHALL

Predominantly Asian. A few shabby Victorian terraces near the main shopping streets but otherwise mostly 1930s semis and terraces huddled together in bleak streets. Norwood Green is popular because it's closest to green space but a lot of the housing stock in Southall is in poor condition and much of it is rented, often to people on benefits who can't find anything to rent elsewhere. Some modern blocks of flats and flats above shops.

ATTRACTS *Members of the Asian community* • **CONSERVATION AREAS** *None*
• **AVERAGE PRICES** *Flats: studio £50,000; 1-bed £60,000; 2-bed £75,000 Houses: 2-bed £90,000+; 3-bed £130,000+; 4-bed £160,000+*
• **AVERAGE RENTS (WEEKLY)** *Flats: studio £140+; 1-bed £150+; 2-bed £175+ Houses: 2-bed £175+; 3-bed £220+; 4-bed £230+.*

BEST POSTCODES

Ealing W5 is the best postcode, covering the smartest parts of North Ealing. West Ealing W13 is less smart than W5 but generally smarter than Hanwell W7. Acton W3 is becoming more acceptable. Middlesex postcodes around Southall and Greenford.

AMENITIES

SCHOOLS * * *

Not a startling overall performance either at primary or secondary level but certainly not scraping the bottom of the barrel. The best schools are highly sought after and operate tight catchment areas. Quite generous state nursery provision for pre-schoolers. A number of private prep and secondary schools.

PRE-SCHOOL PROVISION *104 private day nurseries and playgroups; 50 nursery classes in state and church primary schools; 9 state-run nurseries. Proportion of under-fives in state nurseries: 69%* • **STATE PRIMARY SCHOOLS** *Overall league table position: 85th out of 150. Top scorers: North Ealing (with nursery unit), Pitshanger Village; Mayfield School (with nursery unit), Hanwell; St John Fisher (with nursery unit), Perivale* • **STATE SECONDARY SCHOOLS** *Overall league table position: 77th out of 149. Top scorers: Twyford C of E High (mixed) Acton; Cardinal Wiseman RC (mixed), Greenford; Greenford High, (mixed), Greenford* • **PRIVATE SCHOOLS** *Barbara Speake Stage School (mixed 4-16), East Acton; King Fahad Academy (Muslim, mixed 4-18), Acton; Notting Hill and Ealing High, (girls 5-19), Ealing; Harvington (girls 2-17), Ealing* • **PRIVATE SECONDARY SCHOOLS** *St Augustine's Priory (girls), Ealing; Ealing College Upper School, Ealing; St Benedict's (boys, girls in sixth), Ealing.*

TRANSPORT * * * *

One of the area's big draws. Generally excellent – especially around Ealing and Acton, with trains and tubes, so if one mode of transport isn't working you can use something else. And if one tube line isn't working, it's usually a fairly short walk to an alternative. Hanwell and Southall come off less well, with trains only.

TRAINS *Hanwell Zone 4. Cost of annual season ticket £1104. Average journey time to Paddington 13 minutes. Southall Zone 4. Average journey time to Paddington 13 minutes* • **TUBES** *Acton Town (District and Piccadilly) Zone 3. Cost of annual season ticket £896. Average journey time to Victoria 23 minutes; to Piccadilly Circus 20 minutes. Ealing Broadway (District and Central) Zone 3. Average journey time to Victoria 27 minutes; to Oxford Circus 25 minutes. Greenford (Central) Zone 4. Average journey time to Oxford Circus 29 minutes* • **BUSES** *One or two to town or at least more central areas of London including the 7 from Russell Square to Acton and the 70 from South Kensington Station to Acton. Other than that, buses go to local destinations, shopping centres like Kingston or Brent Cross and Heathrow Airport. Night buses include the N23 to Northolt via Ealing*

Broadway from Trafalgar Square and the N207 from Victoria to Uxbridge via Ealing and Southall ● **TRAFFIC TROUBLESPOTS** *Ealing: The shopping areas around the Broadway are separated by busy roads which doesn't enhance otherwise good shopping. Often snarled up with buses and lorries. The section of the Uxbridge Road between Ealing and Acton can be particularly bad round Ealing Common at the junction with the North Circular. Southall: Bad traffic around the crossroads of the central shopping area. Main Roads: Brilliantly convenient for escaping from town to the west when they're not jammed. Ealing is home to the infamous Hanger Lane gyratory system linking the North Circular to the A40. Traffic on the A40, the main road to Oxford and Birmingham, is sometimes solid; plans to widen the road have been put on ice, leaving gaping holes where homes along the route have been demolished or left boarded up* ● **PARKING** *Controlled parking schemes have spread like a rash in the past two years and now operate in Perivale around the industrial park just north of the A40, around Thames Valley University just south of Ealing Broadway and in Northfields, South Ealing, central Ealing, East Acton, Acton Vale, Ealing Common and Bedford Park (see Hounslow). Cost of annual resident's permit: between £15 and £45.*

LEISURE FACILITIES***

THEATRES & CONCERTS *Plays and stand-up comedy at Drayton Court, West Ealing. Plays at the Questor Theatre in Ealing, which describes itself as 'Britain's most exciting non-professional theatre'. Live music in the summer in Walpole Park and year round in Pitshanger Manor, an elegant Regency villa on the edge of Walpole Park restored by Sir John Soane* ● **CINEMAS** *Lots of screens although unfortunately they usually show many of the same predictable mainstream films. Warner Village at Park Royal and UGC at Ealing Broadway. The BelleVue in West Ealing has Asian films* ● **MUSEUMS & GALLERIES** *An eclectic little collection. Pitshanger Manor has art galleries and workshops, displays of pottery and period furniture. Southall has the railway centre, a trainspotter's dream with collections of rolling stock and engines. Weekends only. Also the archives of the Guinness company at Park Royal* ● **SPORTS FACILITIES** *Well provided for. Leisure centres at Acton, Southall, Hanwell, Greenford, Ealing and Northolt. Pools at Acton (restored Victorian swimming baths), Southall, Ealing and Northolt. Golf at Brent Valley (Hanwell), Ealing, Southall and Horsenden Hill (Perivale)* ● **LIBRARIES** *The most under-used and some of the most poorly resourced in outer London despite a large central library in Ealing, integrated into the Broadway shopping centre, and pleasant branch libraries. All libraries closed on Mondays with several smaller branches closed Wednesdays as well. But following protests from residents, Ealing council reversed its policy of shrinking opening hours and main libraries are open longer in the evenings. 3.91 visits per head. Position in library-use league table: 29th out of 32 (where 1 is best and 32 worst).*

OPEN SPACES****

An excellent variety of space with woods, rivers, meadowland and high viewpoints all within easy striding distance of each other, as well as greenery on a more domestic scale in gardens and tree-lined streets.
VIEWS *Horsenden Hill. One of the high points of suburban west London with views over to Harrow on the Hill and beyond to metroland over a spread of tidy red 1930s roofs below. Part of a wide swathe of open*

space in the north of the borough including Horsenden Wood and golf course • **RIVER WALKS** The Brent Valley walk. Created as a linear riverside park in the 1970s to rescue the river from dereliction. You can now walk from Brentham to Brentford High Street along seven miles of river and canal passing through meadows, parkland and woods as well as getting a spectacular view of Brunel's Wharncliffe Viaduct built to take the Great Western Railway to Bristol across Ealing's fields • **PARKS** Walpole Park. Lush park in the centre of Ealing adorned by Pitshanger Manor and surrounded by salubrious Victorian villas.

SHOPS * * * *

ACTON Uninspiring, trafficky high street, with mostly small chains and local shops, take-aways and discount stores. The Oaks shopping centre has sad looking small shops and an indoor market. There are plans for better pedestrian crossings and other environmental improvements but Acton's main problem is that it's overshadowed by Ealing. Safeway • **EALING** Big choice of well-stocked chains including large M&S and more off-the-wall shops. Two indoor shopping malls on either side of the Broadway, the Broadway and Arcadia. The Broadway has the main library and Safeway. Good middle-of-the-road shopping centre with an attractive entrance via a pedestrianised street of shops and restaurants with Victorian shop fronts. More specialised shops and restaurants in Bond Street and the high street round the green. The trafficky Broadway is the main detraction. A well-used local high street in Brentham. • **SOUTHALL** If you ever need Indian spices, saris, jewellery or Indian sweets, this is the place to come. Two main streets of almost exclusively Asian shops including a huge supermarket with shelves of spices, sacks of rice and drums of cooking oil. Lots of traders spill onto the street with fruit, vegetables, material and jewellery. Dull shopping street transformed into Eastern bazaar • **GREENFORD & HANWELL** Small broadways of chains and local shops. Hanwell is suffering from Ealingitis. Tesco and Sainsbury's at Greenford and retail park by the A40. Tesco in fabulous art deco former Hoover building on the A40, with green lighting at night.

RESTAURANTS * * *

ACTON & EALING Thai and East European restaurants in Acton. Ealing has Café Rouge, All Bar One and all the other ubiquitous restaurant chains you'd expect in a middle-class area plus Chinese, East European and Japanese (for the large Japanese community) • **SOUTHALL** A wide choice of Indian restaurants, Tandoori grills and kebab shops. Take-aways with naan bread rolled in front of your eyes.

CRIME RATES * * *

Position in Metropolitan Police league table: 14th out of 32 (where 1 is worst and 32 best).

THE COUNCIL * * *

POLITICAL AFFILIATION Labour • **MINUS POINTS** Litter in the street not always dealt with quickly. Under-used libraries • **PLUS POINTS** Door to door recycling across the borough of newspapers, glass, tin cans and engine oil. Generous state nursery provision. Energetic policy of bringing empty homes back into use. Recent residents' surveys showed a majority thought *the council was doing a good job* • **PROPERTY SEARCHES CARRIED OUT IN 10 WORKING DAYS** *99.9* • **STANDARD SEARCH FEE** £*122* • **COUNCIL TAX COLLECTED** *94.9%*

• **COUNCIL TAX 2000-2001**

BAND	PROPERTY VALUE	CHARGE	BAND	PROPERTY VALUE	CHARGE
A	up to £40,000	£504	E	£88,001-£120,000	£924
B	£40,001-£52,000	£588	F	£120,001-£160,000	£1,092
C	£52,001-£68,000	£672	G	£160,001-£320,000	£1,260
D	£68,001-£88,000	£756	H	over £320,000	£1,512

ENFIELD

'Golf clubs on one side and deprivation on the other' was Enfield director of housing's recent verdict on London's northernmost borough. Like other London boroughs created by administrative mergers, Enfield is an uneasy mix of affluent and even grand suburbia in the west and, just a short bus ride away, brutal-looking council estates and run-down shopping areas which can compete with London's worst.

The industrial east side stretches up the banks of the River Lea from the tower blocks and Victorian terraces of Edmonton and Ponders End to the suburban sprawl of outer Enfield. But cross the A10 and you're in middle class territory, from the large Edwardian terraces of Palmers Green in the south, reaching up through leafy villagey Winchmore Hill and elegant Enfield Town, to Southgate and the respectable suburbs of Oakwood and Cockfosters. This is where the tube line ends and the fields of Hertfordshire begin, protected by the greenbelt before they could be engulfed in a sea of speculative semis. Tucked away in the countryside is Hadley Wood, favoured haunt of celebrities who like its big houses and greenery.

To look at places like Hadley Wood and Winchmore Hill, it's difficult to believe that unemployment in Enfield is quite high for outer London at 4.7%. It's also difficult to believe that Enfield has significant Afro-Caribbean and Indian communities. Although the borough isn't as multiracial as any of its neighbours, 17% of its population is from an ethnic minority.

But the poorest areas around Edmonton and Ponders End are now receiving large injections of funds from Europe as well as private and public sector money to regenerate former industrial sites along the River Lea, to create new jobs particularly in high tech industries and to bring derelict areas back into use. Between 1995 and 2002, £120 million will be spent on the area. A further £110 million will be spent on demolishing some of the tower blocks dominating the skyline over Edmonton, refurbishing others and giving the depressing Edmonton Green shopping centre a much needed overhaul. The promise is that Edmonton Green will be unrecognisable in 10 years' time, a welcome prospect. Enfield may also play host to a new national sports stadium on the site of the existing Lea Valley leisure complex just east of Edmonton, although nearby residents aren't all thrilled at the prospect of more traffic and crowds converging on the area.

PROPERTY AND ARCHITECTURE

EDMONTON & PONDERS END

Apart from tower blocks, this stretch of the borough has a mixture of small late Victorian terraces (it was built as a workmen's suburb near the Great Eastern railway line which offered workers cheap fares) and messed about 1930s semis with the usual complement of "improvements" in the shape of modern windows, bilious stained glass and ugly porches. Flats in purpose-built blocks and lots of ex-council property. Good for small (nothing much larger than three bedrooms) cheap houses. A first-time buy after which you move out as quickly as you can. Edmonton is slightly more expensive than Ponders End.

ATTRACTS *First-time buyers; loyal locals* • **CONSERVATION AREAS** *Church Street, Edmonton; Ponders End Flour Mills; Turkey Street; Enfield Lock; Montague Cemeteries* • **AVERAGE PRICES** *Flats: studio £50,000; 1-bed £60,000; 2-bed £75,000-£85,000 Houses: 2-bed £65,000+; 3-bed £75,000-£85,000* • **AVERAGE RENTS (WEEKLY)** *Flats: studio £110; 1-bed £120-£130; 2-bed £140-£150 Houses: 2-bed £145-£155; 3-bed £175-£185; 4-bed £230.*

ENFIELD TOWN

More like an attractive county town than part of London, with a high profile local amenity society. This is the beginning of the middle class half of Enfield, with a mix of most styles of property from modest Victorian terraces to larger Edwardian semis around the centre of town and in roads off Chase Side and modern blocks near the grammar school. The jewel in Enfield's crown is Gentlemen's Row, a street of assorted Georgian and early Victorian houses, some set in large gardens, overlooking a grassy sward planted with mature trees. The large detached houses of The Ridgeway to the north west and west of Bush Hill Park station are also sought after. The nearer you are to the A10 the cheaper it is.

ATTRACTS *Families; City workers* • **CONSERVATION AREAS** *Enfield Town; extension to Enfield Town; Bush Hill Park; Forty Hill; Clay Hill* • **AVERAGE PRICES** *Flats: studio £60,000; 1-bed £80,000-£120,000; 2-bed £100,000+ Houses: 2-bed £110,000-£250,000; 3-bed £120,000+; 4-bed £300,000+* • **AVERAGE RENTS (WEEKLY)** *Flats: studio £110-£120; 1-bed £130-£140; 2-bed £160+ Houses: 2-bed £160+; 3-bed £190+; 4-bed £250+.*

WINCHMORE HILL & SOUTHGATE

Winchmore Hill is chic and self-consciously villagey, perched on a hill with far-reaching views from the village green. Mostly Victorian terraces and cottages in roads off the green, with larger, up-market Edwardian and inter-war semis in roads towards Southgate and Palmers Green. Broad Walk is the grandest part of Winchmore Hill, with large detached houses, some vulgar and brash, some hidden behind discreet shrubbery. Popular with celebrities as well as the merely wealthy. Southgate is up-market suburbia, an attractive mix of solid Edwardian semis and half timbered 1930s houses with deep eaves, tall Tudor-style chimneys and neat gardens. Winchmore Hill tends to be more expensive for buyers than Southgate but rents are higher in Southgate because of the tube. Cockfosters and Oakwood are slightly more expensive than Southgate proper because they're nearer the country but still have tubes.

ATTRACTS *Families keen to be close to good schools; young professionals wanting to be close to tubes; minor celebs* ● **CONSERVATION AREAS** *Winchmore Hill Green; Bush Hill Park; Southgate Green; Trent Park* ● **AVERAGE PRICES** *Flats: studio £70,000; 1-bed £85,000-£110,000; 2-bed £120,000+ Houses: 2-bed £170,000-£220,000; 3-bed £220,000-£250,000; 4-bed £275,000-£300,000* ● **AVERAGE RENTS (WEEKLY)** *Flats: studio £120-£130; 1-bed £140-£165; 2-bed £160-£200 Houses: 2-bed £200-£220; 3-bed £220-£300; 4-bed £280+.*

PALMERS GREEN

Once an elegant Edwardian suburb and still mostly Edwardian in roads around the station. Many of the four- and five-bedroom family homes have survived being converted into flats (although this is good flat-hunting territory as well). Further away from the centre, 1930s semis take over. Palmers Green is generally cheaper than Southgate or Winchmore Hill (no tube and less village atmosphere) but parts of it, notably the large Edwardian houses of the Lakes estate off Green Lanes towards Southgate are as pricey as anything in neighbouring areas. South of the north circular there are smaller Victorian terraces around Bowes Park.

ATTRACTS *Families; first-time buyers* ● **CONSERVATION AREAS** *None* ● **AVERAGE PRICES** *Flats: studio £60,000; 1-bed £80,000-£90,000; 2-bed £120,000+ Houses: 3-bed £170,000-200,000+; 4-bed £220,000+* ● **AVERAGE RENTS (WEEKLY)** *Flats: studio £110-£130; 1-bed £140-165+; 2-bed £160-£200+ Houses: 3-bed £180-£280; 4-bed £280-£340.*

HADLEY WOOD

The most expensive part of Enfield. Large detached houses on the edge of greenbelt land yet attached to London by the umbilical cord of the railway line to Moorgate. Surrounded by the greenery and grand Georgian houses of Hadley Common, Hadley Wood looks mostly towards Barnet (see Barnet). Another area popular with minor celebrities, footballers and pop stars. (According to one local agent there are enough footballers to make a team.) The most expensive, mostly 1930s houses, are south of Camlet Way and Beech Avenue, known locally as millionaires' row, with smaller 1960s houses to the north. Few flats.

ATTRACTS *Wealthy families; celebrities* ● **CONSERVATION AREA** *Hadley Wood* ● **AVERAGE PRICES** *Flats: 2-bed £165,000-£175,000; Houses: 2-bed £200,000-£295,000; 3-bed £325,000-£355,000; 4-bed £350,000+;* ● **AVERAGE RENTS (WEEKLY)** *Flats: 2-bed £200+ Houses: 2-bed £250; 3-bed £350+; 4-bed £450+.*

BEST POSTCODES

There are lots of London postcodes here, considering this is outer London. Winchmore Hill N21 is the best code, closely followed by Southgate N14, both of which carry premiums of between 10% and 15% on prices in neighbouring Palmers Green N13. But N13's a good deal better than N9 or N18 (Edmonton and Ponders End). Middlesex codes to the north but EN1 and EN2 are much better than EN3 (east of the A10). Everywhere proximity to tubes (rather than trains) adds to prices.

AMENITIES

SCHOOLS***

Middling performance in school league tables with secondary schools doing better than primary schools, helped by some good selective state and private schools. Some parents send their children over the border to Hertfordshire or Barnet. Below average state provision for pre-schoolers but a wide choice of private nurseries and playgroups. A small number of private prep and secondary schools.

PRE-SCHOOL PROVISION *120 private day nurseries and playgroups; 33 nursery classes in state primaries and church schools. Proportion of under-fives in state nurseries: 53%* • **STATE PRIMARY SCHOOLS** *Overall league table position: 109th out of 150. Top scorers: St George's RC, Enfield; Walker School, Southgate; Hadley Wood, Hadley Wood* • **STATE SECONDARY SCHOOLS** *Overall league table position: 78th out of 149. Top scorers: Latymer School (selective, mixed), Edmonton; Southgate (mixed), Cockfosters; Enfield County School (girls), Enfield* • **PRIVATE PREP SCHOOLS** *Keble Prep (boys), Winchmore Hill; Salcombe Prep (mixed, from 4), Southgate* • **PRIVATE SECONDARY SCHOOLS** *Palmers Green High (girls from 3), Palmers Green.*

TRANSPORT***

Tubes only in the far west of the borough, with the last three stops of the Piccadilly Line linking Southgate, Arnos Grove and Cockfosters with the centre of town. Not only is the tube a vital transport link but its distinctive 1930s tube stations at the Enfield end of the Piccadilly line are a reminder of the days when London Underground took station architecture seriously. Southgate's circular station with its peculiar space-age mast and integrated shopping parade is particularly distinguished. In the south and east of the borough it's trains only, not always very frequent outside rush hour.

TRAINS *Edmonton Green Zone 4. Cost of annual season ticket £1104; average journey time to Liverpool Street 26 minutes. Ponders End Zone 5. Cost of annual season ticket £1332; average journey time to Liverpool Street 23 minutes. Enfield Town Zone 5. Average journey time to Liverpool Street 30 minutes. Winchmore Hill Zone 4. Average journey time to Kings Cross 22 minutes* • **TUBES** *Cockfosters (Piccadilly) Zone 5. Average journey time to Piccadilly Circus 34 minutes. Southgate (Piccadilly) Zone 4. Average journey time to Piccadilly Circus 29 minutes* • **BUSES** *The 149 runs from Ponders End to London Bridge but be prepared for a struggle through some of North London's most trafficky roads (Tottenham High Road and Kingsland Road to name but two). Otherwise buses mostly link different parts of the borough, providing vital west to east services as railway lines run north to south. Night buses include the N29 from Trafalgar Square to Palmers Green, Winchmore Hill and Enfield Town and the N91 from Trafalgar Square to Southgate and Cockfosters* • **TRAFFIC TROUBLESPOTS** *Edmonton: The North Circular road which slashes through the borough from East to West, particularly at the junction with the A10, one of the main roads through North London to the City* • **PARKING** *Five controlled* parking zones in the borough at Enfield Town, Bush Hill Park, Grange Park, Oakwood and Arnos Grove. Cost of annual resident's parking permit: £20-£50. Palmers Green and Southbury Road, Enfield are the next potential candidates for controlled parking zones.

LEISURE FACILITIES***

THEATRES & CONCERT HALLS Two theatres. The Millfield Theatre in Edmonton is now no longer run by the council but has relaunched itself as an independent company with its own theatre school and youth theatre. But it still has family shows, middle of the road plays, the annual Christmas panto, musicals and live music. The Chicken Shed theatre in Southgate has jazz, comedy, musicals and youth theatre workshops. Summer open-air concerts and plays in parks round the borough ● **CINEMA** Improved since the arrival of the Lea Valley Leisure Centre by the River Lea with 12 screen cinema. Mainstream viewing on all screens ● **MUSEUMS & GALLERIES** Small collection. Forty Hall Museum has exhibitions of furniture, ceramics and glass in a handsome 17th century manor house. Collection of early vehicles in the former New River pump house at the Whitewebbs Museum of Transport and Industry in Enfield. Watch truncated opening hours. If you're into gardens, Capel Manor in Enfield is the HQ of the Greater London College of Horticulture and Countryside Studies, with themed gardens, demonstrations and classes. Try also the plant collection at Myddleton House Gardens, Enfield ● **SPORTS FACILITIES** Leisure centres at Enfield, Edmonton, Southgate and Picketts Lock in the Lea Valley, all with pools. Golf, tennis, football and other sports in open spaces across the borough. Discount programme in operation ● **LIBRARIES** Underused, and even the central library in Enfield is small and cramped compared with the modern palaces of learning and culture built by some other boroughs. But staff are pleasant and helpful. Opening hours are patchy, with some branch libraries closed more than they're open, although the central library keeps reasonable hours. No Sunday opening. 6.68 visits per head. Position in library-use league table: 18th out of 32 (where 1 is best and 32 worst).

OPEN SPACES****

No shortage of open space, as London suddenly turns into fields in the startling way it has along its outer edge, demonstrating that the greenbelt, put in place to stop London's growth, really does work. A good choice of parkland and woods, as well as a general feel of green in more built-up areas. Lots of new open space is also opening up along the Lea Valley with the creation of the Lea Valley Park along what were once the derelict banks of the River Lea. The park stretches right down from Hertfordshire through Enfield and down into Docklands (see also Haringey, Hackney and Newham) ● **PARKLAND** Trent Country Park. Rolling hills, woodland (muddy in winter as countryside should be). Only the glimpse of the ugly office block on the skyline at Cockfosters and the whistle of tubes spoils the rural idyll. Try also Forty Hall, the borough's other country park near Enfield ● **RIVER WALKS** The towpath along the River Lea. Great if you like industrial walks right under electricity pylons with the roar of factories on the other side of the river. Frustratingly, there are massive reservoirs just next to the towpath but they're hidden by grass mounds, making the towpath a bit claustrophobic. The New River, which used to bring water supplies to London from Hertfordshire, is also being given a face-lift of its loop around Enfield Town with £1.8 million of lottery money over five years.

SHOPS***

EDMONTON, PONDERS END & ENFIELD OUTSKIRTS *One of the nastiest 1960s shopping centres in London at The Broadway, Edmonton Green, with small, tired shops and greasy spoons along concrete corridors, opening out into a hangar-like central marketplace with stalls selling fruit, vegetables and clothes. Bargain stores and cheap chains predominate. Tesco. Easy to get lost and disoriented and emerge onto a urine-smelling staircase. Due for a big overhaul and about time. More human-scale local shops in Upper Edmonton and Ponders End. Tesco in Ponders End* ● **ENFIELD TOWN** *Instantly likeable town centre, just the right size for a stroll around the market (clothes, food, second-hand books) and along the high street. Mostly chains but with attractive shop fronts. More up-market chains and large M&S in Palace Gardens, the pedestrianised open-air shopping centre tucked so subtly behind the high street that it takes some finding. Antique shops, frame shops and clothes exchanges on Chase Side. Tesco by station, Sainsbury's in shopping centre* ● **WINCHMORE HILL, SOUTHGATE & PALMERS GREEN** *Winchmore Hill is mostly beautiful not useful. Victoriana, antiques and bedsteads are among the attractive cottagey shops on the green. The dull, sensible shops are in Green Lanes, Southgate and Palmers Green. Southgate is sprawling and trafficky and some residents complain, with some justification, that most of the shops seem to have turned into charity shops, restaurants and building societies. Palmers Green's Edwardian shopping streets feel more gracious although the shops aren't very exciting. Tesco and Safeway in Palmers Green.*

RESTAURANTS**

Not very thrilling. A recommended Spanish restaurant in Southgate, Pizza Express and Caffe Uno (stamps of a middle class neighbourhood) in Enfield Town. Otherwise, chains and the usual collection of local restaurants of varying quality.

CRIME RATES****

Position in Metropolitan Police league table: 22nd out of 32 (where 1 is worst and 32 best).

THE COUNCIL***

POLITICAL AFFILIATION *Labour* ● **MINUS POINTS** *No door-to-door recycling collections. Litter in evidence on some streets. Residents complain they aren't issued with wheelie bins or plastic rubbish sacks* ● **PLUS POINTS** *Couldn't be quicker at turning round property searches. Green spaces well kept. Reasonable council tax compared with other outer London boroughs* ● **PROPERTY SEARCHES CARRIED OUT IN 10 WORKING DAYS** *100%* ● **STANDARD SEARCH FEE** *£110.60* ● **COUNCIL TAX COLLECTED** *93.5%* ● **COUNCIL TAX 2000-2001**

BAND	PROPERTY VALUE	CHARGE	BAND	PROPERTY VALUE	CHARGE
A	up to £40,000	£532	E	£88,001-£120,000	£974
B	£40,001-£52,000	£620	F	£120,001-£160,000	£1,152
C	£52,001-£68,000	£709	G	£160,001-£320,000	£1,329
D	£68,001-£88,000	£797	H	over £320,000	£1,595

GREENWICH

No London borough can boast of more newspaper column inches in the last few years than Greenwich, home of the controversial Millennium Dome. The Dome now squats like a giant round insect on the site of the former gasworks, for better or worse one of the most familiar sights in London. Greenwich town centre, Greenwich Park with the distinctive Royal Observatory perched above the Thames and the cluster of buildings around the Royal Naval College are also now known to millions, thanks to energetic millennium year promotion of Greenwich as the home of time. But Greenwich is just a tiny part of Greenwich borough and a pretty unrepresentative part at that.

Greenwich's boundaries stretch east along the river for eight miles beyond the Thames Barrier at Woolwich to the Victorian terraces of Plumstead and the 1960s tower blocks of Thamesmead. East of the Greenwich peninsula, the river front is lined with crumbling warehouses, rusting machinery and weed-choked open spaces, a stark reminder that the Thames at Greenwich and Woolwich was once a hive of industry and that this whole area has been hard hit by the decline in traditional manufacturing.

To the south lie the ancient woodlands of Oxleas Woods and the open spaces and golf courses of suburban Eltham and New Eltham, on the face of it more prosperous than Woolwich and Plumstead but not without problems of their own.

Despite all the tourist attractions of west Greenwich, the borough as a whole is the 11th most deprived in the UK. Greenwich has higher unemployment, at 6.8%, than all the other outer London boroughs with which it's statistically grouped. Greenwich is also on south east London's 'front line', sitting awkwardly between the multiracial inner city and mostly white suburbia. Racial tensions have flared, culminating in the murder of black teenager Stephen Lawrence in Eltham eight years ago. In Greenwich borough as a whole, 16% of residents are from ethnic minorities but some parts, including Eltham, are almost 100% white and can be unpleasant places for anyone who isn't.

The government has been pouring money into the area for several years in a bid to stem the tide of deprivation, rejuvenate the town centres of Greenwich and Woolwich and improve poor transport facilities. The Dome itself will almost certainly go down in history as an expensive flop. But its supporters claim that its presence has at least succeeded in attracting funds to clean up and regenerate the Greenwich Peninsula as well as being the main catalyst for much improved transport links which have put the whole area on the map as a place to live. The arrival of the Docklands Light Railway last year with stations at Cutty Sark and Greenwich has finally provided a direct link with the Isle of Dogs, eliminating the need for a 15 minute walk under the eerily dripping Greenwich foot tunnel. The Jubilee Line extension, finally up and running after being dogged by technical and financial difficulties, links north Greenwich with the West End in 15 minutes. Further west, previously derelict land next to Deptford Creek is also being turned into luxury flats with shops, restaurants, a hotel, a multiscreen cinema and a cruise liner terminal.

PROPERTY AND ARCHITECTURE

WEST GREENWICH & BLACKHEATH

Architecturally the most impressive part of Greenwich borough, with four-storey Georgian terraces in roads west of Greenwich Park and Victorian cottages in roads off Royal Hill and next to the National Maritime Museum. Blackheath Standard (on the opposite side of the A2 from Blackheath Village and duller) has large Victorian houses, many converted into flats. Neighbouring Westcombe Park has a good collection of solid Victorian family homes, popular with people who can't quite afford the space they want in Blackheath proper. Most of Blackheath village is in Lewisham borough (see Lewisham) but the poshest part, on the Cator Estate in Blackheath Village, comes under Greenwich. Here there's a mixture of everything from Georgian cottages, through large stucco early Victorian houses and upmarket early 20th-century family homes to modern Span houses. As a general rule, almost anything on the left side of the A102M motorway looking north is better than anything on the right.

ATTRACTS *Professional couples; families; City workers based in Canary Wharf; people who like to boast that they discovered the area ages ago*
• **CONSERVATION AREAS** *West Greenwich; Greenwich Park; Ashburnham Triangle* • **AVERAGE PRICES** *Flats: 1-bed £90,000+; 2-bed £115,000-£150,000+ Houses: 2-bed £220,000+; 3-bed £330,000+; 4-bed £450,000+* • **AVERAGE RENTS (WEEKLY)** *Flats: studio £125+; 1-bed £150+; 2-bed £195+ Houses: 2-bed £255+; 3-bed £255+; 4-bed £405+.*

EAST GREENWICH

Mostly small two- and three-storey Victorian terraces and council blocks fanning out either side of the traffic-choked Trafalgar and Woolwich Roads. A big contrast to the west Greenwich which tourists see but prices have shot up over the last couple of years, thanks mainly to the arrival of the Jubilee Line station at north Greenwich a short bus ride away. East Greenwich is cheaper than west Greenwich but the gap is closing. The further east you go, the more the area is dominated by the concrete monstrosity of the northbound A102M flyover. There's hardly any property on the Greenwich peninsula yet but an ambitious 'urban village' is taking shape south of the Dome. The Greenwich Millennium Village is intended to be a model of sustainable and energy efficient development with 1,377 homes for sale or to rent.

ATTRACTS *First-time buyers; people who can't afford west Greenwich; investors; loyal locals* • **CONSERVATION AREAS** *East Greenwich* • **AVERAGE PRICES** *Flats: 1-bed £80,000+; 2-bed £110,000+ Houses: 2-bed £150,000+; 3-bed £220,000+; 4-bed £375,000+* • **AVERAGE RENTS**

(WEEKLY) *Flats: 1-bed £150+; 2-bed £195+ Houses: 2-bed £255+; 3-bed £310+; 4-bed £380+.*

CHARLTON

The core of Charlton, around Charlton Village, is Victorian, built up in the last decades of the 19th century. Streets of detached and semi-detached 1920s and 1930s properties dominate in roads further out, interspersed with large-scale council estates and ex-council property. Prices have risen in Charlton as buyers discover how much they can get for their money compared with Blackheath. The roads of Victorian terraces to the north of Charlton Road slope steeply down towards the Thames giving some stunning views of Docklands and the remnants of a once busy working river. Predictably these streets, popular because they're near Charlton Village and a couple of attractive local parks, have been dubbed 'Charlton Slopes' by estate agents.

ATTRACTS *Working families who can't afford Blackheath or west Greenwich; loyal locals; first-time buyers* • **CONSERVATION AREAS** Rectory Field; Charlton Village • **AVERAGE PRICES** *Flats: studio £50,000+; 1-bed £80,000+; 2-bed £110,000+ Houses: 2-bed £130,000+; 3-bed £150,000+; 4-bed £200,000-£250,000* • **AVERAGE RENTS (WEEKLY)** *Flats: 1-bed £140+; 2-bed £160+ Houses: 2-bed £185+; 3-bed £250+; 4-bed £275+.*

WOOLWICH & PLUMSTEAD

A mess of warehouses, council blocks and two- and three-storey Victorian terraces at riverside Woolwich. There's only one way for it to go and that's up. A total of £100 million is being spent on regenerating the area, including more than £43 million developing the handsome listed buildings of the former Royal Arsenal, recently vacated by the Ministry of Defence and now being turned into a mixture of shops, apartments and leisure facilities. Riverside Plumstead, like Woolwich, is a mess of shabby Victorian terraces and council estates. The best properties in Plumstead are up the hill around Plumstead Common, the chain of green space to the east and off Shooters Hill east of the A102(M), where there's a mixture of Victorian cottages and terraces with modern infill and huge flat conversions in Royal Herbert Pavilions, formerly a hospital. Developers have been busy around Woolwich Riverside and Shooters Hill so there's a good choice of new properties. If you're on a tight budget, you can still buy a three-bed ex-council house in Woolwich for around £80,000.

ATTRACTS *First-time buyers; people moving further out of London; people who can't afford Bexleyheath or Charlton; investors; loyal locals* • **CONSERVATION AREAS** Woolwich Common; Plumstead Common; Sun in the Sands; Royal Arsenal Woolwich • **AVERAGE PRICES** *Flats: studio £43,000+; 1-bed £55,000+; 2-bed £65,000+ Houses: 2-bed £65,000-£120,000; 3-bed £85,000-£135,000; 4-bed £100,000+* • **AVERAGE RENTS (WEEKLY)** *Flats: 1-bed £100+; 2-bed £125+ Houses: 3-bed £160+; 4-bed £175+.*

ABBEY WOOD & THAMESMEAD

There are large tracts of council estates at Abbey Wood especially north of the railway line, which means some good bargains if you're on a budget but gives the area a dreary feel. The most popular parts of Abbey Wood are around New Road, which goes through the lovely Lesnes Abbey woods, and around McLeod Road on the early 20th-century co-op estate. Of the half of Thamesmead which comes under Greenwich borough, South Thamesmead is a dispiriting collection of brutal concrete tower blocks built on reclaimed marshland by the GLC in the 1960s. But a rash of housebuilding started to the east and the north when the town was taken over by a resident-controlled trust after the abolition of the GLC in the 1980s and now developers are out in force building everything from starter homes to apartments and townhouses, taking advantage of some of the last remaining stretches of London riverside (see also Bexley). North and east Thamesmead are more attractive than many people give them credit for, with traditional homes built round a network of lakes and canals. But still an area out on a limb despite the arrival of a Safeway a few years ago. Another of London's cheapest areas.

ATTRACTS *First-time buyers; families looking for low-cost housing or part exchange* ● **CONSERVATION AREAS** *None* ● **AVERAGE PRICES** *Flats: studio £45,000+; 1-bed £55,000+; 2-bed £65,000+ Houses: 2-bed £75,000-£90,000+; 3-bed £90,000-£165,000+; 4-bed £75,000-£130,000* ● **AVERAGE RENTS (WEEKLY)** *Flats: 1-bed £90+; 2-bed £125+ Houses: 2-bed £150+; 3-bed £160+; 4-bed £185+.*

ELTHAM & NEW ELTHAM

Mostly 1930s suburbia, sliced through by busy main roads carrying traffic to Kent and the channel ports. But there are roads of handsome family homes round Eltham Palace and the Royal Blackheath Golf Club, and smaller cottage-style properties on the Progress Estate, built in 1915 to house munitions workers. Also worth checking out is the Corbett Estate with Edwardian homes of up to six bedrooms near Oxleas Woods. Roads off the Bexley Road, in the area known to estate agents as Eltham Heights, have large 1920s and 1930s semi-detached and detached houses.

ATTRACTS *Families with children (who want to be near good schools); commuters* ● **CONSERVATION AREAS** *Progress Estate; Eltham Palace; Eltham Green; Well Hall Pleasaunce* ● **AVERAGE PRICES** *Flats: studio £45,000-£50,000; 1-bed £75,000-£85,000; 2-bed £80,000-£125,000 Houses: 2-bed £90,000-£150,000; 3-bed £100,000-£300,000; 4-bed £160,000-£500,000* ● **AVERAGE RENTS (WEEKLY)** *Flats: studio £105+; 1-bed £120-£140; 2-bed £115-£205 Houses: 2-bed £115-£205; 3-bed £140-£275; 4-bed £150-£345.*

BEST POSTCODES

Best postcodes (in descending order): Blackheath SE3, Greenwich SE10, Eltham SE9, Charlton SE7. There are big price differentials between postcodes, particularly between SE3 and SE7. But even SE3 has its downside – it includes the vast and ugly Ferrier estate in Kidbrooke, due for a £22 million overhaul, and council estates on the edge of Eltham.

AMENITIES

SCHOOLS * *

Consistently indifferent performance by state schools in national league tables, particularly at primary level. There's a glut of spare places in Greenwich schools but the council's plans to close one secondary school and three primary schools, rationalise sixth forms and sell off surplus sites worth up to £17 million has angered residents affected. This bleak picture is partly redeemed by a good selection of private schools and relatively generous state nursery provision.

PRE-SCHOOL PROVISION *43 state primary schools with nursery classes; 6 state nursery schools; 90 private and voluntary nurseries and playgroups. Proportion of children in state nurseries: 71%* • **STATE PRIMARY SCHOOLS** *Overall league table position: 144th out of 150. Top scorers: Notre Dame RC, Woolwich; Our Lady of Grace RC, Charlton; St Mary Magdalene CE, Woolwich* • **STATE SECONDARY SCHOOLS** *Overall league position: 138th out of 149. Top scorers: St Ursula's Convent (girls), Greenwich; St Thomas More RC (mixed), Greenwich; St Paul's RC (mixed), Abbey Wood* • **PRIVATE PREP SCHOOLS** *Colfe's Prep, Lee (mixed from 3); St Olave's Prep, New Eltham (mixed); Riverston (mixed from 2), Lee* • **PRIVATE SECONDARY SCHOOLS** *Chart-toppers Blackheath High (girls), Colfe's (mixed).*

TRANSPORT***

The Jubilee Line and DLR have transformed transport links in Greenwich itself but other areas in the borough are not as well served. Thamesmead has no station nearer than Abbey Wood, two and a half miles distant. Woolwich will be better served if hopes of a DLR extension from across the river at Royal Docks and City airport become reality.

TRAINS *Abbey Wood Zone 4. Cost of annual season ticket £1104. Average journey time to London Bridge 27 minutes; to Charing Cross 34 minutes. Woolwich Arsenal Zone 4. Average journey time to London Bridge 22 minutes; to Charing Cross 29 minutes. Charlton Zone 3. Cost of annual season ticket £896. Average journey time to London Bridge 17 minutes; to Charing Cross 24 minutes. Greenwich Zone 2/3. Cost of annual season ticket: £756. Average journey to London Bridge 10 minutes; to Charing Cross 17 minutes. Eltham Zone 4. Average journey time to London Bridge 17 minutes; to Charing Cross 27 minutes; to Victoria 28 minutes* • **TUBES/DLR** *North Greenwich (Jubilee) Zone 3. Average journey time to Westminster 16 minutes. Greenwich Cutty Sark (DLR) Zone 2/3. Average journey time to Canary Wharf 9 minutes; to Bank 20 minutes* • **BUSES** *Not well served with buses to town, particularly from west Greenwich where buses are often crowded with tourists. Services include: 188 from north Greenwich and Greenwich to Russell Square; 53 from Plumstead Common via Woolwich and Charlton to Oxford Circus.* • **BOATS** *Pleasure boats to and from Westminster and down to the Thames Barrier. Free ferry across the river at Woolwich* • **TRAFFIC TROUBLESPOTS** *Greenwich town centre: Not as packed with tourists in millennium year as everyone predicted. But always crowded with pedestrians visiting the sites and markets and clogged with cars using a narrow one way system. Plans for bypass tunnelling under the foreshore in front of the Royal Naval College are on ice for lack of funding. As a compromise there's a ban on heavy lorries through Greenwich. The A2: where the heavy lorries go instead. Carves up Blackheath just outside Greenwich Park. Eltham High Street: often blocked with traffic waiting at the lights at the junction with Well Hall Road. The A102: long queues at the Blackwall Tunnel* • **PARKING** *There are controlled parking zones around Greenwich Town Centre, Eltham Station and Woolwich Town Centre. Cost of annual resident's permit: £44 in Greenwich and Woolwich, £11 around Eltham Station. Residents in the 2.5 mile Dome exclusion zone stretching to Charlton, east Greenwich and Blackheath Standard had free parking last year while the Dome was in operation and some people, especially those in East Greenwich, Maze Hill* and near commuter stations, have voted to retain controlled parking.

LEISURE FACILITIES****

THEATRES & CONCERT HALLS Greenwich Theatre is back with a full programme of plays, musicals and pantomime following a fight by local residents to reopen the theatre when it closed two years ago. The Greenwich Playhouse is a recently opened studio theatre. The Bob Hope Theatre in Eltham offers a mixture of amateur drama, musicals and jazz nights. Stand-up comedy at Up the Creek in Greenwich. For Blackheath venues, see Lewisham • **CINEMAS** Only one, in Greenwich, with three screens, following the demise of cinemas in Eltham and Woolwich. Multiplex planned for Millennium Village on the Greenwich Peninsula • **MUSEUMS & STATELY HOMES** Well provided for. West Greenwich has the National Maritime Museum, the Royal Naval College, the Old Royal Observatory, with its meridian line, the Queen's House and the Rangers House (on Blackheath) containing portraits and a collection of early musical instruments. Eltham Palace just off Eltham High Street, surrounded by trees and a moat, was a royal palace until the time of Charles I. It has now undergone a major refurbishment and restoration by English Heritage of its 1930s art deco interiors. Charlton House, built in 1612, is now a library and community centre. The redevelopment of the Royal Arsenal in Woolwich will include a new Royal Artillery museum • **SPORTS FACILITIES** Good. Eight leisure and fitness centres including the popular Arches in Greenwich in a refurbished 1920s building with pools, gym and baby gym. Other centres at Eltham, New Eltham, Kidbrooke, Plumstead, Thamesmead and Woolwich. Pools at Woolwich, Thamesmead and Eltham. Sailing, fishing and birdwatching on lakes at Thamesmead. Open-air lido at Charlton. Tennis and other sports in parks across the borough • **LIBRARIES** Small and under-resourced, even in the main library at Woolwich. Reasonable opening hours at Woolwich but truncated hours at many branch libraries. Library system under-used: only 4.3 library visits per head. Place in library-use league table: 27th out of 32 (where 1 is best and 32 worst).

OPEN SPACES****

Excellent for parks, woods and open spaces which cover a quarter of the borough's space. Greenwich rises steeply from the Thames and many of its parks have stunning river views. **VIEWS** Greenwich Park. One of the best Royal Parks with excellent views over the Isle of Dogs, Canary Wharf and the Millennium Dome from hills rising above the Thames and the Royal Naval College. Point Hill (Blackheath) has panoramic views over the city. Maryon Park in Charlton is another good viewpoint • **WOODS** Oxleas Woods, one of London's most ancient woodlands, recently reprieved from destruction when plans to build a road through it were abandoned. Oxleas and surrounding greenery all form part of the Green Chain Walk, a 40 mile network of walks across south-east London (see also Bexley, Bromley and Lewisham) • **WIDE OPEN SPACES** Blackheath, (see Lewisham); Avery Hill, Eltham, home of the Avery Hill campus of Greenwich University • **RIVERSIDE WALKS** The Thames Path from Greenwich to the Thames Barrier at Woolwich is a reminder of how industrial this whole stretch once was. More walkways are being opened up and this year new paths should be opened up so that you can walk the whole way round the top of the Greenwich Peninsula and along to Woolwich without having to go inland.

SHOPS***

WEST GREENWICH *Some tourist tat but also some interesting shops including several second-hand bookshops, an antique map shop, second-hand clothes shops and New Age shops and stalls in the covered market. Expanding and lively weekend market opposite and around St Alfege's Church selling books, records, clothes, furniture. Safeway at Blackheath Standard and Asda by the river between Charlton and Woolwich are a bus ride away* ● **EAST GREENWICH** *Mostly small local shops and an energy efficient Eco-Sainsbury on the Peninsula* ● **BLACKHEATH** *See Lewisham* ● **WOOLWICH** *Described by the council as the borough's main shopping area but it currently boasts a sad collection of chain stores and discount shops. The presence of the University of Greenwich has brought a bookshop and a pub or two and M&S is hanging on, much to the surprise of residents. Daily, uninspiring market selling mostly fish, fruit and vegetables in a pedestrianised square. The whole town centre is set for a face-lift as part of the Woolwich Revival Programme. Sainsbury's and Somerfields in Woolwich. Safeway at Thamesmead* ● **ELTHAM** *The high street has improved over the last couple of years. All the main chains are here with a large M&S and WH Smith. The bad news is that Allders department store is closing and being replaced with a discount store. Some interesting local shops in the Arcade. Sainsbury's* ● **OTHER AREAS** *Small shops in Charlton Village; parades at New Eltham and Plumstead. Large electrical goods and DIY stores in Bugsby's Way, Charlton by the river.*

RESTAURANTS***

GREENWICH *A good choice in west Greenwich including Vietnamese and Thai restaurants, Indian, Pizza Express and a number of pubs serving good food and/or providing entertainment* ● **BLACKHEATH** *See Lewisham* ● **ELTHAM** *A couple of local wine bars plus the usual line-up of Indian Tandooris and Chinese take-aways* ● **OTHER AREAS** *Nothing of note.*

CRIME RATES**

Position in Metropolitan Police league table: 13th out of 32 (where 1 is worst and 32 best).

THE COUNCIL***

POLITICAL AFFILIATION *Labour* ● **MINUS POINTS** *Poor schools. Higher Band D council tax than all the surrounding boroughs despite holding tax at 1999 levels. Under-used libraries* ● **PLUS POINTS** *Energetic encouragement for millennium developments which have brought and will bring much needed regeneration money to Greenwich and Woolwich. Generally efficient street sweeping and rubbish collection. Hot on recycling waste to generate heat and power* ● **PROPERTY SEARCHES CARRIED OUT WITHIN 10 WORKING DAYS** *99.5%* ● **STANDARD SEARCH FEE** *£100* ● **COUNCIL TAX COLLECTED** *92.2%* ● **COUNCIL TAX 2000-2001**

BAND	PROPERTY VALUE	CHARGE	BAND	PROPERTY VALUE	CHARGE
A	up to £40,000	£589	E	£88,001-£120,000	£1,080
B	£40,001-£52,000	£687	F	£120,001-£160,000	£1,276
C	£52,001-£68,000	£785	G	£160,001-£320,000	£1,472
D	£68,001-£88,000	£883	H	over £320,000	£1,767

HACKNEY

Hackney is bloody but unbowed. It's cursed with some of the worst poverty in Europe – according to the council, parts of the east of the borough are poorer than Bosnia. It has some of the highest unemployment in London (more than 11% of its residents are out of work) and is the fourth most deprived area in England. Nearly half its residents live in council-owned property, many on grim sink estates. The council has been mired in scandals including child abuse and housing fraud. Its schools were so bad they were taken over by a government hit squad, then partially privatised. Financial mismanagement nearly bankrupted the borough last year. But Hackney is doggedly reinventing itself as a lively, culturally exciting and challenging place to be. Warehouses and factories are being turned into studios and workshops for small, creative businesses. Middle-class homeowners are moving in, not just because it's cheaper than Islington or Docklands (although it still is) but because it's less self-consciously hip than Islington and not full of modern yuppie ghettos like Docklands. And Hackney Council regularly blows up the worst tower blocks on its council estates to cheers from tenants.

At its southern tip, Hackney starts where the wealthy City of London ends, at the clothing factories and warehouses of Shoreditch and Hoxton. North of the Regent's Canal are the Victorian terraces and council blocks of Hackney and some of the borough's best Georgian and Victorian architecture around Victoria Park in the east and De Beauvoir town in the west. North of the mix of small cottagey Victorian terraces and council blocks of Dalston and Shacklewell is recently yuppified Stoke Newington. To the north are the large late Victorian and turn-of-the-century houses favoured by the Orthodox Jewish communities of Stamford Hill and Clapton.

One of the reasons why Hackney has been slow to take off as a place to live is that there's no tube link in the borough (apart from Old Street, almost in the City). Residents have been campaigning for one for years and hopes are high that this omission (bizarre for such a central location) will soon be rectified with the extension of the East London line north from Shoreditch. After years of stalling and refusing to open the public purse, there are hopeful signs that the project might at last take off, particularly as the final decision will rest with Ken Livingstone, the mayor of London, who is under a lot of pressure to produce big improvements in public transport. The extension, which will use existing track, will connect Hoxton, Haggerston and Dalston to the tube network for the first time.

But successive governments and the private sector have invested millions of pounds in the borough for other projects in an attempt to iron out some of Hackney's most pressing problems of derelict properties, menacing streets and unemployment. They include £37.5 million on improving Dalston, with investment in housing, jobs, the environment and better streetscaping, £10 million in neighbouring Haggerston, one of the poorest parts of the borough, and £64 million over seven years in Hackney Wick. Central Hackney will get a face-lift with a new town hall square in Mare Street, dominated by a futuristic £25 million technology and learning centre. There will be funds to stimulate more artistic and cultural activity around Shoreditch and Hoxton on the city fringes and to improve streetscapes and shop fronts (see also Islington).

PROPERTY AND ARCHITECTURE

SHOREDITCH & HOXTON

Loft-living is taking off around here in a big way as former warehouses and factories are converted into living/working spaces or simply huge lofts which make the most of the large windows of former industrial buildings, although artists and others who moved here when it was cheap now complain the area is being gentrified. But this isn't Clerkenwell – yet. The trendy bit only extends into a small grid of streets around Hoxton Square and the triangle between Old Street and Great Eastern Street. There's lot of council property both here, in Hoxton and in Haggerston east of Kingsland Road, some bought under the right-to-buy scheme and now being resold. Big price differences between ex-council and loft spaces, which can sell for half a million pounds or more. Very few houses.

ATTRACTS *Creative types; young single people; some young professionals* • **CONSERVATION AREAS** *South Shoreditch; Shoreditch High Street; Underwood Street; Hoxton Street* • **AVERAGE PRICES** *Flats: 1-bed £140,000-£245,000+; 2-bed £180,000-£285,000+* • **AVERAGE RENTS (WEEKLY)** *(excludes ex-council) Flats: studio £180+; 1-bed £275+; 3-bed £300+.*

DE BEAUVOIR TOWN

The closest part of Hackney to Islington (and with a valuable Islington N1 postcode). Prices are more akin to parts of Islington than Hackney, although compared with central Islington, properties in De Beauvoir Town are a bargain. An attractive enclave of roads of two- and three-storey early Victorian houses centring on De Beauvoir Square with its unusual gabled and diamond-paned semi-detached houses round a central square. A peaceful spot because many roads are cut off from traffic. This area had a narrow escape from planners in the 1960s – if they'd had their way the whole place would now be covered with council blocks as the southern half of De Beauvoir Town is. Mostly houses.

ATTRACTS *Professionals; families* • **CONSERVATION AREAS** *De Beauvoir Town* • **AVERAGE PRICES** *Flats: 1-bed £130,000+; 2-bed £175,000+ Houses: 2-bed £300,000+; 3-bed £400,000+; 4-bed £450,000+* • **AVERAGE RENTS (WEEKLY)** *Flats: 1-bed £140+; 2-bed £250+ Houses: 2-bed £300+; 3-bed £350+; 4-bed £400+.*

HACKNEY & VICTORIA PARK

Immediately east of Mare Street, the spine of the borough, there's a mixture of council estates and standard Victorian two- and three-storey terraces and smaller terraces of cottages. But as you go towards Victoria Park there are some lovely Georgian and early Victorian streets and squares, especially around Cassland Road. As ever, council blocks are around most corners but not as dominant here as in other parts of the borough. Victoria Park to the south is now one of the most sought after parts of Hackney, particularly with people who would live in Islington if they could afford it. Big plus points are the lovely green space of Victoria Park, the Regent's Canal and a good choice of large Victorian semi-detached and terraced houses.

ATTRACTS *Families; young professionals; City workers; people who can't afford Islington* • **CONSERVATION AREAS** *Town Hall Square* • **AVERAGE PRICES** *Flats: studios £95,000+; 1-bed £125,000-£135,000; 2-bed £150,000-£220,000 Houses: 2-bed £180,000-£250,000; 3-bed £175,000-£300,000+; 4-bed £225,000-£400,000+* • **AVERAGE RENTS (WEEKLY)** *Flats: 1-bed £150-£165; 2-bed £170-£220 Houses: 3-bed £250-£330; 4-bed £300+.*

DALSTON & LONDON FIELDS

Parts of Dalston are still pretty scruffy but it will get a big boost if and when it gets its own tube station, so you may get a bargain. Lots of roads of attractive mid-Victorian terraces, particularly west of Hackney Downs and north of Dalston Lane. Roads to the west of the small but lush green space of London Fields are increasingly favoured by the middle classes who like the manageably-sized Victorian terraces and smaller cottages. Some of the most coveted houses are in Albion Square, which has early Victorian terraces around a grassy square. Like most areas of Hackney, 19th-century terraces are cheek-by-jowl with council estates, some now in private hands following right-to-buy sales. But the Holly Street estate, which hit the headlines a couple of years ago as the venue for the launch of Tony Blair's plans to improve Britain's council estates, has been expensively revamped, most of its hated towers pulled down and replaced with new low-rise flats.

ATTRACTS *First-time buyers; people who can't afford Stoke Newington* • **CONSERVATION AREAS** *Albion Square; Graham Road and Mapledene; Broadway Market* • **AVERAGE PRICES** *Flats 1-bed: £70,000-£90,000+; 2-bed £80,000-£180,000 Houses: 3-bed £170,000-£300,000; 4-bed £220,000-£360,000* • **AVERAGE RENTS (WEEKLY)** *Flats: studio £100+; 1-bed flat £130-£150; 2-bed £190+ Houses 3-bed £300+; 4-bed £350+.*

STOKE NEWINGTON

One of London's newly trendy areas, despite having no public transport apart from the 73 bus. Streets of small two- and three-storey Victorian terraces off Stoke Newington Church Street, all sought-after, more expensive and smaller than almost anything further south. Mostly houses, with few flats and some loft apartments. Larger Victorian semis and detached houses north of Clissold Park, around the reservoirs and towards Finsbury Park, many divided into flats (see Haringey).

ATTRACTS *Middle-class families wanting to get their children into one of the borough's few good schools; young singles; young professionals; people who can't afford Islington; loyal locals* • **CONSERVATION AREAS** *Stoke Newington; Clissold Park; Stoke Newington Reservoirs, the filter-beds and New River* • **AVERAGE PRICES** *Flats: studio £70,000+; 1-bed £90,000-£100,000; 2-bed £130,000+ Houses: 2-bed £220,000+; 3-bed £250,000+; 4-bed £300,000+* • **AVERAGE RENTS (WEEKLY)** *Flats: studio £100+; 1-bed £130-£140+; 2-bed £200+ Houses: 2-bed £250+; 3-bed £300+; 4-bed £350+.*

STAMFORD HILL & CLAPTON

Stamford Hill and Upper Clapton are home to many of North London's Orthodox Jewish community. Properties here are much larger than in Stoke Newington (five bedrooms isn't unusual), with roads of late Victorian red brick and Edwardian terraces off Stamford Hill and down towards the marina at the River Lea. Although the houses are large, they're quite densely packed together and the area's still urban rather than suburban. It's been plagued with prostitutes hanging around on street corners (particularly offensive to Orthodox sensibilities) but the council has pledged to clamp down. Properties often change hands privately rather than through agents. A mix of Victorian terraces of varying shapes and sizes further south around Lower Clapton Road

ATTRACTS *Members of the Orthodox Jewish community; families*
● **CONSERVATION AREAS** *Clapton Square; Clapton Pond; Clapton Common*
● **AVERAGE PRICES** *Flats: 1-bed £95,000+; 2-bed £100,000-£150,000 Houses: 3-bed £160,000+; 4-bed £295,000+* ● **AVERAGE RENTS (WEEKLY)** *Flats: 1-bed £130+; 2-bed £150+ Houses: 3-bed £230+; 4-bed £350+.*

BEST POSTCODES

Stoke Newington N16 and the small corner of Finsbury Park N4 in Hackney are the best postcodes in the borough. Hackney E8 suffers from not being neighbouring Islington N1 but is better than Clapton E5.

AMENITIES

SCHOOLS *

Hackney's education department has been chaotic for the last few years, as councillors fell out with officials, a succession of senior officials left or were sacked and a series of government hit squads was brought in. A private company is now in charge of exam and curriculum targets and ethnic minority services. But the borough still languishes near the bottom of the league tables, particularly at primary level. On the plus side, there's good provision for state nursery school places for three- and four-year-olds and a range of private and voluntary nurseries. There is a handful of private selective schools run by the Jewish Community.

PRE-SCHOOL PROVISION *2 council nursery schools; 43 nursery classes in state primary and church schools; 91 private and voluntary day nurseries and playgroups. Proportion of under-fives in state nurseries: 61%* ● **STATE PRIMARY SCHOOLS** *Overall position in league table: 149th out of 150. Top scorers: Our Lady and St Joseph RC, De Beauvoir Town; Avigdor (with nursery unit), Stamford Hill; Grasmere (with nursery unit), Stoke Newington* ● **STATE SECONDARY SCHOOLS** *Overall position in league table: 139th out of 149. Top scorers: Our Lady's Convent High RC (girls), Stoke Newington; Cardinal Pole RC (mixed), South Hackney, Haggerston (girls), Haggerston* ● **PRIVATE SCHOOLS** *Stamford Hill; Yesodey Hatorah (mixed from 2), Stamford Hill; Beis Malka (girls from 2), Stamford Hill; Beis Rochel d'Satmar (girls from 5), Stamford Hill; Lubavitch House (mixed from 2), Stamford Hill.*

TRANSPORT**

Currently transport is poor for an inner London borough, although this should change with the arrival of the new tube line. For now, there are trains only and stations are unevenly scattered, with the west side south of Dalston the most poorly served. The south is best off, with access to Old Street tube (Zone 1) and a good choice of buses.

TRAINS London Fields Zone 2. Cost of annual season ticket £756. Average journey time to Liverpool Street 9 minutes. Hackney Central and Dalston Kingsland Zone 2. Average journey time to Stratford 9-11 minutes; to Highbury & Islington 5-7 minutes. Rectory Road (Stoke Newington/ Stamford Hill) Zone 2. Average journey time to Liverpool Street 12 minutes • **BUSES** A good choice with plenty of buses to the City and West End (there need to be as buses are the borough's lifeline). Services include the 38 to Victoria via Hackney Central and Dalston, the 30 to Marble Arch from Hackney Wick via Hackney Central, Hackney Downs and Dalston, the 48 via Clapton Pond and Hackney Central to London Bridge and the 55 via Clapton and Hackney to Oxford Circus • **TRAFFIC TROUBLESPOTS** Shoreditch: A horrible tortuous one-way system which leaves even seasoned Eastenders confused at times. Lots of traffic, buses and lorries delivering locally (the narrow cobbled streets are often blocked) and heading for the eastern motorways and docks. Dalston Junction: Kingsland High Street, the main street, is another of London's main through roads disguised (not very well) as a shopping street. Too narrow for the amount of traffic it has to carry, backed up with buses valiantly trying to provide transport for Hackney residents and cluttered with delivery and market vans from Ridley Road market. Stoke Newington: The high street is the continuation of Kingsland High Street and just as trafficky. And don't try driving down Stoke Newington Church Street on a Saturday night – it's jammed with restaurant-goers • **PARKING** Controlled parking in most of the south of the borough. Parking in the north around Stoke Newington and Stamford Hill is still not impossible, because most of the properties are houses. There are controlled parking zones around Shoreditch and Old Street, Dalston Junction, central Hackney, Hoxton and Finsbury Park with another being introduced around Manor House. Cost of annual resident's permit: £50.

LEISURE FACILITIES****

THEATRES & CONCERT HALLS The much loved but still struggling Hackney Empire in Mare Street is a variety theatre which stages everything from cabaret to musicals and circuses in a wonderfully florid Victorian building full of red plush, carved wood and marble pillars. Its terracotta exterior was refurbished with lottery money but last year it failed to get more funds and is now trying to raise the £15 million needed to modernise the backstage areas, refurbish the auditorium and provide a new bar, restaurant and other facilities. Live circus performances at the Circus Space, a training school and performance venue in a converted electricity generating station in Shoreditch. Concerts at the Tudor Sutton House in Hackney and the Round Chapel, Clapton • **CINEMAS** As you'd expect in this arts-mad borough, the Lux cinema in a grey industrial style building in Shoreditch and the Rio in Dalston both have repertory and sometimes obscure arthouse films • **MUSEUMS & GALLERIES** A good variety. Galleries in Hackney tend towards the informal. The borough claims to have Europe's largest concentration of artists who open up their studios for public consumption (and purchasing) on a regular basis and several artists have opened galleries, particularly around Dalston and Shoreditch. The Hackney Museum, an excellent local history museum with well-labelled and arranged exhibitions, is temporarily 'on tour' until its new headquarters in the Technology and Learning Centre in Hackney is finished. But the Geffrye Museum chronicling the history of the front room in almshouses in Dalston has just been refurbished. Sutton House, a Tudor townhouse now owned by the National Trust, has original furniture and panelling ● **SPORTS FACILITIES** Leisure Centres in Hoxton, Haggerston and Clapton with gyms and other indoor sports facilities. Pools at Hoxton and Clapton but Haggerston Pool had a bad year last year when it was shut down 'for reasons of health and safety'. A new leisure centre is planned for Stoke Newington. Riding at Lea Valley. Tennis, cricket and other sports in parks round the borough. Stoke Newington West Reservoir is being converted into a £3.2 million watersports centre. The pumping station in a turreted Victorian castle on Green Lanes (no hiding away industrial marvels in concrete boxes for the Victorians) is now a climbing centre ● **LIBRARIES** Under-used although facilities are improving. A new modern library at Shoreditch will be joined by the new library in the Technology and Learning Centre to be built by 2002. Opening hours are long with libraries across the borough open until 8pm during the week. All libraries except Stoke Newington are closed Wednesdays. Stamford Hill library is open Sunday afternoon. 5.68 library visits per head. Position in library-use league table: 22nd out of 32 (where 1 is best and 32 worst).

OPEN SPACES * * *

A much better range than Islington. Victoria Park, one of the area's largest open spaces and firmly attached to Hackney in the public mind, is actually run by neighbouring Tower Hamlets because Hackney and Tower Hamlets councils couldn't agree to run it jointly. Whoever runs it, it's still treasured by Hackney residents. Large swathes of lawn, a huge ornate Victorian drinking fountain and the Regent's Canal running along the bottom make this a special space in an otherwise built-up area.

CEMETERIES Abney Park with an overgrown Victorian cemetery full of crumbling gravestones with a looming derelict chapel in the middle ● **RIVER & CANAL WALKS** The eastern edge of Hackney Marshes after the Lea navigation canal and River Lea divide. Gentle walk along the river, overgrown with reeds and overhung with weeping willows. (Hackney Marsh itself is now a dull, drained expanse used as football pitches.) Also the Regent's Canal from De Beauvoir Town to Victoria Park – more reminders of Hackney's industrial past ● **CHILDREN'S ATTRACTIONS** Clissold Park, which has deer and ducks as well as a recently refurbished playground.

SHOPS * * *

HACKNEY A mixture of small chains including M&S, Boots and Woolworths, and a motley collection of discount stores at the north end of Mare Street, central Hackney's main drag. Trafficky south Mare Street has tatty local shops, a couple of bank branches and some take-aways. Tesco tucked behind St John at Hackney church ● **VICTORIA PARK** A small clutch of craft and pottery shops, antique shops, furniture shops, one or two restaurants and branches of estate agents, all signs of middle-class colonisation ● **DALSTON & KINGSLAND** Dalston has the borough's only indoor shopping centre, the Dalston Cross. Clean and warm with small branches of mostly cheaper chain stores. A total contrast to Ridley Road market next door *where butchers haul carcasses, chickens hang complete with heads and stalls sell ethnic food (particularly Turkish – there's a large Turkish community here), clothes and fruit. Sainsbury's in the shopping centre •* **STOKE NEWINGTON** *The high street has the usual collection of take-aways, Turkish supermarkets and cheap discount stores where everything's £1. Church Street's much more interesting. Lots of New Age shops selling incense, candles, jewellery and cards, several second-hand and new bookshops, a violin shop (even if you can't play, the window display of old and new instruments is interesting). Interior design and furniture shops testify to middle-class presence •* **STAMFORD HILL** *Boring parades around the main junction of Stamford Hill and Amhurst Road, enlivened by Jewish bakers, bagels and kosher butchers' shops. Safeway.*

RESTAURANTS***

SHOREDITCH *Has seen an explosion of new restaurants and bars over the past few years as it moved from being a dump no-one wanted to walk round at night to a hip place to be seen. Some new bars (often filled with City workers), upmarket gastropubs and restaurants with entertainment, although the Blue Note club was forced to move to Islington after complaints from residents about noise •* **HACKNEY & VICTORIA PARK** *Surprisingly, central Hackney's not as good as you'd think, particularly at weekend lunchtimes. But there is good Turkish, Vietnamese and Chinese food and a couple of bars. Restaurants, delis and winebars in Lauriston Road by Victoria Park •* **DALSTON** *Good for Turkish restaurants, as well as bagels •* **STOKE NEWINGTON** *The restaurant capital of the borough. A huge choice including Indian, Far Eastern, Anatolian, French, Italian and Thai all grouped in and around Church Street. Good in the daytime too with cafés and patisseries selling delicious cakes and pubs managing more than a curled-up cheese sandwich for lunch.*

CRIME RATES**

Crime is a problem with levels of robbery, drugs and violence high. Position in Metropolitan Police league table: 4th out of 32 (where 1 is worst and 32 best).

THE COUNCIL**

POLITICAL AFFILIATION *No overall control •* **MINUS POINTS** *Chaotic finances. Terrible schools. Collects less council tax than any other London borough. Standards of street-sweeping and litter collection variable, to put it kindly, with some very bad periods last year due to industrial action. Still trying to disentangle itself from problems caused by years of political infighting on the council. One of the slowest boroughs in London at turning round property searches •* **PLUS POINTS** *Actively working to improve sink estates. Door-to-door recycling collections throughout the borough. Active in seeking regeneration funds and lobbying for tube services. •* **PROPERTY SEARCHES CARRIED OUT IN 10 WORKING DAYS** *78%* **• STANDARD SEARCH FEE** *£100* **• COUNCIL TAX COLLECTED** *74.5%*

• COUNCIL TAX 2000-2001

BAND	PROPERTY VALUE	CHARGE	BAND	PROPERTY VALUE	CHARGE
A	up to £40,000	£561	E	£88,001-£120,000	£1,029
B	£40,001-£52,000	£655	F	£120,001-£160,000	£1,216
C	£52,001-£68,000	£748	G	£160,001-£320,000	£1,403
D	£68,001-£88,000	£842	H	over £320,000	£1,683

HAMMERSMITH AND FULHAM

It's been hard for Hammersmith and Fulham having such grand neighbours on its eastern boundary. Until the 1980s both Fulham and Hammersmith were beyond the pale for thousands of people who refused to consider living anywhere west of Chelsea or South Kensington. Criss-crossed by main roads heading out of London, with large tracts of industrial land, lacking elegant parks or smart shops, they were a distinct second best. Then suddenly in the mid-1980s parts of the borough became fashionable. Nice girls and boys fresh up in London from public school or university colonised the pubs and bought converted flats in the Victorian terraces. Wine bars and shops followed them. Now some of the fickle young have moved on to pastures new in Clapham and Battersea but left Hammersmith and Fulham firmly established.

Most of the borough is Victorian, built up as London spread out over fields and market gardens in the 19th century. The grids of two- and three-storey Victorian houses give some parts of Fulham in particular a claustrophobic and slightly monotonous feel despite attempts to liven things up by painting houses bright colours in some streets. From the elaborate terracotta mansion blocks of Hurlingham by the river, Hammersmith and Fulham reaches west along the river and north to the Victorian terraces of Fulham and the grander red brick terraces of Parson's Green. North of Parson's Green lie the large white, slightly shabby stucco and elaborate brick terraces of West Kensington and beyond the office blocks and flyover of Hammersmith to the west, more Victorian terraces and cottages round Ravenscourt Park and Shepherds Bush. The few roads of Victorian semis and terraces around Wormwood Scrubs and White City in the north are dominated by the grim walls of the prison and the Westway.

There may be wine bars and well-heeled people in Fulham but the borough also ranks as the 18th most deprived area of England. It has higher unemployment, with 5.8% of the population out of work, than all its immediate neighbours except Brent. But millions of pounds are going into regeneration schemes across the borough from White City in the north to Sands End next to the river. A total of £15.2 million is going to White City, one of the poorest parts of the borough, to improve the job prospects and environment of residents. Work is continuing next to Fulham Broadway tube station on a massive £65 million development of shops, restaurants, 12-screen multiplex cinema and health club, which should give a boost to an area surprisingly lacking in big name shops (although there's no shortage of bars and restaurants). Shepherds Bush will also get a much needed shot in the arm with a £450 million development of shops, restaurants, leisure facilities and a new station on the West London Line. And at the borough's southern tip in Sands End, a mix of private and affordable homes, offices, shops, restaurants, a hotel and a fitness centre is being built on the site of the former Imperial Wharf gasworks.

The downside to all this activity is that the new developments will almost certainly generate even more traffic. Heavy traffic on many roads is one of the disadvantages of living in Hammersmith & Fulham and pollution ranks high on residents' list of concerns. The succession of prolonged closures of Hammersmith Bridge, the borough's main gateway to the south, hasn't helped.

PROPERTY AND ARCHITECTURE

CHELSEA HARBOUR

Despite its name, Chelsea Harbour's just in Hammersmith and Fulham (to the disgust of some of its residents who did their darnedest to get the boundary moved so that they could be in Kensington and Chelsea). It's a slightly tired-looking 1980s development of flats and townhouses, a hotel and a landmark 20-storey tower around a glass and marble shopping centre now converted into a one-stop interior design centre after the shopping centre failed to take off. Popular with well-off professionals and City workers who like its river views and burgeoning collection of restaurants and shops nearby but a long trek to good public transport.

ATTRACTS *Young professionals; City workers* • **CONSERVATION AREAS** *None* • **AVERAGE PRICES** *Flats: 1-bed £300,000+; 2-bed £400,000+; 3-bed £700,000+ Houses: 4-bed+ £1.1 million* • **AVERAGE RENTS (WEEKLY)** *Flats: 1-bed £400-£500+; 2-bed £500-£550 Houses: 4-bed+ £1950+.*

FULHAM & PARSONS GREEN

The two- and three-storey bay-windowed Victorian terrace reigns supreme in most of Fulham. Many are still houses with some converted into two or three flats. Some streets, off Fulham Palace Road, for example, have gone multicoloured with houses painted yellow, pink, blue and terracotta to relieve the red brick. Some larger Victorian terraces in Parsons Green, the most desirable part of Fulham, with some of the pleasantest overlooking Eel Brook Common. Roads of large red brick four-bedroom terraces complete with gables and stone lions on the sought-after Peterborough Estate and large mansion blocks, some ornate terracotta and some plainer, by the river at Hurlingham. Once-industrial Sands End has 1990s developments of flats and workshops and, in nearby roads, large red brick Victorian terraces, many converted to flats, mixed with smaller terraces and council blocks. Sands End is now nearly as expensive as the rest of Fulham despite being a long way from public transport. Prices will soar if St George, the developer of the Imperial Wharf gasworks site, manages to persuade Railtrack to build a new station at Sands End.

ATTRACTS *Young well-heeled professionals; well-off first time buyers; mummies and daddies buying properties for their children ('the flat's my pension plan, darling')* • **CONSERVATION AREAS** *Hurlingham; Putney Bridge; Bishops Park; Studdridge Street; Parsons Green; Fulham Park Gardens; Crabtree Estate;*

*Walham Green; Sedlescombe Road; Central Fulham; Colehill Gardens;
Sands End Riverside; Imperial Square* • **AVERAGE PRICES** *Flats: studio
£70,000+; 1-bed £140,000-£250,000; 2-bed £180,000-£350,000
Houses: 2-bed £300,000+; 3-bed £350,000+; 4-bed £450,000+*
• **AVERAGE RENTS (WEEKLY)** *Flats: studio £180+; 1-bed £210-£230; 2-bed
£240+ Houses: 2-bed £300-£325; 3-bed £450+; 4-bed £550-£600+.*

WEST KENSINGTON

Much more similar architecturally to Kensington or Earls Court than Fulham.
Large white stucco houses with pillared porches or tall four- and five-storey
Victorian brick houses with elaborate carved facings. Mostly divided into
flats with many rented out on short lets. A lot of the properties are slightly
unkempt, particularly around West Kensington station and the area has a
transient feel, not helped by the main A4 carving through the middle of it,
carrying four lanes of traffic. But just a few roads away are the grand red
brick mansion blocks of Queen's Club Gardens overlooking private
gardens and tennis courts and the pretty multicoloured terraces in roads off
North End Road known as The Villes to estate agents.

ATTRACTS *Young professionals; people who can't afford Kensington;
investors looking for rental income* • **CONSERVATION AREAS** *Queen's Club
Gardens; Turneville and Chesson; Barons Court; Gunter Estate; Dorcas
Estate; Fitzgeorge and Fitzjames* • **AVERAGE PRICES** *Flats: studio £95,000-
£125,00; 1-bed £170,000+; 2-bed £190,000+ Houses: 2-bed
£300,000+; 3-bed £320,000+; 4-bed £500,000* • **AVERAGE RENTS
(WEEKLY)** *Flats: studio £160+; 1-bed £160+; 2-bed £260+ Houses: 2-bed
£280+; 3-bed £350+; 4-bed £450+.*

HAMMERSMITH & RAVENSCOURT PARK

The residential roads of Hammersmith are a pleasant contrast to the giant
traffic roundabout that is Hammersmith Town Centre. To the east is a
mixture of mansion blocks, cottages, Victorian terraces and conversions
round Olympia, Brook Green and what residents and estate agents call
Blythe Village, centred on Blythe Road. North of the town centre there are
roads of small Victorian terraces around Brackenbury Road and in
Brackenbury Village (another place you'll never find on the A-Z). Victorian
cottages and mid-19th-century multicoloured terraces in roads around
Ravenscourt Park. The riverside at Hammersmith is uncomfortably close to
the flyover but there are some lovely Georgian houses overlooking the
river. Mansion blocks facing the flyover.

ATTRACTS *Families who can't afford a house in Notting Hill or Chiswick;
professionals; some first-time buyers; French people wanting to be near the
French school at Brook Green* • **CONSERVATION AREAS** *Brook Green;
Lakeside/Sinclair/Blythe Road; Hammersmith Odeon; The Mall;
Hammersmith Broadway; King Street (East); Bradmore; Ravenscourt Park;
Melrose; Hammersmith Grove* • **AVERAGE PRICES** *Flats: 1-bed £155,000+;
2-bed £210,000+ Houses: 2-bed £350,000+; 3-bed £430,000+; 4-bed
£550,000+* • **AVERAGE RENTS (WEEKLY)** *Flats: studio £170+; 1-bed £220+;
2-bed £250+ Houses: 2-bed £380+; 3-bed £500+; 4-bed £750+.*

SHEPHERDS BUSH

Shepherds Bush is always being touted as an area 'on the up' but it's got a
bit of a way to go before it reaches the commanding heights of Fulham or
Clapham. Having said that, the area is fairly central, interestingly

cosmopolitan and popular with first-time buyers for the large choice of big Victorian houses converted into flats between the Uxbridge and Goldhawk Roads. Larger Victorian and turn-of-the-century family houses to the west of Askew Road feel more like neighbouring Chiswick than Shepherds Bush. Further north there's a mixture of Victorian terraces, conversions, council and ex-council houses in the bleak roads around Wormwood Scrubs, with the ugly blocks of the White City council estate and the ever-spreading offices of the BBC by the main A40.

ATTRACTS *First-time buyers; young professionals; families who can't afford a house in Notting Hill or Kensington; investors buying for rental income* • **CONSERVATION AREAS** *Coningham Road; Limes Grove; Shepherds Bush: Ingersoll and Arminger; Cleverly Estate; Old Oak and Wormholt; Wood Lane; St Mary's* • **AVERAGE PRICES** *Flats: studio £100,000+; 1-bed £125,000+; 2-bed £165,000+ Houses: 2-bed £250,000+; 3-bed £300,000+; 4-bed £350,000+* • **AVERAGE RENTS (WEEKLY)** *Flats: studio £130-£160; 1-bed £170-£220; 2-bed £200-£280 Houses: 2-bed £270+; 3-bed £270-£360; 4-bed £360-£500.*

BEST POSTCODES

The best postcode is Fulham SW6, followed by West Kensington W14 and Hammersmith W6. But the key issue affecting price is how far away you are from a tube station, because tube provision is patchy, particularly in Fulham. Roads in Sands End (east of Wandsworth Bridge Road) within walking distance of Fulham Broadway tube are just as expensive as anything in Fulham, although Sands End as a whole is still cheaper than the rest of Fulham.

AMENITIES

SCHOOLS***

State secondary schools perform creditably in league tables, although primary schools are more disappointing. There is a choice of private prep and secondary schools in the borough itself, including some famous names like St Paul's Girls, with more in neighbouring boroughs (see Kensington & Chelsea and Wandsworth). Good provision for three- and four-year-olds in state nursery schools and private nurseries.

PRE-SCHOOL PROVISION *5 council-run nursery schools and early years centres; 32 nursery classes in state primary or church schools; 72 private and voluntary day nurseries and playgroups. Proportion of under-fives in state nurseries: 59%* • **STATE PRIMARY SCHOOLS** *Overall league table position: 79th out of 150. Top scorers: Pope John RC (with nursery unit), Shepherds Bush; Good Shepherd RC, (with nursery unit), Shepherds Bush; John Betts, Hammersmith* • **STATE SECONDARY SCHOOLS** *Overall league table position: 51st out of 149. Top scorers: London Oratory School (boys, girls in sixth) (choice of the Blairs), Fulham; Lady Margaret (girls), Parsons Green; Sacred Heart High School (girls, the Blairs' other choice), Hammersmith* • **PRIVATE PREP SCHOOLS** *Bute House (girls), Hammersmith; Latymer Prep (boys), Hammersmith* • **PRIVATE SECONDARY SCHOOLS** *St Paul's Girls, Brook Green; Godolphin and Latymer (girls), Hammersmith; Latymer Upper School (boys), Hammersmith.*

TRANSPORT***

The tube reaches to most parts of the borough but looks better on the map than it actually is. The centre and west are best served by both District and Piccadilly Lines but the south relies on the less frequent and more crowded Wimbledon branch of the District Line. Sands End and Chelsea Harbour are a long way from a tube. The Central Line serves the north of the borough.

TUBES *Fulham Broadway (District) Zone 2. Cost of annual season ticket £756. Average journey time to Embankment 18 minutes. Putney Bridge (District) Zone 2. Average journey to Embankment 22 minutes. Hammersmith (District, Piccadilly, Hammersmith and City) Zone 2. Average journey time to Embankment 17 minutes; to Piccadilly Circus 14 minutes; to Paddington 11 minutes. Shepherds Bush (Central) Zone 2. Average journey time to Oxford Circus 12 minutes* ● **BUSES** *Lots of buses both to town and neighbouring suburbs, with Hammersmith a key interchange and terminus. Services to town include the 9 from Hammersmith to Aldwych, the 11 from Fulham Broadway to Trafalgar Square and Liverpool Street, the 14 via Fulham Broadway to Tottenham Court Road and the 74 via Fulham Palace Road to Baker Street* ● **TRAFFIC TROUBLESPOTS** *Fulham: The junction of Fulham Road, Dawes Road and Fulham Broadway is often choked with traffic including heavy lorries and buses. The end of Fulham Road by Stamford Bridge is trafficky on football match days. In central Fulham, driving along the south part of the North End Road is a nightmare because of the daily market. The junction of Fulham Palace Road and Lillie Road is slow because of blockages further up by the hospital. Hammersmith: A junction of several major main roads including the A4 out of London and a fiendish one-way system through the central shopping area. Frequent long-term closures of Hammersmith Bridge for repairs don't help. Shepherds Bush: The Shepherds Bush roundabout is usually crowded with traffic from the M41 motorway and roads round Shepherds Bush Common are also busy* ● **PARKING** *Controlled parking zones cover most of the borough and parking regulations are strictly enforced. Cost of annual resident's permit: £50.*

LEISURE FACILITIES***

THEATRES & CONCERT HALLS *Fringe theatre and new plays at The Lyric in Hammersmith and at Riverside Studios in Hammersmith. There's also the Bush Theatre at Shepherds Bush and live music and musicals at the Empire, Shepherds Bush and the Apollo, Hammersmith* ● **CINEMAS** *Mainstream cinema complexes in Hammersmith and Fulham and rep at Riverside Studios* ● **MUSEUMS & GALLERIES** *A bit thin on the ground. Museums include the Fulham Palace Museum, housed in Fulham Palace, the borough's oldest building, dating from the 16th century with a peaceful courtyard and fountains and set in riverside gardens. Local activities and guided tours of the palace. William Morris's former house by the river in Hammersmith opens to the public a couple of days a week* ● **SPORTS FACILITIES** *Three leisure centres at Hammersmith, Shepherds Bush and central Fulham – all with fitness centres and indoor sports facilities. Swimming pool at Shepherds Bush. Two whizzy new pools are planned for Fulham as part o an £8 million leisure centre to be run in conjunction with Holmes Place. Football, cricket, tennis and athletics in various combinations at Hurlingham Park, Ravenscourt Park and Wormwood Scrubs. Three major league football clubs – Chelsea, Fulham and QPR – have their grounds in Fulham (all in residential areas which can make Saturdays tricky for* *parking or even walking down the street)* ● **LIBRARIES** *Two main libraries (Fulham, and Hammersmith, in a beautiful building with a carved staircase and stained glass windows), and four branch libraries. Good long opening hours, recently extended to include Sunday opening at Hammersmith and Fulham libraries. Under-used, with only 4.6 library visits per head. Position in library-use league table: 26th out of 32 (where 1 is best and 32 worst).*

OPEN SPACES***

A bit short of open space, especially in comparison with neighbouring boroughs. But the long mostly residential river frontage is a pleasure, although some of the choicest river front is privately owned by the posh Hurlingham Club. If you like to keep abreast of riverfront developments, there's an excellent view from the Thames Path at Sands End of the vast blocks going up along the river at Battersea and Wandsworth
RIVERSIDE WALKS *Prior Bank Gardens and Bishops Park, with a long grassy tree-lined walkway and riverside path looking over to the boathouses of Putney on the south bank. Fulham Palace and grounds are in the park*
● **WIDE OPEN SPACES** *Wormwood Scrubs, a huge featureless flat expanse of common. A good place to stand in and scream without disturbing anyone*
● **FAMILY ATTRACTIONS** *Ravenscourt Park with several play areas, pretty ornamental lake and mature trees.*

SHOPS***

CHELSEA HARBOUR & SANDS END *Up-market and often almost empty galleried shopping centre at Chelsea Harbour now turned over to designer clothes shops and showrooms. Sainsbury's at Sands End* ● **FULHAM** *Several shopping drags. Smart antique shops on the new Kings Road. A handful of antique shops, clothes shops and lots of estate agents around Fulham Broadway but some of it looks down-at-heel, with shops boarded up and heavy traffic. The new Fulham Broadway development (see borough introduction) is much needed. Safeway in North End Road. There is a market at the south end of North End Road six days a week selling mostly fruit, vegetables and cheap clothes. It's struggling and universally considered a blot on the landscape (particularly by residents who have to suffer market lorries and litter at the end of their roads and constant traffic jams)* ● **HAMMERSMITH** *The borough's main shopping centre is here along with two indoor malls and several streets of shops. But the experience is marred by heavy traffic from all directions which can make shopping tricky and unpleasant (lots of waiting to cross the road). The Broadway, incorporating the revamped bus station, is new and smart with a Tesco Metro and bookshop among the chains. Kings Mall is older and shabbier with chains and a large Safeway. King Street has small, tired chain stores. A new pedestrianised square next to the Lyric has improved things a bit – but not a lot* ● **SHEPHERDS BUSH** *Another traffic roundabout masquerading as a shopping centre. Mostly local shops (the usual burger bars and newsagents) round the three sides of Shepherds Bush Common. The grotty little shopping centre is being revamped as part of the White City development. The most interesting shops are further up the Uxbridge and Goldhawk Roads with lots of Middle Eastern supermarkets and ethnic restaurants. Six-day market under the railway arches off Goldhawk Road. Safeway.*

RESTAURANTS ***

FULHAM & PARSONS GREEN *A good choice – particularly round the ends of the Fulham and Kings Roads. Wine bars, pubs and all sorts of restaurants including Spanish and Thai* • **HAMMERSMITH & SHEPHERDS BUSH** *A range for most tastes from pizza to the River Café. A number of up-market restaurants have also sprung up in middle-class enclaves like Brackenbury Village and around the south part of Shepherds Bush Road near Blythe Village. East European, Thai and Far Eastern restaurants around Goldhawk and Uxbridge Roads.*

CRIME RATES **

Position in Metropolitan Police crime league table: 9th out of 32 (where 1 is worst and 32 best).

THE COUNCIL ***

POLITICAL AFFILIATION *Labour* • **MINUS POINTS** *Not always punctilious enough about clearing litter from the streets. Under-used libraries* • **PLUS POINTS** *Piloting boroughwide scheme of kerbside recycling for glass and other items as well as ongoing newspaper scheme. Discounts on home composters. Residents say the council generally does a good job*

• **PROPERTY SEARCHES CARRIED OUT IN 10 WORKING DAYS** *100%* • **STANDARD SEARCH FEE** £*115* • **COUNCIL TAX COLLECTED** *92.3%*

• **COUNCIL TAX 2000-2001**

BAND	PROPERTY VALUE	CHARGE	BAND	PROPERTY VALUE	CHARGE
A	up to £40,000	£586	E	£88,001-£120,000	£1,074
B	£40,001-£52,000	£683	F	£120,001-£160,000	£1,269
C	£52,001-£68,000	£781	G	£160,001-£320,000	£1,464
D	£68,001-£88,000	£878	H	over £320,000	£1,757

HARINGEY

No borough has trendier neighbours than Haringey, with Camden, Islington and Hackney encamped on its southern boundary. But similar fashionableness appears to have eluded much of Haringey, possibly because it's a longer commute to town and has fewer attractive Georgian squares. Blighted more than 15 years ago by the horrific riots on the Broadwater Farm Estate in Tottenham which resulted in the brutal murder of a policeman, Haringey has been keeping a low profile, trying to rebuild bridges between its disparate ethnic communities. Nearly a third of residents are from ethnic minorities, with Afro-Caribbeans the largest single group and large communities of Turks, Greeks and Asians.

Officials have never been able to decide whether Haringey is inner or outer London. But most residents would classify it as inner London psychologically, because it has the inner city's sharp contrasts between rich and poor and the cosmopolitan mix of races and cultures. It contains some of London's richest people in some of its most beautiful houses, as well as some of its poorest who live on alienating 1960s council estates. It stretches from the wooded heights of (parts of) Highgate and the Edwardian splendour of Muswell Hill, Alexandra Palace and Crouch End in the west through to the Victorian railway suburbs of Finsbury Park and Hornsey in the south. Further north on the axis of Victoriana which bisects the borough is Wood Green. Towards the flat expanse of marsh marking the beginning of the Essex flatlands are the council blocks, council houses and small terraces of Tottenham.

The hilly western parts of the borough around Muswell Hill and Crouch End include enough journalists among their middle class residents to ensure a good flow of coverage in the national and regional press about how marvellous the shops are, how friendly the people are and how spacious the family homes.

But Haringey is also the 13th most deprived area in England and 9.1% of its residents are out of work, for which reasons public and private sector money is flowing in to improve some of the borough's derelict and troubled areas, improve training and job prospects and attract business to the area. By 2002 more than £120 million is set to be invested in new shops, leisure facilities and housing on the former railway and gasworks sites between Alexandra Palace and Wood Green. Money will also go towards measures to calm the busy traffic along Wood Green High Road. In Tottenham, funds have been used to improve Tottenham Hale station. There are plans to stimulate the setting up of new businesses in the moribund Upper Lea Valley along the River Lea (see also Enfield, Hackney and Newham), as well as for enviromental improvements and incentives for shops to move into the boarded-up shops along Tottenham High Road.

PROPERTY AND ARCHITECTURE

HIGHGATE

One of London's most desirable areas, much sought after for its views over London, its villagey (although trafficky) high street, and its cosy community feel. An area of active middle class residents' associations and strong amenity groups. Some of its loveliest Georgian houses are in roads just off the High Street. The Edwardian half-timbered houses of the Holly Lodge Estate are outside the borough (see Camden) but there is also a good mixture of property with everything from mews cottages to large Victorian houses, modern blocks and a wide choice of conversion flats.
ATTRACTS Well-off families; city people with big bonuses; some international buyers • **CONSERVATION AREAS** Highgate • **AVERAGE PRICES** Flats: studio £90,000-£100,000; 1-bed £125,000+; 2-bed £170,000+ Houses: 3-bed £350,000+; 4-bed £400,000+ • **AVERAGE RENTS (WEEKLY)** Flats: studio £130-£150; 1-bed £180-£260; 2-bed £220-£350; Houses: 2-bed £250-£400; 3-bed £320-£500; 4-bed £400-£600.

MUSWELL HILL & CROUCH END

Muswell Hill is a good middle class suburb, sought after for its elegant shops, green space and handsome red brick Edwardian houses with lots of carved wooden balconies and porches, many on steep hills sloping downwards from the Broadway or on wide tree-lined streets. Some of the best houses are in roads between Highgate and Muswell Hill. A good range of conversion flats. More modest semis and Victorian terraces towards Alexandra Park, which is becoming more expensive as people move in who have been priced out of Muswell Hill. Plainer Edwardian houses around Bounds Green to the north and some ex-council. Muswell Hill's main drawback is that it's a bus ride (or an extremely brisk walk) to a station. Such enforced self-containment is possibly a reason for residents' community enthusiasm (they even have their own Inside Guide to all the best shops and facilities in the area). Crouch End used to be a part of London that people only knew from the outside of buses but it has grown increasingly fashionable over the past 10 years. Its large Edwardian houses are sought after both as family homes and as generously-sized conversion flats. Like Muswell Hill, the residents pride themselves on being a distinct community.

ATTRACTS *Families; well-off first-time buyers; young professionals; creative types* • **CONSERVATION AREAS** *Alexandra Palace and Park; Bowes Park; Muswell Hill; Fortis Green* • **AVERAGE PRICES** *Flats: studio £65,000-£90,000; 1-bed £115,000-£175,000; 2-bed £120,000-£180,000 Houses: 3-bed £270,000-£360,000; 4-bed £300,000-£600,000* • **AVERAGE RENTS (WEEKLY)** *Flats: studio £120-£140; 1-bed £170-£240; 2-bed £220-£320 Houses: 2-bed £250-£400; 3-bed £320-£450; 4-bed £400-£550.*

WOOD GREEN & HORNSEY

Much of Wood Green consists of Victorian terraces in various stages of repair and 'improvement'. The most historically interesting part of Wood Green (and the cheapest) is Noel Park. Built as model housing for workers in the 19th century, this is an enclave of dead straight avenues between Westbury Avenue and Lordship Lane, lined with red brick Victorian terraces, broken regularly with Dutch or cottage-style gables. To the south of Wood Green are the rows of late Victorian terraces known locally as the Ladder, as this is what the street pattern looks like on the map. Hornsey is more expensive than Wood Green, with a mixture of big Victorian houses, smaller Victorian terraces and modern blocks. The most expensive houses are closest to Crouch End, with which Hornsey shares a postcode.

ATTRACTS *First-time buyers; loyal locals* • **CONSERVATION AREAS** *Noel Park; Wood Green Common; Lordship Lane; Hornsey High Street; Hornsey Water Works and Filter Beds* • **AVERAGE PRICES** *Flats: studio £75,000-£90,000; 1-bed £95,000-£105,000; 2-bed £120,000-£145,000 Houses: 2-bed £150,000+; 3-bed £180,000-£200,000; 4-bed £250,000-£325,000* • **AVERAGE RENTS (WEEKLY)** *Flats: studio £120-£150; 1-bed £150-£170; 2-bed £190-£210 Houses: 2-bed £200-£220; 3-bed £250-£320; 4-bed £350+.*

FINSBURY PARK

Fifteen years ago most people wouldn't have been seen dead around here. The unsavoury reputation of the south end of Seven Sisters Road as a poor and vicious place long predated the grim council estates built to replace slums. But the 1980s boom had a lasting effect, with developers eagerly dividing up the larger Victorian houses round the park into spacious flats, and young professionals discovering how good its transport links were. Lots of conversions. Large houses are rare. Some of the area is still run-down and the area round the station particularly is a bit sleazy. But socially Finsbury Park is more like parts of Islington or Camden (indeed parts of it fall into both these boroughs). Upwardly mobile buyers like to think the Victorian terraces of Stroud Green are a cut above Finsbury Park although there's minimal difference in prices.

ATTRACTS *Young single people working in town; young professional couples; buyers who can't afford Islington or Crouch End* ● **CONSERVATION AREAS** *None* ● **AVERAGE PRICES** *Flats: studio £85,000+; 1-bed £120,000+; 2-bed £150,000+; Houses: 3-bed £250,000+; 4-bed £300,000+* ● **AVERAGE RENTS (WEEKLY)** *Flats: studio £120+; 1-bed £160+; 2-bed £220+ Houses: 3-bed £300; 4-bed £400.*

TOTTENHAM

Tottenham spreads across the east side of the borough and is its cheapest part. There is a mixture of Victorian and Edwardian terraces in the middle around Bruce Grove and towards Seven Sisters as well as roads of 1930s semis with modern council infill further north around White Hart Lane and Northumberland Park. The notorious Broadwater Farm estate, now revamped, is just west of Bruce Grove. The nearer you get to the marshes and the run-down warehouses lining the canal near the reservoirs, the bleaker the roads are. South Tottenham near Seven Sisters tube is one of the most expensive parts of Tottenham because of good transport links. Downhills Park near Turnpike Lane tube is also popular. Around White Hart Lane is the cheapest.

ATTRACTS *First-time buyers; people who can't afford Finsbury Park or Hornsey; investors* ● **CONSERVATION AREAS** *Bruce Castle; Campsbourne Cottage Estate; Clyde Circus; North Tottenham; Tottenham Bruce Grove; Tottenham Cemetery; Tottenham Green; Tottenham High Road and Scotland Green; Peabody Cottages* ● **AVERAGE PRICES** *Flats: studio £40,000-£55,000; 1-bed £65,000-£85,000; 2-bed £80,000-£110,000 Houses: 2-bed £100,000-£125,000; 3-bed £110,000-£170,000; 4-bed £140,000-£175,000* ● **AVERAGE RENTS (WEEKLY)** *Flats: studio £90+; 1-bed £130+; 2-bed £160+ Houses: 2-bed £160+; 3-bed £185+; 4-bed £240+.*

BEST POSTCODES

Highgate N6 and Muswell Hill N10 are, not surprisingly, the smartest postcodes in Haringey. Hornsey N8 is generally considered better than the part of Finsbury Park N4 which is in Haringey. South Tottenham N15 is smarter than Tottenham N17. Good transport links affect property prices more than postcodes.

AMENITIES

SCHOOLS * *

Dismal performance by primary and secondary schools alike, only partially redeemed by well-above-average state nursery provision. A handful of private prep and secondary schools.

PRE-SCHOOL PROVISION *3 state nursery centres; 41 nursery classes in state primary and church schools; 82 private and voluntary nurseries and playgroups. Proportion of under-fives in state nursery schools: 74%* ● **STATE PRIMARY SCHOOLS** *Overall position in league tables: 145th out of 150. Top Scorers: Tetherdown, Muswell Hill; Our Lady of Muswell Hill RC (with*

nursery unit), Muswell Hill; St James' CE (with nursery unit), Muswell Hill
• **STATE SECONDARY SCHOOLS** *Overall position in league tables: 144th out of 149. Top scorers: Fortismere (mixed), Muswell Hill; Hornsey School (girls), Hornsey; Highgate Wood School (mixed), Hornsey* • **PRIVATE PREP SCHOOLS** *Channing (girls), Highgate; Highgate Junior School (boys, girls to seven), Highgate* • **PRIVATE SECONDARY SCHOOL** *Highgate (boys), Highgate.*

TRANSPORT * * *

Unevenly spaced with some areas (Muswell Hill, parts of Hornsey, parts of South Tottenham) a long way from a station. It's worth being near a tube because two of the best lines (Victoria and Piccadilly) go through the centre of the borough. Finsbury Park almost certainly has the best transport, with excellent tube, bus and rail links, and mainline trains often stop there on their way north and east. Tottenham has three railway stations.

TRAINS *Finsbury Park Zone 2. Cost of annual season ticket £756. Average journey time to Kings Cross 9 minutes. Alexandra Palace Zone 3. Cost of annual season ticket £896. Average journey time to Kings Cross 15 minutes. Bruce Grove (Tottenham) Zone 3. Average journey time to Liverpool Street 20 minutes* • **TUBES** *Finsbury Park (Piccadilly, Victoria) Zone 2. Average journey time to Kings Cross 6-8 minutes. Wood Green (Piccadilly) Zone 3. Average journey time to Kings Cross 14 minutes. Tottenham Hale (Victoria) Zone 3. Average journey time to Kings Cross 12 minutes* • **BUSES** *Pretty good although buses from town can get tied up in traffic, giving you more time to absorb Archway Road, Wood Green High Road or Tottenham High Road than you'd ever need. Services to town include the 43 via Muswell Hill and Highgate to London Bridge, the 29 via Wood Green, Turnpike Lane and Green Lanes to Trafalgar Square*
• **TRAFFIC TROUBLESPOTS** *Finsbury Park: A tortuous one-way system through once-quiet residential roads. Always clogged with buses and cars around the station. Highgate: Often long queues on Highgate Hill into Highgate Village with lots of buses and lorries struggling up the hill from Archway. The village itself has far more traffic than its narrow main street can manage, with lots of parked delivery vans and buses. The Archway Road can also be a long haul, particularly in the rush hour. Wood Green: trafficky and unpleasant High Road particularly around the station. Lots of buses, shoppers and cars. Turnpike Lane can also be busy, with parked cars on both sides and late-night shoppers at the Asian supermarkets. Tottenham: The High Road doubles as the main A10. Another of London's depressingly polluted, traffic-dominated shopping streets with several lanes of traffic each way* • **PARKING** *So far, there are three controlled zones in Haringey, around Wood Green High Road, Green Lanes and at Seven Sisters. Another zone in Bounds Green/Bowes Park looks set to go ahead and consultations are going on in Muswell Hill. Plans for a zone in Finsbury Park have been postponed due to local opposition. Cost of annual resident's permit: £50.*

LEISURE FACILITIES * *

THEATRES & CONCERT HALLS *No dedicated indoor theatre but two theatres, the Mountview Conservatoire for the Performing Arts (Hornsey) and Jackson's Lane Community Centre (Highgate) have regular performances of a mix of professional and amateur productions. The North London Performing Arts Centre in Muswell Hill has theatre courses and performances. No permanent concert venue but rock concerts and annual*

Irish Fleadh in Finsbury Park (much to the disgust of some residents who object to the noise and litter) ● **CINEMAS** *The Muswell Hill Odeon shows mainstream films and there's a new multiplex cinema in Wood Green as part of the revamp of the Shopping City shopping centre* ● **MUSEUMS & GALLERIES** *Not a huge choice. Local history museum at Bruce Castle, a handsome Grade I listed Tudor building in lush grounds, a startling contrast to the roads of Victorian terraces around it. Art and craft exhibitions in the Alexandra Gallery at Alexandra Palace, the massive Edwardian pile which dominates Alexandra Park and whose television mast winks at its counterpart in faraway Crystal Palace. 'Ally Pally', as it's called locally, has had a chequered history. It has suffered two fires, the most recent in 1980 which gutted half the building and from which it's still recovering. Now there are plans for a 200-bed hotel at the south west corner of the palace but parts of the main building like the Victorian theatre are still waiting to be restored* ● **SPORTS FACILITIES** *Three leisure centres at Wood Green, Tottenham and Hornsey. Swimming pools at Hornsey and Tottenham. Hornsey has indoor and outdoor pools. Ice-skating at Alexandra Palace. Football matches at White Hart Lane (Tottenham Hotspur's home ground – residents who aren't fans dread match days). Tennis courts and other facilities at parks throughout the borough* ● **LIBRARIES** *Under-funded and under-used. Even the borough's largest library in Wood Green hasn't been refurbished for a long time and it shows. Branch libraries are small and struggling and local residents have been fighting council proposals to close branch libraries. Opening times are among the most truncated of any borough with some branches closed almost as often as they're open. 4.38 library visits per head. Position in library-use league table: 25th out of 32 (where 1 is best and 32 worst).*

OPEN SPACES ****

Everything from woods to marshes to parks, and no area is too far from an interesting space. Finsbury Park, one of the largest open spaces in the borough and the largest run directly by the council, could get a much-needed face-lift to its lake, flower gardens and general appearance if a £1.5 million heritage lottery fund bid is successful.
VIEWS *Alexandra Park, no contest. When it's clear, you can see to the hills of Crystal Palace and beyond and there are excellent views of the City, West End and Canary Wharf* ● **WOODS** *Highgate Woods. A treasure of mature woodland between Highgate and Muswell Hill (although the woods do make coming out of Highgate Station late at night a bit creepy). Run by the Corporation of London. The Parkland Walk, along the old railway line from Finsbury Park to Alexandra Palace, runs from the woods to Finsbury Park. Good views of people's back gardens* ● **RIVER WALKS** *The towpath on the River Lea. The river runs through the Lea Valley Regional Park, an area of grassy marshland dominated by electricity pylons. The towpath runs alongside the canal which is a diversion of the River Lea with locks and rows of moored houseboats (none of your posh Islington stuff here though – these houseboat owners have broken-down old cars parked on the bank and washing hanging out to dry).*

SHOPS ***

HIGHGATE *Attractive villagey shops in the High Street including several bookshops (the second-hand one is deceptively spacious), clothes shops, and local grocery and food shops among others. But a constant flow of* *traffic up and down the hill blights an otherwise pleasant shopping experience* • **MUSWELL HILL & CROUCH END** *Muswell Hill manages to combine the interesting and the practical, making this one of the best shopping areas in the borough. Local bookshops, furniture and interior design shops with items you can actually imagine living with and reasonably-priced clothes shops are mixed with the dull but necessary banks, building societies and other chains. Sainsbury's. Crouch End has some similarly interesting shops north of the Clocktower – the Broadway itself is fairly predictable. Budgens* • **WOOD GREEN & HORNSEY** *Wood Green is the borough's official flagship shopping centre which is fine if you like indoor malls full of chain stores (mostly at the cheaper end of the market). Shopping City, an ugly red brick building with multi-storey car-park, looms above on either side of the High Road, joined by a pedestrian bridge. It has recently had a much needed revamp with new shops including Next and HMV. Sainsbury's. The High Road itself has local shops with a lot of take-aways and small supermarkets. Turnpike Lane is much more interesting, with mostly Indian-run shops, full of bright saris and materials, exotic bakeries, Halal butchers and boxes of fruit and vegetables spilling onto the pavement. Hornsey has a couple of antique shops, a piano shop and furniture auction rooms in a High Street running either side of a small green* • **FINSBURY PARK & TOTTENHAM** *Mostly local shops along wide trafficky roads. Ethnic supermarkets, including a lot of Turkish shops around Green Lanes in Finsbury Park. Sainsbury's by Harringay and Green Lanes station. Lots of Afro-Caribbean shops in Tottenham including hairdressers and soul record shops. Tesco in Tottenham High Road. A new retail park by Tottenham Hale station is part of the area's regeneration, with office and electrical goods stores.*

RESTAURANTS***

HIGHGATE *Chains like Café Rouge alongside locally popular French and Italian restaurants and winebars* • **MUSWELL HILL & CROUCH END** *A good choice of everything from pizza and pasta chains to individual winebars and brasseries and a widely praised French restaurant* • **ELSEWHERE** *Lots of Turkish and Greek restaurants of varying quality, particularly in Finsbury Park, Wood Green and Hornsey. The best are often little more than cafés from the outside but offer good value and freshly-cooked food.*

CRIME RATES**

Position in Metropolitan Police league table: 11th out of 32 (where 1 is worst and 32 best).

THE COUNCIL**

POLITICAL AFFILIATION Labour • **MINUS POINTS** *Some of the worst schools in London. The highest band D council tax in London in 2000-2001. Poorly resourced and used libraries. Not always thorough at sweeping the streets (lots of old black refuse sacks with rubbish bursting out of them across the borough) and has the highest level of missed household rubbish collections in outer London* • **PLUS POINTS** *Experimenting with a door-to-door recycling scheme in 25,000 homes. Energetic promotion of the borough to businesses and government and encouragement of regeneration*
• **PROPERTY SEARCHES CARRIED OUT IN 10 WORKING DAYS** 98.3%
• **STANDARD SEARCH FEE** £110 • **COUNCIL TAX COLLECTED** 85%
• **COUNCIL TAX 2000-2001**

BAND	PROPERTY VALUE	CHARGE	BAND	PROPERTY VALUE	CHARGE
A	up to £40,000	£621	E	£88,001-£120,000	£1,139
B	£40,001-£52,000	£725	F	£120,001-£160,000	£1,346
C	£52,001-£68,000	£828	G	£160,001-£320,000	£1,553
D	£68,001-£88,000	£932	H	over £320,000	£1,864

HARROW

Harrow (to people who don't live there) means Harrow School, alma mater to prime ministers, poets and peers, whose buildings sprawl up and down the narrow streets of Harrow on the Hill and whose uniform of dark blazers and straw boaters would be instantly recognisable to the Victorians who presided over the school's 19th-century expansion.

But Harrow on the Hill is one of the borough's high points, both physically and architecturally. Walk down the hill and you plunge into miles of streets of anonymous mostly inter-war suburbia across the south part of the borough around Harrow itself and in Wealdstone, Harrow Weald and South Harrow. To the north around Pinner in the west and Stanmore in the east, however, the densely packed houses start to thin out, giving way to the large detached houses, well preserved high streets and open space of Harrow's metroland, before London rises up over its northern hills to meet Hertfordshire.

This is the beginning of the north-west London commuter belt, with more than half the borough's residents travelling outside the borough to go to work every morning. They're mostly a solid lot, big in white collar industries like banking, finance and public administration. Not surprisingly, the council's keen to tempt others in and has been enthusiastically pressing the attractions of Harrow (good transport links and schools, green space) on the service and manufacturing sectors. Unemployment is low at 2.7%.

As in neighbouring Hillingdon and Ealing, Harrow's large Indian community has made its mark, particularly on otherwise fairly uninspiring local shopping parades, although Harrow has nothing to compare with Southall (see Ealing). More than a quarter of the borough's population is from an ethnic minority, with Indians the largest single group. A large Jewish population, particularly round Stanmore, Northwood and Pinner, adds to a melting pot of cultures which preserves Harrow from being socially just another bland bit of suburbia.

The borough's main shopping centre in Harrow got a big face-lift five years ago with the addition of the St George's shopping and entertainment complex to complement the existing St Ann's centre at the other side of the pedestrianised shopping street. Designers at St George's eschewed the obvious glass ceiling and lifts in favour of a vaulted church-like roof with arched brick window surrounds and a series of iron railinged walkways on upper floors rising from the ground floor like tiers of theatre balconies. Harrow now has one of the largest shopping centres for miles around, to compete with the lure of Brent Cross just over the border in Barnet, with the council claiming Harrow as one of the top ten retail centres in Greater London.

PROPERTY AND ARCHITECTURE

HARROW ON THE HILL

Spectacularly set on a wooded hill with church spire, overlooking a sea of red suburban roofs below and a dramatic point of reference for miles around. In contrast to surrounding areas, a lot of Harrow on the Hill is Victorian and Edwardian, mixed with some beautiful Georgian townhouses. The picturesque main streets of the Hill, as locals call it, are dominated by the buildings of Harrow School (small notices indicating Matron's Entrance are a give-away that a building is a boys' boarding house rather than a desirable residence) so most of the properties for mere mortals are in roads running up to the village street at the top. A good mix of flats (many in new developments), and houses, but don't expect a bargain.

ATTRACTS *Wealthy families; young professionals; first time buyers prepared to commute for the sake of more space* • **CONSERVATION AREAS** *Roxeth Hill; Harrow School; Harrow Park; Harrow on the Hill village; South Hill Avenue; Mount Park Estate; Roxborough Park* • **AVERAGE PRICES** *Flats: studio £75,000+; 1-bed £110,000-£140,000; 2-bed £175,000-£240,000 Houses: 2-bed £185,000-£200,000+; 3-bed £250,000-£300,000+; 4-bed £500,000+* • **AVERAGE RENTS (WEEKLY)** *Flats: 1-bed £160+; 2-bed £185+ Houses: 2-bed £195+; 3-bed £345+; 4-bed £575+.*

HARROW & WEALDSTONE

On paper Harrow has a number of different parts – North Harrow, South Harrow, Harrow Weald and Harrow itself. But they're all more or less suburban, with streets of mostly 1930s semis further away from Harrow, mixed with Victorian and Edwardian two-storey terraces around Wealdstone. In descending order of desirability, the pecking order is roughly: North Harrow (because it borders on smarter Pinner); Harrow (good shops and transport); Wealdstone; South Harrow. Harrow Weald is the smarter part of Wealdstone (or the more down-market end of Stanmore if you prefer). Some bargains to be had in South Harrow and Wealdstone if you want a cheap house. Good choice of modern blocks of flats in Harrow.

ATTRACTS *First-time buyers; families; members of the Asian communities (especially Wealdstone)* • **CONSERVATION AREAS** *Brookshill, Harrow Weald; West Drive, Harrow Weald* • **AVERAGE PRICES** *Flats: studio £60,000; 1-bed £75,000-£105,000; 2-bed £90,000-£150,000 Houses: 2-bed £115,000-£145,000; 3-bed £135,000-£200,000; 4-bed £175,000-£350,000* • **AVERAGE RENTS (WEEKLY)** *Flats: 1-bed £125+; 2-bed £140 Houses: 2-bed £250+; 3-bed £275+.*

PINNER & HATCH END

Superior metroland, with well-spaced detached and semi-detached 1930s houses built in what their first owners were happy to believe was a 'country' style – Tudor beams, leaded lights, tall chimneys and deep sloping eaves. Now on the edge of greenbelt land, maybe the speculative builders were more accurate than they knew. Modern estates of small 1960s and 1970s townhouses and new blocks in roads leading to the centre of Pinner, which, with its attractive hilly Tudor high street, could certainly pass muster as a prosperous Hertfordshire or Buckinghamshire town. Cosy village community in Pinner if you want to get involved.

ATTRACTS *Families; commuters; young professionals; members of the Jewish community* • **CONSERVATION AREAS** *Pinner High Street; Tookes Green; Pinnerwood Park Estate; Waxwell Lane; Waxwell Close, East End Farm; Pinnerwood Farm; Moss Lane; Pinner Hill Estate; West Towers* • **AVERAGE PRICES** *Flats: 1-bed £130,000+; 2-bed £130,000-£160,000 Houses: 2-bed £150,000-£200,000+; 3-bed £150,000-£300,000; 4-bed £200,000-£400,000* • **AVERAGE RENTS (WEEKLY)** *Flats: 1-bed £140+; 2-bed £175+ Houses: 2-bed £185+; 3-bed £330+; 4-bed £565+.*

STANMORE

Blessed with some of the borough's most attractive green space, Stanmore includes some of the grandest houses in Harrow in the private roads between Stanmore Common and Bentley Priory open space. Huge houses with iron gates, double drives and houses with bewildering numbers of wings, gables and entrances. Just to make it clear who's top dog, some of the grass verges outside the houses warn anyone who's odd enough not to be in a car to keep off the grass. A mixture of well-kept Edwardian, 1920s and 1930s semis and detached houses further south in roads off Uxbridge Road, around the Broadway and around Canons Park.

ATTRACTS *Families wanting good schools and green space; members of the Jewish community; members of the Asian community* • **CONSERVATION AREAS** *Little Common; Stanmore Hill; Old Church Lane; Kerry Avenue; Canons Park Estate* • **AVERAGE PRICES** *Flats: 1-bed £140,000-£160,000; 2-bed £160,000+ Houses: 2-bed £160,000+; 3-bed £185,000+; 4-bed £360,000+* • **AVERAGE RENTS (WEEKLY)** *Flats: 1-bed £125+; 2-bed £175+ Houses: 3-bed £230+; 4-bed £275+.*

BEST POSTCODES

Postcodes are largely irrelevant as the whole borough is in Middlesex. Proximity to transport links has a significant impact on prices.

AMENITIES

SCHOOLS ★ ★ ★ ★

Harrow's school system works differently from all the other London boroughs, in that it operates a three-tier school system with primary, middle and high school. Merton, the only other borough to operate three tiers, is changing over to a more traditional two-tier system (see Merton). Harrow's high schools finish at 16 and there are no council-run sixth form colleges. There's also a system of 'links' between primary and middle schools and high schools to control entry. Not everyone approves of these unusual arrangements but there are no signs that they work to Harrow's detriment, with very good results especially at secondary school level. A good selection of top performing private schools. Below average provision for under-fives in state nurseries but a decent choice of private nurseries.

PRE-SCHOOL PROVISION *68 private nurseries and playgroups; 25 state primary and church schools with nursery places. Proportion of under-fives in state nurseries: 48%* ● **STATE PRIMARY SCHOOLS** *Overall league table position: 13th out of 150. Top scorers: Newton Farm (with nursery unit), South Harrow; West Lodge, Pinner; Grimsdyke, Pinner* ● **STATE SECONDARY SCHOOLS** *Overall league table position: 14th out of 149. Top scorers: Nower Hill High (mixed), Pinner; Park High (mixed), Stanmore; Bentley Wood High (girls), Stanmore* ● **PRIVATE PREP SCHOOLS** *Alpha Prep (mixed), Harrow; Inellan House (mixed) Pinner; Reddiford (mixed), Pinner; Quainton Hall (boys), Harrow; Orley Farm (mixed), Harrow on the Hill* ● **PRIVATE SECONDARY SCHOOLS** *Harrow School (boys); John Lyon (boys), Harrow; Buckingham College (boys, girls in 6th), Harrow; Heathfield (girls from 3), Pinner; Peterborough and St Margaret's (girls), Stanmore; North London Collegiate (girls), Canons Park.*

TRANSPORT★★★★

Well served by tube (as you'd expect in a borough which largely exists as a result of tube line building) with Jubilee, Metropolitan and Bakerloo Lines running through it. These are all good tube lines but the Metropolitan Line is a better bet than the Bakerloo from Harrow for a fast trip into town – only about half the Bakerloo Line trains come out as far as Harrow and Wealdstone and the train stops at every station, unlike the fast trains from Harrow on the Hill. Trains only around Hatch End in the far north of the borough unless you fancy a brisk walk to Pinner.

TRAINS *Hatch End Zone 6. Cost of annual season ticket £1456. Average journey time to Euston 35 minutes* ● **TUBES** *Harrow on the Hill (Metropolitan) Zone 5. Cost of annual season ticket £1332. Average journey time to Baker Street 16-20 minutes. Pinner (Metropolitan) Zone 5. Average journey time to Baker Street 24 minutes. Harrow and Wealdstone (Bakerloo) Zone 5. Average journey time to Oxford Circus 34 minutes. Stanmore (Jubilee) Zone 5. Fastest journey time to Westminster 36 minutes* ● **BUSES** *Brent Cross is about as near as you'll get to the glittering lights of town during the day on a bus from Harrow. But links between different parts of the borough are generally good, particularly around Harrow itself. Services tail off a bit around Stanmore and there can be long waits. Night buses include the N18 from Trafalgar Square via Harrow and Harrow Weald, the N98 from Trafalgar Square to Stanmore* ● **TRAFFIC** *Rare among outer London boroughs in that it escapes the blight of motorways and dual carriageways which turn into motorways. But its main shopping areas don't escape traffic, particularly as the borough has a lot of 1930s parades built directly onto busy roads* ● **TRAFFIC TROUBLESPOTS** *Harrow & Harrow on the Hill: There can be long waits at the lights at the bottom of Harrow on the Hill heading for the main shopping centre. The shopping centre itself is pedestrianised which inevitably means more traffic building up in roads immediately outside it. Pinner: The streets around the station and Sainsbury's can get clogged with traffic* ● **PARKING** *There are controlled parking zones in Pinner; Rayners Lane; Harrow; Harrow on the Hill; Wealdstone; Stanmore and Harrow Weald. Cost of annual resident's permit: £25.*

LEISURE FACILITIES***

THEATRES & CONCERT HALLS *Of local appeal. The Travellers Theatre and Elliot Concert Hall are both housed in the Harrow Arts Centre, an attractive Queen Anne-style red brick building in Hatch End. Travellers Theatre has a mixture of plays by visiting companies, children's shows, drama workshops and live music. Elliot has middle-of-the-road concerts and Mum and Gran's favourite stars. Concerts and Sunday bands at Headstone Manor (see below). Gilbert and Sullivan evenings at Grim's Dyke House, Harrow Weald, once owned and lived in by W S Gilbert* ● **CINEMAS** *Much improved choice since the arrival of the nine-screen Warner Village cinema at the St George's Centre, Harrow, although if black and white arts cinema's your thing, you'd better head for the tube station. The Safari Cinema in Harrow shows Asian films only* ● **MUSEUMS & GALLERIES** *A small selection but there are plans for a big expansion of the local history museum and heritage centre at Headstone Manor with a £1.5 million lottery grant. The manor, a 14th-century manor house with barns and a granary already has some local history displays (including mock-ups of 1930s front rooms) but the borough plans a whole historical sweep of displays from medieval to present day. Cat obsessives should head for the Cat Museum in Harrow on the Hill (antique porcelain and glass rather than warm fur). Art gallery in the Old Speech Room at Harrow School (limited opening hours)* ● **SPORTS FACILITIES** *One leisure centre in Harrow. Tennis, football, basketball, cricket in parks throughout the borough* ● **LIBRARIES** *Below average use although the central library at the Civic Centre is large and well laid out. Opening hours are erratic around the borough with several opening in the middle of the afternoon on some days. Everything's closed on Wednesdays and half the borough's branch libraries are closed on Fridays, with those that open in the morning closing in the afternoon. No Sunday opening. 7 library visits per head. Position in library-use league table: 16th out of 32 (where 1 is best and 32 worst).*

OPEN SPACES****

Fields, woods, hills, parks – you want it, it's here. As in other outer London boroughs, the northernmost reaches are the greenest, as built-up London gives way to greenbelt but there are excellent views from Harrow on the Hill in the south as well.

VIEWS *The lawns by the library at Harrow School (if you're permitted access – this is private property). Beautiful views across to London from one of the area's most prominent hills. Also the top of the climb by the deer park in Bentley Priory Open Space (if the views aren't obscured by trees). Cattle with villainous-looking horns grazing by the path help the rural effect. Bentley Priory is otherwise a bit of a disappointment because much of it's now owned by the Ministry of Defence and fenced off* ● **GARDENS** *Canons Park – once the grounds of a grand mansion which is now the North London Collegiate School. Peaceful gardens (despite tubes passing regularly) with poplars, weeping willows and a walled garden with formal flower beds* ● **WOODS** *Stanmore and Harrow Weald Commons. Good walks through mature woods (although attempts to cut across the grounds of Bentley Priory from one side to the other don't work).*

SHOPS***

HARROW ON THE HILL *Pretty high street of whitewashed cottages and Victorian shopfronts, including the inevitable Harrow School outfitters, as* *well as antique shops, a few restaurants, estate agents and other local shops. Beautiful rather than useful* • **HARROW** *Just at the bottom of the hill and a total contrast. Harrow itself is visually nothing to look at – a mess of office blocks and shops of different vintages – but there's a large choice of decent chains both in the pedestrianised St Ann's Road and in the St Ann's and St George's shopping centres, once you've crossed the nasty busy road by the station. Nothing startlingly original but a pleasant place to shop. Tesco* • **WEALDSTONE** *Down the road from Harrow and suffering for it. A partially pedestrianised street of small shabby shops. Cheap clothes, Halal butchers and pile 'em high, sell 'em cheap discount stores, occupying empty shops until someone catches up with them. All this could change if plans go ahead for a new Sainsbury's with car park and flats, along with improved pedestrian access to the high street and a revamped railway station* • **PINNER** *Very up-market and Home Counties. The best shops gleam discreetly from under the overhanging Tudor eaves of the high street (and some of this is real Tudor, not Tudorbethan). Designer clothes, jewellery, galleries, a bookshop and (of course) estate agents. Sainsbury's by the station and more ordinary local shops in roads off the high street. Safeway at Hatch End* • **STANMORE** *Disappointing shops for such a smart area. Mostly local shops including a real butcher, a baker and a couple of clothes shops but mysteriously, a Lidl discount store, normally found in more down-market areas than this.*

RESTAURANTS***

A couple of good Indian restaurants in Harrow as well as Thai and Chinese. Otherwise local brasseries and restaurants in Harrow on the Hill, and a handful of ye olde worlde pubs and Pizza Express in Pinner. W S Gilbert's former home at Grim's Dyke House is now a hotel with a restaurant.

CRIME RATES*****

Position in Metropolitan Police league table: 32nd out of 32 (where 1 is worst and 32 best).

THE COUNCIL***

POLITICAL AFFILIATION *Labour. To the amazement of local residents, even true blue Harrow on the Hill returned a Labour member in the last council elections for the first time in living memory* • **MINUS POINTS** *One of the most expensive boroughs in London for property searches. Has had problems with missed rubbish collections* • **PLUS POINTS** *Excellent schools. Generally rated by residents as efficient and effective. Expanding programme of kerbside recycling collections and home composters* • **PROPERTY SEARCHES CARRIED OUT IN 10 WORKING DAYS** *100%* • **STANDARD SEARCH FEE** *£126* • **COUNCIL TAX COLLECTED** *96.9%*

• **COUNCIL TAX 2000-2001**

BAND	PROPERTY VALUE	CHARGE	BAND	PROPERTY VALUE	CHARGE
A	up to £40,000	£568	E	£88,001-£120,000	£1,042
B	£40,001-£52,000	£663	F	£120,001-£160,000	£1,232
C	£52,001-£68,000	£758	G	£160,001-£320,000	£1,422
D	£68,001-£88,000	£853	H	over £320,000	£1,706

HAVERING

If you're one of the many people who thinks there's no life east of Islington, you've probably never heard of Havering. London's easternmost borough is a large chunk of Essex fields, marshland, big skies and industrial Thames which suburban sprawl hasn't yet managed to overwhelm. Many of its built-up areas are the prosaic result of decades of speculative development round tube and train lines but there's more open space in relation to built-up areas than in almost any other London borough.

At Havering's western boundary is Romford, the main shopping and administrative centre, surrounded by the attractive garden suburb of Gidea Park. To the east of Romford is the post-war council estate of Harold Hill before countryside takes over around Havering Atte Bower right in the north. To the south are Upminster and Hornchurch, once distinctive towns in their own right but engulfed in waves of building at the beginning of the century. Surrounded by marshland and fields in the south of the borough are the industrial estates of Rainham, reaching down to the Thames.

This is where multiracial London finally dies out as Essex takes over. Only three per cent of Havering's population is from an ethnic minority, the lowest in London. Its other vital statistics are low too: crime rates are the second lowest in the capital and unemployment stands at just 2.4%, the fifth lowest in London. Statistically it has most in common with wealthy western and northern boroughs like Richmond, Sutton and Barnet. But Havering doesn't drip prosperity. Its suburbs don't have the cachet even of old East London suburbs like Woodford or Wanstead, although there are some large houses lived in by people not short of a bob or two. This is solid, semi-detached Essex, still making more than a tenth of its money from manufacturing, although the borough is keen to push its credentials (good transport links, space) to white collar industries.

But despite lots of manufacturing activity on the Thames waterfront, vast tracts of marshland lie derelict as its future hangs in the balance. Last year, the Royal Society for the Protection of Birds bought more than 850 acres of marshland, hoping to create a nature reserve. But Havering council, which owns large tracts of neighbouring marshland, is keen to attract development to build up the local economy, which campaigners for a nature reserve fear will destroy wildlife.

Inland there are plans to revamp Romford town centre with a big development on the site of the 19th century Romford Brewery in the High Street which closed in 1992. Work has started on the development of one-, two- and three-bed loft style apartments, some in the converted brewery building. The latest proposals for the £118 million development include a hypermarket, 16 screen multiplex cinema, health and fitness centre and a new museum to be leased to the council. This should perk up a part of Romford which is currently looking a bit tired.

PROPERTY AND ARCHITECTURE

ROMFORD

Romford grew up around the railway which reached it in the 1850s and bears all the familiar traits of suburban building although there are still a few reminders of its past as a market town. A mix of Victorian terraces and more recent 1930s terraces round the centre, many bearing the mark of ubiquitous 'improvements'. 1930s semis and bungalows predominate in Collier Row to the north. Some blocks of modern flats, a good choice of conversion flats and some new developments deliberately aimed at City workers who can't afford more central loft living.

ATTRACTS *First-time buyers; loyal locals; City workers* • **CONSERVATION AREAS** *Romford* • **AVERAGE PRICES** *Flats: studio £50,000; 1-bed £65,000-£70,000+; 2-bed £75,000-£85,000+ Houses: 2-bed £100,000-£110,000; 3-bed £120,000-£150,000; 4-bed £175,000-£250,000* • **AVERAGE RENTS (WEEKLY)** *Flats: studio £95+; 1-bed £105-£130; 2-bed £125-£180 Houses: 2-bed £138-£230; 3-bed £180+; 4-bed £180-£270.*

GIDEA PARK

Gidea Park was developed as a garden suburb at the beginning of this century. The most sought-after part around the golf course is called the Exhibition Estate, after an architectural competition and exhibition in 1911 which resulted in 100 individually designed houses. Handsome Edwardian half-timbered detached houses in tree-lined streets and private drives are a big contrast to Romford just a few minutes' drive away. An established area. More modest mostly 1930s houses south of Main Road are popular for proximity to the station.

ATTRACTS *Families; wealthy commuters* • **CONSERVATION AREA** *Gidea Park and Railway Extension* • **AVERAGE PRICES** *Flats: 2-bed £80,000+ Houses: 3-bed £160,000-£240,000; 4-bed+ £250,000-£450,000* • **AVERAGE RENTS (WEEKLY)** *Flats: 2-bed £150; Houses: 2-bed £140-£230; 3-bed £180+; 4-bed £340+*

HAROLD HILL

A sprawling council estate started after the Second World War to house overspill tenants from London. A fussy series of cul-de-sacs, crescents and loop roads lined with low red brick barrack-like terraces. A good bus ride away from decent shops and without a car you could be marooned, with Harold Wood station on the other side of the A13. But local estate agents estimate that 65% of the estate is now private after many were sold to tenants under the right-to-buy scheme and sold on. A good area for cheap houses and lots of space for your money.

ATTRACTS *Bargain hunters; local first-time buyers; people from the East End; people who can't afford Romford* • **CONSERVATION AREAS** *none* • **AVERAGE PRICES** *Flats: studio £50,000; 1-bed £50,000-£55,000; 2-bed £55,000 Houses: 2-bed £80,000-£85,000; 3-bed £85,000-£105,000* • **AVERAGE**

RENTS (WEEKLY) *Flats: studio £80; 1-bed £95; 2-bed £115 Houses: 2-bed £120; 3-bed £125.*

HAVERING ATTE BOWER

Pronounced Havering Atty Bower. No more than a cluster of (mostly large) houses, a couple of pubs and a church but set very attractively on the edge of undulating fields and Havering Country Park. Large gardens and a feeling of being in the middle of the country rather than in London are powerful attractions. A car is vital. Lettings are rare and so are flats.

ATTRACTS *Wealthy people with cars; families; people moving out of Romford or Gidea Park to be nearer the country* ● **CONSERVATION AREAS** *Havering Atte Bower* ● **AVERAGE PRICES** *Flats: 2-bed £100,000+ Houses: 3-bed £200,000-£250,000+; 4-bed £300,000+.*

HORNCHURCH

A respectable suburb with a proper town centre. Ordinary 1930s semis along the main road to Hornchurch and in Hornchurch itself, mixed with some Victorian and modern blocks. A good choice of flats and maisonettes south of the high street. The largest houses are in Emerson Park north of the railway line (it has its own station) with every combination of half timbering, red brick, sloping roofs and large gardens. This is where the new money is in Havering.

ATTRACTS *Families; new money* ● **CONSERVATION AREAS** *St Leonards; RAF Hornchurch; also south of South Hornchurch: Rainham* ● **AVERAGE PRICES** *Flats: 1-bed £75,000-£90,000; 2-bed £90,000-£155,000 Houses: 2-bed £115,000-£130,000; 3-bed £125,000-£225,000; 4-bed £175,000+* ● **AVERAGE RENTS (WEEKLY)** *Flats: 1-bed £105+; 2-bed £125+ Houses: 2-bed £185; 3-bed £185-£300; 4-bed £340+.*

UPMINSTER

Familiar to most people as the destination at the end of the eastbound District Line, Upminster is a step above Hornchurch, partly because of the good transport links (District Line and trains) and partly for its good schools. North of the tube and railway line lies another of the garden suburbs built for the professional middle classes at the beginning of the century, with a mix of large Edwardian houses in wide roads round the golf course. More modest houses south of the railway line.

ATTRACTS *Families wanting good schools and good transport links; City workers; people progressing up from Dagenham and East Ham* ● **CONSERVATION AREAS** *Cranham; North Ockenden; Corbets Tey* ● **AVERAGE PRICES** *Flats: 2-bed £85,000+ Houses: 2-bed £120,000-£140,000; 3-bed £150,000-£200,000; 4-bed £250,000+* ● **AVERAGE RENTS (WEEKLY)** *Flats: 2-bed £150+ Houses: 2-bed £180+; 3-bed £190+; 4-bed £270+.*

BEST POSTCODES

Irrelevant, as the whole borough has Essex postcodes.

AMENITIES

SCHOOLS★★★★

Good performance overall in league tables by both primary and secondary schools. Below average state provision for under-fives. A couple of independent schools.

PRE-SCHOOL PROVISION *14 nursery classes in state primary schools; 95 private day nurseries and playgroups. Proportion of under-fives in state nursery schools: 50%* ● **STATE PRIMARY SCHOOLS** *Overall position in league tables: 32nd out of 150. Top scorers: Dame Tipping CE, Havering-atte-Bower; Scotts, Hornchurch; Engayne Junior, Upminster* ● **STATE SECONDARY SCHOOLS** *Overall position in league tables: 21st out of 149. Top scorers: Coopers Company and Cobourn (mixed), Upminster; Sacred Heart of Mary (girls), Upminster; Campion (boys, girls in sixth), Hornchurch.*

TRANSPORT★★★

Upminster and Hornchurch are the best served, by the fairly reliable District Line as well as by trains at Upminster. Trains only (although fast and quite frequent) to Romford.

TRAINS *Romford Zone 6. Cost of annual season ticket £1456. Average journey to Liverpool Street 27 minutes* ● **TUBES** *Upminster (District) Zone 6. Average journey to Tower Hill 40 minutes. Hornchurch (District) Zone 6. Average journey to Tower Hill 36 minutes* ● **BUSES** *No buses to town (tubes and trains do it much better) unless you're travelling at night when there's the N15 to Romford from Trafalgar Square and the N25 to Romford and Harold Hill from Trafalgar Square. Buses criss-cross the borough, although travel to outlying parts can be tricky, and there are regular buses to the huge Lakeside shopping centre at Thurrock. A car is possibly the most useful form of transport, unenvironmental though it may be, particularly as the M25 is so close* ● **TRAFFIC TROUBLESPOTS** *Gallows Corner: Where four main roads meet, bringing traffic from Romford in one direction and the M25 in the other. Hornchurch High Street: Too narrow for the amount of traffic travelling down it, along with buses and delivery vans* ● **PARKING** *Two controlled parking zones at Romford (divided into six sectors with six separate controlled zones) and Harold Wood. Cost of annual resident's permit: £6.60 for two years.*

LEISURE FACILITIES★★

THEATRES & CONCERT HALLS *The Queen's Theatre Hornchurch has a good reputation for staging new plays as well as West End shows, live music and jazz, pantomimes and childrens' shows, although it has been struggling financially* ● **CINEMAS** *Two, an ABC and an Odeon, in Romford, both multiscreen. With this many screens already, it's not quite clear why developers think the town needs 16 more on the planned Brewery site* ● **MUSEUMS & GALLERIES** *Museums are thin on the ground with nothing run by the borough itself until the proposed museum opens in the Brewery. The 15th century thatched Upminster tithe barn has a display of local history exhibits and the early 19th century Upminster Windmill is open to the public. Run by local historical society. Opening hours limited. Rainham Hall, an elegant Georgian house in Rainham, is owned by the National Trust* ● **SPORTS FACILITIES** *Two leisure centres at Rainham and Hornchurch, both with swimming pools and fitness centres. Pool at Harold Hill with* weight training. Public golf course at Romford, skating rink at Romford, greyhound racing at Romford and tennis, football, cricket and other games in parks across the borough • **LIBRARIES** Under-used and a bit under-resourced. The main library in Romford is a good size with helpful staff although it's separated from the main shopping areas by busy roads and accessible via subways, not the best way of tempting people in. Patchy and inconsistent opening hours, with lots of closing for lunch and on various days during the week. Romford central library has the best opening hours. 7.12 library visits per head. Position in library-use league table: 15th out of 32 (where 1 is best and 32 worst).

OPEN SPACES * * * * *

Half the borough's area is greenbelt land, with gentle fields stretching out on either side of narrow country lanes in the north and flat marshland in the south. There are also country parks which are more country than park and miles of river frontage.

PARKS Havering Country Park. Tucked into fields by Havering Atte Bower with mature woodland and glimpses of nothing but rural countryside. Great for rides and walks in the park or across the fields to Hainault Forest Country Park (see Redbridge). Hornchurch Country Park at the edge of fields at Hornchurch has walks through the meadows by the River Ingrebourne. Once an airfield for Battle of Britain spitfires, it still has concrete reminders of the old defence system • **RIVER WALKS** The Havering Riverside Path, a path along part of Havering's three mile industrial river frontage. Views of bleak beauty on a sunny day across to Thamesmead and Erith (see Bexley) while mechanical diggers bite into the piles of aggregrate behind you.

SHOPS * *

ROMFORD Where most of Havering's shopping's at. Seriously unpromising approaching from the outside, with a mess of concrete multistorey car parks, office blocks and a gaping hole where most of the brewery used to be. But more interesting than you'd expect in the centre, with a couple of Essex clapboard cottages and pedestrianised marketplace. Once this was a livestock market, now there's an all-purpose market on Wednesday, Friday and Saturday. For permanent shopping, there's less of a single shopping mall and more of a series of arcades all linking up with each other although this only becomes obvious when you've passed the same shop several times. Mostly chain store shopping here and in the newer Liberty 2 shopping centre. Indoor shopping hall and local shops overlooking the market place. Sainsbury's • **HORNCHURCH & UPMINSTER** Hornchurch is nothing spectacular but at least it's a proper high street with local shops. Some attractive cottages in the centre but spoilt by heavy traffic. Sainsbury's. The usual collection of off-licences, banks and take-aways around Upminster Station, interspersed with some more interesting individual shops.

RESTAURANTS *

Of strictly local appeal.

CRIME RATES * * * * *

Position in Metropolitan Police league table: 31st out of 32 (where 1 is worst and 32 best).

THE COUNCIL * * *

POLITICAL AFFILIATION *Labour minority* • **MINUS POINTS** *One of the most expensive for property searches in London* • **PLUS POINTS** *Good schools. Recently introduced boroughwide scheme for kerbside collections of plastic bottles, paper and textiles. One of the most efficient rubbish collection systems in London. The cheapest residents' parking in London* • **PROPERTY SEARCHES CARRIED OUT IN 10 WORKING DAYS** 96% • **STANDARD SEARCH FEE** £130 • **COUNCIL TAX COLLECTED** 96.8%

● **COUNCIL TAX 2000-2001**

BAND	PROPERTY VALUE	CHARGE	BAND	PROPERTY VALUE	CHARGE
A	up to £40,000	£569	E	£88,001-£120,000	£1,043
B	£40,001-£52,000	£663	F	£120,001-£160,000	£1,232
C	£52,001-£68,000	£758	G	£160,001-£320,000	£1,422
D	£68,001-£88,000	£853	H	over £320,000	£1,706

HILLINGDON

It can be a good thing to have the world's busiest airport on your doorstep. No struggling through the traffic or sitting on the tube to get to the airport, a bewildering choice of destinations at your fingertips and a quick pop home when you arrive back from holiday exhausted. But for residents of Hillingdon who don't want to go anywhere and don't depend on Heathrow for their livelihood, the presence of the airport spreading over the bottom third of their borough is a mixed blessing. Low-flying aircraft, constant traffic jams in roads round the airport and the prospect of a fifth terminal make Heathrow a noisy and disagreeable neighbour. As if one airport wasn't enough, Hillingdon is also home to Northholt Aerodrome, scene of many wartime sorties and arrivals.

But Metroland, that 1930s dream of comfortable suburban living and escape from the city smog, still survives almost unscathed in many parts of a borough which looks more to the rolling hills of the Chilterns and the Thames Valley than London, 14 miles to the east. Hillingdon is London's second biggest borough. Around Heathrow, the air throbs with the roar of planes. Further north, warehouses and factories cluster round the Grand Union Canal and stretch up to Hayes (in Middlesex and not to be confused with Hayes, Kent). To the west are the Victorian terraces of Uxbridge opening out into fields and hills and the village of Ickenham to the north. Salubrious Ruislip and Eastcote give way to wealthy Northwood, spiritually in Hertfordshire and only a few steps from the edge of London. Large properties, abundant green space and children in neat school uniforms breathe prosperity.

Northwood, Northwood Hills and Ruislip are Hillingdon's

metroland, linked umbilically to London by the rattling Metropolitan Line tube bringing thousands of commuters to town every morning. Many more work at Heathrow, a major employer. The south around Hayes and West Drayton, once a busy manufacturing area, is now reinventing itself as a magnet for high tech, retail and other white collar service industries looking for space and good transport links. Not surprisingly, the unemployment rate is low at 2% but more than £21 million of public and private money has been injected into improving employment prospects and the environment and cutting crime in the area.

Uxbridge, the borough's retail and adminstrative centre, is also set for a massive face-lift. On the north side of the high street a vast new shopping centre, The Chimes, is rising up behind the carefully restored facades of existing high street buildings and will bring a Debenhams, 75 other new shops and a nine-screen multiplex cinema to the town. If the £150 million centre looks somehow familiar when it's done, it's not necessarily that you're getting jaded about the predictability of outer London shopping (although this would be quite understandable). The company working on Uxbridge was also responsible for The Glades in Bromley and Lakeside in Thurrock.

PROPERTY AND ARCHITECTURE

HAYES

Hayes falls into two parts, the more commercial Hayes Town to the south around the station and the more villagey Hayes proper around the 13th-century church to the north. 1930s semis mixed with modern blocks, small estate houses and council houses predominate around Hayes Town. The older part of Hayes around the church is more attractive, set at the edge of Barra Hall Park, with Victorian cottages straggling down narrow streets. But the few shops on Church Road have long given up the unequal struggle and have been converted to houses. A good area to buy a cheap house although it's a bus ride away from the nearest station. 1930s semis, many 'improved' with pebble-dash and picture windows in West Drayton.
ATTRACTS First-time buyers; families; members of the Asian community • **CONSERVATION AREAS** Hayes Village; Botwell (East and West Walk); Bulls Bridge; West Drayton Green • **AVERAGE PRICES** Flats: studio £55,000; 1-bed £75,000+; 2-bed £85,000-£95,000 Houses: 2-bed £105,000+; 3-bed £120,000+ • **AVERAGE RENTS (WEEKLY)** Flats: studio £115+; 1-bed £140+; 2-bed £160 Houses: 2-bed £160; 3-bed £185.

UXBRIDGE & HILLINGDON

The centre of Uxbridge is almost completely commercial, a mix of narrow winding streets with ugly 1960s multistorey car parks grafted on. Roads of mostly Victorian and Edwardian terraces predominate around the centre of this once important market town with some modern apartment blocks on main roads. 1930s semis take over on the fringes. Hillingdon manages to preserve some of its former village feel, with some gracious Georgian buildings and shops in a red brick parade, despite being carved up by the main Ealing to Uxbridge Road. It has its share of 1930s semis but also some large detached houses.

ATTRACTS *Families, loyal locals; first-time buyers who want to be close to tubes and shops* • **CONSERVATION AREAS** *Old Uxbridge; The Greenway; Cowley Lock; Cowley Church* • **AVERAGE PRICES** *Flats: studio £55,000+; 1-bed £65,000+; 2-bed £80,000+ Houses: 3-bed £150,000+; 4-bed £185,000+* • **AVERAGE RENTS (WEEKLY)** *Flats: studio £105+; 1-bed £115+; 2-bed £140+ Houses: 2-bed £175+; 3-bed £195+; 4-bed £230+.*

RUISLIP & EASTCOTE

This is where things get more up-market as industry and built-up streets give way to greenbelt land. South Ruislip, Ruislip Gardens and Ruislip Manor are less posh than central and west Ruislip and the nearer you are to Northolt Aerodrome and the A40, the cheaper it is. All these areas were mostly built up in the 1930s but Ruislip and West Ruislip have roads of middling and large detached houses among the semis, giving these areas a more spacious feel than other suburban parts of London. Well-cared-for family houses near Ruislip town centre in every kind of style known to the 1930s speculative builder (half-timbered, diamond-paned windows, small wooden panes with shutters, red brick manorial). Attempts at a Ruislip Garden Suburb petered out but the results are still there around Manor Way just off Eastcote Road, with characteristic cottage-style houses grouped round green space. The grandest houses in Ruislip are just by the Common, while Eastcote's most sought-after area is the Eastcote Park Estate. Mostly family houses rather than flats. Temporary residents of Ruislip include Americans employed at the nearby airbase.

ATTRACTS *Families* • **CONSERVATION AREAS** *Ruislip Village; Manor Way Ruislip; Eastcote Village* • **AVERAGE PRICES** *Flats: studio £65,000+; 1-bed £90,000+; 2-bed £110,000-£130,000+ Houses: 2-bed £130,000+; 3-bed £150,000-£250,000; 4-bed £220,000+* • **AVERAGE RENTS (WEEKLY)** *Flats: studio £115+; 1-bed £125-£145; 2-bed £150-£185 Houses: 2-bed £185+; 3-bed £195+; 4-bed £345+.*

ICKENHAM

Suspended on a band of greenbelt north of Uxbridge and south of Ruislip, Ickenham likes to think of itself as superior to the sea of suburbia around it although it too was mostly built up in the 1930s. But it does still have a village pump and pond and a discernible centre with a handful of shops and cottages. Akin in many respects to Ruislip, it also has some roads grand enough to compete with anything posher Northwood can offer. The area west of Long Lane is most sought after for its large houses and because it is near one of the borough's best schools, Vyners.

ATTRACTS *Families wanting good schools and green space* • **CONSERVATION AREAS** *Ickenham Village* • **AVERAGE PRICES** *Flats: 1-bed £85,000-£95,000; 2-bed £115,000-£160,000 Houses: 2-bed £140,000-£160,000; 3-bed £200,000-£350,000; 4-bed £250,000-£450,000* • **AVERAGE RENTS (WEEKLY)** *Flats: 1-bed £125-£145; 2-bed £150-£185 Houses: 2-bed £185-£190; 3-bed £195-220; 4-bed £345+.*

NORTHWOOD

Includes the crème-de-la-crème of the borough's property, particularly in the roads between the golf course and Ruislip Common. Wide roads lined with mature trees and houses which aren't ashamed to be huge. Neo-Georgian, stockbroker Tudor, Hacienda style – it's all there. Houses have names like Wildwood and Oak Lodge and there are lots of wrought iron gates and olde worlde carriage lamps. Slightly less exalted houses around the centre of Northwood and Northwood Hills, which sounds as though it should be posher than Northwood but isn't.

ATTRACTS *The wealthy; families wanting good schools and green space; loyal locals; wealthy internationals* • **CONSERVATION AREAS** *Northwood* • **AVERAGE PRICES** *Flats: 1-bed £85,000-£180,000; 2-bed £120,000-£300,000 Houses: 2-bed £150,000; 3-bed £180,000-£300,000; 4-bed £220,000+* • **AVERAGE RENTS (WEEKLY)** *Flats: 1-bed £125-£145; 2-bed £150-£185 Houses: 2-bed £185-£190; 3-bed £195-3220; 4-bed £345+.*

BEST POSTCODES
Hillingdon is all well beyond the reach of London postcodes.

AMENITIES

SCHOOLS***
Overall league table performance is quite good, particularly at primary level, without being startling. A number of excellent private schools around Northwood. Below-average provision of nursery places for under-fives but a reasonable choice of private and voluntary day nurseries.

PRE-SCHOOL PROVISION *1 state nursery school; 6 state primary and church schools with nursery classes; 103 private day nurseries and playgroups. Proportion of under-fives in state nurseries: 46%* • **STATE PRIMARY SCHOOLS** *Overall league table position: 35th out of 150. Top scorers: St Swithun Wells RC, Ruislip; St Catherine RC, West Drayton; Bourne, Ruislip* • **STATE SECONDARY SCHOOLS** *Overall league table position: 68th out of 149. Top scorers: Bishop Ramsey C of E (mixed), Ruislip; Haydon (mixed), Eastcote; Vyners (mixed), Ickenham* • **PRIVATE PREP SCHOOLS** *St John's (boys), Northwood; St Martins (boys) Northwood* • **PRIVATE SECONDARY SCHOOLS** *Chart-topper St Helens Northwood (girls from 4); Northwood College (girls from 4) Northwood; Merchant Taylors (boys) Northwood; Guru Nanak Sikh College (mixed from 3), Hayes.*

TRANSPORT***
Much better in the middle and north of the borough than the south, where large tracts of residential areas in Yeading and Hayes are a bus ride away from a not terribly good rail service. The north has the Metropolitan and Piccadilly lines, both fairly reliable although it's a bit of a slog to the end of the line, stopping at every station, and not all trains go that far.

TRAINS *Hayes and Harlington Zone 5. Cost of annual season ticket £1332. Average journey time to Paddington 19 minutes* • **TUBES** *Ruislip (Metropolitan and Piccadilly) Zone 6. Cost of annual season ticket £1456. Average journey time to Baker Street 34 minutes; to Piccadilly Circus 46 minutes. Uxbridge (Metropolitan and Piccadilly) Zone 6. Average journey time to Baker Street 40 minutes; to Piccadilly Circus 53 minutes. Northwood (Metropolitan) Zone 6. Average journey to Baker Street 29 minutes* • **BUSES** *Good choice of services to Heathrow, as you'd expect. But* *otherwise buses mostly link suburbs and there are no regular daytime services all the way into central London. It's difficult to get from one end of the borough to the other without changing buses. Night buses include the N97 to Heathrow from Trafalgar Square and the N207 from Trafalgar Square to Uxbridge via Hayes and Hillingdon* ● **TRAFFIC TROUBLESPOTS** *Heathrow: The A4 alongside the airport perimeter always has several lanes of traffic, often sitting in tailbacks from traffic lights and roundabouts trying to get onto other main roads. Uxbridge: A depressing confluence of main roads meets at a large roundabout just south of the town's main shopping area. Often jammed with traffic waiting at a series of confusing traffic lights. Uxbridge town centre itself isn't too bad for traffic – a pleasant contrast to some other London shopping streets* ● **PARKING** *There are four controlled parking zones: north of Uxbridge Town Centre, Northwood, Eastcote and the Heathrow fly-drive area. Cost of annual resident's permit: £20 for the first car, £30 for the second, £50 for the third and £100 for a fourth or subsequent.*

LEISURE FACILITIES* * *

THEATRES & CONCERT HALLS *Two theatres, the Beck Theatre in Hayes, and the Compass Theatre in Ickenham, with a mix of plays, children's shows, bands and music recitals. Plays also at the Winston Churchill Hall, Ruislip. Theatre groups meet at Southlands Arts Centre in West Drayton, started by local residents in the 1960s in despair that there was nothing to do in Hillingdon* ● **CINEMAS** *A poor show. Only one, the Uxbridge Odeon, strictly mainstream although there will be another nine screens when The Chimes shopping centre is finished* ● **MUSEUMS & GALLERIES** *Local art galleries at the Cow Byre Gallery, Ruislip and the Atrium Gallery in Uxbridge's large and impressive central library, as well as exhibitions at the Southlands Arts Centre and Brunel University. Only one museum, or more accurately a couple of display cases, of local history in Uxbridge Central Library. RAF Uxbridge occasionally allows the public a glimpse of the underground control centre used to direct the Battle of Britain. Also for plane enthusiasts, there's the visitor centre at Heathrow, with flight simulators and a mock-up cockpit* ● **SPORTS FACILITIES** *Well provided for. Leisure centres in Hayes, Ruislip, Harefield and Northwood. Pools at Hayes, Harlington and Ruislip. Four public golf courses at Northwood, Ruislip, Uxbridge and Stockley Park, West Drayton. Water sports at Ruislip Lido, an attractive 40 acre lake surrounded by Ruislip Woods and golf courses. Dry ski slope at Uxbridge* ● **LIBRARIES** *Used less than average although Uxbridge has a large modern library and Ruislip's beautiful little library is housed in a 16th-century barn with hammer-beamed roof and stained glass windows. But opening hours across the borough are gappy, which could account for lower usage. Lots of lunchtime closing in smaller branch libraries. Most libraries are closed on Wednesdays. 5.3 library visits per head. Position in library-use league table: 23nd out of 32 (where 1 is best and 32 worst).*

OPEN SPACES* * * *

This is where Hillingdon really scores. It has large tracts of rolling greenbelt land within its boundaries particularly in the north west, where it borders on the beginnings of the Chilterns, as well as some excellent woodland walks between Ruislip and Northwood. Many of its houses have large gardens and roads are lined with mature trees. Even though the south is more built up it still has woods, open space and rivers running along past the backs of houses, although some of its parks could do with some TLC. The Victorian mansion of Barra Hall in Barra Hall Park. Hayes for example is sorely in need of a coat of paint although it's set for a face-lift, and the open-air theatre is derelict. Hillingdon's section of the Grand Union Canal is industrial for most of its length.

WOODS Ruislip Woods. Now a national nature reserve. The council claims this is the single largest unbroken stretch of mature woodland in London, which is easy to believe if you set off for a walk there just before lunch with no provisions, then get slightly lost. Beech trees and mud, just like a real Chiltern walk. Ruislip Lido is an attractive stretch of water deep in Park Woods, Ruislip, with its own sandy beach and a miniature steam railway running round the back.

SHOPS***

HAYES One of Hillingdon's two main shopping centres. Pedestrianised shopping centre and shopping in streets around Hayes Town. Fairly predictable, with mostly chains at the cheap end of the market, take-aways and burger bars. More shops along Uxbridge Road, again predictable (but useful) ● **UXBRIDGE** Where it's at for Hillingdon shopping. The pedestrianised area outside the handsome art deco Uxbridge station with a couple of pavement cafés is a good welcome for new arrivals and it's not difficult to imagine Uxbridge as the market town it once was. Chain stores and indoor market stalls selling cheap clothes and leather bags at the Pavilions Shopping Centre. The centre is looking a bit tired and it's questionable whether the new Chimes shopping centre will be much help to its future (although the new shops should perk up Uxbridge). Much more interesting small shops in the narrow old Windsor Road including antique shops, jewellers, evening dress hire and, defiantly, a sex shop. Look back at the bottom of Windsor Road for a depressing view of the back of the Pavilions and horrible 1960s multistorey car park. Sainsbury's ● **RUISLIP** More like the high street of a Buckinghamshire town than London with a good mix of the useful (chains) and the individual (long established local shops). Provincial rather than trendy. Tidy streets lined with half-timbered and red brick parades on both sides, including a baker, a local bookshop, a couple of old-fashioned clothes shops and a furniture shop. Waitrose ● **NORTHWOOD** A sloping high street of mostly well-manicured local shops and charity shops promising ex-fashion show stock. Lots of estate agents and a large Waitrose. Shabbier shopping parades in Northwood Hills.

RESTAURANTS*

A bit of a culinary desert. The usual collection of local restaurants, brasseries, pizza and pasta chains and take-aways. If you fancy a curry, your best bet is to pop over the borough border into Southall (see Ealing).

CRIME RATES***

Position in Metropolitan Police league table: 20th out of 32 (where 1 is worst and 32 best).

THE COUNCIL***

POLITICAL AFFILIATION Conservative minority ● **MINUS POINTS** Residents have complained about the state of some of the parks and open spaces. One of the slowest boroughs in London at turning round property searches while

charging a lot for the privilege ● **PLUS POINTS** *Got the thumbs up in recent surveys from three quarters of residents for a generally good performance, particularly on rubbish collections and libraries (surprising, given the low library use in the borough). Kerbside recycling pilot being expanded*
● **PROPERTY SEARCHES CARRIED OUT IN 10 WORKING DAYS** 44% ● **STANDARD SEARCH FEE** £125 ● **COUNCIL TAX COLLECTED** 95.7%

● **COUNCIL TAX 2000-2001**

BAND	PROPERTY VALUE	CHARGE	BAND	PROPERTY VALUE	CHARGE
A	up to £40,000	£549	E	£88,001-£120,000	£1,007
B	£40,001-£52,000	£641	F	£120,001-£160,000	£1,190
C	£52,001-£68,000	£733	G	£160,001-£320,000	£1,374
D	£68,001-£88,000	£824	H	over £320,000	£1,648

HOUNSLOW

The transport planners haven't been kind to Hounslow. Not only is the northern part of the borough carved up by the M4 and the A4 (both running almost parallel to each other, just to turn the knife) but the sleep of its residents is regularly shattered by incoming planes landing at Heathrow. The prospect of a fifth terminal at Heathrow is chilling for those with homes under the flight path. Hounslow has some of the best westward road and air connections of any borough but this is cold comfort to people who live there and want to stay put rather than force their way out.

But is Hounslow worth staying in? Yes and no. It has miles of frankly dull suburbs thrown up during London's westward expansion in the 1930s, as a glance out of the window of a Heathrow-bound tube over a sea of tiled roofs will confirm. But it also has some of the prettiest riverside in London, some elegant parks and some good schools.

Its boundaries stretch from middle class Victorian Chiswick in the east down to the Thames, across to once-industrial Brentford and the pretty riverside village of Isleworth. To the north are the large family homes of Osterley by Osterley Park and to the west from Hounslow outwards are the amorphous 1930s suburbs of Feltham and Heston.

Hounslow has some posh bits but it's more a white collar worker enclave than part of the stockbroker commuter belt. Unemployment is comfortably low by London standards at 2.5%, with many residents employed at nearby Heathrow or British Airways or in media jobs at the BBC or Sky, both of which have offices a short commute away. Nearly a quarter of the population is from an ethnic minority, the vast majority of whom are Indian. Although the Indian community adds interest to what is otherwise a fairly staid area, its mark is not obvious as in nearby Southall (see Ealing).

Middle class homeowners have been colonising Chiswick for years, attracted by its closeness to the river and good tube links. Now they're turning their attention to neighbouring Brentford, which is set for a series of major face-lifts over the next five years in a bid to improve the town centre, rehabilitate rivers and canals from industrial dereliction and bring life to the area in the evening. A total of £136 million is being invested in Brentford. On the north side of the High Street at Brentford Lock, owned by British Waterways, there are plans to build apartments, restaurants and a hotel around the canal. On the south side of the High Street between the town and the Thames, developers want to demolish part of Brentford High Street and the old warehouses behind to make way for a £50 million development of homes, a superstore, leisure facilities, a multiplex cinema and car parking. At the other end of the High Street, more riverside industrial sites will be turned into a mixture of housing, shops and offices with a large element of the affordable housing the council wants to encourage.

PROPERTY AND ARCHITECTURE

CHISWICK & GUNNERSBURY

Streets of well-kept Victorian cottages and terraces and later Edwardian terraces in roads off and around Chiswick High Road. Mansion blocks on the High Road. Much larger Victorian semi-detached and detached houses nearer the river in Grove Park near Chiswick Station in wide tree-lined roads. Some of the houses are now flats but many still have original stained glass windows and ornate woodwork porches and balconies. Along Strand on the Green, on the river towpath, there is a lovely mix of Georgian and early Victorian cottages and larger houses, some of the most sought-after in Chiswick. Equally sought-after is Bedford Park (the less smart part of which is in Ealing), a suburb of Queen Anne-style detached houses and smaller cottages built as an artists' colony in the 1870s. Bedford Park's active local amenity society has angered some residents who resent their zealous guardianship of the conservation area.

ATTRACTS *Young professionals; young families; people who are disenchanted with or can't afford Fulham; workers from the BBC*

• **CONSERVATION AREAS** *Old Chiswick; Chiswick House; Strand on the Green; Turnham Green; Stamford Brook; Bedford Park; Gunnersbury Park*

• **AVERAGE PRICES** *Flats: studio £170,000; 1-bed £170,000+; 2-bed £210,000-£250,000+ Houses: 2-bed £260,000-£360,000; 3-bed 350,000+; 4-bed £440,000+* • **AVERAGE RENTS (WEEKLY)** *Flats: studio £160; 1-bed £220+; 2-bed £270+ Houses: 2-bed £280-£350; 3-bed £350+; 4-bed £400+.*

BRENTFORD & ISLEWORTH

Brentford still bears many traces of its industrial past, with factories and riverside warehouses, more recently joined by tower blocks. But there are some roads of attractive small terraces and cottages off the main road, particularly in the conservation areas around St Paul's recreation ground. The area has improved a lot in the last ten years. The best part of Brentford is The Butts, large Victorian houses set back from a wide road leading to an almost-perfect square of Georgian townhouses (many of which are now offices). Expensive flats at Brentford Dock. Old Isleworth around Church

Road feels more like part of an old seaside town with the Thames on one side and a street of white painted and brick houses and cottages on the other. Further inland there's a mix of modern estate houses and Victorian terraces. A good choice of small flats. Osterley, the best part of Isleworth around the park, has some large Victorian and Edwardian houses among 1930s houses in Jersey Road.

ATTRACTS *Young professionals (including employees of the BBC); families* • **CONSERVATION AREAS** *Isleworth Riverside; St Paul's Brentford; The Butts; Osterley Park* • **AVERAGE PRICES** *Flats: studio: £75,000-£80,000; 1-bed £90,000-£140,000; 2-bed £100,000-£200,000 Houses: 2-bed £130,000-£170,000; 3-bed £170,000-£220,000; 4-bed £250,000+* • **AVERAGE RENTS (WEEKLY)** *Flats: studio £140+; 1-bed £160; 2-bed £185+ Houses: 2-bed £215; 3-bed £230+; 4-bed £275.*

HOUNSLOW, FELTHAM & HANWORTH

A lot of central Hounslow is Victorian, with roads of large and small terraces near the shopping centre. West Hounslow is mostly 1930s semis as is the area around Hounslow Heath. Further south, almost the only good thing that can be said about Feltham and Hanworth is that they're cheap. Shabby 1930s semis on wide, treeless, rather bleak roads broken by parades of uninspiring local shops predominate and there are a couple of local council estates which should be avoided. Local agents say the area has become an airport workers' colony. Lots of local authority flats and nothing much bigger than a three-bed house. The best parts of Hanworth are near the border with Hampton (see Richmond) where parents can send their children to schools just over the border in Richmond.

ATTRACTS *Families; airport workers; loyal locals (a recent survey found that more than half the people questioned had lived in Feltham ten years or more); investors (Hounslow)* • **CONSERVATION AREAS** *St Paul's Hounslow; St Stephen's Hounslow; Hounslow Cavalry Barracks; Feltham Town Centre; Hanworth Park* • **AVERAGE PRICES** *Flats: studio £60,000-£70,000; 1-bed £80,000-£90,000; 2-bed £90,000-£110,000 Houses: 2-bed £120,000+; 3-bed £135,000-£150,000; 4-bed (Hounslow): £200,000+* • **AVERAGE RENTS (WEEKLY)** *Flats: studio £95+; 1-bed £125-£150; 2-bed £145 Houses: 3-bed £185; 4-bed (Hounslow) £275.*

BEST POSTCODES

Largely irrelevant as most of the borough is technically in Middlesex. Chiswick W4 is one of London's sought-after postcodes.

AMENITIES

SCHOOLS***

Both primary and secondary schools perform creditably overall in league tables. But there are several chart-topping state schools all of which are oversubscribed. Primary schools all operate catchment areas (called Priority Admissions areas) to keep schools local. Above average provision of state nursery school places. A couple of private schools in the borough itself but there's also a good choice in neighbouring boroughs (see Richmond and Ealing).

PRE-SCHOOL PROVISION *45 nursery units in state and church primary schools; 64 private nurseries and playgroups. Proportion of under-fives in state nurseries: 66%* • **STATE PRIMARY SCHOOLS** *Overall league table position:*

83rd out of 150. Top scorers: Sparrow Farm, Feltham; Belmont (with nursery unit), Chiswick; St Mary's RC (with nursery unit), Chiswick • **STATE SECONDARY SCHOOLS** Overall league table position: 76th out of 149. Top scorers: Gumley House Convent (girls), Isleworth; Green School (girls), Isleworth; St Mark's RC (mixed), Hounslow • **PRIVATE SCHOOLS** Arts Educational School (mixed to 16), Chiswick; Ashton House (mixed, from 3), Isleworth.

TRANSPORT★★★

Good tube services in the centre and east of the borough with Chiswick and Hounslow particularly well served, although the travelling in on the Piccadilly line from Heathrow with the gangways cluttered by the unwieldy suitcases of long-haul air passengers can be tedious. In the west and south some areas (parts of Hanworth for example) are a long way from a station. **TRAINS** Brentford Zone 4. Cost of annual season ticket £1104. Average journey time to Waterloo 29 minutes. Feltham Zone 6. Cost of annual season ticket £1456. Average journey time to Waterloo 27-31 minutes • **TUBES** Turnham Green (Chiswick) (District) Zone 2. Cost of annual season ticket £756. Average journey time to Embankment 22 minutes. Gunnersbury (District) Zone 3. Cost of annual season ticket £896. Average journey time to Embankment 24 minutes. Hounslow Central (Piccadilly) Zone 4. Average journey time to Piccadilly Circus 33 minutes • **BUSES** Mostly linking one suburb with another, particularly shopping suburbs like Kingston. The nearest you'll get to town without a change is Shepherds Bush or Hammersmith. But there are good links to Heathrow. The N97 night bus goes from Trafalgar Square via Turnham Green, Brentford, Isleworth and Hounslow • **TRAFFIC TROUBLESPOTS** Chiswick: The A4 Great West Road and Hogarth Roundabout. One of the oldest and still one of the nastiest pieces of road in London. Fast, merciless traffic. No-one has yet worked out an alternative to the makeshift-looking bridge carrying traffic over the roundabout. The A4 carves Chiswick in two, creating an ugly barrier between the centre and the river. Chiswick High Road is also often chock-a-block. Hounslow: The main London Road between Hounslow and Isleworth can be very slow, particularly at rush hour and school times. Feltham: Traffic bottlenecks can build up during the rushhour around the railway bridge and at the junction of Hounslow and Harlington Roads • **PARKING** Controlled parking zones operate in Hounslow West, Hounslow Central, Brentford around The Butts, East Chiswick, Isleworth and Bedford Park. The council is consulting about a second controlled parking zone in Brentford, amid opposition from some residents. Cost of annual resident's permit: Hounslow West £35; Hounslow Town Centre £35; East Chiswick £75; Bedford Park £75; The Butts £50; Isleworth £50.

EISURE FACILITIES★★★★

THEATRES & CONCERT HALLS Two theatres in the borough, the Paul Robeson in Hounslow which has a lot of family shows, pantomimes and regular Asian shows (attended by Asians from all around west London), and the Watermans Art Centre on the riverside at Brentford which has a wide variety of theatre, contemporary dance and live music. Regular plays and shows also at Feltham Assembly Hall. • **CINEMAS** Repertory cinema at the Watermans Art Centre; 14 screen Cineworld at Feltham showing mainstream films; nine screen cinema planned for Brentford • **MUSEUMS & GALLERIES** A surprisingly good choice. Hounslow was once a favoured choice as a country seat for the aristocracy and rich merchants and several of their stately homes survive as reminders that the borough wasn't always a mere extension of London. They include Chiswick House, the elegant white Palladian house of Lord Burlington; Gunnersbury House, once the home of the Rothschilds and now housing a small local history museum (often seen by motorists from the vantage point of the Chiswick flyover); the slightly forbidding grey mass of Syon House in Brentford, home of the Duke of Northumberland, and Osterley Park House. If stately homes pall, there's the Kew Bridge Steam Museum in a Victorian pumping station with water tower. There are also the weird and wonderful automatic musical instruments at the Musical Museum and tours of Fullers Brewery at Chiswick ● **SPORTS FACILITIES** Leisure centres with pools at Brentford, Feltham, Isleworth, Chiswick and Heston. Golf at Hounslow, mini-golf at Gunnersbury Park as well as tennis, football and other outdoor sports in parks across the borough. ● **LIBRARIES** The central library in Hounslow is conveniently situated in the main Treaty shopping centre just next to the Paul Robeson theatre. Opening hours much improved over the past year but most libraries are closed on Wednesday and some on Friday. No Sunday opening. Few long evening openings. Position in library-use league table: no information supplied; Hounslow becomes bottom of league table by default.

OPEN SPACES ★ ★ ★ ★

One of the borough's best features despite all attempts by traffic planners to site motorways next to or across beautiful parks like Gunnersbury or Osterley. A good choice of parks with manicured lawns, noble trees, elegant conservatories and so on.

RIVER WALKS The section of the Thames Path running along most of the borough's waterfront. Takes in the riverside 'villages' of Strand on the Green and Old Isleworth as well as the warehouses of Brentford with views over some of the Thames' most rural stretches. Also the tangle of islets around Brentford leading to the towpath along the Grand Union Canal, a canalised section of the River Brent. Overgrown with tall grass and with houseboats moored under the trees, its industrial past has faded. But the concrete pillars of the raised M4 motorway rearing up overhead still come as a shock ● **WILD HEATHLAND** Hounslow Heath. Once one of the dodgiest areas around London, stalked by highwaymen. Now a tangle of woods, brambles and open heathland, a welcome break in the surrounding suburbia. Paths along the Crane River to the west have been restored and improved with more to come, so you should be able to walk from the junction of the Grand Union Canal west of Paddington to the Thames at St Margaret's (see Richmond).

SHOPS ★ ★ ★

CHISWICK Where most of the borough's most interesting shops are. An up-market collection of antiques, furniture shops (futons and minimalism rather than World of Leather), bookshops, designer clothes and respectable chains like M&S and Waterstones. Spoilt by several lanes each way of horrible and constant traffic, a serious disincentive to energetic shopping. Sainsbury's ● **BRENTFORD & ISLEWORTH** Brentford is dull, as even its supporters admit, which is why there are plans to gee it up by knocking some of it down. A dispiriting collection of take-aways, small cafés and local shops with lots of empty shops in modern and 1950s parades.

Somerfields • **HOUNSLOW** *The official flagship, with a large indoor shopping centre at The Treaty and more shops in the adjoining pedestrianised shopping street. A good shopping environment, generally clean and litter-free, and The Treaty's large atrium saves it from being overwhelming or claustrophobic. Mostly chain stores although some of the branches are of good size. There are plans to expand Hounslow's shopping and leisure facilities with a new development just up the high street from The Treaty although residents are concerned about the impact of extra traffic in an area where the main street is pedestrianised and everything has to go round the outside. Tesco* • **FELTHAM** *So dull that it's depressing even to be there. A long street of chain stores and local shops, broken by a 1960s concrete and glass shopping precinct overlooked by slab blocks of offices and flats. Fortunately there are plans to revamp the town centre under the Feltham First regeneration initiative and there are plans for new shops, as well as offices, a new library and leisure facilities.*

RESTAURANTS***

CHISWICK *Any yuppie restaurant chain that hasn't yet set up a branch in or around Chiswick High Road yet will doubtless soon get in on the act. The usual suspects – All Bar One, Pitcher and Piano et al are already there and there's a huge choice of other brasseries, wine bars, pubs with large picture windows and restaurants including a good Thai* • **HOUNSLOW** *The usual pizza and pasta chains among other local places* • **ELSEWHERE** *Nothing of note.*

CRIME RATES**

Position in Metropolitan Police league table: 12th out of 32 (where 1 is worst and 32 best).

THE COUNCIL***

POLITICAL AFFILIATION *Labour* • **MINUS POINTS** *Not always thorough in litter collection and street-sweeping; accused by some residents of neglecting parts of the borough like Brentford and Feltham* • **PLUS POINTS** *Door-to-door recycling; among the most efficient outer London boroughs for refuse collections; 100% efficiency in turning round property searches within target times (although it charges a lot for it)* • **PROPERTY SEARCHES CARRIED OUT WITHIN 10 WORKING DAYS** *100%* • **STANDARD SEARCH FEE** *£125* • **COUNCIL TAX COLLECTED** *93.5%*

• **COUNCIL TAX 2000–2001**

BAND	PROPERTY VALUE	CHARGE	BAND	PROPERTY VALUE	CHARGE
A	up to £40,000	£573	E	£88,001-£120,000	£1,051
B	£40,001-£52,000	£669	F	£120,001-£160,000	£1,242
C	£52,001-£68,000	£765	G	£160,001-£320,000	£1,434
D	£68,001-£88,000	£860	H	over £320,000	£1,720

ISLINGTON

Until the 1960s, Islington was beyond the pale to the middle classes. It was poor, full of run-down, crumbling rented terraces, surrounded by other poor areas, and worst of all, on the wrong (i.e. not west) side of London. Now, thirty years later, in one of the subtle shifts in which London specialises, Islington itself has been colonised by City and West End workers, politicians and opinion formers, who covet its elegant Georgian and Victorian terraces, its proximity to the centre, shops, bars, restaurants and innovative arts scene. So complete has the takeover been in people's minds that the very word Islington has become shorthand for a certain type of self-consciously New Labour middle-class hipness, the 'sun-dried tomato effect' as one cynic calls it. In retrospect, Islington was the only place where Tony and Cherie Blair could have lived. Those who can't afford Islington's rocketing house prices have turned their attention north to Tufnell Park, signalled by the inexorable appearance of antique fireplace shops in the Holloway Road.

But like its surrounding neighbours, Camden, Hackney and Haringey, the borough of Islington is more complex than the rather one-sided media coverage would suggest. It's not all trendy chatterers seeing and being seen in the eateries of Upper Street. It's a melting pot of races (nearly a fifth of the population is from an ethnic minority). The poor haven't left Islington; they live next door to the rich. Unemployment is the fifth highest in London at 8.8% and the borough ranks as the tenth most deprived in England. Islington Council, now under Liberal Democrat control for the first time in living memory and still trying to jettison its reputation as one of the loony left councils of the 1980s, is spending millions on refurbishing some of its worst estates.

The borough of Islington stretches from the newly trendy warehouses and workshops of Clerkenwell up through the council blocks of Finsbury, touching Kings Cross before reaching the beautiful Georgian terraces of Islington itself. North of Islington are the elegant squares and terraces of Barnsbury, Canonbury and Highbury. They then give way to the densely packed Victorian terraces of Archway to the east of Holloway Road and the more salubrious Victorian enclave of Tufnell Park to the west.

The past few years have seen large injections of private and public money into the borough to regenerate Kings Cross (see Camden) and the now trendy city fringe areas of Clerkenwell, Shoreditch and Hoxton (see Hackney) and Spitalfields (see Tower Hamlets). Islington, Hackney, Tower Hamlets and their private sector partners are spending up to £15 million over eight years to help the unemployed and small businesses and to revamp streetscapes and lighting. In Islington, Cowcross Street by Farringdon Station and Exmouth Market are the chief beneficiaries of new streetscaping. They are included in proposals by Railtrack to improve the cross-London Thameslink line with new platforms and a smart new ticket office for Farringdon Station if a public enquiry on the Thameslink improvements gives the go-ahead. Public money is also helping to fund a new 'cultural quarter' in Clerkenwell, encouraging the use of urban spaces (warehouses, streets) for public art and cultural events, cutting traffic and making it pleasanter to walk round the area.

PROPERTY AND ARCHITECTURE

CLERKENWELL & FINSBURY

A hotchpotch of council blocks, Georgian terraces and former warehouses converted into dramatically spacious loft apartments. Ten years ago this area was full of boarded-up and bombed-out industrial buildings, deserted by the printers and watchmakers who used to work in them. Then it took off in a big way as loft-living caught on. Developers bought up the warehouses and the yuppies moved into spaces (not flats, please) full of exposed brick and industrial steel fittings. There are some beautiful Georgian terraces in Clerkenwell in the triangle between St John's Street and Farringdon Road, particularly in Sekforde Street. Humbler but still attractive Georgian properties in Finsbury. Warehouses and lofts mostly in and around main roads including St John's Street and Clerkenwell Road. When the supply of real lofts ran low, developers leapt into the breach with 'loft style' apartments, now filling almost every available space in Clerkenwell. Clerkenwell was once the centre of London's Italian community and the Italian church in Clerkenwell Road still provides a focus for Italian festivals and celebrations.

ATTRACTS *Young well-off single people; creative types; City workers wanting to be central* • **CONSERVATION AREAS** *Clerkenwell Green; Charterhouse Square; Hat and Feathers; Bunhill Fields and Finsbury Square; Moorfields; St Luke's; Northampton Grove* • **AVERAGE PRICES** *Flats: studio £120,000-£150,000; 1-bed £140,000+; 2-bed £270,000+ Houses: 2-bed £325,000; 3-bed £500,000; 4-bed £550,000+* • **AVERAGE RENTS (WEEKLY)** *Flats: studio £180-£225; 1-bed £220-£350; 2-bed £300-£325.*

ISLINGTON & HIGHBURY

Sought after and expensive, particularly Islington and its satellite Barnsbury, which have delectable streets of tall Georgian and early Victorian flat-fronted terraces and cottages, many carefully restored with their owners leaving the curtains open at dusk so that passers-by can admire their exquisite taste. Canonbury has some large Victorian villas with large gardens as well as elegant terraces. Cheaper Highbury has some splendid houses overlooking Highbury Fields, with a mixture of mansion blocks and Victorian terraces, many converted into flats in roads around. Progressively shabbier four-storey Victorian houses and smaller terraces towards Arsenal football ground.

ATTRACTS *The right-on, wealthy New Labour; young professionals; City workers; well-off families who can afford to send their children to private school; empty nesters who are bored in the country and want some life in the evening* • **CONSERVATION AREAS** *Duncan Terrace and Colebrooke Row;*

The Angel; Chapel Market and Penton Street; Arlington Square; East Canonbury; Canonbury; Upper Street North; Barnsbury • **AVERAGE PRICES** *Flats: studio £80,000-£130,000; 1-bed £140,000-£230,000; 2-bed £155,000-£225,000+ Houses: 2-bed £200,000-£450,000; 3-bed £285,000-£800,000; 4-bed £325,000+ •* **AVERAGE RENTS (WEEKLY)** *Flats: studio £120-£160; 1-bed £180-£350; 2-bed £280-£450 Houses: 2-bed £350-£550; 3-bed £380-£800; 4-bed £425+.*

TUFNELL PARK

Once an obscure web of Victorian residential streets west of the Holloway Road but now considered an acceptable alternative by people who've been priced out of Islington, Hampstead or Dartmouth Park (see Camden), and sought after by families who like the close knit atmosphere and one of Islington's best schools on their doorstep. Wide tree-lined roads with a mixture of large houses converted into flats and three- and four-bed family homes set back from the street with small front gardens. Wooden slatted blinds, carefully restored original features and freshly painted exteriors are evidence of middle-class colonisation. The further away you are from the Holloway Road the better.

ATTRACTS *First-time buyers; young professionals; families •* **CONSERVATION AREAS** *Tufnell Park; Hillmarton; Mercers Road and Tavistock Terrace •* **AVERAGE PRICES** *Flats: studio £90,000-£100,000; 1-bed £125,000-£180,000; 2-bed £150,000+ Houses: 3-bed £360,000-£400,000; 4-bed £500,000-£700,000 •* **AVERAGE RENTS (WEEKLY)** *Flats: studio £130-£150; 1-bed £180-£200; 2-bed £230-£270 Houses: 3-bed £350+; 4-bed £400+.*

UPPER HOLLOWAY

This segment of streets to the east of Holloway Road and Archway Road is a mixture of potentially posh and pretty shabby. Large Victorian family houses further north in roads off Archway Road in the Whitehall conservation area would be seriously expensive if they were picked up and placed over the postcode border into Highgate N6, so they're an excellent buy if you can put up with the indignity of N19 on your letterhead. They give way further south to narrow streets of tall, densely packed Victorian terraces divided into flats in streets east of the Holloway Road (although this is good flat-hunting ground). This area is home to wholesale clothing stores and factories and there are several council estates.

ATTRACTS *First-time buyers; young professionals; families who can't afford Tufnell Park •* **CONSERVATION AREAS** *Whitehall; Highgate Hill and Hornsey Lane; St John's Grove •* **AVERAGE PRICES** *Flats: 1-bed £110,000-£130,000; 2-bed £140,000-£180,000; 3-bed £175,000-£200,000 Houses: 3-bed £250,000-£350,000; 4-bed £325,000-£425,000 •* **AVERAGE RENTS (WEEKLY)** *Flats: 1-bed £180-£200; 2-bed £230-£270 Houses: 3-bed £350+; 4-bed £400+.*

BEST POSTCODES

Islington N1 is generally the best, although it includes some of the sleazy areas of Kings Cross, followed by Highbury N5. The relative social cachet of postcodes further north then gets seriously confusing. To quote a local estate agent: 'The part of Tufnell Park that's in N7 is better than Archway N19 (near Highgate), which in turn is better than Upper Holloway N19. This is better than Lower Holloway N7.' Got that? Good.

AMENITIES

SCHOOLS*

A generally dismal performance, with secondary schools among the worst in the country, let alone London. Parents of secondary school age children flee to other boroughs rather than suffer their children to be educated in Islington. Primary schools don't do quite as badly but this isn't saying much. School performance has been so consistently bad that the council has ceded control to a firm of private education consultants. No private prep schools and only one private (specialist arts) secondary school in the borough. A relatively small range of private nursery schools but an above-average number of places in state nursery schools.

PRE-SCHOOL PROVISION *3 state nursery schools; 40 nursery classes in state primary and church schools; 91 private or voluntary nurseries and playgroups. Proportion of under-fives in state nurseries: 66%* • **STATE PRIMARY SCHOOLS** *Overall league table position: 122nd out of 150. Top scorers: St Peter's and St Paul's RC (with nursery unit), Clerkenwell; Canonbury School, Canonbury; Hanover (with nursery unit), Islington* • **STATE SECONDARY SCHOOLS** *Overall league table position: 147th out of 149. Top scorers: Mount Carmel RC (girls), Archway; Highbury Fields (girls), Highbury; Elizabeth Garrett Anderson (girls), Islington* • **PRIVATE SECONDARY SCHOOLS** *Italia Conti Academy of Theatre Arts (mixed), Clerkenwell.*

TRANSPORT****

Very good transport links to most parts of the borough although the north-west has to rely on the unpleasant Northern Line tube from High Barnet. The east has the much better Piccadilly and Victoria Line. A good choice of buses.

TUBES *Central services Zone 1. Cost of annual season ticket £636. Clerkenwell: Farringdon (Circle and Metropolitan). Islington: Angel (Northern). Further out Zone 2. Cost of annual season ticket £756. Highbury. Highbury and Islington (Victoria). Average journey time to Oxford Circus 8 minutes; Victoria 12 minutes. Upper Holloway: Holloway Road (Piccadilly). Average journey time to Piccadilly Circus 12 minutes. Tufnell Park (Northern). Average journey time to Tottenham Court Road 11 minutes; to London Bridge 18 minutes* • **BUSES** *A good selection of services to the northern suburbs, into town and beyond. The best choices are at Upper Street and Archway (the terminus for many buses from town). Services include the 19 via Highbury and Islington to Piccadilly Circus and Battersea, the 38 via Islington to Victoria, the 43 via Archway, Holloway and Islington and the 10 from Archway via Tufnell Park to Kings Cross and Hammersmith* • **TRAFFIC TROUBLESPOTS** *Islington: The junction of roads near Angel tube station at the south end of Upper Street. Often long tail-backs up Upper Street because of short traffic lights. Holloway Road: The main A1 out of London. Several lanes of traffic in each direction, often jammed. Archway: The continuation of the A1 with a massive ugly traffic roundabout, clogged with buses and lorries which then have problems hauling themselves up the hill at Archway Road. Frequent attempts to widen the Archway Road have floundered in the face of huge opposition by residents whose property would be demolished* • **PARKING** *Pretty difficult and getting worse as residents' controlled parking zones spread. There are controlled parking zones around Old Street, Clerkenwell, Angel and Highbury. Further zones are proposed for the areas of Finsbury Park* *controlled by Islington council (see Haringey for details of Finsbury Park) and for the area around the Arsenal football stadium on match days. Parking permits are the most expensive in London at £95 a year.*

LEISURE FACILITIES★★★★

THEATRES & CONCERT HALLS *A good choice. Sadlers Wells, the borough's best-known theatre, has re-opened after a long closure for a complete overhaul and specialises in dance and opera. Islington is also one of the best places for fringe, pub and off-the-wall theatre in London. The Almeida theatre in Islington currently being refurbished, specialises in new plays and productions. New plays, music and exhibitions at the refurbished Victorian music hall Rosemary Branch theatre. Lots of other smaller theatre groups* ● **CINEMAS** *Currently not a huge choice in the borough itself but there are plenty of cinemas in the West End and neighbouring boroughs. Screen on the Green, Islington shows a mixture of mainstream and fringe films. The Holloway Odeon is definitely mainstream, although the art deco exterior of the building is stunning. But there are plans for a nine-screen cinema as part of a huge new shopping development at Angel behind Upper Street* ● **MUSEUMS & GALLERIES** *A small, eccentric but fascinating selection, ranging from the House of Detention in Clerkenwell, an underground prison which was the site of the last public execution, to the Museum of Methodism in City Road with the chapel and house of Methodism's founder, John Wesley. The London Canal Museum is in a 19th-century ice house on the Kings Cross canal basin. Art exhibitions in Berry House, a former warehouse in St John's Street in Clerkenwell's 'cultural quarter'. Islington now has its own local history museum in the Town Hall in Upper Street* ● **SPORTS FACILITIES** *Well provided for with seven leisure centres in Archway, Kings Cross, Finsbury, Highbury, Clerkenwell, Upper Holloway and Islington. All managed by a charitable trust funded by Islington Council. Pools at Archway, Kings Cross, Highbury and Clerkenwell. Tennis at Islington and skating at the Sobell Centre, Upper Holloway. Tennis and football at parks across the borough. Highbury is home to Arsenal FC (can be hell on matchdays for residents in nearby streets who aren't football fans – and Arsenal is trying to expand its facilities)* ● **LIBRARIES** *Well-used libraries (the daytime population is swollen by workers and there are a lot of students). Threats of cuts in the library budget angered residents so much that the borough was forced to backtrack on plans for branch closures and instead extend opening hours and experiment with Sunday opening. 7.76 library visits per head. Position in library-use league table: 10th out of 32 (where 1 is best and 32 worst).*

OPEN SPACES★

Less open space than any other borough in London. Densely built-up and populated, Islington can be awful on a hot day. But as a compensation, the cool oasis of the Regents Canal flows through Islington itself.

CANAL WALKS *The Regents Canal. Excellent walks along the towpath from the canal basin at Kings Cross, then through the streets of Islington as the canal goes through a long early 19th-century tunnel, and then joins the towpath again below the Georgian houses of Colebrooke Row. Great views of people's back gardens stretching down to the water and colourfully painted houseboats moored by the bridge* ● **URBAN RELIEF** *Highbury Fields, gently sloping grass and mature trees bring welcome relief from hard tarmac. Tennis courts and swimming pool.*

SHOPS * * *

CLERKENWELL *Has improved over the past few years with the influx of people with money to spend and there should be more to come as new mixed developments of shops, restaurants, flats and offices come on stream. Cowcross Street now has a big bookshop alongside the coffee bars and wine bars, and small parades of shops, including some useful shops like hardware shops around Farringdon station, are still hanging on. More small shops in Exmouth Market. Clerkenwell has good Italian delis. Daily market at Exmouth Market* • **ISLINGTON** *Great for small, unusual shops especially furniture, interior design, antiques (Camden Passage off Upper Street with its furniture, silver and jewellery shops is a haven for antique afficionados). Upper Street, with pavements at the south end conveniently raised to separate shoppers from the remorseless traffic, is a pleasant place to shop with small branches of chains and bookshops opening late. But a bit of a dearth of larger, national chains, a gap which should be filled by the new Angel shopping development. Fruit, veg and clothes market in Chapel Market just off Upper Street. Large Sainsbury's in Liverpool Road* • **HOLLOWAY & ARCHWAY** *Holloway Road is trafficky and depressing – boarded-up shops are frequent, and there's the usual motley collection of fast food joints, cafés, small newsagents and shops offering international phone calls, testifying to the large numbers of residents with overseas links. The presence of the University of North London has at least brought a proper bookshop and a bit of life to the street. The building which used to house Jones Bros, Holloway's department store, is now home to Waitrose. Big Safeway further up the street. Some signs of gentrification around Tufnell Park including a large antique fireplace shop. Islington council is keen to attract developers wanting to build an indoor shopping mall near Archway roundabout but there have been no immediate takers. And there's no sign yet of what everyone would really like – the demolition of the eyesore tower block by the roundabout.*

RESTAURANTS * * * *

CLERKENWELL *New wine bars and restaurants springing up, particularly around Cowcross Street and Exmouth Market (one reason why the latter was such a culinary desert until recently was that council planners had a policy of restricting restaurants). Now a total volte-face, encouraged by the re-opening of Sadlers Wells and the prospect of lots of pre- and post-theatre diners as well as the influx of young affluent residents with plenty of money and inclination to eat out. Restaurants include the Quality Chop House, once the purveyor of Noted Cups of Tea and stodgy puddings to nearby postal workers and now serving up-market British food* • **ISLINGTON** *If you can't find something to eat in Upper Street, you're very fussy. Residents complain there are too many restaurants but it's great for visitors. Every sort of restaurant from chains like Pizza Express, the Dome and Café Flo to Granita, scene of the famous leadership meeting between Tony Blair and Gordon Brown. Cuban, Vietnamese and Belgian are among other choices. The pavements are thronged with people and diners eating and drinking at outside tables. One of London's best attempts at café society – even the traffic becomes an exciting part of urban living rather than a drag after a couple of glasses of wine* • **HOLLOWAY** *Choice of ethnic restaurants around the Holloway Road including Eastern European, Korean and North African, as well as Spanish and pie and mash.*

CRIME RATES*

Position in Metropolitan Police league table: 3rd out of 32 (where 1 is worst and 32 best) although large daytime populations can distort the figures.

THE COUNCIL**

POLITICIAL AFFILIATION *Liberal Democrat* • **MINUS POINTS** *The most expensive residents' parking permits in London. Some of the worst schools in London. Very lax at street-sweeping and emptying bins, with low levels of satisfaction among residents. The second highest council tax in inner London* • **PLUS POINTS** *Borough-wide recycling scheme being implemented following a successful pilot. LibDem administration trying to get to grips with council finances and improve efficiency. Council tax cut in 2000-2001. One of the more efficient boroughs in inner London in turning round property searches* • **PROPERTY SEARCHES CARRIED OUT IN 10 WORKING DAYS** 99.9% • **STANDARD SEARCH FEE** £115 • **COUNCIL TAX COLLECTED** 88.9% • **COUNCIL TAX 2000-2001**

BAND	PROPERTY VALUE	CHARGE	BAND	PROPERTY VALUE	CHARGE
A	up to £40,000	£591	E	£88,001-£120,000	£1,084
B	£40,001-£52,000	£690	F	£120,001-£160,000	£1,281
C	£52,001-£68,000	£788	G	£160,001-£320,000	£1,478
D	£68,001-£88,000	£887	H	over £320,000	£1,774

KENSINGTON & CHELSEA

Kensington and Chelsea is the borough with everything – beautiful and varied architecture (70% of its territory is a conservation area), properties to die for, excellent transport links, a wealth of museums, galleries, parks and gardens, a range of shops from the eclectic to the practical and some of the most up-to-the-minute bars and restaurants. So what's the downside? It's one of the most expensive parts of London, it tends to get crowded with tourists and coaches especially in summer, it can compete with anywhere else for the most traffic-clogged roads, and the simple act of parking outside your own front door can be a nightmare.

Up from the river and at its southern boundary the borough stretches from the red-bricked Dutch-gabled elegance of Chelsea's Cadogan Estate in the east around Sloane Square tube station past the artists' studios, early-Victorian stucco terraces and cottages of central Chelsea to Chelsea Harbour in the south-west corner, built on a former industrial site next to Lots Road power station (see Hammersmith & Fulham). Further north, West Chelsea gives way to the shabbier, hotel-lined roads of transient Earls Court before smartening up again around the museums and porticoed streets of South Kensington and moving north to the white stucco and multi-coloured cottages of Notting Hill. Beyond the Westway, built when cars were in and conservation and the environment were out, lie the more modest brick and stucco terraces of North Kensington, mixed with council estates.

Kensington and Chelsea appears to be one of the most affluent boroughs of London. Its residents are not just domestic but international, from businessmen to diplomats. The south of the borough is the preferred home of well-off middle-class families and well-off young professionals, many armed with fat bonuses from the City. It's the home of royalty at Kensington Palace (although this didn't prevent it from supporting its formidable and articulate residents in a campaign against the proposal for a memorial garden for the late Diana, Princess of Wales, in Kensington Gardens). Unemployment is the third lowest in inner London at 4.4%. But there are still pockets of poverty, unemployment and poor housing, particularly in the north of the borough.

Popular areas like South Kensington, Kensington and the Sloane Square end of Chelsea have never fallen from grace and their popularity has rippled out over the years to the far western reaches of Chelsea and to Notting Hill, once both considered near-slums. North Kensington, traditionally the least affluent part of the borough, is the latest to feel the ripple effect as more people priced out of Notting Hill venture north of the Westway. North Kensington has also received £35 million of government regeneration money since 1993, matched by £127 million from the public and private sectors. An area which people used to have to nerve themselves up to visit is now more stimulatingly cosmopolitan than threatening. Kensington and Chelsea has one of the smallest ethnic minority populations of inner London at 16% but there is still a significant West Indian community in Notting Hill and north Kensington as well as Spanish and Portuguese. The south of the borough is popular with expatriates from other parts of Europe, particularly the French and the Italians.

PROPERTY AND ARCHITECTURE

CHELSEA & WEST CHELSEA

A long east–west swathe of some of the most desirable real estate in London. Thirty years ago, Chelsea was considered raffish and arty. Rising prices and an increasingly international clientele have smartened it up but it's still less staid than Kensington. Flats in imposing red brick mansion blocks with elaborate gables and carving in streets around Sloane Street and Pont Street, owned by the Cadogan Estate. West of Sloane Square and in streets off Kings Road, there are small but expensive Victorian terraces. Larger, more formal houses around the Royal Hospital and big red brick family homes north of Kings Road. Streets opposite the Worlds End council estate in West Chelsea have four-bedroom white stucco family houses which were once beyond the pale because of the council estate and the distance from transport – but no more.

ATTRACTS *Well off buyers including young professionals and families; those* *wanting pieds-à-terre; glitterati* • **CONSERVATION AREAS** *Royal Hospital; Cheyne; Chelsea Park and Carlyle; Sloane and Stanley; Chelsea; Hans Town; Sloane Square* • **AVERAGE PRICES** *Flats: studio £150,000-£180,000; 1-bed £220,000-£285,000; 2-bed £280,000+; Houses: 2-bed £500,000+; 3-bed £600,000-£800,000; 4-bed £1 million+;* • **AVERAGE RENTS (WEEKLY)** *Flats: studio £225+; 1-bed £300+; 2-bed £500+ Houses: 3-bed £850+; 4-bed £1200+.*

SOUTH KENSINGTON

Where all mothers would like their children to live when they come to London. Safe, smart and respectable as well as fun. Gracious streets of four- and five-storey stucco wedding cake houses, many converted to flats, off Old Brompton Road and Gloucester Road. Many have private garden squares. Much of South Kensington is owned by the Wellcome Trust Estate, which has strict rules about what people can do with property. Some huge grand houses between the Fulham and Brompton Roads where houses change hands for millions. South Kensington has more flats than Chelsea but is getting too expensive for first-time buyers, unless they're buying with Daddy's money. Some smaller houses in streets north of Fulham Road.

ATTRACTS *Expatriate Europeans, particularly French wanting to be near the French lycée; English families and professionals; people wanting a pied-à-terre* • **CONSERVATION AREAS** *The Boltons; Thurloe; Wellcome; Brompton* • **AVERAGE PRICES** *Flats: studio £160,000+; 1-bed £250,000+; 2-bed £300,000+ Houses: 2-bed: £600,000+; 3-bed £750,000+; 4-bed £900,000+* • **AVERAGE RENTS (WEEKLY)** *Flats: studio £250+; 1-bed £325+; 2-bed £550+ Houses: 3-bed £950+; 4-bed £1300+.*

EARLS COURT

Traditionally the scruffy bit between South Kensington and Kensington proper. But improving all the time as seedy hotels are replaced by luxury flat conversions or turned back into houses. East of Earls Court Road, tall red brick gabled terraces and squares of large stucco houses are almost as smart as Kensington. More transient to the west with backpackers, tourists and short-stay tenants but there are several popular garden squares here including Earls Court Square and Nevern Square. Victorian cottages in and around Kenway Road off Earls Court Road.

ATTRACTS *People who can't afford Kensington or Chelsea; well-off first-time buyers* • **CONSERVATION AREAS** *Courtfield; Earls Court Square; Nevern Square; Philbeach; Earls Court Village* • **AVERAGE PRICES** *Flats: studio £140,000+; 1-bed £160,000+; 2-bed £225,000+ Houses 3-bed £550,000+* • **AVERAGE RENTS (WEEKLY)** *Flats: studio £230+; 1-bed £300+; 2-bed £450+.*

KENSINGTON & HOLLAND PARK

Like South Kensington, safe, pretty and fun – if you can afford it. Less hip than Notting Hill. Streets of white stucco three- and four-storey terraces, many still family homes, in roads both sides of Kensington High Street, alongside some streets of red brick Queen Anne terraces. Mansion blocks and luxury apartments in and around Kensington High Street. Further up around Holland Park there are some massive Victorian houses, now mostly converted into flats and some attractive terraces up around Campden Hill Square. Family houses in roads around Addison Avenue.

ATTRACTS *Wealthy British and internationals; families* • **CONSERVATION**

AREAS *Edwardes Square, Scarsdale and Abingdon; Lexham Gardens; Kensington Square; Kensington Court; De Vere; Holland Park; Kensington; Kensington Palace* • **AVERAGE PRICES** *Flats: studio £140,000+; 1-bed £190,000+; 2-bed £230,000+ Houses: 3-bed £650,000+; 4-bed £1million+* • **AVERAGE RENTS (WEEKLY)** *Flats: studio £220+; 1-bed £300+; 2-bed £425+ Houses: 2-bed £500+; 3-bed £700+; 4-bed £1000+.*

NOTTING HILL

Currently the hippest part of the borough and sufficiently daring without being dangerous to attract well-off young single professionals, celebrities and trustafarians – rich young things living off family trust money. A magnet for people who want to see and be seen in one of the area's many new restaurants. Thirty years ago, Notting Hill was cheap and scruffy, populated with immigrants forced into crumbling overcrowded terraces. Now it's expensive and beautiful. So far, it's the only area of London to have a film named after it, which has proved a mixed blessing as rents and prices rise and the area is overrun with American tourists. Lots of white stucco and private garden squares and some lovely multicoloured terraces and cottages around Portobello Road.

ATTRACTS *The young; the well-off buying with their own or other people's money; glitterati* • **CONSERVATION AREAS** *Norland; Ladbroke; Pembridge* • **AVERAGE PRICES** *Flats: studio £100,000+; 1-bed £160,000+; 2-bed £200,000+ Houses: 2-bed £325,000+; 3-bed £450,000+; 4-bed £650,000+* • **AVERAGE RENTS (WEEKLY)** *Flats: studio £220+; 1-bed £270+; 2-bed £300+ Houses: 2-bed £450+; 3-bed £500+; 4-bed £550+.*

NORTH KENSINGTON

Still a bit down-at-heel north of the Westway but improving as it gets attention from people looking for cheap(ish) property in Kensington. But don't expect massive bargains. Prices have risen sharply over the past two years and are now closer to those in Notting Hill. Three- and four-bedroom Victorian terraces in streets off Ladbroke Grove just north of the Westway. Large terraces around St Charles Square. Council estates further east but even some of these have become trendy, particularly Trellick Tower, a massive tower block now apparently great to live in but still monstrous from the outside.

ATTRACTS *Young professionals wanting to live on the front line; families* • **CONSERVATION AREAS** *Oxford Gardens; Kensal Green Cemetery* • **AVERAGE PRICES** *Flats: studio £100,000+; 1-bed £145,000+; 2-bed £165,000+ Houses: 2-bed £250,000-£325,000; 3-bed £300,000+; 4-bed £350,000+* • **AVERAGE RENTS (WEEKLY)** *Flats: studio £180-£200; 1-bed £220+; 2-bed £250+ Houses: 2-bed £400+; 3-bed £450+; 4-bed £500+.*

BEST POSTCODES

Several pecking orders within the borough. In South Kensington SW7 is best, followed by SW10 then SW5 (Earls Court). In Chelsea, SW3 is better than SW10. In Kensington and Notting Hill, W8 is better than W11 which is better than W14. Some huge price anomalies, particularly around the boundary of W11 and W14.

AMENITIES

SCHOOLS ★ ★ ★

State primary schools score very well but there's a falling off at secondary level, possibly because of some creaming off to private schools. There are only four state secondary schools. The lowest provision for pre-school children in state nurseries of any borough in London although there's a good choice of private nurseries and nursery classes linked to voluntary-aided or grant-maintained schools. Good for prep schools and there is a number of private secondary schools.

PRE-SCHOOL PROVISION *4 state nursery schools; 21 nursery classes in state primary or church schools; 66 private nurseries and playgroups. Proportion of under-fives in state nurseries: 34%* ● **STATE PRIMARY SCHOOLS** *Overall league table position: 3rd out of 150. Top scorers: Our Lady of Victories (with nursery unit), South Kensington; Oratory RC, Chelsea; Servite RC (with nursery unit), Chelsea* ● **STATE SECONDARY SCHOOLS** *Overall league table position: 67th out of 149. Top scorers: Cardinal Vaughan Memorial School (boys), Holland Park; Sion Manning RC (girls), North Kensington* ● **PRIVATE PREP SCHOOLS** *Sussex House (boys), Chelsea; Hellenic (Greek 2-16) (mixed); Cameron House (mixed), Chelsea; Falkner House (girls), South Kensington; Glendower Prep (girls), South Kensington; Hampshire Schools (mixed), South Kensington; St James Junior (mixed), South Kensington; Hill House (mixed), Chelsea* ● **PRIVATE SECONDARY SCHOOLS** *More House (girls), Chelsea; Mander Portman Woodward (mixed), South Kensington; Queens Gate (girls from 4), South Kensington; St James (girls), Notting Hill; Lycée français Charles de Gaulle, (mixed), South Kensington.*

TRANSPORT ★ ★ ★ ★

One of the most central residential areas in London with plentiful tube and bus services to most parts of the borough. West Chelsea is the worst served, with long walks to the nearest tube at Sloane Square. High Street Kensington can be a frustrating journey from the city with only the slow Circle Line going direct.

TUBES *Central area Zone 1. Cost of annual season ticket £636* ● **BUSES** *Constant flow of buses to town down the main arteries of the borough with the best choice in the south. Buses to town include the 9 to Aldwych via Kensington High Street, the 10 via Kensington High Street to Kings Cross, the 52 via Ladbroke Grove and Notting Hill Gate to Victoria, the 14 via South Kensington to Piccadilly and the 11 from west Chelsea via Sloane Square, Charing Cross and Liverpool Street* ● **TRAFFIC TROUBLESPOTS** *Chelsea: Sloane Square and all the way down Kings Road. Four roads flow into Sloane Square often jamming it on all sides and a press of traffic, delivery vans and buses often blocks Kings Road. Earls Court & Chelsea: Three lines of traffic often stationary on the Warwick Road, the northbound section of the notorious Earls Court one-way system. Southbound the traffic is often forced into one lane by parked cars, delivery vans and a narrowed bridge over the tube lines. The one-way system uses Gunter Grove and Finborough Road in Chelsea going north and Redcliffe Gardens and Edith Grove going south. Jams continue south along Cheyne Walk and north along Cromwell Road. Kensington: Long tail-backs at the lights at the junction of Kensington Church Street and Kensington High Street because* of traffic, buses and shoppers • **PARKING** Problem areas. Parking is a serious problem in the borough and even having a resident's permit won't insulate you from driving round and round trying to find a parking space. But permits are much prized because, uniquely of all boroughs, there are no zones and once you have a permit you can park in any resident's parking bay in the borough. This is all the more useful because hours of permit-only parking have been extended later into the evening in some areas, much to the fury of non-resident theatre goers and diners. There are controlled parking zones around Sloane Square, Kings Road, Knightsbridge, Earls Court and around Kensington High Street. Cost of annual resident's permit: £70.

LEISURE FACILITIES * * * * *

THEATRES & CONCERT HALLS The Royal Court has reopened after years closed for refurbishment and is renowned for avant garde and controversial plays. Plays, play readings and workshops at the Chelsea Centre Theatre and plays at The Gate, Notting Hill. Holland Park Theatre has its own in-house opera company and orchestra. And the West End is just down the road • **CINEMAS** A good choice. Mostly mainstream viewing at Kensington High Street, Fulham Road and the Notting Hill Coronet. A chance of more off-beat offerings at the Chelsea Cinema and The Gate at Notting Hill. The Electric Cinema in the Portobello Road has finally reopened after a refurbishment • **MUSEUMS & GALLERIES** The place to be. The pantheon of the natural history, science, geological and V&A museums housed in wonderful buildings in Prince Albert's favourite venue of South Kensington. The National Army Museum is at the Royal Hospital. Several smaller but fascinating places including the Linley Sambourne House, a 19th-century middle-class house with all the furniture and fittings preserved, and the Leighton House Museum, the former home of one of the leading lights of the Pre-Raphaelite movement • **SPORTS FACILITIES** Two leisure centres at Ladbroke Grove and Chelsea (both fairly recently refurbished). Pools, gym, classes and racquet sports. Tennis and cricket in Holland Park and other parks across the borough • **LIBRARIES** The main library is in Kensington High Street in a handsome classical-style building next to the town hall. Generously long opening hours, particularly in the main library, but watch Wednesday afternoons when all borough libraries are closed. Libraries well used at 7.6 visits per head. Place in library-use league table: 11th out of 32 (where 1 is best and 32 worst).

OPEN SPACES * * * *

Very good for public open space but also excels in the garden square and the hidden communal garden. Access to these is often restricted to residents but passers-by can get tantalising glimpses behind railings and walls. Residents who live in garden squares and qualify for a key guard their privileges jealously, often with strict rules about dogs, ball games and parties. **GARDEN SQUARES** Kensington Square, Kensington; Markham Square, Chelsea; Earls Court Square, Earls Court, all with lawns, mature trees and a satisfying feel of privacy without isolation • **PARKS AND GARDENS** Kensington Gardens, famous to television viewers the world over as the scene of mass wreath-laying after the death of Diana, Princess of Wales. But also much loved by residents for its lawns, mature trees and round pond. Holland Park has open space, woodland and peacocks. Try also the Chelsea Physic Garden, a wonderful hidden space founded in the 17th century by the Society of Apothecaries of London for the cultivation of medicinal herbs • **RIVER VIEWS** Cremorne Gardens, Chelsea, a small patch of green with great views of the changing riverbank at Battersea • **CANAL WALKS** The towpath beside the Paddington branch of the Grand Union Canal, dominated by Trellick Tower. A reminder that not all of Kensington is a smart residential suburb • **CEMETERIES** Kensal Green. Victorian cemetery, less wild than Highgate but monthly tours of the catacombs with all-too-real lead coffins stacked on shelves.

SHOPS * * * * *

KINGS ROAD, CHELSEA Not as ground-breaking as it was in the 60s (it's even got an M&S and tourists have muscled in on the Chelsea set) but still lots of designer clothes and shoe shops, expensive furniture and soft furnishings, and up-market second-hand clothes. Big Waitrose and of course, Peter Jones, the department store whose contents adorn so many middle-class homes in the area • **FULHAM ROAD** Has smartened up considerably in the past 15 years, particularly at the Fulham end. Lots of antique furniture shops, art galleries and bookshops among the bars and restaurants • **SOUTH KENSINGTON & EARLS COURT** Smartish shops around South Ken station at the top of Old Brompton Road, particularly a French patisserie and bookshop in Harrington Road opposite the lycée français. Earls Court Road is still shabby and full of cheap restaurants, take-aways and bureaux de change. Sainsbury's in Cromwell Road and gleaming white Tesco in Warwick Road • **KENSINGTON & HOLLAND PARK** Getting better all the time in Kensington High Street although marred by the difficulty of crossing the road. A good range of mid-range clothes chains with upmarket stock. Antique shops in Kensington Church Street • **NOTTING HILL & NORTH KENSINGTON** Antique and clothes shops in and around Portobello Road with what is claimed to be the largest antiques market in the world on Saturdays, when stalls stretch beyond the Westway. Crammed with tourists at weekends. There are bargains but you have to know where to look. Second-hand record and book exchanges in Notting Hill Gate, specialist cookery and travel bookshops in Blenheim Road. In short one of the most eclectic collections of shops in London. But there are widespread fears that individual traders could be forced out by high rents as landlords take advantage of Notting Hill's media star status following the success of That Film. Shabbier, local shops in north Ladbroke Grove. Sainsbury's at Ladbroke Grove by the canal, Tesco Metro in Portobello Road.

RESTAURANTS * * * * *

CHELSEA A huge choice – from the humble Stockpot in Kings Road to Terence Conran's Bluebird restaurant. Lots of eateries including Thai now in Chelsea Harbour (river views) which used to be dead after 9pm • **SOUTH KENSINGTON & EARLS COURT** Choice of ethnic restaurants, crêperies and winebars of varying quality in Earls Court. Good fish and Italian restaurants round the junction of Earls Court and Old Brompton Roads. Spoilt for choice in South Kensington with everything including French, Japanese and Polish • **KENSINGTON & HOLLAND PARK** Also spoilt for choice, with lots of new restaurants opening up around Kensington Church Street especially • **NOTTING HILL** An explosion of new restaurants and trendy bars in and around Portobello Road and North Kensington. Locals are getting more and more blasé about spotting celebrities.

CRIME RATES*

Position in Metropolitan Police league table: 7th out of 32 (where 1 is worst and 32 best).

THE COUNCIL****

POLITICAL AFFILIATION *Conservative* • **MINUS POINTS** *Very strict and some would say picky about granting planning permission for extensions or other alterations to property. But this is a plus for those keen to preserve the area. Low provision of state nurseries* • **PLUS POINTS** *Very hot on recycling and street-cleaning, although the borough's normally excellent record on rubbish collections has been dented by industrial disputes. At least rubbish collections are twice weekly so missing one isn't as painful as it might be. A twice weekly door-to-door recycling service — the only one in London so far – collecting cans, tins, bottles, newspapers and cartons. Good primary schools. One of the most efficient boroughs at carrying out land searches. Low council tax* • **PROPERTY SEARCHES CARRIED OUT IN 10 WORKING DAYS** *100%* • **STANDARD SEARCH FEE** £115 • **COUNCIL TAX COLLECTED** 95.2% • **COUNCIL TAX 2000-2001**

BAND	PROPERTY VALUE	CHARGE	BAND	PROPERTY VALUE	CHARGE
A	up to £40,000	£416	E	£88,001-£120,000	£762
B	£40,001-£52,000	£485	F	£120,001-£160,000	£900
C	£52,001-£68,000	£554	G	£160,001-£320,000	£1,039
D	£68,001-£88,000	£623	H	over £320,000	£1,247

KINGSTON UPON THAMES

Kingston is the most southwesterly point of a huge swathe of suburbia reaching upwards and outwards around West London. Well known to any motorist trying to escape from the capital to Surrey and the south coast, the Kingston bypass bisects the borough from east to west with roads of undistinguished 1930s semis ribboning out from it in all directions. The jewel in the borough's crown, the medieval Surrey market town of Kingston itself, lies well hidden to the north through miles of anonymous streets, busy through-roads, a barricade of ugly concrete office blocks and the backside of its huge shopping centre. In short, Kingston doesn't do itself many architectural favours.

The north of the borough is dominated by Kingston, mostly Victorian in the middle, giving way to middling and up-market Edwardian and 1930s houses to the north west and large detached properties around leafy Coombe to the north east. East of Kingston lies New Malden, Victorian in its best roads but shading off in other areas to shabby 1930s. Surbiton is south of Kingston, claiming the title of Queen of the Suburbs (although if this is awarded for being respectable but slightly dull, Surbiton has plenty of competition in outer London). Tatty Tolworth is carved up by the gyratory systems, underpasses and bridges of the A3. In the south, where the borough narrows to a point, the council houses and 1930s semis of Chessington give way to open fields and green space as London slips into Surrey.

Kingston is mostly affluent, mostly white collar and mostly white (although it has Indian, and more recently Korean communities). Just 9% of the population is from an ethnic minority and unemployment is the second lowest in London at 1.9%. The nomination of Kingston as top town in the 1995 Guinness Guide to the best place to live in the UK successfully brought in a number of large companies who have their headquarters in the borough. Kingston has always been commuter country and the borough's good schools, good shops, good transport and quick access to green space and the river have made it a popular middle-class choice.

For similar reasons, developers have moved in, snapping up desirable riverside sites to build luxury homes. Not always uncontroversially – plans by Fairclough Homes a few years ago to chop down a row of picturesque poplars by the river at Kingston to give their buyers an unimpeded view met with angry protests from locals and a band of eco-warriors who chained themselves to trees to prevent them being felled. But this hasn't stopped other developers from buying up former industrial sites along the river and inland for new supermarkets, cinemas, hotels and homes. One of the highest profile developments to date is Charter Quay, a mixed development of more than 200 apartments and townhouses, with shops, restaurants, new public space and a theatre on derelict land between the high street and the Thames, along the banks of the Hogmill River. The theatre is sorely needed in Kingston, which lacks such a facility at the moment, but some residents think the development, which will dominate the town just behind the historic marketplace, is too large.

PROPERTY AND ARCHITECTURE

KINGSTON & COOMBE

Streets of mostly well-kept Victorian and Edwardian terraces near the centre of town with some handsome Victorian semis overlooking the Fairfield recreation ground to the south. A good choice of flats, mostly in modern and newly built blocks near the river and around Kingston College. Further north, mostly 1920s and 1930s semis and terraces including the streets known as the Tudors around Tudor Drive, lined with dizzying rows of mock-Tudor black and white semis. Coombe, north east of Kingston, is the grandest part of the borough with large detached houses, many built to order by their owners, in big gardens.

ATTRACTS *Families wanting to be near Richmond Park (see Richmond) and close to good schools (Tiffin Girls, one of Kingston's best schools, is just round the corner from the Tudors); people who can't afford Richmond*

• **CONSERVATION AREAS** *Kingston Old Town; Fairfield and Knights Park;*

Richmond Road; Grove Crescent; Coombe Wood; Coombe Hill; Coombe House • **AVERAGE PRICES** *Flats: studio £75,000+; 1-bed £110,000; 2-bed £125,000+ Houses: 2-bed £145,000+; 3-bed £200,000+; 4-bed £330,000* • **AVERAGE RENTS (WEEKLY)** *Flats: studio £125+; 1-bed £150+; 2-bed £190+ Houses: 2-bed £195+; 3-bed £275+; 4-bed £346+.*

NEW MALDEN

A mixture of everything from Victorian to 1970s, a legacy of bombing during the Second World War. Some large detached Victorian villas on the Kingston Road coming into the centre, now mostly converted into flats or offices and some roads of modest two-storey Victorian and Edwardian terraces in roads off the High Street. Some of the best roads are in the conservation area of The Groves north of Kingston Road. South of Kingston Road there are mostly modest 1930s semis or terraces, some shabby and many 'improved' with metal-framed picture windows or new front doors, making the houses uglier than they were ever intended to be. A lot of council property near the railway line.

ATTRACTS *Families; local first-time buyers; members of the Korean community* • **CONSERVATION AREAS** *The Groves* • **AVERAGE PRICES** *Flats: 1-bed £115,000+; 2-bed £135,000+ Houses: 2-bed £160,000+; 3-bed £200,000+; 4-bed £330,000+* • **AVERAGE RENTS (WEEKLY)** *Flats: studio £115+; 1-bed £138+; 2-bed £185+ Houses: 2-bed £195; 3-bed £250+; 4-bed £320+.*

SURBITON

Some large, ornate Victorian houses in roads around the Upper Brighton Road and Ewell Road – a good place for generously-sized conversion flats and studios. Large detached 1930s houses in the sought-after Southborough conservation area. Berrylands to the east of the busy Ewell Road has some solid Edwardian semis overlooking the Fishponds open space before giving way to well-tended 1930s suburbia (neatly mown grass frontages, front gardens with crazy paving, cars parked straight in drives). Technically, Berrylands is part of cheaper Tolworth but residents like to call it Surbiton.

ATTRACTS *Families; commuters* • **CONSERVATION AREAS** *Cadogan Road; Claremount Road; St Andrews Square; Surbiton Town Centre; Surbiton Hill Park; Southborough; Oakhill; Christchurch; Victoria Avenue* • **AVERAGE PRICES** *Flats: studio £85,000-£90,000; 1-bed £120,000-£175,000; 2-bed £140,000+ Houses: 2-bed £130,000+; 3-bed £190,000+; 4-bed £400,000* • **AVERAGE RENTS (WEEKLY)** *Flats: studio £125+; 1-bed £160+; 2-bed £170+ Houses: 3-bed £320+; 4-bed £460+.*

TOLWORTH & CHESSINGTON

The scrag end of the borough around and south of the A3 Kingston bypass. Mostly a 1930s sprawl with modern infill, cut up with dual carriageways and main roads in every direction, carrying motorists out of London or to Chessington World of Adventure. Even many of the quieter residential roads are wide and bleak, unrelieved by trees or any obvious greenery. Lots of modest council houses mixed with bungalows in the south of Chessington around Garrison Lane.

ATTRACTS *Loyal locals; families wanting to be near Tolworth Girls School (tight catchment area and very sought-after); people looking for affordable properties* • **CONSERVATION AREAS** *None* • **AVERAGE PRICES** *Flats: studio*

£70,000; 1-bed £80,000-£85,000; 2-bed £100,000-£110,000 *Houses:*
2-bed £120,000; 3-bed £175,000; 4-bed £200,000 (Tolworth)
• **AVERAGE RENTS (WEEKLY)** *Flats: studio £105+; 1-bed £125; 2-bed £150;*
3-bed £185 Houses: 2-bed £160+; 3-bed £185.

BEST POSTCODES

Out of town postcodes throughout the borough – so largely irrelevant.
Proximity to stations, shops and schools is more important.

AMENITIES

SCHOOLS****

Some excellent selective state secondary schools and private schools push
Kingston to dizzying heights in the GCSE and A level league tables and
attract parents and children from miles around, making the best schools
fiercely competitive to get into. Primary schools are also some of the best in
London. A good range of private schools. Provision of pre-school places in
state nursery schools and a reasonable selection of private and voluntary
nurseries for the under-fours. The borough participated in a pilot scheme to
test-drive baseline testing for four-year-olds and is an enthusiastic supporter
of the policy.

PRE-SCHOOL PROVISION *1 state nursery school; 16 nursery classes in state*
primary and church schools; 63 private and voluntary nurseries and
playgroups. Proportion of under-fives in state nurseries: 61% • **STATE PRIMARY**
SCHOOLS *Overall position in league tables: 17th out of 150. Top scorers:*
Christ Church CE, Surbiton; Grand Avenue (with nursery unit), Surbiton; St
Agatha's RC (with nursery unit), Kingston • **STATE SECONDARY SCHOOLS** *Overall*
position in league tables: 5th out of 149. Top scorers: Tiffin Girls (selective),
Kingston; Tiffin School (boys, selective), Kingston; Coombe Girls, New
Malden • **PRIVATE PREP SCHOOLS** *Holy Cross (girls), Kingston; Rokeby (boys),*
Kingston; The Study School (mixed), New Malden; Shrewsbury House (boys)
Surbiton • **PRIVATE SECONDARY SCHOOLS** *League table leaders Kingston*
Grammar School (mixed), Kingston; Surbiton High (girls), Surbiton; Canbury
School (mixed), Kingston; Marymount International (girls), Kingston.

TRANSPORT***

Trains only throughout the borough, although stations are well spaced and
nowhere is desperately far from a station. Surbiton and New Malden are
best served.

TRAINS *Kingston Zone 6. Cost of annual season ticket £1456. Average*
journey time to Waterloo 25 minutes. New Malden Zone 4. Cost of annual
season ticket £1104. Average journey time to Waterloo 20 minutes.
Surbiton Zone 6. Average journey time to Waterloo 20 minutes.
Chessington South Zone 6. Average journey time to Waterloo 31 minutes
• **BUSES** *Most services link neighbouring suburbs. Surprisingly frequent and*
efficient, even in the most far flung parts of the borough. But no buses go
further into town than Streatham or Tooting. At night the N9 goes to
Kingston from Trafalgar Square and the N77 goes from Trafalgar Square
to Tolworth via New Malden, Kingston and Surbiton • **BOATS** *Run between*
Kingston, Hampton Court and Richmond during the summer • **TRAFFIC**
TROUBLESPOTS *Any road leading off the A3, including Ewell Road and*
Hook Road through Surbiton. Long waits to get onto roundabouts to cross

over the main road for traffic that doesn't want to use the A3. The A3 itself has a constant stream of traffic and can get snarled up, particularly on Friday nights. Kingston: Despite the bypass, the town centre is criss-crossed by busy roads and has an alienating one-way system which forces motorists miles out of their way. Pedestrians face several sets of lights every time they want to cross the road away from the pedestrianised centre. New Malden: Often trafficky around the roundabout next to the pub at the east end of the High Street ● **PARKING** According to residents, difficult even where it shouldn't be, in Kingston Shopping Centre. There are four residents' parking zones in the borough in Kingston town centre, The Grove around Kingston University, Canbury Gardens along Kingston riverside and Surbiton. Cost of annual resident's permit: £60.

LEISURE FACILITIES***

THEATRES & CONCERT HALLS Currently no theatre in Kingston itself, although the Charter Quay development by the river is expected to include a 550-seat theatre. Off-the-wall touring plays, workshops, dance and music at the Douglas Centre, Tolworth. Regular concerts at All Saints Church, Kingston ● **CINEMAS** Only one, the Options ABC in Kingston, showing mostly mainstream films. Residents have to travel to other boroughs for more choice (see Richmond and Merton for example). There are plans for a multiplex cinema on the site of the old bus station by Kingston railway station ● **MUSEUMS & GALLERIES** Thin on the ground, although the Kingston Museum, housed in an elegant 'listed' red brick Edwardian building next to the library, has a fascinating, well laid out and well labelled exhibition of the borough's history from the remains of early wooden boats to the mayoral chain and mace of the now-defunct boroughs of Malden and Coombe and Surbiton. Kingston is very conscious of its long history and its status as a Royal Borough (seven Saxon Kings were crowned there) which, it hopes, sets it apart from other simply suburban boroughs. Local art exhibitions in the library next door ● **SPORTS FACILITIES** Four indoor leisure centres at Tolworth, Chessington, Malden and Kingston with pools, fitness suites and other sports facilities. Watersports including canoeing and sailing at Albany Park Canoe and Sailing Centre, Kingston; outdoor and indoor sports pitches at the Hawker Centre, Kingston. Golf on public courses at New Malden and Chessington. For more passive leisure, Chessington World of Adventure has rides, attractions and the Big Circus (and big traffic jams during school holidays) ● **LIBRARIES** Disappointingly under-used for a middle-class area. Erratic opening hours in some branch libraries (is this the reason for low use or vice versa?) with late opening limited and most libraries closed on Wednesdays. Kingston main library (housed in a listed building next to the museum) and children's library are open on Sunday afternoon. 5.2 library visits per head. Position in library-use league table: 24th out of 32 (where 1 is best and 32 worst).

OPEN SPACES***

A three-star rating may seem mean for a borough surrounded by as much open space as Kingston but many of the spaces most loved by residents (Bushy Park and Richmond Park to the north and Wimbledon Common to the east, for example) are outside the borough boundary (see Richmond and Merton). It scores for its large tracts of open greenbelt land in the south but many of its parks and open spaces are small and flat, pleasant enough but without much character.

RIVER WALKS Canbury Gardens. A pretty slice of green between Kingston town centre and the river. The approach from town is offputting at the moment along a road lined with a couple of derelict houses but developers are working on it. Views across the river to Hampton Wick with handsome Victorian houses and carved wooden boathouses • **WIDE OPEN SPACES** Hogsmill Open Space, Surbiton. The Hogsmill River winds down from the Thames via Kingston to this lush tract of grass, a fleeting rural idyll before suburban houses reappear through the trees.

SHOPS****

KINGSTON Shopping is one of the town's main raisons d'être. Historically a market town, it has now expanded greatly. Its massive Bentall centre set the seal on Kingston as a paradise for shopaholics when it opened in 1992. Three floors of up-market branches of chain stores (many stores testing out the UK market start in Kingston). More shops at the Eden Walk shopping centre and along the network of pedestrianised streets joining the two centres. Big branch of John Lewis. But shoppers confess they find the indoor centres a bit overwhelming. The pleasantest shopping environment is around the Market Place where modern suddenly gives way to medieval with narrow streets and half-timbered houses with smaller, more individual shops and a fruit, vegetable and clothes market. Waitrose and Sainsbury's in the shopping centre • **NEW MALDEN** Official claims that New Malden is 'villagey' are stretching it a bit – it's basically a long, straight high street, mostly lined with chain stores. A Korean supermarket and a couple of Korean restaurants testify to a Korean community here, smaller since boom turned to bust in the Far East a couple of years ago but still noticeable. Big Waitrose near the station • **SURBITON** The 1930s modernist station and forecourt lend an air of elegance to what is essentially another suburban shopping street with small branches of chains, charity shops and banks. Some attractive 19th century terracotta buildings and more manageable than Kingston for a quick pop to the shops. Waitrose and Sainsbury's • **TOLWORTH & CHESSINGTON** Depressing inter-war parades of take-aways, newsagents, chains and building society and bank branches. They are either on busy roads or very nearby. Some boarded-up shops around Tolworth.

RESTAURANTS**

KINGSTON A range of brasseries, patisseries and pubs, with a locally praised (but overpriced) French brasserie by the river near Kingston Bridge. Good Thai on Kingston Hill. But tends to be a bit dead at night and people say they don't always feel safe. There have been some problems with teenage drunkenness outside pubs and clubs • **NEW MALDEN** The place to go locally for Korean food • **SURBITON** A couple of wine bars, pizza chains.

CRIME RATES****

Position in Metropolitan Police league table: 24th out of 32 (where 1 is worst and 32 best).

THE COUNCIL★★★

POLITICAL AFFILIATION *No overall control – Conservative administration*
● **MINUS POINTS** *Under-used library service. One of the most expensive boroughs for property searches* ● **PLUS POINTS** *Excellent schools. Generally efficient and approachable. Door-to-door paper recycling. Efficient rubbish collections* ● **PROPERTY SEARCHES CARRIED OUT IN 10 WORKING DAYS** *99.1%*
● **STANDARD SEARCH FEE** *£133.10* ● **COUNCIL TAX COLLECTED** *91.9%*
● **COUNCIL TAX RATES 2000-2001**

BAND	PROPERTY VALUE	CHARGE	BAND	PROPERTY VALUE	CHARGE
A	up to £40,000	£576	E	£88,001-£120,000	£1,055
B	£40,001-£52,000	£672	F	£120,001-£160,000	£1,247
C	£52,001-£68,000	£768	G	£160,001-£320,000	£1,439
D	£68,001-£88,000	£864	H	over £320,000	£1,727

LAMBETH

Lambeth is one of the few boroughs that even non-Londoners have heard of, and what they've heard isn't flattering. Scene of the Brixton riots in 1981, the borough hit the headlines again later in the same decade when the left-wing councillors running the self-styled People's Republic of Lambeth refused to set annual rates. Tales of incompetent and corrupt councillors and officers continued into the 1990s, culminating in the high-profile appointment of a new chief executive (who has since moved on) to shake up the borough from top to bottom. So far results have been patchy. Residents are noticing improvements in core services like street sweeping and rubbish collections, and council tax levels are now among the lowest in London instead of among the highest. But other vital services like good schools and efficient collection of council tax are still lacking.

Lambeth has assumed an increasingly high profile, thanks partly to the popularity of the Millennium Wheel, which has nearly doubled the number of visitors to the borough's riverfront. There are ambitious plans to revamp the South Bank Arts complex and developers are crowding in to build swanky new riverside apartments in Waterloo and Vauxhall. All very exciting but even Lambeth's biggest supporters admit that Waterloo and Vauxhall are still a trafficky mess. Both these areas are set to benefit from big cash injections totalling £27 million, which will be spent on environmental improvements and a 'state of the art' transport interchange at Vauxhall Cross, giving better pedestrian access to transport links. There are also plans to improve shopping centres, open spaces, public buildings and leisure facilities in the borough's more suburban areas of Norwood and Streatham, as well as in Clapham and Brixton, now firmly on the map as desirable and/or trendy places to live.

Lambeth's section of riverfront in the north of the borough stretches along the south bank from Waterloo's eclectic mix of luxury apartments, council blocks and tucked-away Victorian terraces to the traffic maelstrom of Vauxhall. Inland are the Georgian and

Victorian terraces of Kennington and Stockwell, mixed with more council blocks. Brixton to the south still carries reminders of the smart Victorian suburb it used to be, with many substantial houses and grand public buildings alongside the crumbling terraces and council estates. To the west lie the well-kept Victorian terraces of Clapham Park and the Georgian townhouses of Clapham Old Town. Suburbia begins with Streatham, as 1930s semi-detached and detached houses compete with smart and not-so-smart Victorian and Edwardian houses. At Lambeth's south-eastern tip lie the Victorian villas and terraces of West Norwood and Gipsy Hill which lead up the hill to Crystal Palace.

Despite the recent middle-class influx, Lambeth is still one of the poorest boroughs in London. It's the 12th most deprived area of England and unemployment is high at 8.8%. Crime levels are some of the highest in London. People used to be considered brave for ignoring such downsides and moving to the Lambeth front line. But good transport links, a good choice of still reasonably cheap property, lively street life and energetic ethnic markets are proving a winning combination and turning the area around, particularly in Brixton. Nearly a third of Lambeth's population is from an ethnic minority with a significant Afro-Caribbean community. Kennington and Stockwell are home to supposedly the largest Portuguese community outside Portugal. So if you like your London cosmopolitan and multicultural, this is one of the best places to be.

PROPERTY AND ARCHITECTURE

WATERLOO & KENNINGTON

No one really used to live in Waterloo, an area of dull office blocks dominated by Waterloo Station and an appalling 1960s concrete roundabout with underpasses leading to Waterloo Bridge. Now many of the redundant office blocks and commercial buildings, including the former home of the Greater London Council at County Hall, have been converted into luxury apartments, attracting a new affluent clientele who want to live centrally. Tracts of previously vacant industrial land next to Lambeth and Vauxhall Bridges are being covered with futuristic glass and steel buildings in which penthouses sell for half a million pounds or more. Even the notorious concrete Bullring roundabout has been converted into the IMAX cinema. Period properties are rare in Waterloo, apart from a perfect group of small early-Victorian terraces around Roupell Street just by Waterloo East. Newer houses round Coin Street built after a long battle by local people for homes not offices. Lots of council and ex-council flats in Kennington as well as a mixture of Victorian terraces and handsome Georgian terraces and squares in streets off the Kennington Road.

ATTRACTS *Young professionals wanting to be central; MPs wanting a London base* • **CONSERVATION AREAS** *Waterloo; Roupell Street; South Bank; Mitre Road and Ufford Street; Lambeth Palace; Lambeth Walk and China Walk; Renfrew Road; Walcot; Vauxhall; St Marks* • **AVERAGE PRICES** *Flats: studio £100,000; 1-bed £145,000+; 2-bed £170,000-£300,000 Houses: 2-bed*

£300,000+; 3-bed £350,000+; 4-bed £500,000-£700,000 • **AVERAGE RENTS (WEEKLY)** *Flats: studio £150-£200; 1-bed £180-£220; 2-bed £220-£300 Houses: 2-bed £300+; 3-bed £350-£500; 4-bed £450-£600.*

STOCKWELL & BRIXTON

Lots of still reasonably priced Georgian and Victorian family houses in both areas as well as flats in converted houses. Some of the best houses in Stockwell are in Stockwell Park, an enclave of Georgian family houses off the Clapham Road slightly marred by their proximity to the Stockwell Park council estate. On the other side of the Clapham Road, there are some roads of handsome detached Regency villas among the council property. Brixton is more Victorian with roads of two- and three-storey terraces as well as larger family houses but there are plenty of surprises off the busy main roads, including small Georgian terraces in Trinity Square just behind Brixton Road. Good-sized Victorian terraces in roads off Brixton Water Lane and just north of Brockwell Park off Railton Road, in what estate agents call Poets Corner (the streets are named after poets). Some large Victorian houses by Brockwell Park in cheaper Tulse Hill with lots of council property around the station.

ATTRACTS *Young professionals; creative and media types; City workers who like to think they live on the front line; some families; members of the Afro-Caribbean community* • **CONSERVATION AREAS** *Brixton Road; Stockwell Green; Brixton; Angell Town; Loughborough Park; Trinity Gardens; Brixton Water Lane; Brockwell Park; Rush Common and Brixton Hill; Minet Estate* • **AVERAGE PRICES** *Flats: studio £85,000+; 1-bed £100,000-£140,000+; 2-bed £165,000+ Houses: 2-bed £105,000-£250,000; 3-bed £200,000-£400,000; 4-bed £280,000-£400,000* • **AVERAGE RENTS (WEEKLY)** *Flats: studio £120+; 1-bed £160-£180; 2-bed £200-£240 Houses: 2-bed £250+; 3-bed £300+; 4-bed £400+.*

CLAPHAM

Rapidly displacing Fulham as *the* place for young respectable people to live when they first come to London. But it's also popular with middle-class mums and dads despite the awful reputation of many of Lambeth's schools. Some of the most sought-after properties are well-kept Victorian terraces, some still houses and others converted, around Abbeville Road in Clapham Park. This area is dubbed Abbeville Village by estate agents, enthusiastically backed by residents who claim it feels like a village even if it doesn't look like it. Some marvellous Georgian townhouses overlooking Clapham Common on Clapham Common North Side. The Old Town has a mixture of Georgian and Victorian terraces including the surprising white stucco Grafton Square which wouldn't look out of place in Kensington. Roads of mansion blocks, late Victorian terraces and some early Victorian two-storey Cubitt terraces (many ex-council) around Clapham Manor Street in cheaper Clapham North, where Clapham turns into Stockwell.

ATTRACTS *Young professionals, especially from the City; well off first-time buyers; families* • **CONSERVATION AREAS** *Clapham; Clapham Road; Clapham High Street; The Chase; Clapham Park Road, Northbourne Road; La Retraite* • **AVERAGE PRICES** *Flats: studio £100,000+; 1-bed £140,000-£160,000; 2-bed £185,000-£200,000 Houses: 2-bed £220,000-£330,000; 3-bed £300,000-£400,000; 4-bed £450,000+* • **AVERAGE RENTS (WEEKLY)** *Flats: studio £170-£200; 1-bed £250-£275; 2-bed £300-£325 Houses: 2-bed £350-£400; 3-bed £400-£475; 4-bed £600-£1000.*

STREATHAM

More suburban (and duller) than Clapham but increasingly sought after by families for its large Victorian, Edwardian and 1930s homes as well as first-time buyers who are drawn to the conversion flats. Prices have risen sharply in Streatham as buyers priced out of Clapham and Balham head down here instead. Cheaper 1930s homes in Streatham Vale and grander Victorian and Edwardian detached and semi-detached in streets off Streatham High Road. Some of the best and largest houses are in roads off Streatham Common and in the Telford Park area off Streatham Hill. Newly-converted flats are getting rarer as the council clamps down following the 1980s proliferation of small flats.

ATTRACTS *Families who can't afford the space they want in Clapham or Balham; other buyers who can't afford anything in Balham or Clapham; some first-time buyers* ● **CONSERVATION AREAS** *Hyde Farm; Telford Park; Streatham Hill; Garrads Road; Sunnyhill Road; Leigham Court Road; Streatham Common* ● **AVERAGE PRICES** *Flats: studio £55,000-£65,000; 1-bed £75,000-£100,000; 2-bed £85,000-£120,000 Houses: 2-bed £130,000-£180,000; 3-bed £200,000+; 4-bed £240,000-£300,000* ● **AVERAGE RENTS (WEEKLY)** *Flats: studio £115-£125; 1-bed £150+; 2-bed £175+ Houses: 3-bed £220+; 4-bed £220+.*

WEST NORWOOD & GIPSY HILL

One of the main advantages of this area is that it's very hilly and the views over London are wonderful. A mixture of large Victorian terraces, many converted into flats in the 1980s and others refurbished as single family homes. Victorian cottages in roads in and around more up-market Gipsy Hill and some elegant villas and white stucco terraces. A strong local community feel in roads around Westow Hill, currently united in opposition to plans to build a leisure centre in Crystal Palace Park (see Bromley). West Norwood has roads of Victorian terraces in roads off Norwood High Street with pleasant streets of Edwardian semis in roads to the west of West Norwood station.

ATTRACTS *First-time buyers; families* ● **CONSERVATION AREAS** *Lancaster Avenue; Rosendale Road; West Norwood; Gipsy Hill; Westow Hill North Side* ● **AVERAGE PRICES** *Flats: studio £50,000-£55,000; 1-bed £75,000-£100,000; 2-bed £90,000-£150,000 Houses: 2-bed £120,000-£150,000; 3-bed £140,000-£350,000; 4-bed £200,000-£400,000* ● **AVERAGE RENTS (WEEKLY)** *Flats: studio £105+; 1-bed £150+; 2-bed £175+ Houses: 3-bed £230+; 4-bed £300+.*

BEST POSTCODES

The best postcode is Clapham SW4 followed by Streatham SW16. There can be some big price differences between property in SW4 and neighbouring Brixton SW2. The dividing line between Lambeth and Wandsworth also creates big price differences with people prepared to pay several thousand pounds more to live in cheap, efficient Wandsworth.

AMENITIES

SCHOOLS*

Generally a depressing picture although there are reports that the borough is trying to get to grips with low academic achievement and truancy. State schools both at primary and secondary level consistently perform poorly in league tables and are among London's worst. Middle-class parents fight to get their children into the good schools of neighbouring Wandsworth, Bromley or Croydon or bankrupt themselves to send them to private school in Dulwich. No private prep schools and only one private secondary school. The third lowest proportion of under-fives in state nurseries of any inner London borough but a reasonable selection of private and voluntary nursery schools.

PRE-SCHOOL PROVISION *5 state nurseries; 42 nursery classes in state primary or church schools; 81 private or voluntary nursery schools. Proportion of under-fives in state nurseries: 47%* • **STATE PRIMARY SCHOOLS** *Overall league table position: 136th out of 150. Top scorers: Macaulay C of E (with nursery unit) Clapham; St Mary's RC, Clapham; Corpus Christi RC, Brixton* • **STATE SECONDARY SCHOOLS** *Overall league table position: 141st out of 149. Top scorers: La Retraite RC (girls), Clapham; Dunraven (mixed), Streatham; Bishop Thomas Grant (mixed), Streatham* • **PRIVATE SECONDARY SCHOOLS** *Streatham Hill and Clapham High (girls), Streatham.*

TRANSPORT****

Good, particularly in the north of the borough with a wide choice of tubes and trains. The borough includes Waterloo station. South of Brixton and Clapham there are only trains. Talk of extending the East London line south to Dulwich and Streatham, giving these areas a tube for the first time, could finally be on the cards after years of inaction if Ken Livingstone the mayor of London gives the go-ahead.

TRAINS *Waterloo Zone 1. Cost of annual season ticket £636. Trains to south-west London, south coast as well as Paris and Brussels (Eurostar). Streatham Zone 3. Cost of annual season ticket £896. Average journey time to London Bridge 21 minutes. Gipsy Hill Zone 3. Average journey time to London Bridge 21-24 minutes* • **TUBES** *Waterloo (Bakerloo, Northern and Jubilee) Zone 1. Stockwell (Northern and Victoria) Zone 2. Cost of annual season ticket £756. Average journey time to Charing Cross 11 minutes; to Oxford Circus 10 minutes. Brixton (Victoria) Zone 2. Average journey time to Oxford Circus 12 minutes. Clapham Common (Northern) Zone 2. Average journey time to Charing Cross 14 minutes; to London Bridge 13 minutes* • **BUSES** *An excellent selection in the northern half of the borough with buses converging from all directions. Fewer in the south, around Streatham and Norwood, where many link suburbs rather than going to central London. Buses to town include the 2 from Crystal Palace via West Norwood, Tulse Hill, Brixton, Stockwell and Vauxhall to Marylebone, the 3 from Crystal Palace to Oxford Circus via Brixton and Kennington and the 133 from Streatham Hill via Brixton and Kennington to Liverpool Street* • **TRAFFIC TROUBLESPOTS** *Vauxhall: A horrible traffic interchange, one of the worst legacies of 1960s planners, with one-way systems requiring motorists to change lanes constantly and roads narrowing suddenly from three lanes to one. There are plans to improve the junction for pedestrians and cyclists. Brixton: Very trafficky around the* lights at the junction of the main shopping streets around the town hall where there are too many buses, delivery lorries, cars and pedestrians. There are plans to improve pedestrian crossings on Brixton Road and Brixton Hill which doubles as the main A23. Clapham: Heavy traffic on roads all around Clapham Common and up Clapham High Street. Suffers badly from being at the junction of several major through-roads including the south circular and the A3 to the south coast. Streatham: Like Brixton and Clapham, its main shopping street doubles as a main road. Jams are almost constant at the junction with the south circular. Streatham High Road is the second busiest bus route in London so there are loads of buses but when they're backed up taking on passengers they create traffic jams of their own ● **PARKING** The council is tightening up to discourage commuters from parking and riding. Controlled parking zones are gradually being extended into the south of the borough and already spread over most of the north. There are controlled parking zones throughout Waterloo, Vauxhall, Kennington, Stockwell, Clapham and West Norwood. Parts of Brixton are also controlled. Cost of annual resident's permit: £60.

LEISURE FACILITIES * * * *

THEATRES & CONCERT HALLS Excellent choice of venues, particularly on the South Bank in the north of the borough. Discussions have been going on for years to find ways of making the concrete building of the arts complex and its surroundings more welcoming and some of the high level concrete walkways have been dismantled but it looks as if this one will run and run. The complex includes the National Theatre, (considered part of the West End) as well as concert halls at the Royal Festival Hall, Queen Elizabeth Hall and Purcell Room. The Old Vic and Young Vic theatres are just the other side of Waterloo Station from the National. Open-air theatre at the Rookery, Streatham Common. Live music at The Fridge, Brixton and the Brixton Academy ● **CINEMAS** A very good selection: the repertory National Film Theatre at the South bank complex, the Clapham Picture House, showing a mixture of mainstream and more off-the-wall films, and the Ritzy repertory cinema in Brixton, now grandly restored with government grant money. The ABC and Odeon in Streatham show mainstream films. A huge new multiscreen IMAX cinema showing 3D films on what is claimed to be the largest screen in the UK has been built in the middle of the Bullring roundabout in Waterloo ● **MUSEUMS & GALLERIES** A varied selection, mainly in the north of the borough, ranging from the Aquarium at the former headquarters of the Greater London Council to the quieter pleasures of the Museum of Garden History at Lambeth Palace and the Florence Nightingale Museum at St Thomas's Hospital. Major art exhibitions at the Hayward Gallery ● **SPORTS FACILITIES** Four leisure centres in Brixton, East Brixton, Streatham and Clapham. Indoor swimming pools at Clapham, Brixton and Streatham (which has recently had a £350,000 revamp to improve changing facilities and introduce new health suite and gym facilities). Outdoor swimming at the popular and trendy Brockwell lido (as seen on TV). Football, tennis, cricket and other sports in parks across the borough; ice skating at Streatham Rink which could do with a face-lift but is popular with locals ● **LIBRARIES** The most under-used in London, and old fashioned. But residents' protests against cuts in hours and attempted closures appear to have paid off, with a 14% increase in opening hours last year and a programme of modernisation underway. Hours are still patchy in some branch libraries with widespread closing on Monday mornings as well as all day Thursday. Sunday opening at Streatham and Brixton. 3.1

library visits per head. Position in library-use league table: 31st out of 32 (no information supplied by Hounslow which becomes bottom by default).

OPEN SPACES * * *

Not as generously endowed as neighbouring boroughs and many of its most-loved open spaces (Streatham and Clapham Commons for example) are blighted by being right next to busy main roads. But there are some hidden surprises.

VIEWS *The Rookery, Streatham Common. A secluded walled series of terraced gardens, a riot of floral colour in summer, opening out to great views over south London and Surrey* • **WIDE OPEN SPACES** *Brockwell Park, less flat and trafficky than either Clapham Common or the open parts of Streatham and an excellent antidote to relentlessly urban Brixton. The smaller Kennington Park with mature trees and tennis courts is also worth a visit, as is Myatts Fields, a small gem with Victorian bandstand, surrounded by handsome Victorian houses, between Brixton and Camberwell* • **CEMETERIES** *West Norwood. Not as Gothic as Highgate or Nunhead but pleasantly Victorian.*

SHOPS * * *

WATERLOO, KENNINGTON & VAUXHALL *Mostly shabby local shops on busy main roads, although there are plans to build new shops around Waterloo Station and Vauxhall as part of the huge regeneration effort in the area. Market in Lower Marsh behind Waterloo Station* • **BRIXTON** *The centre of Brixton has had £37.8 million of government money spent on it in the five years to 1998 as part of the Brixton Challenge and there are plans to spend another £1.6 million on environmental improvements. It's now got a much better choice of shops including a big Woolworths, M&S and a Morley's department store to replace the late-lamented Bon Marché (now turned into a number of smaller shops). A new shopping centre around the tube station will bring more high street stalwarts. But it's the lively indoor and outdoor markets in and around Electric Avenue which make shopping in Brixton interesting. Stalls sell Afro-Caribbean food and materials, clothes and fruit and a series of small businesses including Afro-Caribbean hairdressers and a radical bookshop operate from neighbouring railway arches. Tesco in Acre Lane* • **CLAPHAM** *Plentiful shops and restaurants in Clapham High Street although some of it is slightly shabby and down-market, particularly towards Clapham North and the street is trafficky. Mostly chains, including banks and several off-licences, although the local bookshop is holding on. Sainsbury's in strange pointed glass and metal building. Smarter shops around The Pavement in the Old Town, including a delicatessen, picture framer and real butcher, and a handful of up-market local shops in Abbeville Road.* • **STREATHAM** *The shops straggle along the main A23 making shopping here an unpleasant experience. Lots of small branches of chains, ethnic clothes shops and local shops but the high road looks tired with boarded-up shops, particularly down the Common end. Big new Sainsbury's by the Common. Safeway by Streatham Station* • **WEST NORWOOD & GIPSY HILL** *Dull shops at West Norwood with the usual collection of hardware stores, newsagents and Chinese take-aways, a Co-op and Kwiksave. Things get more interesting at the top of Gipsy Hill at Westow Hill, an attractive villagey street with restaurants, clothes and furniture shops among the chains (see also Croydon).*

RESTAURANTS***

WATERLOO *A huge explosion of trendy new restaurants along the South Bank including the Oxo Tower restaurant and the People's Palace at the South Bank complex. Also a good choice around Gabriel's Wharf and The Cut by the Old and Young Vics* • **BRIXTON & STOCKWELL** *A couple of good Portuguese restaurants in Stockwell (there's a significant Portuguese community here and in Vauxhall where there are also good Portuguese restaurants). Bars, Far Eastern, Afro-Caribbean and vegetarian are among a big choice of eateries in Brixton which never seems to go to bed* • **CLAPHAM** *Lots of new restaurants have sprung up to cater for the middle classes especially round the Old Town and in Abbeville 'Village'. Brasseries and pavement cafés lend a European feel to the area and there's a choice of every type of cuisine from Europe to the Far East* • **STREATHAM** *Pizza Express and the usual Indian and Chinese restaurants of varying quality.*

CRIME RATES*

Position in Metropolitan Police league table: 5th out of 32 (where 1 is worst and 32 best).

THE COUNCIL**

POLITICAL AFFILIATION *Labour* • **MINUS POINTS** *Poor schools. Widespread reports from residents of administrative inefficiency. Patchy record of sweeping the streets and collecting rubbish. Poorly-resourced libraries. Charges more than any other inner London borough except Westminster for property searches. Collects less council tax than any other London borough except Hackney* • **PLUS POINTS** *Finally trying to get to grips with the chaos created by years of giving higher priority to ideological dogma than the needs of local people. The fourth lowest council tax in London after cuts. Growing enthusiasm for weekly kerbside recycling of almost anything including glass, cans and textiles as well as newspapers*

- **PROPERTY SEARCHES CARRIED OUT WITHIN 10 WORKING DAYS** *83.8%*
- **STANDARD SEARCH FEE** *£125.70* • **COUNCIL TAX COLLECTED** *80.3%*
- **COUNCIL TAX 2000-2001**

BAND	PROPERTY VALUE	CHARGE	BAND	PROPERTY VALUE	CHARGE
A	up to £40,000	£437	E	£88,001-£120,000	£802
B	£40,001-£52,000	£510	F	£120,001-£160,000	£948
C	£52,001-£68,000	£583	G	£160,001-£320,000	£1,093
D	£68,001-£88,000	£656	H	over £320,000	£1,312

LEWISHAM

Lewisham spent last year promoting itself as the Millennium Fringe, hoping to bask in the reflected glory of neighbouring Greenwich. As everyone now knows, the Millennium celebrations were a damp squib. But Lewisham still entered the 21st century on an upbeat note as long-awaited transport links materialised, partly thanks to the arrival of the Dome. Growing numbers of affluent Londoners working a few stops up the Docklands Light Railway in Canary Wharf took the drastic step of moving south of the river for the first time, property prices rose sharply and no newspaper article or television piece about up-and-coming London was complete without mention of Lewisham.

Shaped like a badly drawn map of the British Isles, the borough of Lewisham has only a tiny slice of riverfront at once-industrial Deptford before it spreads south uphill over the Thames ridge into Victorian suburbia. South of Deptford are the large shabby Victorian houses of New Cross, Brockley and Lewisham itself. On the hill above Lewisham is Blackheath, the jewel in Lewisham's crown, its picturesque village and heath the only part of Lewisham familiar to people from other parts of London. The Victorian villas of Forest Hill and Sydenham cover the hills of south-west Lewisham up to Crystal Palace, giving way to smaller Victorian and Edwardian terraces around Catford and Hither Green. In the south east, 1930s semis take over at Lee and Grove Park as inner city Lewisham changes into outer London at the borders of Bromley.

Lewisham has its middle-class and wealthy enclaves (Blackheath and the best parts of Lee particularly). It likes to characterise itself as an average inner London borough and statistically the incomes of its residents come closest to the London average of any borough. But it's still the 14th most deprived local authority in England. Unemployment stands at 7.3 per cent, and of those who do work, two thirds commute out.

During the past few decades, many of the once elegant houses and shopping centres which testified to Lewisham's 19th-century status as a smart suburb were left to decay gently. At the same time, the riverside and manufacturing industries which had sustained Deptford for centuries gradually disappeared, leaving high unemployment and poverty in their wake. But then successive governments started pumping millions of pounds into the borough, starting with £38 million for Deptford and New Cross to bring in new businesses and improve streetscapes and traffic layout. Lewisham town centre was pedestrianised a few years ago in a bid to make shopping pleasanter and lure shoppers back from Bromley and Bluewater. The town centre is now set to get a £16 million cash injection to expand shopping and leisure facilities, including possibly even a cinema to replace the late lamented Odeon.

For those who relish a good mix of cultures, Lewisham doesn't quite manage the zany atmosphere of Brixton or Peckham, but nearly a quarter of its population comes from an ethnic minority, with substantial Afro-Caribbean, Turkish and Irish communities.

PROPERTY AND ARCHITECTURE

BLACKHEATH & LEE

Blackheath Village is the best part of Lewisham. Unlike many London 'villages', this is the real thing, with pleasing roads of 19th-century shops and cottages sprawling down the hill from the green space of Blackheath, church spires at each end and cafés and restaurants with tables on the wide pavements. A mix of flats above shops, cottages and small, expensive Victorian terraces in the centre of the village. Look for large family houses and generously proportioned converted flats in the streets off the heath towards Lewisham to the west and Kidbrooke to the east. The large Victorian houses in the most desirable parts of Lee around Micheldever, Southbrook and Handen Roads are full of people who can't quite afford to live in Blackheath but aren't short of a bob or two. Lee gets cheaper and more suburban the further south (away from Blackheath) you go, with dull streets of mostly 1930s semis and Victorian terraces where it shades into Hither Green to the west. The closer to Blackheath you are generally, the more expensive it is because you can call it Blackheath borders. Blackheath Standard (named after the Royal Standard pub at its centre) is on the north side of the heath (see Greenwich).

ATTRACTS *Intellectuals and media types who can't afford Hampstead (or don't want to – Glenda Jackson MP for Hampstead and Highgate is a long-standing resident); families who value the open spaces and good primary schools* ● **CONSERVATION AREAS** *Blackheath (around the village and heath); Lee Manor* ● **AVERAGE PRICES** *Flats: studio £65,000-£85,000; 1-bed £80,000-£165,000; 2-bed £100,000-£250,000 Houses: 2-bed £125,000+; 3-bed £150,000-£300,000+; 4-bed £220,000-£450,000+* ● **AVERAGE RENTS (WEEKLY)** *Flats: studio £110-£150; 1-bed £150-£185; 2-bed £180-£205+ Houses: 2-bed £195-£255; 3-bed £195-£300; 4-bed £275+.*

DEPTFORD

Tower blocks dominate the skyline, a reminder of ruthless slum clearance schemes in the 1960s and 1970s. But housing associations and the council are now actively building low-rise homes on a more human scale. There are bargains to be had for first-time buyers prepared to buy ex-council homes sold under the right-to-buy scheme, as well as 1980s starter homes and increasingly flats above shops brought into use as part of the area's regeneration programme. Roads of small attractive Victorian cottages off Brookmill Road in the St John's conservation area and Victorian terraces in roads around Elverson Road DLR station. The arrival of the new Docklands Light Railway link with stations here and at Deptford Bridge has given the whole area a boost.

ATTRACTS *First-time buyers; loyal locals; bargain hunters prepared to move to fringe areas; members of the Afro-Caribbean community* ● **CONSERVATION AREAS** *Deptford High Street; St Paul's [Church]; St John's, Brookmill Road* ● **AVERAGE PRICES** *Flats: studio £45,000+; 1-bed £60,000-£90,000; 2-bed £75,000-£125,000 Houses: 2-bed £100,000-£160,000; 3-bed £115,000-£200,000; 4-bed £155,000-£200,000* ● **AVERAGE RENTS (WEEKLY)** *Flats: studio £85-£150; 1-bed £115-£160; 2-bed £125+; 3-bed £140-£185 Houses: 2-bed £185+; 3-bed £160-£255; 4-bed £230+.*

NEW CROSS & BROCKLEY

Home of some of the best property bargains if you want space. This area has lost out in the past because of the lack of shops and transport links but this has already improved with the advent of Sainsbury's and the DLR extension a short walk away at Deptford Bridge. If the East London Line at New Cross and New Cross Gate is extended up to Hackney and down to

Croydon and Wimbledon as seems likely, prices will soar. The most
sought-after areas are in the conservation areas of New Cross around
Telegraph Hill and Brockley around Hilly Fields, which is laid out with wide
roads lined with large double-fronted Victorian villas. Some have been
converted into flats but others remain as houses, although many of them
need a lot of money spent. The roads around Hilly Fields are becoming
increasingly popular with middle-class families who love the large houses
with many original features still intact. Roads of middle-sized Victorian
terraces and turn of the century semis, many 'improved' with replacement
windows and doors around Honor Oak, south of Brockley.

ATTRACTS *First-time buyers; people who want space; members of the Afro-Caribbean community* • **CONSERVATION AREAS** *Telegraph Hill, Brockley, Hatcham* • **AVERAGE PRICES** *Flats: studio £50,000-£80,000; 1-bed £50,000-£100,000; 2-bed £85,000-£150,000 Houses: 2-bed £115,000+; 3-bed £145,000-£250,000; 4-bed £200,000-£400,000* • **AVERAGE RENTS (WEEKLY)** *Flats: studio £115+; 1-bed £125-£160; 2-bed £140+ Houses: 3-bed £205+; 4-bed+ £275.*

LEWISHAM

A mishmash of council estates and former industrial sites alongside
Victorian terraces and the occasional road of startlingly handsome villas,
particularly to the east of Lewisham High Street. You get a lot of space for
your money. The most expensive properties are on the roads up the hill
towards Blackheath where there are large Edwardian and Victorian villas,
many still family homes. Roads round Granville Park close (but not too
close) to the railway line and the DLR have seen big price rises over the last
year and now are almost as expensive as Blackheath. There are some
good-sized Victorian houses and conversion flats in roads off the high
street to the west in Ladywell and down towards Catford and Hither Green
to the east, mixed in with modern bomb infill and low-rise council estates.

ATTRACTS *First-time buyers; City people working in Canary Wharf who want a quick commute; people who can't afford the space they want in Blackheath or Lee; members of the Afro-Caribbean community* • **CONSERVATION AREAS** *None* • **AVERAGE PRICES** *Flats: studio £50,000+; 1-bed £60,000-£85,000; 2-bed £80,000-£110,000 Houses: 2-bed £130,000+; 3-bed £160,000-£250,000; 4-bed £220,000+* • **AVERAGE RENTS (WEEKLY)** *Flats: studio £95-£105; 1-bed £120+; 2-bed £150+ Houses: 2-bed £155+; 3-bed £185+; 4-bed £230+.*

CATFORD & HITHER GREEN

Mostly two- and three-storey Victorian terraces in Hither Green, many
'improved' with ugly modern windows and pebble-dashing. The effect is
pretty bleak. Parts of Catford are better with large and sought-after
Edwardian family houses on the Corbett Estate and round the Culverley
Green conservation area in Catford in roads off the Bromley Road. There
are smaller terraces in roads off Rushey Green and the south circular. Both
areas have plentiful supplies of conversion flats. Roads round Manor House
Gardens are the best in Hither Green, with some large Victorian and
Edwardian houses. Hither Green is generally more expensive than Catford.

ATTRACTS *First-time buyers, couples trading up to a house from a flat in a more expensive area* • **CONSERVATION AREAS** *Culverley Green* • **AVERAGE PRICES** *Flats: studio £50,000+; 1-bed £60,000-£85,000; 2-bed £70,000+ Houses: 2-bed £120,000+; 3-bed £140,000+; 4-bed+ £170,000-*

*£250,000 • **AVERAGE RENTS (WEEKLY)** Flats: studio £85+; 1-bed £115+; 2-bed £145+ Houses: 2-bed £150+; 3-bed £170+; 4-bed £225+.*

FOREST HILL & SYDENHAM

Once considered very smart by the Victorians, who believed the position high on a ridge above the Thames was health-giving. Many of the huge Victorian villas are now flats but there are still family houses of all types and ages. Some of the best are in the roads round the Horniman Museum and to the west at Upper Sydenham where some have spectacular views. The cheapest properties are in roads off the south circular, which are lined with flat conversions and smaller terraces. These areas are worth watching, particularly if you want a large period property because they will be linked up to the tube network for the first time if the East London line extension goes ahead.

ATTRACTS *Families wanting big houses, gardens and open space, first-time buyers* • **CONSERVATION AREAS** *Forest Hill, Sydenham Park, Sydenham Hill and Jews Walk* • **AVERAGE PRICES** *Flats: studio £55,000-£68,000; 1-bed £75,000-£110,000; 2-bed £90,000-£135,000 Houses: 2-bed £140,000+; 3-bed £160,000-£180,000; 4-bed £200,000-£250,000* • **AVERAGE RENTS (WEEKLY)** *Flats: studio £105+; 1-bed £125+; 2-bed £140-£175 Houses: 3-bed £175-£220; 4-bed £230+.*

GROVE PARK

Where inner London shades off into suburbia. The roads of Grove Park are lined mainly with respectable if dull 1930s family homes and pleasant roads of Edwardian semis. A large number of ex-council properties in neighbouring Downham, a low rise estate of mostly two- and three-bed houses built by the London County Council at the beginning of the 20th-century, come onto the market regularly.

ATTRACTS *Couples moving from inner London, many without children (those with children try to buy over the border in Bromley to get their children into Bromley's sought-after schools); retired people; first-time buyers* • **CONSERVATION AREAS** *None* • **AVERAGE PRICES** *Flats: 1-bed £65,000-£85,000; 2-bed £80,000-£100,000 Houses: 2-bed £90,000-£130,000; 3-bed £100,000-£180,000; 4-bed £180,000+* • **AVERAGE RENTS (WEEKLY)** *Flats: 1-bed £125-£145; 2-bed £150-£185 Houses: 2-bed £150+; 3-bed £195+; 4-bed £230+.*

BEST POSTCODES

Blackheath SE3 is head and shoulders above other postcodes except the parts of Lee SE12 and Lewisham SE13 nearest Blackheath which are nearly as good. Forest Hill SE23 and Sydenham are respectable codes. Prices depend mainly on proximity to open space, good transport links and the cachet of being in a conservation area. Properties in the Brockley, Telegraph Hill and Hatcham conservation areas are a lot more expensive than neighbouring properties outside, say local agents.

AMENITIES

SCHOOLS**

Undistinguished, with state primary and secondary schools consistently languishing near the bottom of the league tables. Above average state nursery provision and a handful of private prep and secondary schools. **PRE-SCHOOL PROVISION** 57 nursery classes in state primary and church schools; 95 private or voluntary nurseries and playgroups; 2 state nurseries. Proportion of under-fives in state nurseries: 64% • **STATE PRIMARY SCHOOLS** Overall league table position: 128th out of 150. Top scorers: All Saints C of E, Blackheath; Kelvin Grove (with nursery unit), Sydenham; Christ Church CE (with nursery unit), Sydenham • **STATE SECONDARY SCHOOLS** Overall league table position: 131st out of 149. Top scorers: Haberdashers' Aske's Hatcham College (mixed), New Cross; Prendergast (girls), Hilly Fields; Sydenham (girls), Sydenham • **PRIVATE PREP SCHOOLS** St Dunstan's Prep (mixed), Catford; Sydenham High Junior (girls) Sydenham • **PRIVATE SECONDARY SCHOOLS** Chart-topper Sydenham High (girls), Sydenham and St Dunstan's College (mixed), Catford.

TRANSPORT***

TRAINS Until the DLR extension opened, the borough's only connection with the tube network was on the East London Line at New Cross. But the DLR has improved links at Deptford and Lewisham dramatically. Train services, by contrast, are variable, with Lewisham and Hither Green best served. Blackheath Zone 3. Cost of annual season ticket £896. Average journey time to London Bridge 12 minutes; to Charing Cross 21 minutes; to Victoria 22 minutes. Deptford Zone 2. Cost of annual season ticket £756. Average journey time to London Bridge 8 minutes; to Charing Cross 15 minutes. New Cross Zone 2. Average journey time to London Bridge 6 minutes; to Charing Cross 14 minutes. Lewisham Zone 2. Average journey time to London Bridge 10 minutes; to Charing Cross 17 minutes; to Victoria 20 minutes. Hither Green Zone 3. Average journey time to London Bridge 13 minutes; to Charing Cross 21 minutes. Forest Hill Zone 3. Average journey time to London Bridge 14 minutes; to Charing Cross 22 minutes; to Victoria 30 minutes. Grove Park Zone 4. Cost of annual season ticket £1104. Average journey time to London Bridge 15 minutes; to Charing Cross 23 minutes • **TUBES** New Cross and New Cross Gate (East London). Average journey time to Whitechapel 12 minutes • **DLR** Lewisham Zone 2. Average journey time to Bank 27 minutes • **BUSES** An estimated 100 buses an hour pass through Lewisham town centre mostly linking suburbs and providing services to shopping areas like Bromley. Services to town include the 36 from Lewisham via New Cross to Victoria, the 21 from Lewisham to London Bridge and Moorgate and the 47 from Catford to Shoreditch via Deptford. The 53 crosses Blackheath on its journey to Oxford Circus via Deptford and the 185 goes via Forest Hill and Lewisham to Victoria • **TRAFFIC TROUBLESPOTS** Lewisham town centre: The main part of the high street was pedestrianised five years ago as part of a £37 million revamp of the town centre. Shopping is pleasanter but traffic jams are frequent on the roads skirting the area. The large roundabout recently built by the bus station is where several main roads meet and badly-timed traffic lights at Lewisham High Street clog up traffic. Deptford: Carved up by trafficky roads including the main A2 from London to Dover. The south circular: Runs through Catford and Forest Hill much of the time on residential roads not built for the volume of traffic. Blackheath: Delivery vans and badly parked cars frequently block the narrow roads of Blackheath Village and clumsily sited residents' parking bays frequently force traffic coming into the village to a standstill. The A2 road across Blackheath suffers from heavy lorries banned from using Greenwich • **PARKING** There are controlled parking zones around Lewisham town centre and residential roads around the station to stop unofficial park-and-riding, and in Blackheath. Parking in either centre is a nightmare on Saturdays and wardens are strict. Cost of annual resident's permit: £25, valid only in the zone for which it's issued.

LEISURE FACILITIES***

THEATRES & CONCERT HALLS The Blackheath Concert Halls, in a beautiful Victorian building constructed for the purpose, were rescued from closure four years ago after a campaign raised £50,000 from members of the public, which brought promises of further funding. The halls are the borough's main venue for classical concerts, jazz and theatre. The Lewisham Theatre in Catford has middle-of-the-road plays, family shows, pantomimes and musicals. But it's looking a bit tired and it's to have £2 million spent on it over the next three years to revamp its seating and generally perk it up. The Albany Theatre in Deptford, also recently recovered from funding problems, specialises in community plays and performances. Pub theatre at the Brockley Jack in Brockley and concerts by students at the Blackheath Conservatoire • **CINEMAS** Currently a poor show – the Catford ABC (mainly blockbusters) is the only cinema in the borough. There are plans for a new 12-screen multiplex cinema in Lewisham town centre • **MUSEUMS** Just one museum, the Horniman, housed in a brilliant art nouveau building with a rounded stone tower high on the slopes of Forest Hill. It has an eclectic selection of stuffed birds, skeletons, tribal masks and other objects brought together by Victorian tea merchant and MP Frederick Horniman. The museum's gardens have panoramic views over south London. An ambitious building programme is underway to improve visitor facilities and build new galleries for the famous musical instrument collection and the anthropology collection • **SPORTS FACILITIES** Four leisure centres at Deptford, Brockley, Sydenham and Ladywell and pools at Forest Hill and Deptford. There is a new fitness centre and revamped pool at Ladywell but it and the other centres are still shabby and cramped and compare unfavourably with provision in neighbouring boroughs (notably Greenwich). Downham could get a new state of the art library, leisure and health centre à la Peckham Pulse (see Southwark) if Lewisham council succeeds in getting private sector cash. Greyhound racing at Catford. Golf at Beckenham Place Park and tennis and other sports in parks across the borough. Millwall Football Club has its ground at Deptford • **LIBRARIES** A new central library with modern computer systems and referencing equipment was installed in Lewisham High Street six years ago and is now well-used, well-stocked and open reasonable hours. Some smaller branch libraries have come under repeated threat over the past few years and only huge opposition from residents succeeded in halting the closure of branches in Blackheath, Lee and Grove Park. Library use has fallen sharply over the past year. 5.85 library visits per head. Position in library-use league table: 21st out of 32 (where 1 is best and 32 worst).

OPEN SPACES***

Lewisham may not look its best from the window of a bus, train or car but there are more than 40 parks and 15% of the borough is green space. The borough is built on hills so there are some excellent views over London. But some of the parks and green space show signs of neglect, with litter and graffiti. Blackheath fights a constant battle against litter and illegal car parking. **VIEWS** *Blackheath. A large grassy, windswept plateau with views over to Docklands and the City to the north and south London to the south. You either dismiss Blackheath as featureless and trafficky or love it for its big skies and space. Hilly Fields in Brockley also has excellent all round views. Good views amid attractive surroundings at Horniman Gardens*
- **CHILDREN'S ATTRACTIONS** *The Zoo at Horniman Gardens* • **GARDENS** *Manor House Gardens in Lee have just been overhauled and it's now a pleasure to stroll by the cleaned up lake. The gardens are the setting for the 18th-century Manor House, once the home of Sir Francis Baring of the banking family. Beckenham Place Park in the very south of the borough is also worth a visit. Lewisham's largest park, it has a good variety of woodland and open space and a public golf course. The park is part of the Green Chain Walk, which has 40 miles of paths linking south east London's green spaces (see also Greenwich, Bexley and Bromley). Rumours last year that a kangaroo was roaming loose at Beckenham Place proved unfounded.*

SHOPS***

BLACKHEATH *Some interesting independent shops line the Victorian streets of the village including a bookshop, a kitchen shop, antique shops and an up-market Oxfam. But high rents are forcing independent traders out and they're being replaced by branches of restaurant chains (Café Rouge, Costa Coffee) and branches of estate agent chains. Late night shopping at Costcutter* • **DEPTFORD** *Shabby but interesting shops in Deptford High Street, now mostly pedestrianised. A big Afro-Caribbean and African presence, with fruit and vegetable stalls selling yams and sweet potato, clothes shops selling African clothes, lots of small discount traders and ethnic take-aways and restaurants. Raucous Wednesday and Saturday market with stallholders giving vigorous demonstrations of their wares. Kitchen equipment, clothes and food figure heavily. Antique furniture shops along Deptford Broadway. Sainsbury's superstore at New Cross*
- **LEWISHAM** *Frequently touted (mainly by the council) as south-east London's premier shopping centre but has been steadily losing ground over the past ten years to Bromley, Lakeside at Thurrock and Bluewater (to which, ironically there is a direct bus service from Lewisham High Street). Pedestrianisation was meant to revive Lewisham's fortunes but branches of chain stores are mainly small, stock is limited and there are too many tell-tale empty shops filled with fly-by-night traders selling cheap goods. There's a huge gap in the middle of the high street which was the late and lamented Army & Navy, Lewisham's last department store. Plans to build a high security police station here met with outcries from residents but three years on no-one knows what will fill the hole. Daily market selling mainly fruit, vegetables and flowers. Tesco by the station, Sainsbury's in the shopping centre* • **CATFORD** *Currently as tired as Lewisham with its main shops housed in a 1960s concrete shopping centre below council flats. A major revamp of the area is planned, with new shops and facilities, pedestrianisation of the space between town hall buildings and the creation of a new arts centre at Lewisham Theatre. But so far the results*

*have been dreary. A large McDonalds has sprung up by the one-way system opposite a terrace of bricked up Victorian houses waiting to be repaired. Tesco in the shopping centre ● **OTHER AREAS** Forest Hill, Hither Green and Sydenham have mainly local parades of shops with people going elsewhere for major shopping. Lee has several good pine furniture shops in the high road. Sainsbury's at Lee Green.*

RESTAURANTS***

BLACKHEATH *A big choice of restaurants (too big say many residents, who have seen shops disappear to be replaced by restaurants). The range includes Thai, Indian, Italian, French, Vietnamese and Chapter Two, a widely praised modern European restaurant ● **DEPTFORD & NEW CROSS** Deptford has pie and mash, Indonesian and a couple of good noodle bars. There are signs of a small but growing middle class presence with the arrival of an Internet café and other cafés which rise above the greasy spoon level. New Cross has good Turkish and Thai restaurants ● **FOREST HILL & SYDENHAM** Recommended Indian, Thai and Turkish restaurants ● **ELSEWHERE** Little of note. Lewisham and Catford are virtually dead after about nine o'clock.*

CRIME RATES**

Place in Metropolitan Police league table: 18th out of 32 (where 1 is worst and 32 best).

THE COUNCIL***

POLITICAL AFFILIATION *Labour* ● **MINUS POINTS** *Poor performing schools. Variable standards of street-sweeping and litter collection with lots of old rubbish sacks and uncollected litter in corners particularly in Lewisham town centre* ● **PLUS POINTS** *General efficiency much improved over the last decade. Has stepped up its efforts to encourage feedback from residents on issues like council spending and efficiency of litter collections and was one of the first boroughs to create a Citizens' Panel. Energetically fighting back against 'enviro-crimes' – graffiti, flytipping, dog fouling. The first London borough to set out proposals for a directly elected mayor. Cheaper council tax than neighbouring inner London boroughs (although not cheaper than Bromley). Door-to-door recycling scheme being expanded* ●
PROPERTY SEARCHES CARRIED OUT IN 10 WORKING DAYS *91%*
● **STANDARD SEARCH FEE** *£115* ● **COUNCIL TAX COLLECTED** *90.6%*
● **COUNCIL TAX 2000-2001**

BAND	PROPERTY VALUE	CHARGE	BAND	PROPERTY VALUE	CHARGE
A	up to £40,000	£532	E	£88,001-£120,000	£976
B	£40,001-£52,000	£621	F	£120,001-£160,000	£1,153
C	£52,001-£68,000	£710	G	£160,001-£320,000	£1,330
D	£68,001-£88,000	£798	H	over £320,000	£1,597

MERTON

Merton isn't all dull suburbia. But much of it could be anywhere in the layer of outer London built up in the last 20 years of the 19th century and the first 30 years of the 20th. The streets of small semis and terraces, some lined with trees and some without, the tangle of crescents and cul-de-sacs turning onto busy main roads, the tatty parades of shops, the roadhouse-style pubs strategically placed at roundabouts, will all be familiar to anyone who's ever passed through the outskirts of any major city, not just London. All of which is why Wimbledon village, an attractive Victorian sprawl of small shops and cottages on the edge of one of London's best commons, doesn't feel part of the borough at all.

Wimbledon, mostly Victorian around the centre and in the village with big detached houses further towards Wimbledon Common, dominates the north west of the borough and is familiar to anyone who has ever trudged for miles or queued to get into the All England tennis ground during Wimbledon fortnight. Around Wimbledon is the amorphous Victorian sprawl of South Wimbledon to the east, relieved by the attractive garden suburb of Merton Park and the late Victorian and Edwardian terraces of Raynes Park to the west. In Mitcham, the satisfying open space of Mitcham Common breaks the monotony of 1930s semis which reaches round to Morden.

People commute from Merton but it isn't classic middle-class commuter-belt country like parts of neighbouring Sutton or Kingston. It's more ethnically diverse for a start, with 16% of its population coming from an ethnic minority and significant communities of Indians and Afro-Caribbeans. Unemployment is higher, at 2.7%, although this is still lower than some outer boroughs in north London. Unlike other suburban boroughs, its most favoured and wealthiest parts are those closest to London rather than as far away from the inner city as possible.

An abundance of green space and good transport links, particularly in the north, are major draws for middle class parents, although the schools haven't performed as well as neighbouring boroughs in the past and there's a fair bit of migration across borough boundaries. Wimbledon itself has become a popular follow-up move to Clapham or even Fulham, favoured by young couples and professionals who like the shops and restaurants and the quick train and tube links to town without the noise and dirt of the inner city.

Escaping traffic isn't, however, that simple. Traffic is one of Merton's big problems. It has its fair share of through roads out to the M25 and beyond, many of which double up as shopping centres, and residents themselves have high levels of car ownership. It remains to be seen whether the gleaming red and white trams now whizzing up and down the eastern side of the borough from Wimbledon to Croydon via Mitcham and Morden will persuade more people to abandon their cars in favour of public transport.

PROPERTY AND ARCHITECTURE

WIMBLEDON & WIMBLEDON VILLAGE

Wimbledon isn't all smart. It's sprawling and includes some roads of very ordinary Victorian and Edwardian terraces. But it also includes Wimbledon Village, the most expensive and sought-after part of Merton borough, with a mix of Victorian cottages and large detached and semi-detached houses of all vintages from Victorian to modern. Lots of modern apartment blocks and new developments on Wimbledon Hill Road. Victorian and Edwardian family homes and huge detached houses in tree-lined roads off Parkside between Wimbledon Common and Wimbledon Park, with discreetly large gardens behind high walls or hedges. Some have panoramic views across the park towards London.

ATTRACTS *Families; first-time buyers; young professionals; people wanting more space for their money than they could get in Clapham or Fulham; Norwegians wanting to be near the Norwegian School* ● **CONSERVATION AREAS** *North Wimbledon; Bathgate Road; Wimbledon Windmill; Wimbledon Hill Road; Vineyard Hill Road; Kenilworth Avenue; Leopold Road; Wimbledon Broadway; South Park Gardens* ● **AVERAGE PRICES** *Flats: studio £80,000; 1-bed £140,000-£165,000; 2-bed £180,000-£200,000 Houses: 2-bed £240,000-£350,000; 3-bed £250,000+; 4-bed £340,000+* ● **AVERAGE RENTS (WEEKLY)** *Flats: studio £130+; 1-bed £160+; 2-bed £195+ Houses: 2-bed £205-£230+; 3-bed £255+; 4-bed £330+.*

RAYNES PARK & SOUTH WIMBLEDON

The further north you go in Raynes Park the better it is because you're that bit nearer Wimbledon. Once you get north of Worple Road you can call it West Wimbledon. A mix of family houses on the hill up towards Wimbledon and smaller semis and Victorian semis near the railway line. Lots of semi-detached three- and four-bedroom 1930s houses in roads off Grands Drive further south, overlooking rather bleak, flat recreation grounds. In the grid of 12 roads known as the Apostles off Kingston Road by Raynes Park station there are small Edwardian terraces. The usual assortment of terraces and semis in small gardens is interrupted by Merton Park, an attractive mixture of Victorian cottages and villas laid out in the 1870s near the lovely Morden Hall Park. Prices here are more akin to Wimbledon proper.

ATTRACTS *Families; first-time buyers; people who can't afford Wimbledon* ● **CONSERVATION AREAS** *West Wimbledon; Drax Avenue; Copse Hill; Durham Road; Lambton Road; Dunmore Road; Wool Road; John Innes Merton Hall Park; John Innes Wilton Crescent; Quintin Avenue and Richmond Avenue; Merton Hall Road* ● **AVERAGE PRICES** *Flats: studio £70,000; 1-bed £110,000+; 2-bed £120,000-£130,000 Houses: 2-bed £180,000+; 3-bed £195,000+; 4-bed £230,000+* ● **AVERAGE RENTS (WEEKLY)** *Flats: studio £130+; 1-bed £160+; 2-bed £195+ Houses: 3-bed £205+; 4-bed £255+.*

COLLIERS WOOD, MITCHAM & MORDEN

Mitcham is the cheapest of these three because there's no tube, trains go from Mitcham Junction rather than the more central Mitcham and the tram, although welcome, goes to Wimbledon rather than central London. The tube is the main attraction of Colliers Wood, marginally the most expensive of the three areas. It has mostly streets of Victorian terraces and 1930s semis in various stages of misguided 'improvements' and/or in need of painting, and council blocks. Worth looking at for reasonably cheap houses and conversion flats. Its supporters claim that it has a good community spirit. Mitcham has some attractive Victorian cottages in roads along the east side of the common and near the centre around Cricket Green but this soon gives way to more suburbia and modern blocks. Much of Morden is occupied by the St Helier estate (see Sutton) which is good for small, cheap houses.

ATTRACTS *Loyal locals; first-time buyers; people who can't afford Tooting or Streatham* • **CONSERVATION AREAS** *Wandle Valley; Mitcham Cricket Green; Upper Morden* • **AVERAGE PRICES** *Flats: studio £60,000-£80,000; 1-bed £80,000-£95,000; 2-bed £100,000-£120,000 Houses: 2-bed £125,000-£140,000; 3-bed £135,000-£170,000; 4-bed £165,000-£192,000* • **AVERAGE RENTS (WEEKLY)** *Flats: studio £85-£100; 1-bed £110-£140; 2-bed £140-£175 Houses: 2-bed £170+; 3-bed £170+*

BEST POSTCODES

Not really an issue as most of the borough has Surrey postcodes. Wimbledon SW19 is a smart London postcode and better than West Wimbledon SW20.

AMENITIES

SCHOOLS ***

Merton's schools are set to undergo massive upheaval in the next few years as the borough converts from its existing three-tiered system of primary (5–8), middle (9–13) and high school (13–19) to a more usual two tiered primary/secondary school pattern. Merton pioneered the three tier system in the late 1960s in the fond hope that everyone was going to follow suit. They didn't, and now that the national curriculum and key stage tests have been brought in, the set-up is looking increasingly cumbersome. The change, which has widespread local support, has been approved by the Secretary of State and will cost £40 million in new school buildings and general reorganisation. Possibly because of the current structure, league table performance isn't as good as in other outer London boroughs, particularly at primary level. There is however some of the most generous state pre-school provision anywhere in London as well as a good range of private nursery education and some excellent private secondary schools.

PRE-SCHOOL PROVISION *37 nursery classes in state primary or church schools (all Merton schools have nursery units); 55 private or voluntary nurseries and playgroups. Proportion of under-fives in state nurseries: 85%* • **STATE MIDDLE SCHOOLS** *Overall league table position: 77th out of 150. Top scorers: Wimbledon Chase, Wimbledon; St Catherine's RC, West Wimbledon; Park House, Wimbledon* • **STATE HIGH SCHOOLS** *Overall league table position: 106th out of 149. Top scorers: Ricards Lodge (girls), Wimbledon; Ursuline Convent RC (girls), Raynes Park; Wimbledon College*

*RC (boys), Wimbledon • **PRIVATE PREP SCHOOLS** Hazelhurst (girls, to 16),
Wimbledon; Kings College Junior School (boys), Wimbledon; The Study
Prep (girls), Wimbledon • **PRIVATE SECONDARY SCHOOLS** Wimbledon High
(girls), Wimbledon; Kings College (boys), Wimbledon.*

TRANSPORT * * *

Wimbledon has an excellent train service and is on the District Line for
tubes. Elsewhere it's not so good. The Northern Line extends to Morden
and Colliers Wood although it's a long tedious journey to town. Mitcham
is worst off, with no decent train or tube service less than a bus ride away.
Transport has improved with Tramlink which gives Mitcham at least a direct
link to Wimbledon and Croydon and points beyond (see Croydon).
TRAINS *Wimbledon Zone 3. Cost of annual season ticket £896. Average
journey time to Waterloo 16 minutes. Mitcham Junction Zone 4. Cost of
annual season ticket £1104. Average journey time to Victoria 19 minutes;
to Blackfriars 28 minutes. Raynes Park Zone 4. Average journey time to
Waterloo 20 minutes • **TUBES** Wimbledon (District) Zone 3. Average
journey time to Victoria 25 minutes. Colliers Wood (Northern) Zone 3.
Average journey time to Waterloo 22 minutes • **TRAMLINK** Wimbledon.
Average journey time to East Croydon 25 minutes • **BUSES** Wimbledon has
the best bus service – many pass through and some terminate there.
Elsewhere in the borough, there's a choice of just one or two buses, mostly
linking neighbouring suburbs, and the most central destinations are
Streatham, Tooting or Brixton. The N155 night bus goes from Trafalgar
Square to Colliers Wood, Merton, South Wimbledon and Morden
• **TRAFFIC TROUBLESPOTS** Wimbledon & Wimbledon Village: Heavy traffic
including buses and delivery lorries in the centre of Wimbledon itself where
none of the shopping streets are pedestrianised. Wimbledon Hill and
Wimbledon Village have constant streams of cars and heavy lorries, rather
spoiling the otherwise pleasant experience of eating al fresco in the
Village. Merton High Street: Long tail-backs at the junctions with Haydons
Road and Merton Road and trafficky around the junction with the A24,
which slices through Merton on its way to Sutton and beyond. Morden: The
main shopping street in Morden, London Road, doubles as the A24 which
is often jammed with traffic • **PARKING** A rapid spread of controlled
parking zones across the borough in the last two years. There are now 13
separate zones in Wimbledon, and further zones in Raynes Park (two) and
Morden (four). A further two are set to be implemented in Wimbledon
Park. Cost of annual resident's permit: £27.50 for the first car; £50 for a
subsequent car.*

LEISURE FACILITIES * * *

THEATRES & CONCERT HALLS *The recently revamped Wimbledon Theatre in
an ornate Edwardian building on the Broadway has a range of plays and
family shows, as does the Polka Children's Theatre. Fringe theatre at The
Studio, Wimbledon. The Colour House Theatre in a former industrial dye
house at Merton Abbey Mills (see below) has more off-beat and fringe
shows • **CINEMAS** Currently only one, the Odeon in Wimbledon, showing
mainstream films • **MUSEUMS & GALLERIES** A fun selection of small specialist
museums including the Wimbledon Lawn Tennis Museum relating the story
of how tennis changed from a polite amateur pitpat to 200 mile an hour
service games. The Wimbledon Windmill Museum on Wimbledon
Common with exhibitions on the working of windmills and the Wimbledon
local history museum (only open on Saturdays). The complex of former*

industrial buildings at Merton Abbey Mills, on the river Wandle, which used to be a Liberty silk-printing mill, has a small exhibition on the history of the river and its industries (William Morris rented workshops here for printing his designs) • **SPORTS FACILITIES** Leisure centres in Mitcham and Wimbledon with fitness centres, classes and pools. Riding on Wimbledon Common. Tennis, football, cricket and facilities for other team games in parks and open spaces across the borough • **LIBRARIES** Well used, well spaced around the borough. There have been battles with residents over library closures but opening hours have recently been tidied up (no more scrappy half day or lunchtime closing) and extended, adding an estimated 39 hours of open library time a week. No one day when all the borough's libraries are closed, except Sunday. 8.6 library visits per head. Position in library-use league table: 6th out of 32 (where 1 is best and 32 worst).

OPEN SPACES****

A very good range of open spaces, including most of Wimbledon Common, with its woods, open land and golf courses.

RIVER WALKS The Wandle Trail along the River Wandle through Merton Abbey Mills and Morden Hall Park. A peaceful walk beside a (mostly) clear-flowing river with reedy banks, overhanging trees and rows of electricity pylons to remind you that you're really in a city (see also Wandsworth). Morden Hall Park belongs to the National Trust and has the usual craft and tea shops, carefully labelled direction arrows and well-kept parkland overlooked by Morden Hall, a handsome white stucco house built in 1770 • **WIDE OPEN SPACES** Wimbledon Park. Duller than the Common but with good views across London over a landscaped lake and lawns designed by Capability Brown. Mitcham Common, a large tract of open heathland • **WOODS** Wimbledon Common. As well as extensive open spaces, there are plentiful walks up and down hills through mature woods where you feel 100 miles from London.

SHOPS***

WIMBLEDON & WIMBLEDON VILLAGE The best shopping areas in the borough. The Centre Court shopping centre right next to Wimbledon station has several storeys of mostly up-market chains (particularly clothes shops) and a large Debenhams. Less overwhelming than Croydon or even Sutton. More good branches of chain stores in streets around the shopping centre. More shops and leisure facilities are being built at the east end of the Broadway, as an added incentive to travel to Wimbledon by Tramlink and traffic calming measures are having some impact. The shops get smaller and more specialist (furniture, antiques, designer clothes and shoes) up Wimbledon Hill Road and into Wimbledon Village. Safeway and Tesco metro in central Wimbledon • **MITCHAM** Dull parades of local shops. The usual selection of take-aways, newsagents, charity shops and branches of banks and building societies • **MERTON & COLLIERS WOOD** More dreary high streets with empty shops to let, take-aways and hardware shops. Tesco in Colliers Wood. But Merton has Merton Abbey Mills, with craft shops, a second-hand bookshop and weekend antique market all housed in carefully restored former industrial buildings. Sainsbury's Savacentre at Merton and retail park at Colliers Wood with Boots and Next • **MORDEN** An ugly, busy shopping street (aka the A24) lined with charity shops, greasy take-aways, predictable chains and lots of shops to let. Bleak and dominated by the grim curving tower block of the civic centre.

RESTAURANTS ★ ★ ★

WIMBLEDON & WIMBLEDON VILLAGE *Every yuppie restaurant and bar chain in the book in Wimbledon Village including Dôme, Café Rouge, Pizza Express and All Bar One (down the hill towards Wimbledon) as well as a selection of local brasseries and restaurants. Most have tables outside for a touch of café society. A bit predictable if you want something out of the ordinary but pleasant. A good Indian in Wimbledon Hill Road and a couple of good winebars in Wimbledon itself* ● **ELSEWHERE** *Nothing special. An assortment of variable ethnic (read the usual Indian and Chinese restaurants, burger bars and fast food joints).*

CRIME RATES ★ ★ ★ ★

Position in Metropolitan Police league table: 28th out of 32 (where 1 is worst and 32 best).

THE COUNCIL ★ ★ ★

POLITICAL AFFILIATION *Labour* ● **MINUS POINTS** *Complex school system which no longer fits in with National Curriculum. Has had big problems with rubbish collections but these seem to have been resolved* ● **PLUS POINTS** *Enthusiastically green and keen on recycling. Planning to extend green box recycling scheme throughout the borough. Couldn't be quicker at turning round land searches* ● **PROPERTY SEARCHES IN 10 WORKING DAYS** *100%* ● **STANDARD SEARCH FEE** £*130* ● **COUNCIL TAX COLLECTED** *95.1%*
● **COUNCIL TAX 2000-2001**

BAND	PROPERTY VALUE	CHARGE	BAND	PROPERTY VALUE	CHARGE
A	up to £40,000	£578	E	£88,001-£120,000	£1,059
B	£40,001-£52,000	£674	F	£120,001-£160,000	£1,252
C	£52,001-£68,000	£770	G	£160,001-£320,000	£1,444
D	£68,001-£88,000	£867	H	over £320,000	£1,733

NEWHAM

'Where's Newham?' is the first question many people, including Londoners, ask. And with some justification. Even its most fervent supporters wouldn't call it architecturally exciting. It has few obvious tourist attractions to draw people into the borough and being out in the hinterland of the old docks to the east has put it beyond the pale for many who refuse to venture further from the centre of town than Canary Wharf.

This is the part of the East End the tourists don't see. It's not trendy and arty like Spitalfields or full of people with 'lifestyles' like the Isle of Dogs. It stretches from the traffic-clogged roads and tangled railway lines of Stratford East across to the suburbs of Forest Gate and Manor Park, criss-crossed with mind-boggling miles of straight, flat streets of late Victorian and 1930s terraces. Slightly to the south, the larger double-fronted Victorian houses of Woodgrange Park temporarily relieve the architectural tedium which takes over again throughout much of East Ham, West Ham and Plaistow. To the south around the old Royal Docks, brash new homes are springing up around Beckton, east of the council sprawls of Canning Town and Custom House. Almost forgotten, sandwiched between the docks and the river, is the Victorian huddle of North Woolwich.

The only leagues headed by Newham are deprivation leagues. It is ranked as the second most severely deprived district in England. Levels of unemployment, at 9.2%, are the third highest in London.

But the last few years have witnessed a whirl of regeneration activity in Newham. Massive sums of government money are pouring into regeneration schemes across the borough, hit hard by the decline of the docks and traditional manufacturing industry. The money is intended to improve transport links and infrastructure, cut crime and improve education and employment chances.

One of the chief beneficiaries is Stratford, with a huge £15 million glass station to incorporate its new Jubilee Line link, a £3 million refurbishment of its shopping centre, an £8 million performing arts centre to expand the existing Theatre Royal and a £3.3 million library. It will also be the major London interchange for the long awaited Channel Tunnel Rail Link. Canning Town, one of the poorest parts of Newham, is having £100 million spent on it over the next five years and access to central London and Stratford has already improved dramatically with an architect-designed station for the Jubilee Line extension. A huge exhibition centre and a business park are being built alongside the Royal Victoria Dock at Beckton in the south of the borough and the University of East London's Docklands campus at the Royal Albert Dock is finished.

All this, coupled with some of the cheapest property in London, is already making Newham popular with people working in the city who value quick transport to town. The borough is also one of the most multicultural in London – more than half of its inhabitants come from ethnic minorities, which injects a bit of interest into the drab Victorian streets.

PROPERTY AND ARCHITECTURE

STRATFORD

Stratford has improved a lot in the past couple of years. It still has grim tower blocks and crumbling 1960s office blocks around the bus and rail stations but many of these are being bought up and redeveloped as flats. The tube/rail station itself is an elegant construction of steel and glass and the town centre round the church has been tidied up although it's still trafficky. There are roads of mostly two-storey Victorian terraces off main roads out of the town centre. Check out roads near the station off West Ham Lane and Romford Road for reasonably-priced two- and three-bedroom houses near good transport links. Larger five-bedroom Victorian houses further up Romford Road are mostly rented out or converted into flats. Prices are rising as money is pumped into the area and promised transport links open up.

ATTRACTS *Growing numbers of young, up-market people working in the City; bargain hunters; lawyers working in the nearby courts wanting pieds-à-terre; first-time buyers; investors* • **CONSERVATION AREAS** *University; Three Mills* • **AVERAGE PRICES** *Flats: studio £70,000; 1-bed £85,000+; 2-bed £90,000+ Houses: 2-bed £110,000-£120,000; 3-bed £135,000-£170,000; 4-bed £200,000+* • **AVERAGE RENTS (WEEKLY)** *Flats: studio £100; 1-bed £130; 2-bed £160 Houses: 2-bed £180; 3-bed £220; 4-bed £250.*

FOREST GATE & UPTON

North of the Forest Gate and Woodgrange Park railway line, roads of Victorian and 1930s terraces stretch out in every direction, their monotony broken up only by 'improvements' wrought by successive home owners (louvred windows, pebble-dash and elaborate front doors). Good cheap house and flat-buying territory. Much larger and more attractive Victorian houses are south of the railway line and west of Woodgrange Road in what's known as the Woodgrange Estate. Many are detached and double-fronted with large front gardens. This together with Capel Road, opposite Wanstead Flats (in Redbridge) is widely considered one of the best parts of Newham. More terraces to the south in Upton, mostly with two and three bedrooms.

ATTRACTS *First-time buyers; people wanting a lot of space for their money; members of the Asian community* • **CONSERVATION AREAS** *Woodgrange; Capel Road and City of London Cemetery* • **AVERAGE PRICES** *Flats: 1-bed £65,000+; 2-bed £70,000+ Houses: 2-bed £95,000-£105,000+; 3-bed £125,000+; 4-bed £160,000-£220,000* • **AVERAGE RENTS (WEEKLY)** *Flats: 1-bed £110-£150; 2-bed £165+ Houses: 2-bed £185; 3-bed £200+.*

MANOR PARK & EAST HAM

Larger three- and four-bedroom Victorian and 1930s properties in East Ham on the Burges estate to the east of High Street North and also on the Central Park estate around East Ham Central Park to the west, both sought-after areas. Elsewhere in East Ham mostly Victorian terraces and 1930s terraces and semis. East Ham is slightly grander than Manor Park, which has mostly smaller two-storey Victorian terraces, many 'improved' for better or worse in straight tree-lined streets, with the occasional struggling corner shop or small parade of shops to break the pattern.

ATTRACTS *First-time buyers; loyal locals; members of the Asian community (particularly Manor Park); people who can't afford Hackney or Tower Hamlets* • **CONSERVATION AREA** *Durham Road* • **AVERAGE PRICES** *Flats: studio £60,000; 1-bed £65,000-£70,000; 2-bed £75,000 Houses: 2-bed £100,000-£110,000; 3-bed £130,000+; 4-bed £170,000+* • **AVERAGE RENTS (WEEKLY)** *Flats: 1-bed £120; 2-bed £140 Houses: 2-bed £160; 3-bed £200; 4-bed £230.*

PLAISTOW & WEST HAM

Two-storey, two- and three-bedroom Victorian terraces predominate in Plaistow, although there is a handful of newly-built blocks of purpose-built flats. A number of new estates in West Ham, mostly built on former industrial sites, otherwise roads of the ubiquitous two- and three-bedroom terraces around the tube station (now grandly upgraded to receive the Jubilee Line). West Ham has better transport than Plaistow, which makes it popular with people working in town. Some of the best properties (large Victorian houses) are in roads round West Ham Park.

ATTRACTS *First-time buyers; city workers wanting good transport; loyal*

locals; members of the African and Afro-Caribbean communities
● **CONSERVATION AREAS** *None* ● **AVERAGE PRICES** *Flats: 1-bed £60,000-£70,000; 2-bed £75,000 Houses: 2-bed £80,000+; 3-bed £110,000+; 4-bed £170,000+* ● **AVERAGE RENTS (WEEKLY)** *Flats: 1-bed £120; 2-bed £140 Houses: 2-bed £160; 3-bed £200; 4-bed £230.*

BECKTON

Almost entirely new housing here around the docks on the site of the old gasworks. Beckton is the last part of Docklands to be regenerated and the process is still very much ongoing, giving the area a somewhat bleak feel. You won't get anything more than 18 years old here. Mostly two- and three-bedroom houses on modern estates with some four-bedroom houses. There's a newly built urban village at Silvertown with more than 1,000 new private and housing association-owned homes, shops, restaurants, a primary school and a community centre, and a lot more building is planned particularly on the south side of the Royals. The problem with the south side at the moment is that transport links are terrible but this should change if a suggested extension of the Docklands Light Railway to City Airport goes ahead. If you long for Victoriana down here, head for the riverside enclave of North Woolwich which has some two-bedroom Victorian terraces and cottages by Royal Victoria Gardens.

ATTRACTS *Some professional people; second-time buyers wanting to trade up to houses; watersports enthusiasts (on the nearby docks); investors wanting to rent out their properties* ● **CONSERVATION AREAS** *Bargehouse Road, North Woolwich* ● **AVERAGE PRICES** *Flats: studio £50,000; 1-bed £65,000+; 2-bed £70,000-£85,000 Houses: 2-bed £90,000-£110,000; 3-bed £95,000-£130,000; 4-bed £140,000-£175,000*
● **AVERAGE RENTS (WEEKLY)** *Flats: studio £95-£110; 1-bed £110-£135; 2-bed £135-£170 Houses: 2-bed £200; 3-bed £170-£250; 4-bed £300+.*

BEST POSTCODES

Postcodes are not a big issue in a borough where price differences between areas are minimal. But in descending order of preference, the best postcodes are East Ham E6, Stratford E15 and Forest Gate E7.

AMENITIES

SCHOOLS**

Historically poor performance in league tables particularly at primary level. But the borough is pulling itself up by its bootstraps and recently received glowing reports from Ofsted for refusing to let poverty and language difficulties stand in the way of achievement. Unfortunately these accolades have yet to make themselves felt in primary school performance which is currently the worst in London. There is an above-average proportion of under-fives in nursery school. No private prep or secondary schools.

PRE-SCHOOL PROVISION *8 state nursery schools; 52 nursery classes in state primary or church schools; 52 private and voluntary nurseries and playgroups. Proportion of under-fives in state nurseries: 77%* ● **STATE PRIMARY SCHOOLS** *Overall league table position: 141st out of 150. Top scorers: St Edward's RC, East Ham; Calverton (with nursery unit), Custom House; St Winefride's RC, Manor Park* ● **STATE SECONDARY SCHOOLS** *Overall league table position: 123rd out of 149. Top scorers:*

St Angela's Ursuline Convent (girls), Forest Gate; St Bonaventure's RC
(boys), Forest Gate; Plashet School (girls), East Ham.

TRANSPORT★★★★

Newham has done better out of new transport links than any other
borough (except possibly Greenwich) and is now very well connected, with
the Docklands Light Railway at Beckton, Custom House and Stratford, and
the Jubilee Line at Canning Town, Stratford and West Ham. The DLR looks
set to expand round the south side of the Royal Docks to City Airport.
Central, District and Hammersmith and City Line tubes run to the west and
middle of the borough but further north and east it's trains only.
TRAINS Stratford Zone 3. Cost of annual season ticket £896. Average
journey time to Liverpool Street 8 minutes; to Highbury and Islington 15
minutes. Forest Gate Zone 3. Average journey time to Liverpool Street 14
minutes. West Ham Zone 3. Average journey time to Fenchurch Street 9
minutes; to Highbury and Islington 20 minutes • **TUBES** Stratford (Central,
Jubilee). Average journey time to Liverpool Street 10 minutes. East Ham
(District, Hammersmith & City) Zone 3. Average journey time to Tower Hill
19 minutes; to Liverpool Street 19 minutes • **DOCKLANDS LIGHT RAILWAY**
Stratford. Average journey time to Canary Wharf 10-15 minutes. Beckton
Zone 3. Average journey time to Tower Gateway 27 minutes • **BUSES**
Mostly suburban services and trafficky roads across most of the borough
can mean long journeys. Services to town include the 25 from Ilford to
Oxford Circus via Manor Park, Forest Gate and Stratford and the 15 from
Canning Town or East Ham to Paddington • **AIRPORTS** London City Airport
at the Royal Docks • **TRAFFIC TROUBLESPOTS** The junction of High Street
South, East Ham and the A13: Single lane traffic leads to long southbound
delays. Road widening to three lanes planned as part of a series of
improvements along the A13. The area around Stratford shopping centre:
Lots of main roads meet here and there can be long waits at junctions.
Upton Park: Streets around West Ham United's ground off Green Street on
match days are also trafficky • **PARKING** Controlled parking zones in East
Ham around the station, Upton Park, Stratford town centre and in Prince
Regent Road and West Ham. Consulations with residents are taking place
for further controlled parking zones in Manor Park and Forest Gate. In
Upton Park, East Ham and Stratford an annual resident's permit is free for
the first car; the second car is £30 and the third car is £50. In Prince
Regent Road and West Ham the first car is £15, the second car is £30
and the third car is £50.

LEISURE FACILITIES★★

THEATRES & CONCERT HALLS The Theatre Royal Stratford East is being
refurbished and a new performing arts centre, Stratford Circus, is taking
shape. This will be a venue for theatre training, comedy, music, dance and
clubbing as well as plays. The Circus will be the centrepiece of a new
cultural quarter for Stratford. Live music at the Rex, a recently-converted
cinema in Stratford • **CINEMAS** The new four-screen Stratford Picture House
is just opposite the Theatre Royal and next to the shopping centre and has
art films as well as more mainstream offerings. Asian films at the Boleyn on
the corner of Green Street and Barking Road. The Showcase at Beckton
shows mostly blockbusters • **MUSEUMS & STATELY HOMES** Thin on the
ground. The North Woolwich Old Station Museum for railway buffs is
housed in an old Victorian station building, its well-looked-after exterior a

sad contrast to the shabbiness of the rest of the area. Elsewhere, local history at the Manor Park Museum • **SPORTS FACILITIES** Three indoor leisure centres including two in Plaistow and the new Atherton leisure centre in Stratford. All with fitness centres and pools. Another £15 million leisure centre is planned on the site of the old baths at East Ham, with three pools, sports hall, badminton court and café. Water sports (including water-skiing and jet-ski) on the water at the Royal Docks where an international rowing centre is also planned. Dry ski slope at Beckton. • **LIBRARIES** Improving with the help of regeneration money. The largest lending and reference libraries are in the new library at Stratford and at East Ham in the wonderful Victorian Gothic town hall building. Sunday opening at Stratford, Beckton and Green Street. Investment in the library system is paying off, with library use sharply up on previous years. 6.6 library visits per head. Place in library-use league table: 19th out of 32 (where 1 is best and 32 worst).

OPEN SPACES***

Short on open space generally. Small parks and open spaces dotted around the borough have a slightly municipal feel although they're generally tidy and cared for. But fascinating walks along the footpaths of the tangle of rivers and canals south of Stratford do a lot to make up for lack of greenery. Cemeteries provide an attractive space to walk in, like the City of London cemetery, the only green space in the borough big enough to get lost in, although it's duller and less Gothic Victorian than others like Highgate or Nunhead.

CHILDREN'S ACTIVITIES Newham City Farm, Custom House; Plashet Park and Zoo; Nature Reserve, East Ham, with nature trail and museum by walled church graveyard • **FOOTPATHS** The Greenway, a path running literally over the top of the main Northern outfall sewer carrying London's sewage from West Ham to East Ham via Plaistow. Excellent views of people's back gardens and the remnants of the East End's industrial past • **CANALS** The Bow Back Rivers, a network of once busy industrial rivers and canals, has been cleaned up and made accessible as part of the Lower Lea Project (see also Enfield, Haringey and Hackney). At a confluence in the network is the restored Three Mills mill, once used to grind corn for breweries and now converted to offices behind the preserved exterior.

SHOPS**

STRATFORD The 1960s concrete shopping centre has been overhauled and is lighter and brighter. But the shops are still uninspiring, mostly chain stores. The inside market stalls sell clothes, jewellery, leather goods and food. Sainsbury's superstore and new Safeway next to the new library • **GREEN STREET** This is the place to come for all things Indian. Sari and silk shops, jewellery shops, bakeries selling fresh bhajis and sickly Indian sweets, market stalls in Queen Street market selling fruit, vegetables and Asian and African goods. Currently a grim 1960s building but due for a face-lift. The most colourful and interesting shopping street in Newham. Tesco's by Upton Park station • **EAST HAM** Pedestrianised shopping street at High Street North, with mostly chain stores and a covered market. Tends towards small branches with cheap stock. Sainsbury's • **ELSEWHERE** Forest Gate has mostly local shops including new and second-hand furniture shops. Local shops in Romford Road. West Ham and Plaistow have just local shops. Beckton has a large Asda and Savacentre, part of a complex of three new retail centres. Across the borough there are small corner *shops, often Asian-run, selling groceries, newspapers and second-hand goods.*

RESTAURANTS**

FOREST GATE *Good Indian restaurants around Green Street* • **STRATFORD** *A handful of cafés including The Courtyard in the courtyard of the old town hall building. A cybercafé, pubs, Pizza Express at the Stratford Picture House and the occasional winebar, all symbols of regeneration. But café society is not here quite yet* • **ELSEWHERE** *Plentiful ethnic restaurants and take-aways of varying quality.*

CRIME RATES**

Position in Metropolitan Police league table: 10th out of 32 (where 1 is worst and 32 best).

THE COUNCIL***

POLITICAL AFFILIATION *Labour* • **MINUS POINTS** *One of the most inefficient boroughs in London at collecting council tax, needed for essential services* • **PLUS POINTS** *Not complacent about its problems. One of the first to set up an Education Action Zone to raise standards and get results. The first council to launch a door-to-door recycling service. Energetic support for regeneration initiatives. Household rubbish collections are some of the most efficient in London* • **PROPERTY SEARCHES CARRIED OUT WITHIN 10 WORKING DAYS** *100%* • **STANDARD SEARCH FEE** *£100* • **COUNCIL TAX COLLECTED** *83.1%*

• **COUNCIL TAX 2000-2001**

BAND	PROPERTY VALUE	CHARGE	BAND	PROPERTY VALUE	CHARGE
A	up to £40,000	£512	E	£88,001-£120,000	£939
B	£40,001-£52,000	£597	F	£120,001-£160,000	£1,110
C	£52,001-£68,000	£683	G	£160,001-£320,000	£1,280
D	£68,001-£88,000	£768	H	over £320,000	£1,536

REDBRIDGE

By rights, Redbridge should be pretty smart. It has its fair share of well-to-do and wealthy suburbs and good transport links, it's on the edge of the greenbelt with Epping Forest on its doorstep, its schools are good and until the last local elections it was a bastion of Conservatism. But its problem is that it's East London, not west, or even south. It borders on Essex, still trying to live down its barrow boy reputation. It's the home of the aspirational and self-made, those who grew up in the University of Life in the East End and moved to Redbridge when they made good. And however much government planners talk about the renewal of the east and Thames gateways, Londoners obstinately rate the west higher than the east as a place to live.

But for those who can overcome such snobbery, property is cheaper, the commute to the city and beyond is quick and escape to the country easy. The downside is that the borough's shopping is often dull and/or depressing and the miles of small Victorian terraces in the less salubrious areas get you down pretty quickly. Redbridge's territory stretches from the Victorian and Edwardian terraces of Ilford, the borough's main adminstrative and shopping centre, to the meaner workmen's terraces of Seven Kings and Goodmayes. North of Ilford are the larger Edwardian and inter-war semis of Gants Hill and tucked into the borough's northern border on the edge of the greenbelt are the council houses of Hainault. To the west, around Woodford and down into Wanstead, it's a different world, with large detached and semi-detached houses and handsome Victorian terraces in tree-lined streets.

As a staging post on many a journey out of the East End to the suburbs and beyond, Redbridge is a mix of many cultures, with significant Asian and Jewish communities. Just over a fifth of its population is from an ethnic minority, in stark contrast to surrounding boroughs to the east (see Barking and Dagenham and Havering) which are predominantly white. Mosques, synagogues and shops selling exotic spicy foods add a much needed dash of colour.

This isn't a borough with the huge unemployment problems of some parts of inner London (unemployment stands at 3.9%, lower than most of its neighbours) but equally it lacks the sleek prosperity of some of the richest commuter suburbs. The arrival of the Channel Tunnel rail link at Stratford just along the railway line to the west of Ilford would give the south of the borough a much needed boost (see Newham and Camden).

PROPERTY AND ARCHITECTURE

ILFORD

Ilford developed as a Victorian railway suburb and roads of Victorian, Edwardian and 1920s terraces spread away from the town centre either side of the railway line. North of the tracks, on the posher side, the houses are larger, some with ornate metal-trellissed porches. Many were turned into flats before the council clamped down on conversions. But the once-handsome houses are grievously defaced by some truly horrible 'improvements' – fake stained glass and modern windows and ill-fitting front doors abound and there's hardly a house left in its original state. Grids of small bay-windowed and flat-fronted terraces south of the tracks off Ilford Lane. In a neat twist, roads named to recall Victorian imperial triumphs – Bengal Road, Madras Road – are now lived in by Asians. Some of the best houses in Ilford are in the enclave of roads between Valentines Park and Cranbrook Road on the Garden City estate.

ATTRACTS *Families, loyal locals, local first-time buyers* • **CONSERVATION AREAS** *Valentines Park & Mansion* • **AVERAGE PRICES** *Flats: studio £60,000; 1-bed £60,000-£65,000; 2-bed £75,000-£80,000 Houses: 2-bed £110,000+; 3-bed £125,000-£200,000; 4-bed £150,000-£275,000* • **AVERAGE RENTS (WEEKLY)** *Flats: studio £100-£110; 1-bed £120-£140;*

2-bed £150-£170 Houses: 2-bed £150-£170; 3-bed £180-£300; 4-bed £250-£400.

SEVEN KINGS & GOODMAYES

More down-market than Ilford and generally the shabbiest parts of the borough. More roads and grids of small Victorian terraces in Seven Kings, built as a 'people's suburb' to house workers travelling to town on the Great Eastern Railway. Goodmayes has its share of Victorian speculative building but to relieve the tedium, roads to the south of Green Lane are lined with larger Edwardian terraces and 1930s bungalows, many with original features intact. Bungalows may not be that thrilling but here they're a welcome change. The easternmost corner of Goodmayes is the beginning of the massive Becontree council estate (see Barking and Dagenham). Some good house bargains to be had.

ATTRACTS *Families; members of the Asian community (especially Seven Kings)* • **CONSERVATION AREAS** *Mayfield (Seven Kings bungalow estate)* • **AVERAGE PRICES** *Flats: 1-bed £60,000+; 2-bed £75,000+ Houses: 2-bed £110,000+; 3-bed £120,000; 4-bed £140,000* • **AVERAGE RENTS (WEEKLY)** *Flats: studio £100-£110; 1-bed £120-£140; 2-bed £150-£170 Houses: 2-bed £150-£170; 3-bed £180-£300; 4-bed £250-£400.*

GANTS HILL & CLAYHALL

Gants Hill grew up around the new roads being laid in the borough in the 1920s and has mostly middling and large 1920s and 1930s semis, many sporting timber-framed gables, diamond-paned windows and other 'country' touches. Larger houses in more expensive Clayhall, with some of the most sought-after roads off Longwood Gardens, in the catchment area for good local schools and known as the Woods estate because all the roads have 'wood' in their name. Gants Hill is home to many of the borough's Jewish community, one of the largest in London. Mostly houses rather than flats in Clayhall, although the former Claybury hospital has recently been converted to luxury apartments. Flats and houses in Gants Hill.

ATTRACTS *Families; members of the Jewish community; professionals* • **CONSERVATION AREAS** *Barnadoes Village Homes; Little Heath* • **AVERAGE PRICES** *Flats: 1-bed £55,000-£65,000; 2-bed £75,000-£80,000 Houses: 3-bed £135,000-£250,000; 4-bed £200,000-£300,000* • **AVERAGE RENTS (WEEKLY)** *Flats: 1-bed £120+; 2-bed £150+ Houses: 3-bed £180+; 4-bed £250+.*

HAINAULT

A wonderful setting on the edge of Hainault Forest Country Park and greenbelt land for a council estate which was originally flung up as temporary accommodation during the post-war housing shortage. The estate has been rebuilt in red brick, a big improvement. An estimated three quarters of the properties are now in private hands having been sold to tenants under the right-to-buy scheme and sold on. Some ex-council bargains here, mostly three-bedroom houses. Better to the west of Fencepiece Road, with larger private houses on the Tudor estate (the group of roads including Wolsey, Aragon and Boleyn Roads).

ATTRACTS *Locals; people needing cheap houses; families* • **CONSERVATION AREAS** *None* • **AVERAGE PRICES** *Flats: 1-bed £65,000-£70,000; 2-bed £75,000-£85,000 Houses: 2-bed £85,000-£95,000; 3-bed £110,000+; 4-bed £150,000-£200,000* • **AVERAGE RENTS (WEEKLY)** *Flats: 1-bed £120-*

£140; 2-bed £150-£170 Houses: 2-bed £150-£170; 3-bed £180-£300; 4-bed £250-£400.

WOODFORD & SOUTH WOODFORD

Some of the best parts of the borough and highly sought after for its excellent schools. Roads on the ridge where London stops and Essex begins are lined with huge houses boasting the full panoply of half-timbering, diamond-paned windows, and several wings (useful for the personal workout room). This is where the unashamedly nouveau riche live. Large, well looked after detached Edwardian and 1930s houses in tree-lined roads around Woodford and Woodford Green, with a handful of roads of Victorian cottages around the green itself. Some of the best roads are on the Monkhams estate, which has large detached early 20th century houses within easy walking distance of Woodford tube station. South Woodford has a mixture of good Edwardian terraces and 1930s houses and more flats than more expensive Woodford.

ATTRACTS *Barrow boys made good; families; young professionals; City workers* • **CONSERVATION AREAS** *Woodford Bridge; Woodford Wells; Woodford Green; Woodford Broadway; South Woodford; George Lane* • **AVERAGE PRICES** *Flats: 1-bed £100,000+; 2-bed £120,000+ Houses: 2-bed £170,000+; 3-bed £170,000-£350,000;4-bed £280,000* • **AVERAGE RENTS (WEEKLY)** *Flats: 1-bed £140-£150; 2-bed £160-£170 Houses: 2-bed £180-£200; 3-bed £205-£230; 4-bed £275+.*

WANSTEAD

Another of Redbridge's most classy areas. Lots of large handsome Victorian and Edwardian houses, some now converted into flats. Prices depend on a whole lot of factors important to its middle class population, including proximity to tubes and the best parts of Wanstead High Street and inclusion in school catchment areas. Large houses on the Firs Estate, snuggling up to Epping Forest (see Waltham Forest) are sought after. Other good (read expensive) areas, both with large Edwardian detached houses, are the Warren Estate just north of Wanstead golf course and the Aldersbrook Estate tucked between Wanstead Park and Wanstead flats. Not many first-time buyer bargains here.

ATTRACTS *Families; young professionals; City people; the upwardly-mobile from Ilford and points east* • **CONSERVATION AREAS** *Snaresbrook; Wanstead Village; Wanstead Park* • **AVERAGE PRICES** *Flats: 1-bed £100,000+; 2-bed £120,000+ Houses: 2-bed £170,000+; 3-bed £200,000+; 4-bed £280,000+* • **AVERAGE RENTS (WEEKLY)** *Flats: 1-bed £140-£150; 2-bed £160-£170 Houses: 2-bed £180-£200; 3-bed £205-£230; 4-bed £275+.*

BEST POSTCODES

Most of Redbridge is outside the London postcode area. Of the parts that aren't, Woodford E18 is probably better than Leytonstone E11 (which includes Wanstead but also parts of dreary Leytonstone). But both are fairly obscure codes to most Londoners and prices depend far more on closeness to shops and transport and inclusion in school catchment areas.

AMENITIES

SCHOOLS * * *

Great performance in secondary school league tables, thanks mainly to the borough's two remaining selective grammar schools and a number of independent schools. Overall performance at primary level is much less spectacular. Possibly this has something to do with parents' reports that many people are so desperate to get their children through the borough's tests for the grammar schools that they opt for one of a growing number of private prep schools specialising in cramming for the exam. The grammar schools are very oversubscribed and admission depends on being in the right catchment area as well as results. Improving amounts of provision for under-fives in state nursery schools.

PRE-SCHOOL PROVISION *37 nursery classes in state primary and church schools; 81 private day nurseries and playgroups, including Christian and Jewish. Proportion of under-fives in state nurseries: 60%* • **STATE PRIMARY SCHOOLS** *Overall position in league tables: 50th out of 150. Top scorers: Wanstead C of E (with nursery unit), Wanstead; Our Lady of Lourdes RC (with nursery unit), Wanstead; Wells (with nursery unit), Woodford Green* • **STATE SECONDARY SCHOOLS** *Overall position in league tables: 7th out of 149. Top scorers: Woodford County High (girls, selective), Woodford Green; Ilford County High (boys, selective), Ilford; Ilford Ursuline High (girls), Ilford* • **PRIVATE PREP SCHOOLS** *Woodford Green Prep (mixed), Woodford Green; St Aubyn's (mixed, from 3), Woodford Green; Glenarm College (mixed, from 3); Ilford* • **PRIVATE SECONDARY SCHOOLS** *Chart topper Bancrofts' (mixed), Woodford Green; Cranbrook College (boys), Ilford; Park (girls), Ilford; Ilford Ursuline High (girls), Ilford.*

TRANSPORT * * *

Well spaced throughout the borough. The south (Ilford, Seven Kings and Goodmayes) has a fairly reliable service to Liverpool Street. The north of the borough has the distinctive eastern loop of the Central line which has improved after a recent bad patch.

TRAINS *Ilford Zone 4. Cost of annual season ticket £1104. Average journey time to Liverpool Street 16 minutes. Goodmayes Zone 4. Average journey time to Liverpool Street 21 minutes* • **TUBES** *Wanstead (Central) Zone 4. Average journey time to Liverpool Street 19 minutes. Woodford (Central) Zone 4. Average journey time to Liverpool Street 22 minutes* • **BUSES** *Buses into town exist (the main service is the 25 from Ilford via Aldgate to Oxford Circus) but the journey can be slow and frustrating. Other buses mainly join shopping centres or neighbouring suburbs. Night buses include the N8 from Trafalgar Square to Woodford and Gants Hill* • **TRAFFIC TROUBLESPOTS** *Wanstead: The new M11 link road between Redbridge and Hackney runs along the bottom of Wanstead High Street, completed at the end of 1999 after years of upheaval and protest (see also Waltham Forest). Traffic on the road itself is fast flowing but contractors tunnelled under Wanstead's treasured George Green so the overall impact on Wanstead is reduced and the high street is quieter than before the road was built. Ilford: Pedestrianised shopping streets mean that all the traffic is forced onto surrounding roads around the station and Cranbrook Road* • **PARKING** *Currently there's only one parking zone in the borough, around South Woodford shopping centre. Cost of annual resident's permit: £20* *for the first car; £35 for a subsequent car.*

LEISURE FACILITIES ***

THEATRES & CONCERT HALLS The Kenneth More theatre in Ilford has mainstream plays by local theatre companies, musicals and opera. Concerts at Ilford's wonderfully florid Victorian town hall, local churches and Ilford's oldest building, the medieval hospital chapel of St Mary and St Thomas of Canterbury ● **CINEMAS** Two, the Ilford Odeon and the Woodford ABC, both showing mainstream films. ● **MUSEUMS & GALLERIES** Sadly devoid of any museums at present but a new local history museum was set to open at the end of 2000 in the Central Library in Ilford complete with mock-up of rooms from 1900 and 1930s homes ● **SPORTS FACILITIES** Well provided for. Three leisure centres in Ilford, Wanstead and Redbridge with gyms, weights and indoor tennis at Redbridge. Pools at Barkingside and Ilford. Athletics ground at Ilford and tennis, football and other outdoor sports in parks around the borough. Watersports and riding at Fairlop Waters, a lake created on a former gravel plain, surrounded by greenbelt land. Proposals to create a racecourse at Fairlop have had a mixed reception from residents. Golf on public courses at Fairlop and Hainault. ● **LIBRARIES** Well used and well resourced with an upgraded computer system. Handsome central library in Ilford. Generally long opening hours, particularly in the central library but respectable elsewhere. Many branch libraries are closed on Wednesdays. 10.2 library visits per head. Position in library-use league table: 3rd out of 32 (where 1 is best and 32 worst).

OPEN SPACES ****

Lots of it and there are even excellent views from the northern ridge of the borough just before it turns into Essex (a surprise for those who think Essex is flat). Much of the north-east corner is rural, with mostly open fields.
PARKS Valentines Park, the borough's largest park, is in Ilford, with two lakes and lots of lush green open space with mature trees. Once the grounds of Valentines Mansion, a 17th century mansion. The future of the mansion became a cause célèbre in Ilford when it was no longer needed for council offices. A bid to turn it into a pub failed and the council is now considering recommendations drawn up by community groups in Redbridge's widest ranging public consultation exercise to date. Apart from a restaurant, the house could be used for adult education classes and rented out commercially for wedding receptions and business conferences
● **WIDE OPEN SPACES & VIEWS** Hainault Forest Country Park. Sloping meadows and woods surrounded by greenbelt land. A haven for wildlife. Easy to forget you're in London (albeit on the very edge). Excellent views from the top of Dog Kennel Hill, Redbridge's highest point ● **RIVER WALKS** The Roding runs down the west side of the borough from Ray Park to Ilford with the pleasantest parts meandering through a wonderful mixture of woods and grassland at the edge of Epping Forest in Wanstead Park. Further north by the M11 access to the river is being improved and previously contaminated land by the river landscaped as part of a £9 million regeneration scheme in the surrounding area over the next five years (see also Barking and Dagenham).

SHOPS ***

ILFORD The main shopping area. Mostly chains in the town's indoor shopping mall, the Exchange, built seven years ago, and in the neighbouring pedestrianised shopping streets. Pleasant enough but longstanding residents blame the shopping centre for sucking the life out of the rest of the town, especially Cranbrook Road, which was once the smartest part of Ilford with four department stores, but is now shabby and run-down, with lots of empty shops. But Ilford Lane partly makes up for it with a whole street of Asian supermarkets and shops selling glittering fabrics and saris. Sainsbury's in Ilford • **GOODMAYES** Where to come if you want to buy a used car, as every other shop is a second-hand car sales showroom. Otherwise, Asian supermarkets, furniture shops and more empty shops. Tesco • **GANTS HILL & BARKINGSIDE** A couple of kosher food shops at Gants Hill but otherwise the usual collection of take-aways, supermarkets and banks in parades round a busy roundabout by the tube station. More shops at Barkingside, useful rather than beautiful. Tesco and Sainsbury's at Barkingside • **WOODFORD & WANSTEAD** Much more up-market small shops along the Broadway in Woodford including a charcuterie/fromagerie. Somerfields. Wanstead also has good shops in an attractive Edwardian High street, with a couple of patisseries and antique shops. Chains and local shops in South Woodford. Sainsbury's and Waitrose's.

RESTAURANTS**

A recommended bagel bakery in Gants Hill and a popular Chinese restaurant in Ilford but apart from that mostly local restaurants with the familiar choice of Chinese, Indian, Italian and Greek of varying quality. Winebar country in Woodford and Wanstead.

CRIME RATES****

Position in Metropolitan Police league table: 23rd out of 32 (where 1 is worst and 32 best).

THE COUNCIL****

POLITICAL AFFILIATION No overall control (Conservative minority rule) • **MINUS POINTS** Recovering from years of rather sleepy Tory control during which inefficiencies crept in, according to residents. Seen by residents as remote (although trying to counteract this with the creation of 'citizens' juries'). Slow on property searches • **PLUS POINTS** Excellent secondary schools. Well used libraries. Door-to-door recycling scheme started in 1995 with collections of cans, tins and bottles as well as newspapers. Special deals on home composters. Generally efficient rubbish collection with some of the lowest levels of missed collections in London • **PROPERTY SEARCHES CARRIED OUT IN 10 WORKING DAYS** 61% • **STANDARD SEARCH FEE** £95 • **COUNCIL TAX COLLECTED** 96.1%

• **COUNCIL TAX 2000-2001**

BAND	PROPERTY VALUE	CHARGE	BAND	PROPERTY VALUE	CHARGE
A	up to £40,000	£541	E	£88,001-£120,000	£939
B	£40,001-£52,000	£597	F	£120,001-£160,000	£1,171
C	£52,001-£68,000	£683	G	£160,001-£320,000	£1,352
D	£68,001-£88,000	£768	H	over £320,000	£1,622

RICHMOND-UPON-THAMES

If Richmond doesn't feel much like London this could be because much of it technically isn't London at all but Surrey or Middlesex. The borough is one of the greenest in the capital, including within its boundaries Kew Gardens, Richmond Park and Hampton Court Park, to name but three, as well as 18th- and 19th-century cottages, narrow lanes, towpaths and duckponds which wouldn't be out of place in far more rural areas than Surrey, let alone London.

The Thames both divides and links the different areas of the borough, one of the most sprawling in London. In the north the large Victorian houses of Castelnau give way to the small cottages and winding high street of Barnes village, self-contained in a deep bend of the river. In the next bend to the west lies Kew, another village made famous by the floral displays and greenhouses of the Royal Botanic Gardens. Past the large Edwardian homes of East Sheen, the even grander houses of Richmond Hill occupy a commanding position overlooking the river at the edge of Richmond Park. Around Hampton Court Park and Bushy Park to the south are the Victorian houses and cottages of Teddington, Hampton Wick and Hampton Village, giving way to inter-war suburbia at Whitton and Hampton.

Richmond is among the most thriving boroughs in London. Unemployment is the lowest in the capital at 1.8 per cent. Its good transport links, schools and open spaces are a magnet for professional families who commute to town every day, and those who work in the borough tend to be white collar office workers or self-employed people running their own businesses. Only 5 per cent of Richmond's population comes from an ethnic minority, the third lowest in the whole of Greater London.

One major blot on the landscape is the ever-present noise of jumbo jets coming in to land at Heathrow Airport to the west. The noise affects residents of Barnes, Kew, Sheen, Richmond, St Margarets and Twickenham and there is growing local concern over the outcome of the long-running inquiry into the building of a fifth terminal at Heathrow. Residents fear that a fifth terminal will increase noise and traffic congestion and reject the claims of the British Airports Authority that noise levels have already improved and that only a small number of people will be affected.

Hammersmith Bridge, normally the umbilical link between Barnes and Hammersmith's shops and transport, has had a troubled couple of years. Closed for repairs to its delicate Victorian construction for two years, it opened again only to fall victim to a terrorist attack which once again closed Barnes' main exit route to the north side of the Thames. The closures have divided local opinion. Some residents love the traffic-free roads but others say the bridge is vital to bring business to Barnes.

PROPERTY AND ARCHITECTURE

BARNES

An expensive enclave with handsome Victorian family homes in roads around Barnes Common and Castelnau and Lonsdale Roads to the north of the high street. Large Regency houses facing the river are lovely but suffer constant traffic noise. There are smaller early Victorian cottages in roads off the high street and around the pond on Barnes Green. Multi-coloured cottages in roads off Whitehart Lane (known as Little Chelsea) are some of the smartest.

ATTRACTS *Families with children; arty, media and intellectual types. Prides itself on its community atmosphere to the extent that it has been accused of insularity. Also popular with residents from overseas, particularly Swedes wanting to be near the Swedish school in Barnes* ● **CONSERVATION AREAS** *Barnes Green; Castelnau; Mill Hill; Barnes Common; Thorne Passage; Whitehart Lane* ● **AVERAGE PRICES** *Flats: 1-bed £170,000+; 2-bed £240,000+ Houses: 2-bed £250,000+; 3-bed £400,000+; 4-bed £500,000+* ● **AVERAGE RENTS (WEEKLY)** *Flats: 1-bed £185+; 2-bed £230+ Houses: 2-bed £320+; 3-bed £460+; 4-bed £575.*

EAST SHEEN & MORTLAKE

Small Victorian cottages and Victorian terraces in roads north and south of the railway line at Mortlake with larger houses in First and Second Avenue. The trafficky south circular at Upper Richmond Road splits East Sheen in two and the best properties are well away from the main road to the south near Richmond Park in Fife Road and surrounding streets. Big gardens and lots of space in a mixture of Edwardian and 1930s properties in this area, known as Parkside. Smaller mostly 1930s properties to the north of the south circular.

ATTRACTS *Families looking for green space and good schools (often refugees from more urban Notting Hill and Fulham); the glitterati (East Sheen)* ● **CONSERVATION AREAS** *Mortlake; Mortlake Green; Queen's Road; Model Cottages; East Sheen Avenue; Christchurch Road* ● **AVERAGE PRICES** *Flats: studio £100,000; 1-bed £145,000+; 2-bed £170,000-£240,000 Houses: 2-bed £225,000+; 3-bed £350,000-£400,000; 4-bed £425,000+* ● **AVERAGE RENTS (WEEKLY)** *Flats: studio £150+; 1-bed £185+; 2-bed £230+ Houses: 2-bed £275+; 3-bed £392; 4-bed £460.*

KEW

Lots of modern purpose-built blocks appeared among the Georgian and Queen Anne gems after the area was heavily bombed during the war but central Kew around the station is still mostly Victorian. Large Victorian family houses in the best roads including Litchfield and Broomfield Roads just opposite Kew Gardens and a mixture of property from Queen Anne to modern around Kew Green at the north tip of Kew Gardens. Cheaper properties, mostly 1930s to the east in North Sheen including some ex-

council although the three-bedroom Edwardian houses in roads off Lower
Richmond Road near the cemetery are becoming gentrified.
ATTRACTS *Families; young professionals; a substantial contingent from the
arts and the media; loyal locals* • **CONSERVATION AREAS** *Kew Green; Royal
Botanic Gardens; Old Deer Park; Kew Gardens; Lawn Crescent; Kew
Road; Kew Foot Road* • **AVERAGE PRICES** *Flats: 1-bed £175,000+; 2-bed
£200,000+ Houses: 2-bed £220,000+; 3-bed £250,000-£500,000; 4-
bed £400,000+* • **AVERAGE RENTS (WEEKLY)** *Flats: studio £135+; 1-bed
£175+; 2-bed £220+ Houses: 2-bed £275+; 3-bed £405; 4-bed £645+.*

RICHMOND & ST MARGARETS

Richmond has everything from conversion flats and period cottages in
roads off Sheen Road to some of London's most beautiful Georgian houses
around Richmond Green and along Richmond Hill. Richmond Hill also has
some of the best large Victorian houses in the area. It's not unusual to see
properties for sale here for more than £1 million. On the other side of the
river, slightly cheaper and more suburban St Margaret's has substantial
mansion blocks fronting the river and large Victorian and Edwardian
family homes in roads behind. The most sought-after properties in St
Margaret's are in roads backing onto the Trust Grounds by the river.
ATTRACTS *Families wanting green space, shops and schools; young
professionals wanting easy access to town and shops; overseas residents
relocated by their companies; Germans wanting to be near the German
school at Petersham* • **CONSERVATION AREAS** *Richmond Green; Central
Richmond; St Margarets; Richmond Riverside; Richmond Hill; Richmond
Park* • **AVERAGE PRICES** *Flats: studio £90,000-£120,000; 1-bed £160,000-
£260,000; 2-bed £250,000-£400,000 Houses: 2-bed £275,000-
£350,000; 3-bed £375,000-£600,000; 4-bed £500,000+* • **AVERAGE
RENTS (WEEKLY)** *Flats: studio £185+; 1-bed £230+; 2-bed £320+ Houses:
2-bed £320+; 3-bed £530+; 4-bed £800+.*

TWICKENHAM & STRAWBERRY HILL

More famous as a rugby ground than a residential area, Twickenham is
mostly late Victorian interspersed with 1930s properties. Less exciting
architecturally than Richmond but it can still boast some Georgian gems in
East Twickenham around Marble Hill. More expensive Strawberry Hill is
leafily suburban with a mixture of Victorian, Edwardian and inter-war
houses. Look for first-time buyer flats above shops in the high street or in
conversions around the centre of Twickenham. Some good value ex-council
houses on the Fulwell Avenue and Meadway estates towards Hanworth.
ATTRACTS *Young professionals working in town; families with young
children wanting good schools* • **CONSERVATION AREAS** *Twickenham
Riverside; Cambridge Park; Queens Road, Twickenham; Amyard Park
Road* • **AVERAGE PRICES** *Flats: studio £95,000+; 1-bed £130,000-
£145,000; 2-bed £135,000+ Houses: 2-bed £200,000+; 3-bed
£200,000-£350,000; 4-bed £230,000-£325,000* • **AVERAGE RENTS
(WEEKLY)** *Flats: studio £115+; 1-bed £150; 2-bed £175+ Houses: 2-bed
£205-£270; 3-bed £205+; 4-bed £275+.*

HAM & PETERSHAM

The poshest houses are in Petersham which is set in beautiful meadows
running down to the river and has Victorian cottages and larger Georgian
and Victorian family houses. Expect to pay Richmond prices, especially in

roads near Richmond Park. If you're looking for cheap property near Richmond or Kingston try Ham for ex-council properties on the Ashburnham Estate west of Ham Street towards the river or in the 1960s Wates estate in roads opposite Ham Common. Distance from a station is a disadvantage of the area.

ATTRACTS *First-time buyers (Ham); actors and glitterati (Petersham); families; Germans wanting to be near the German school at Petersham*

● **CONSERVATION AREAS** *Ham Common; Ham House; Petersham* ● **AVERAGE PRICES** *Flats: 1-bed £85,000-£110,000; 2-bed £100,000-£135,000 Houses: 2-bed £150,000+; 3-bed £185,000+; 4-bed £220,000+*

● **AVERAGE RENTS (WEEKLY)** *Flats: studio £155; 1-bed £155-£160; 2-bed £175 Houses: 2-bed £205+; 3-bed £285+.*

TEDDINGTON & THE HAMPTONS

Grouped round Bushy Park and Hampton Court Park in the south of the borough. Mostly Victorian properties in Teddington and Hampton Wick, the most desirable and expensive parts of this area, with riverfront properties in Teddington commanding premium prices. Look for first-time buyer flats in roads round Teddington Station. A cheaper mix of Victorian, inter-war and modern property at Hampton Hill, further from good shops and train services. Some handsome family houses in roads around Hampton Station in the area known as Hampton Village but to the west Hampton turns flat and boringly suburban.

ATTRACTS *Families wanting good schools, easy access to the City and a quiet life* ● **CONSERVATION AREAS** *Teddington Lock; Park Road; Normansfield; Hampton Village; Hampton Court Park; Hampton Court Green; Hampton Wick; Bushy Park* ● **AVERAGE PRICES** *Flats: studio £90,000; 1-bed £120,000-£150,000; 2-bed £135,000-£200,000 Houses: 2-bed £200,000-£280,000; 3-bed £260,000-£350,000; 4-bed £375,000+* ● **AVERAGE RENTS (WEEKLY)** *Flats: studio £105+; 1-bed £150+; 2-bed £170+ Houses: 2-bed £205+; 3-bed £205+; 4-bed £275+.*

WHITTON

The cheapest part of Richmond with a variety of mostly 1930s three-bed semi-detached and terraced houses. Victorian cottages round Colonial Road and Whitton Dean. Prices are held down by the main Chertsey Road which carves through the middle of the area.

ATTRACTS *People who can't afford Twickenham; families wanting to be in Richmond rather than Hounslow for the schools* ● **CONSERVATION AREAS** *None* ● **AVERAGE PRICES** *Flats: 1-bed £80,000-£100,000; 2-bed £100,000-£120,000 Houses: 3-bed £170,000-£200,000; 4-bed £250,000-£280,000* ● **AVERAGE RENTS (WEEKLY)** *Flats: studio £105; 1-bed £135+; 2-bed £160 Houses: 2-bed £195+; 3-bed £195+; 4-bed £265+.*

BEST POSTCODES

Not a burning issue in a borough where more than half the area is outside London. Of the areas that are in London Barnes SW13 is generally considered better than Mortlake SW14, although the latter contains East Sheen Parkside where properties easily compete with Barnes for grandeur.

AMENITIES

SCHOOLS★★★★

State schools are widely praised and sought after by residents. Consistently high performance in league tables particularly at primary level. A drop-off at state secondary school level, possibly due to excellent private provision. Below average number of state nurseries; expect to pay for children up to four years old.

PRE-SCHOOL PROVISION 16 nursery classes in state primary or church schools; 1 state nursery school; 3 under-fives centres; 102 private and voluntary nurseries and playgroups. Proportion of under-fives in state nurseries: 45% ● **STATE PRIMARY SCHOOLS** Overall league table position: 1st out of 150. Top scorers: St Stephen's CE, Twickenham; St Elizabeth's RC, Richmond; Queen's C of E, Kew ● **STATE SECONDARY SCHOOLS** Overall league table position: 41st out of 149. Top scorers: Waldegrave (girls), Twickenham; Teddington School (mixed), Teddington; Grey Court (mixed), Ham ● **PRIVATE PREP SCHOOLS** Colet Court (St Paul's Prep), Barnes; Tower House (boys), Sheen; Denmead (boys), Hampton; Twickenham prep (mixed); Mall (boys), Twickenham; Newland House (mixed), Twickenham; St Catherine's RC (boys 3-5, girls 3-16), Twickenham; Kings House (boys), Richmond; Old Vicarage (girls), Richmond; Unicorn (mixed), Kew ● **PRIVATE SECONDARY SCHOOLS** Chart-topper and academic powerhouse St Paul's Boys, Barnes; Hampton (boys); Lady Eleanor Holles (girls), Hampton.

TRANSPORT★★★

Choice of tube (District Line) or rail at Richmond and Kew; rail only in the rest of the borough. Fast and frequent services to Richmond; less so to some other parts.

TRAINS Barnes Zone 3. Cost of annual season ticket £896. Average journey time to Waterloo from Barnes 19 minutes; from Barnes Bridge 22 minutes. Mortlake Zone 3. Average journey time to Waterloo 21 minutes. Kew Zone 3. Average journey time to Waterloo from Kew Bridge 25 minutes; average journey time to Highbury and Islington from Kew Gardens (North London Line) 37 minutes. Richmond Zone 4. Cost of annual season ticket £1104. Average journey time to Waterloo 17-25 minutes; to Highbury and Islington 40 minutes. Twickenham Zone 5. Cost of annual season ticket £1332. Average journey time to Waterloo 22-30 minutes. Teddington Zone 6. Cost of annual season ticket £1456. Average journey time to Waterloo 32 minutes. Hampton Zone 6. Average journey time to Waterloo 39 minutes. Whitton Zone 5. Average journey time to Waterloo 27-36 minutes ● **TUBES** Richmond (District). Average journey time to Embankment 30 minutes. Kew Gardens (District). Average journey time to Embankment 27 minutes ● **BUSES** Mostly suburban services, many infrequent, particularly to points south of Richmond. No buses direct to the centre of town. Services include the 391 from Richmond to West Kensington and Fulham Broadway and the 33 from Fulwell to Hammersmith ● **BOATS** Passenger boats from Westminster to Kew, Richmond and Hampton Court; from Richmond Pier to Kingston, Hampton Court, Kew and Teddington Lock. Foot ferries at Twickenham (Marble Hill to Ham House) and Hampton ● **TRAFFIC TROUBLESPOTS** Upper Richmond Road (south circular): Clogged with traffic most of the way from Mortlake to Richmond with Sheen bearing the brunt. Chiswick Bridge: Suffering extra traffic as commuters try to find a way round repeated closures of

Hammersmith Bridge. Richmond Town Centre: Usually trafficky and queues build up at the entrance to the one way system. King Street and Richmond Road, Twickenham: Long queues particularly during rush hour and at the end of the school day as cars, buses and lorries mix with shoppers and pedestrians • **PARKING** There are controlled parking zones all over the borough. In central Barnes, Twickenham, many parts of Richmond, St Margarets and Hampton Wick an annual permit costs £60. In central Richmond and Hampton Court the cost is £80 and in North Barnes, £35.

LEISURE FACILITIES * * * *

THEATRES & CONCERT HALLS Richmond has two theatres, both of which have recently been feeling the pinch financially but are still hanging on in there. The Orange Tree moved from cramped premises in the Orange Tree pub to a modern theatre in 1991 and performs obscure classics and new plays. Richmond Theatre is an elaborate Victorian building on Richmond Green offering opera, comedy shows and pantomime. Teddington Theatre Club, an amateur theatre company, puts on a variety of plays and organises workshops, play readings and theatre visits. Open-air concerts at Kew and evening concerts at Marble Hill • **CINEMAS** Three in Richmond, including the Richmond Filmhouse showing arty & unusual films and the Odeon showing mostly blockbusters • **MUSEUMS & STATELY HOMES** One of the best-endowed boroughs, scattered with reminders that the area was long a favoured country seat of royals and aristocrats. Hampton Court Palace in Hampton Court Park, a tudor palace built for Cardinal Wolsey and extended by Henry VIII with the famous maze, galleries and state apartments. Kew Palace bought by George III. Queen Charlotte's cottage stands in the grounds of Kew Gardens. Riverside stately homes include the 17th-century Ham House and Marble Hill House • **SPORTS FACILITIES** Three leisure centres at East Sheen, Teddington and Whitton with gyms and indoor sports facilites; indoor pools at Teddington and Richmond Park; outdoor pool at Hampton; golf at Richmond, Twickenham and Mortlake; riding in Richmond Park; rugby at Twickenham. • **LIBRARIES** Well-equipped and helpful main library and community information centre at Richmond and friendly branch libraries, some in wonderfully florid 19th-century Carnegie buildings. But library opening hours have recently been truncated in more outlying areas. As compensation Richmond lending library now opens on Sunday afternoons. All libraries closed on Mondays. Libraries well used with 8.15 visits per head. Position in library-use league table: 8th out of 32 (where 1 is best and 32 worst).

OPEN SPACES * * * * *

Brilliant, in a word. Four large, beautiful and interesting parks including Richmond Park (with deer), the Royal Botanic Gardens at Kew, Hampton Court Park and the lower profile but still lovely Bushy Park, as well as delightful commons and riverside meadows.

VIEWS Richmond Park. A huge undulating swathe of green with woods, grassland and gardens (there are particularly attractive gardens at the Isabella Plantation). Excellent views over London and Surrey. A haven for horses and riders as well as the resident deer • **RIVERSIDE WALKS** The Thames Path through Ham Riverside and Petersham Meadows up to Richmond. Tree-lined river, cattle-grazing – you don't feel anywhere near London. But plans to flood Petersham meadows to attract wetland wildlife *caused an outcry among residents who love the stroll through the riverside meadows* ● **GARDENS** *Kew Gardens. The famous glasshouses contain enough exotic plants to keep the most ardent enthusiast happy and there is plenty of space for peaceful walks down to the river.*

SHOPS * * * *

BARNES *Villagey high street of small local shops including a butcher, cheese shop and kitchen shop, as well as a handy supermarket. Useful branches of banks and building societies and estate agents. Waitrose and Safeway in Upper Richmond Road (Sheen)* ● **MORTLAKE & SHEEN** *Interesting shops in Sheen Lane beyond the level crossing including a second-hand bookshop, brasseries, cafés and antique shops. Duller but more practical shops around the corner in Upper Richmond Road which has all the usual chain stores including late-night opening* ● **KEW** *Interesting shops around the station reflecting eclectic population – a good bookshop, butcher, health food shop and antique shop. Supermarkets at Upper Richmond Road. Out-of-town-style shopping at Kew Retail Park where M&S's moves to start selling food have fuelled fears among local retailers that they will be put out of business* ● **RICHMOND** *A middle-class mecca and natural home for Tesco Metro and Habitat as well as long-standing stores like Dickins and Jones. Good for buying clothes, books and presents – check out the narrow streets leading to Richmond Green. Some older residents complain of a lack of practical shops. Antique shops on Richmond Hill. Waitrose in the town centre* ● **TWICKENHAM** *Victorian high street lined mainly with chain stores and a couple of furniture shops. Church Street which winds down to the river has more individual shops plus a choice of restaurants* ● **TEDDINGTON** *More up-market than Twickenham with a Liberty's, smart furniture and brassware shops as well as the usual chain stores including Tesco and a late-opening convenience store* ● **OTHER AREAS** *Parades or streets of mainly local shops in Hampton Hill, Hampton Village, Hampton Wick, Ham and Whitton. Shopping centre at Nurserylands (Hampton).*

RESTAURANTS * * *

RICHMOND *A good choice including Chinese, French, Italian and Spanish as well as branches of the usual chains (Pizza Express, All Bar One). Pubs by the river* ● **TWICKENHAM** *Usual line-up of pubs, Indian restaurants and take-aways and a good fish restaurant* ● **TEDDINGTON & HAMPTON** *A range of locally popular wine bars and restaurants plus recommended French restaurant in Hampton Hill* ● **ELSEWHERE** *Nothing of note.*

CRIME RATES * * * *

Position in Metropolitan Police league table: 27th out of 32 (where 1 is worst and 32 best).

THE COUNCIL * * *

POLITICAL AFFILIATION *Liberal Democrat* ● **MINUS POINTS** *The second highest Band D council tax in London in 2000-2001. Has faced criticism over its handling of contracts with private rubbish collectors and the costs it incurred after guaranteeing a refurbishment loan to Richmond Theatre. Truncated library hours* ● **PLUS POINTS** *Excellent primary schools. Improved house-to-house rubbish collection after initial glitches with private contractors. Fortnightly collection of newspaper for recycling with planned* *extension to cans and bottles* ● **PROPERTY SEARCHES CARRIED OUT WITHIN 10 WORKING DAYS** *81.6%* ● **STANDARD SEARCH FEE** £*115* ● **COUNCIL TAX COLLECTED** *96.2%*

● **COUNCIL TAX 2000-2001**

BAND	PROPERTY VALUE	CHARGE	BAND	PROPERTY VALUE	CHARGE
A	up to £40,000	£606	E	£88,001-£120,000	£1,111
B	£40,001-£52,000	£707	F	£120,001-£160,000	£1,312
C	£52,001-£68,000	£808	G	£160,001-£320,000	£1,514
D	£68,001-£88,000	£909	H	over £320,000	£1,817

SOUTHWARK

Most people have set foot in Southwark at some time in their lives even if they haven't realised it. If you commute across London Bridge or Tower Bridge to the City in the morning, walk along the river to one of the pubs or restaurants springing up along the South Bank or visit the new Tate Modern art gallery, you've been to Southwark. This is part of south London's newly trendy riverside, a stone's throw from the City. It's full of expensively converted warehouses, designer shops and fashionable restaurants under the 19th-century railway arches and in the narrow cobbled streets which were once a hive of industrial riverside activity.

But travel five miles south on the number 40 bus to the leafy suburb of Dulwich and you're still technically in Southwark. This is a borough of huge contrasts. It stretches for four miles along the river from the Oxo Tower in the west to the jumble of council blocks and warehouse conversions of Bermondsey and Rotherhithe in the east before reaching down through the concrete nightmare of the Elephant and Castle roundabout. South of the Elephant, the Victorian suburbs of Peckham and Camberwell are finding a new lease of life after years blighted by 1960s planners, poverty and racial tension. Between Peckham and Dulwich lie the Victorian terraces of East Dulwich and Nunhead and Edwardian Herne Hill. At the very southern tip of Southwark is Dulwich Village, one of the middle-class jewels in south London's slightly tatty crown.

Despite the affluence of Dulwich, however, Southwark is the eighth most deprived area in the country. A total of 9.1% of its workforce is unemployed, the fourth highest in London.

Until fairly recently, many people would have greeted the idea of living anywhere in Southwark (except Dulwich) with a shudder, equating most of it with poor transport links, high crime and tatty shops. But the new Jubilee Line extension with stations at Bermondsey and Canada Water has finally put the developments around the old Surrey Docks at Rotherhithe and Bermondsey on the map, after a slow start when redevelopment of the areas started in the 1980s. At the same time Southwark's efforts to promote its section of riverfront as 'south London's answer to Covent Garden' is paying off. Now dubbed 'Bankside' by estate agents, the river front is benefiting from £12 million in lottery and government grants for environmental improvements to the riverfront, a new river pier and the Millennium Bridge which now links St Paul's with Tate Modern and the Globe Theatre (although walking on it is a wobbly experience). Old warehouses around London Bridge, Tower Bridge and Bermondsey have been colonised by yuppies, artists, photographers and people running small high tech businesses.

Further south, the good news for those who hate the Elephant and Castle roundabout (i.e. almost everyone) is that most of it is to be razed to the ground and transformed as part of a £1 billion redevelopment which will include a new shopping centre, gardens, offices, and a traffic free piazza. The bad news is that the redevelopment will take nearly ten years. Meanwhile £260 million is being poured into Peckham, demolishing loathed tower blocks, installing CCTV to cut crime and improving training and job opportunities. Peckham will also be a major beneficiary of the planned extension to the East London Line, which will bring tubes to this part of south-east London for the first time if the line goes ahead. Neighbouring Camberwell is starting to get serious attention from people discovering the area's stock of Georgian and Victorian houses a short bus ride away from town and the vibrancy of its multiracial community. A quarter of Southwark's population is from an ethnic minority, with significant communities of Afro-Caribbeans, West Africans, Turkish and Vietnamese.

PROPERTY AND ARCHITECTURE

BERMONDSEY & ROTHERHITHE

For years this was an almost forgotten corner of London after the closure of the Surrey Docks, but it's now been rejuvenated by trendy restaurants and shops around Shad Thames, east of Tower Bridge and more recently the Jubilee Line. Almost all the homes are new in more expensive Rotherhithe around the old dock basins, with some beautiful warehouse conversions. The place is pretty dead during the day as residents zip off to the City or Canary Wharf to work so probably not a good choice if you're at home all day and like a bit of life around you. Bermondsey's still a tangle of grim council estates and old warehouses not yet turned into Manhattan-style lofts. But plenty have been converted, either into live/work units or just massive apartments. Check out streets off Southwark Park Road for small Victorian cottages.

ATTRACTS *First-time buyers; creative types who want studio space near town; watersports enthusiasts; young professionals; loyal locals (Bermondsey)* • **CONSERVATION AREAS** *St Mary's, Rotherhithe; Wilson Grove; St Saviours Dock* • **AVERAGE PRICES** *Flats: studio £70,000-£115,000+; 1-bed £80,000-£165,000+; 2-bed £110,000-£180,000+ Houses: 2-bed £150,000+; 3-bed £175,000-£220,000; 4-bed £220,000+* • **AVERAGE RENTS (WEEKLY)** *Flats: studio £150+; 1-bed £170+; 2-bed £200+ Houses: 2-bed £200+; 3-bed £260+; 4-bed £320+.*

BOROUGH & ELEPHANT & CASTLE

The oldest part of Southwark, stretching down from London Bridge. Cobbled streets and warehouses by the river where developers are now fighting over old warehouses 'ripe for conversion' and any site which can be turned into loft style apartments. Even small apartments here sell for upwards of £250,000 or more, especially if they have river views. The further away from the river you are, the cheaper it generally is. A mix of streets and squares of Georgian and Victorian terraces among the council blocks around the Elephant and Castle roundabout near the Imperial War Museum. Behind the Inner London Crown Court are the beautiful Trinity Church and Merrick Squares, a Georgian treat in the surrounding sea of council blocks. Streets of small early and mid-Victorian terraces off the Walworth Road near East Street market and down the Old Kent Road.

ATTRACTS *First-time buyers; City workers who want to be central; loyal locals; some professionals; creative types (Borough); people who can't afford Kennington* • **CONSERVATION AREAS** *Trinity Church Square; West Square; Borough High Street; Thrale Street; Bear Gardens; Pages Walk; Sutherland Square* • **AVERAGE PRICES** *Flats: studio £70,000-£80,000; 1-bed £90,000-£200,000+; 2-bed £120,000+ Houses: 2-bed £140,000+; 3-bed £200,000-£600,000* • **AVERAGE RENTS (WEEKLY)** *Flats: studio £150+; 1-bed £180-£320; 2-bed £230-£400 Houses: 2-bed £230-£400; 3-bed £275-£550.*

CAMBERWELL

Getting trendier by the minute, helped by the presence of a large student population from Kings College Hospital and Camberwell School of Art. One or two almost perfect terraces of four-storey Georgian houses in Camberwell Grove and Grove Lane near Camberwell Green as well as the Georgian Addington Square just off the busy Camberwell Road. Houses like this will probably set you back at least £500,000. Elsewhere, there are three- and four-storey Victorian houses in roads off Coldharbour Lane on the way to Brixton and around the attractive green space of Myatts Fields (see Lambeth), and some Victorian survivors mixed up with council blocks and hospital buildings at the top of Grove Lane.

ATTRACTS *First-time buyers; professional and creative people who like the idea of living 'on the front line'; students who can afford not to live in Peckham* • **CONSERVATION AREAS** *Addington Square; Camberwell Green; Camberwell Grove; Sceaux Gardens* • **AVERAGE PRICES** *Flats: studio £65,000-£70,000; 1-bed £75,000+; 2-bed £85,000-£200,000 Houses: 2-bed £140,000-£200,000; 3-bed £180,000-£215,000+; 4-bed £280,000+* • **AVERAGE RENTS (WEEKLY)** *Flats: studio £95+; 1-bed £125-£160; 2-bed £160-£195 Houses: 2-bed £185-£205; 3-bed £205-£275; 4-bed £275.*

PECKHAM & NUNHEAD

Sooner or later Londoners playing their favourite game of Where's On the Up always mention Peckham. Parts of it have certainly improved, with some of the worst tower blocks in North Peckham being pulled down and replaced with new street level houses and a futuristic new library and health centre just off the high street. But it's still not for the faint hearted, especially north of the Peckham Road. The best surprises in Peckham are south of Queens Road in roads off Rye Lane, where there are early Victorian houses with gardens. This whole area is part of the Bellenden Renewal Area, a ten year council project to improve housing and the environment. Large four-bedroom Victorian houses overlooking Peckham Rye Common and Park. Mostly two- and three-bedroom Victorian terraces around Nunhead, the posher face of Peckham, with the best in roads around the cemetery. People are already paying premium prices for properties in Peckham anticipating the arrival of the East London Line, which would link the area to the tube network for the first time.

ATTRACTS *People who can't afford a house in Camberwell or East Dulwich; first-time buyers; families (Nunhead)* • **CONSERVATION AREAS** *Holly Grove; Nunhead Cemetery* • **AVERAGE PRICES** *Flats: studio £50,000-£60,000; 1-bed £85,000-£100,000; 2-bed £105,000-£130,000 Houses: 2-bed £155,000-£175,000; 3-bed £175,000-£225,000; 4-bed £185,000-£260,000* • **AVERAGE RENTS (WEEKLY)** *Flats: studio £105+; 1-bed £140-£150; 2-bed £160 Houses: 2-bed £195+; 3-bed £220+; 4-bed £230+.*

EAST DULWICH

Traditionally the poor relation of Dulwich proper but now appealing to people in its own right and becoming positively 'buzzy' in the words of one resident. Where Dulwich residents come for more interesting nightlife. Mostly three-bedroom Victorian terraces in roads off Lordship Lane with larger four- and five-storey Victorian terraces overlooking the slightly trafficky Goose Green and Peckham Rye Common. Solid late 19th-century family houses in and off Barry Road leading up to Peckham Rye. This is another area hoping to benefit from the East London Line extension and prices have risen sharply in anticipation. A good choice of generously sized conversion flats.

ATTRACTS *People who want Dulwich without the smugness; professionals; families who want to be close to Dulwich schools; people who can't afford Dulwich, or want more for their money than they can get in south-west London* • **CONSERVATION AREAS** *The Gardens* • **AVERAGE PRICES** *Flats: studio £65,000; 1-bed £95,000-£115,000; 2-bed £115,000-£145,000 Houses: 2-bed £175,000-£200,000; 3-bed £200,000-£250,000; 4-bed £230,000-£280,000* • **AVERAGE RENTS (WEEKLY)** *Flats: studio £105+; 1-bed £140+; 2-bed £160+ Houses: 2-bed £195-£205; 3-bed £220; 4-bed £230+.*

DULWICH

Green, leafy and expensive. Semi-detached and detached Victorian and Edwardian properties with crunchy gravel drives and well-cared-for gardens, substantial 1920s and 1930s homes and some modern property in roads leading off and up to Dulwich Village. Mostly modern properties in roads east of Dulwich Woods. One or two handsome Georgian mansions just south of the village near the park. The Dulwich College Estate still owns most of Dulwich and has strict rules about what residents can and can't do with their properties which has led to run-ins with some residents. Roads of mostly substantial Victorian and Edwardian terraces interspersed with 1920s semis in neighbouring Herne Hill, some converted into flats.

ATTRACTS *Families keen on green space and good schools* • **CONSERVATION AREAS** *Dulwich Village; Dulwich Woods* • **AVERAGE PRICES** *Flats: 1-bed £120,000+; 2-bed £180,000+ Houses: 2-bed £200,000-£250,000; 3-bed £250,000-£350,000; 4-bed £350,000-£450,000+* • **AVERAGE RENTS (WEEKLY)** *Flats: 1-bed £150-£185; 2-bed £185-£220 Houses: 2-bed £205+; 3-bed £230+; 4-bed £300+.*

BEST POSTCODES

Dulwich SE21 wins hands-down, with East Dulwich SE22 and Herne Hill SE24 tying for second place as long as the roads are in the parts near Dulwich. Roads near the border with SE21 have prices to match, with roads at the other side of SE22 near Peckham reflecting much lower prices there. It's the same story with roads in the west of SE24 next to Brixton (see Lambeth).

AMENITIES

SCHOOLS * *

State schools are consistently near the bottom of the league tables at primary level. Performance is marginally better at secondary level, possibly due to good numbers of private schools in the borough, which go some way towards redeeming the borough's performance. Above-average proportion of children with places in state nurseries.

PRE-SCHOOL PROVISION *5 state nurseries; 53 nursery classes in state primary or church schools; 96 private or voluntary nurseries and playgroups. Proportion of under-fives in state nurseries: 66%* ● **STATE PRIMARY SCHOOLS** *Overall league table position: 147th out of 150. Top scorers: St John's RC (with nursery unit), Rotherhithe; Boutcher C of E (with nursery unit), Bermondsey; Friars, Borough* ● **STATE SECONDARY SCHOOLS** *Overall league table position: 140th out of 149. Top scorers: Bacon's College (mixed), Rotherhithe; Notre Dame RC (girls), Elephant and Castle; St Saviour's and St Olave's CE (girls), Elephant and Castle* ● **PRIVATE PREP SCHOOLS** *Alleyn's Junior (mixed), Dulwich; James Allen's Prep (mixed), Dulwich; Dulwich College Prep (boys), Dulwich; Oakfield Prep (mixed), Dulwich; Rosemead Prep (mixed), Dulwich* ● **PRIVATE SECONDARY SCHOOLS** *James Allen's Girls (JAGS), Dulwich; Dulwich College (boys); Alleyn's (mixed), Dulwich.*

TRANSPORT * * *

Excellent in the north of the borough around London Bridge and Elephant & Castle. The Jubilee Line extension has dramatically improved access to Docklands and the West End for the whole of Southwark's river front, particularly Rotherhithe (at Canada Water) and Bermondsey. But other parts of the borough have to rely on trains and buses until and unless an extension to the East London tube line from New Cross materialises. Herne Hill has Thameslink, which gives travellers a useful cross-London link.

TRAINS *Denmark Hill (Camberwell) Zone 2. Cost of annual season ticket £756. Average journey time to Victoria 13 minutes; to London Bridge 11 minutes. Peckham Rye Zone 2. Average journey time to Victoria 13-17 minutes; to Blackfriars 11 minutes. East Dulwich Zone 2. Average journey to London Bridge 11 minutes. North Dulwich (for Dulwich Village) Zone 3. Cost of annual season ticket £896. Average journey time to London Bridge 13 minutes. Herne Hill Zone 3. Average journey time to Victoria 9 minutes; to City Thameslink 16 minutes* ● **TUBES** *Elephant & Castle (Bakerloo and Northern) Zone 1. Cost of annual season ticket £636. Rotherhithe (East London) Zone 2. Cost of annual season ticket £756. Average journey time to Shoreditch 8 minutes. Canada Water (Jubilee) Zone 2. Average journey time to London Bridge 5 minutes; to Westminster 11 minutes. Bermondsey (Jubilee) Zone 2. Average journey time to London Bridge 3 minutes; to*

Westminster 9 minutes • **BUSES** *Well-endowed for services to town, particularly in the north and middle of the borough, including the 36 via Peckham and Camberwell to Victoria, the 45 via Camberwell to Kings Cross, the 63 via Peckham to Kings Cross and the 47 via Surrey Quays to London Bridge. Further south, the main services, often held up by traffic, are the 12 to Oxford Circus from Dulwich via Peckham and Camberwell and the 185 via Dulwich, East Dulwich and Camberwell to Victoria*
• **TRAFFIC TROUBLESPOTS** *The south circular across Dulwich Common: Heavy traffic almost constant with long waits sometimes at lights at junction with Dulwich Village. Dulwich Village: Big jams, especially at school finishing time. Roads into Camberwell including Camberwell Road and Camberwell Church Street: A busy junction of four main roads with buses and delivery vans often blocking Denmark Hill by the main shopping area. Elephant and Castle: One of London's ugliest and most trafficky roundabouts*
• **PARKING** *There are controlled parking zones at Borough/Bankside, London Bridge, Bermondsey, Canada Water, Surrey Quays, Camberwell and Walworth. Cost of annual resident's permit: £72, only valid for the zone for which it's issued.*

LEISURE FACILITIES****

THEATRES & CONCERT HALLS *The Globe Theatre built on the site of the original theatre has Shakespeare plays in authentic Elizabethan surroundings. The Southwark Playhouse, in a 19th-century warehouse, specialises in new writing, directing and acting. The Blue Elephant in Camberwell has an eclectic mix of youth theatre, dance, plays, films and exhibitions. Concerts and a good choir at Southwark Cathedral* • **CINEMAS** *six-screen mainstreamer at Peckham* • **MUSEUMS & GALLERIES** *Very well provided for, especially in the north of the borough which is now well on the tourist map. The list includes the Shakespeare Museum at the Globe, the Design Museum at Butlers Wharf, the Britain at War Experience at London Bridge, the Imperial War Museum, HMS Belfast, the Tower Bridge experience, the Clink Prison Museum, the Old Operating Theatre, Museum and Herb Garrett (with gruesome displays of old surgical instruments), the London Dungeon and the Tate Modern, London's wonderful new gallery of modern art in the former Bankside Power Station building. Bankside Gallery has works by the Royal Watercolour Society. Further south Dulwich Picture Gallery, Britain's oldest picture gallery, housed in an attractive old building opposite Dulwich Park, has reopened after a £9 million face-lift*
• **SPORTS FACILITIES** *Indoor leisure centres at Camberwell, Dulwich, Bermondsey, Peckham and Rotherhithe. A new leisure centre is promised for the Elephant and Castle and a new £11 million health and fitness centre, Peckham Pulse, has taken shape in a huge glass building behind Peckham High Street as part of the area's regeneration. Watersports and marina at Greenland and South Dock, Rotherhithe. Outdoor sports stadium at Herne Hill* • **LIBRARIES** *Many branch libraries closed on Wednesdays and unpredictable opening hours at other times so check before you go. Dulwich, Newington and Peckham libraries are now open on Sundays. The architecture of the new library at Peckham is more exciting than its content. Excellent local history library in Borough High Street. High levels of satisfaction continue to be recorded from residents in library-use surveys but system use is average at 6.95 visits per head. Place in library-use league table: 17th out of 32 (where 1 is best and 32 worst).*

OPEN SPACES★★★★

Generous amounts of open space in the south of the borough around
Dulwich. More poorly provided for in the north, except for Burgess Park,
carved out of a densely-packed area after the Second World War. A
valuable green space in a built-up area but rather flat and featureless,
relieved only by the unexpected and attractive enclave of Chumleigh
Gardens, a square of almshouses which houses the park ranger service.
WOODS *Dulwich Wood; Sydenham Hill Nature Reserve with part of the old
railway line which used to run to Crystal Palace and remains of Victorian
villas which once stood at the edge of the wood* ● **PARKS** *Dulwich Park at
the edge of Dulwich Village has gardens and a boating lake. Burgess Park
has a display of gardens from around the world next to the almhouses at
Chulmleigh Gardens* ● **CEMETERIES** *Nunhead, an overgrown and mysterious
Victorian cemetery, has a full complement of mourning angels, cracked
urns and trailing ivy. It is now being restored with the help of a £1.25
million lottery grant.*

SHOPS★★★

BERMONDSEY & ROTHERHITHE *Designer food shops, clothes shops and
bookshop in restored warehouses at Shad Thames near Terence Conran's
group of restaurants. Antique shops and Friday antiques market around
Bermondsey Street. Large Co-op and other chains on Southwark Park
Road. Surrey Quays shopping centre at Rotherhithe with Tesco* ● **ELEPHANT
& CASTLE** *The ugly 1960s shopping centre was painted a shocking red a
few years ago in a desperate bid to brighten it up but this only succeeded
in drawing attention to its ugliness. Slightly improved in the last ten years
with a Tesco Metro replacing the previous 'pile 'em high sell 'em cheap'
store and some ethnic food stalls but still mostly dull chains. Residents can
only hope the planned new shopping centre will be better. Walworth Road
has cheap clothes and household goods and an active local market in East
Street* ● **PECKHAM** *Pedestrianised shopping street in Rye Lane with all the
usual chain stores. Mostly cheap stock and a lot of discount stores. Big
injections of government money have gone into encouraging stores to
locate here, especially Safeway. Small local shops in Peckham High Street
with Afro-Caribbean and Asian foodstores, clothes shops and takeaways* ●
CAMBERWELL *The small uninspiring shopping centre in the centre of
Camberwell is set for a revamp if planners give the go-ahead. The new
centre would include a six-screen cinema, a larger Safeway and a bigger
car park. A couple of interesting shops elsewhere, although of the three
secondhand bookshops in and around Camberwell Church Street, only
one survives. Small junk market off Camberwell New Road and a couple of
secondhand furniture shops. Big Sainsbury's at the bottom of Dog Kennel
Hill* ● **EAST DULWICH** *Lordship Lane has a good variety of ethnic restaurants
alongside the usual banks, chains and a branch of Somerfields. Signs of
middle class habitation include antique shops in North Cross Road and
Melbourne Grove* ● **DULWICH** *Not as villagey as the name suggests, at least
not around the shops. Two parades of shops along a rather trafficky road.
Mostly up-market local shops including a delicatessen, handfinished dry
cleaning, artists materials, clothes and a baby and children's wear shop.*

RESTAURANTS***

BERMONDSEY *The Conran restaurants at Shad Thames (if you have deep pockets or an expense account). Bermondsey Street is also becoming a good place to eat with a choice of pubs and relaxed restaurants popular with the lunch time crowd. Good Italian in Southwark Park Road* ● **BOROUGH** *London Bridge and Borough used to be a dead loss if you wanted somewhere decent to eat but now wine bars and restaurants are burgeoning under the arches of London Bridge station and along the river. All Bar One at London Bridge station. Thai restaurant by the river at Hay's Galleria, a collection of up-market shops, restaurants and market stalls in a former Thameside warehouse* ● **CAMBERWELL** *A number of restaurants and bars have opened recently around Camberwell Church Street and its junction with Camberwell Grove although some have closed again equally rapidly. Good choice of ethnic restaurants* ● **EAST DULWICH & DULWICH** *A locally-praised Thai restaurant. A big choice of Indian restaurants of varying quality. Number of chains in Dulwich Village including Pizza Express and a widely-praised restaurant at Belair House, a former mansion in parkland near Dulwich College.*

CRIME RATES*

Position in Metropolitan Police league table: 8th out of 32 (where 1 is worst and 32 best).

THE COUNCIL**

POLITICAL AFFILIATION *Labour* ● **MINUS POINTS** *Some of the worst schools in London. Not always as efficient as it should be in sweeping the streets and mending roads and pavements. Collects less council tax than any other London borough except Hackney* ● **PLUS POINTS** *Energetically working on regeneration of some of its poorest areas and collaborating with other boroughs to bring more tourists to the South Bank and rejuvenate the riverside* ● **PROPERTY SEARCHES CARRIED OUT IN 10 WORKING DAYS** *97.3%* ● **STANDARD SEARCH FEE** £95 ● **COUNCIL TAX COLLECTED** *81.3%* ● **COUNCIL TAX 2000-2001**

BAND	PROPERTY VALUE	CHARGE	BAND	PROPERTY VALUE	CHARGE
A	up to £40,000	£564	E	£88,001-£120,000	£1,033
B	£40,001-£52,000	£658	F	£120,001-£160,000	£1,221
C	£52,001-£68,000	£752	G	£160,001-£320,000	£1,409
D	£68,001-£88,000	£845	H	over £320,000	£1,691

SUTTON

It's tempting to think that Sutton was only included in the administrative area of Greater London to fill in what would have otherwise been an awkward gap in London's roughly circular shape. Uniquely among London boroughs, it's surrounded by affluent neighbours (Merton, Kingston and Croydon). It harbours no chunks of Victorian inner suburb within its boundaries. Overwhelming inner city problems of crime, high unemployment and poor housing are safely away from its borders. It's mostly white (only 6 per cent of its population is from an ethnic minority) and working (unemployment stands at just 1.9%, joint second lowest in London, along with Kingston). A pleasant part of the Surrey commuter belt, it's safe, cosy and green, but a bit dull for those who crave more excitement than whether they'll get a seat on the 7.45.

At its northern tip is the turn-of-the-century council estate of St Helier with small cottages set attractively around greens. To the west are the 1930s semis and small detached houses of North Cheam. Just below is Cheam, with some attractive cottages among the inter-war building which grew up around its station. To the north east is Sutton, the shopping and administrative centre of the borough. Villagey Carshalton, whose clapboard houses and ponds spanned by delicate hump-backed bridges would be picture-postcard if the roads weren't so busy, gives way to Carshalton Beeches, classic well-off stockbroker-belt territory. In the east are the more modest terraces of Wallington and Beddington, and Sutton's only tower blocks at Roundshaw, in the process of being demolished and replaced with low-rise housing as part of a £100 million regeneration programme.

Like many other outer London boroughs, one of Sutton's biggest problems (and residents' biggest grumbles) is traffic. The mostly affluent residents collectively have one of the highest rates of car ownership in the UK and the borough is bisected with busy roads filled with through-traffic.

PROPERTY AND ARCHITECTURE

ST HELIER

One of the largest council estates built by the London County Council in the 1920s and 1930s. Mostly terraces in typical LCC cottage estate-style with gables, steeply-pitched roofs and arched doorways set in generous amounts of green space. Many of these houses and some more recent additions built in the 1950s were bought by their tenants under the right-to-buy scheme and are now coming back onto the market. Local agents estimate that up to three quarters of the properties are privately owned. Homes nearest the tube at Morden (see also Merton) are the most sought after. A good place to find a cheap house. Mostly two- and three-bedroom terraces – flats are rare.

ATTRACTS *Families; first-time buyers* • **CONSERVATION AREAS** *None* • **AVERAGE PRICES** *Houses: 2-bed £105,000-£120,000; 3-bed £110,000-£125,000* • **AVERAGE RENTS (WEEKLY)** *Houses: 2-bed £140-£150; 3-bed £160+.*

NORTH CHEAM & CHEAM

North Cheam is predominantly 1930s semis with the best properties in roads round Churchill Road. Popular for schools, with some top performing primary schools in the area. Cheam itself is more villagey and up-market than North Cheam, with a proper centre just north of the station. Among the predictable 1930s semis it has some beautifully preserved 16th century clapboard houses in roads just near Cheam Park. South of Cheam, the enclave of Belmont, west of Burdon Lane, has some of the handsomest houses in the area. Everything here from neo-Georgian to overgrown cottages with rustic chimneys and tilehung fronts.

ATTRACTS *Families; commuters; people moving further out of London from areas like Tooting and Mitcham* • **CONSERVATION AREAS** *Cheam Village* • **AVERAGE PRICES** *Flats: 1-bed £90,000+; 2-bed £110,000+ Houses: 2-bed £140,000+; 3-bed £150,000+; 4-bed £215,000* • **AVERAGE RENTS (WEEKLY)** *Flats: 1-bed £130+; 2-bed £155+ Houses: 2-bed £160+; 3-bed £185; 4-bed £230.*

SUTTON

Some large and lovely Victorian and Edwardian houses near the centre of Sutton around St James's Road, some now converted into flats, as well as roads of Victorian terraces and cottages. South Sutton is the most sought-after, with spacious detached and semi-detached houses in the best roads east of Brighton Road. Elsewhere in Sutton there's a good choice of modern blocks and 1960s and 1970s houses as well as everything from Victorian onwards. Turn-of-the-century cottage-style houses around Oak Close and Meadow Close north of Sutton are the result of an early planning experiment which created the Sutton Garden Suburb.

ATTRACTS *Families; local first-time buyers* • **CONSERVATION AREAS** *Landseer Road; Grove Avenue; Sutton Garden Suburb* • **AVERAGE PRICES** *Flats: studio £55,000-£70,000; 1-bed £80,000-£100,000; 2-bed £90,000-£140,000 Houses: 2-bed £115,000-£160,000; 3-bed £130,000-£250,000; 4-bed £170,000+* • **AVERAGE RENTS (WEEKLY)** *Flats: studio £100-£120; 1-bed £120-£145; 2-bed £150-£185 Houses: 2-bed £150-£185; 3-bed £195+; 4-bed £275+.*

CARSHALTON VILLAGE & CARSHALTON BEECHES

Roads of Victorian and Edwardian terraces and semis off the High Street in Carshalton Village and pretty white clapboard 16th century cottages in Pound Street, as well as roads of 1930s semis. Some handsome late Victorian and Edwardian semis in roads around Park Hill in more expensive Carshalton Beeches. Elsewhere in Carshalton Beeches (known as The Beeches to distinguish it from The Village) is archetypal stockbroker-belt, occasionally trembling into Southfork in some of the grandest roads. Big detached houses of every permutation (red brick, Tudorbethan, white plastered, you name it) in large gardens in Pine Walk West and East with a large swathe of grass and trees shielding inhabitants from their neighbours on the other side.

ATTRACTS *Families; local first-time buyers (Carshalton); loyal locals moving up-market from the less-grand north of the borough; people moving out of inner London boroughs like Wandsworth* • **CONSERVATION AREAS** *Wrythe Green; Carshalton Village; Carshalton Park; Park Hill* • **AVERAGE PRICES** *Flats: Studio £60,000-£80,000; 1-bed £80,000-£100,000; 2-bed £100,000-£130,000 Houses: 2-bed £105,000-£140,000; 3-bed £160,000-£220,000; 4-bed £240,000-£300,000* • **AVERAGE RENTS (WEEKLY)** *Flats: 1-bed £130+; 2-bed £150+ Houses: 2-bed £165-£205 3-bed £195+; 4-bed £230+.*

WALLINGTON & BEDDINGTON

Much of Wallington is Victorian, a reminder of its beginnings as a 19th century railway suburb. Large Victorian houses, many converted into flats in roads north of the railway, which used to be the smartest area. Now South Wallington is smarter with roads of large and small Victorian houses in roads off Stafford Road and around Mellows Park. Woodcote Avenue is the poshest road in Wallington with large Edwardian detached houses. Beddington is cheaper than Wallington with a mix of everything from Victorian to blocks of modern flats. Wallington is home to some of the best selective schools.

ATTRACTS *Families; commuters; local first-time buyers* • **CONSERVATION AREAS** *Wallington Green; Beddington Village; Church Lane; Carew Manor* • **AVERAGE PRICES** *Flats: studio £55,000-£60,000; 1-bed £70,000-£90,000; 2-bed £85,000-£140,000 Houses: 2-bed £110,000-£140,000; 3-bed £140,000+; 4-bed £200,000+* • **AVERAGE RENTS (WEEKLY)** *Flats: 1-bed £125+; 2-bed £150+ Houses: 2-bed £160+; 3-bed £175+; 4-bed £205.*

BEST POSTCODES

Largely irrelevant in a borough with Surrey rather than London postcodes. Proximity to a good train service to town, good schools and green space are much more important.

AMENITIES

SCHOOLS★★★★

Excellent overall performance in league tables particularly at secondary level, where the marks are lifted by some seriously academic selective grammar schools. Lots of competition to get into the best schools, although being surrounded by outer London boroughs with some pretty good schools of their own means there's not as much pressure on numbers from parents in neighbouring boroughs. A fair selection of private schools. You're likely to end up paying for nursery education as Sutton has the second lowest proportion of under-fives in nursery education in outer London.

PRE-SCHOOL PROVISION *1 state nursery; 31 nursery classes in state primary and church schools; 71 private and voluntary nurseries and playgroups. Proportion of under-fives in state nurseries: 38%* • **STATE PRIMARY SCHOOLS** *Overall position in league tables: 33rd out of 150. Top scorers: St Dunstan's CE (with nursery unit), Cheam; Dorchester (with nursery unit), Worcester Park; Westbourne (with nursery unit), Sutton* • **STATE SECONDARY SCHOOLS** *Overall position in league tables: 2nd out of 149. Top scorers (all selective): Nonsuch High (girls), Cheam; Wilson's School (boys), Wallington; Wallington High (girls), Wallington* • **PRIVATE PREP SCHOOLS** *Collingwood (mixed), Wallington; Glaisdale (mixed), Cheam; Homefield (boys) Sutton;* • **PRIVATE SECONDARY SCHOOLS** *Chart-topper Sutton High (girls from 4), Sutton; Stowford College (mixed, children from 7), Sutton.*

TRANSPORT★★★

Trains only throughout the borough with the middle better served than the outer reaches. Services from town can be tediously slow at weekends and outside rush hour, and there are lots of complaints about slow and crowded rush hour services from Sutton. Some areas, such as North Cheam, are some distance from a decent station. Connections in the far north-east corner of the borough have improved a bit with the Croydon Tramlink (see Croydon).

TRAINS *Cheam Zone 6. Cost of annual season ticket £1456. Average journey time to London Bridge 45 minutes; to Victoria 23-29 minutes. Sutton Zone 5. Cost of annual season ticket £1332. Average journey time to London Bridge 39 minutes; to Victoria 20-26 minutes; to Blackfriars 36 minutes. Carshalton Zone 5. Average journey time to London Bridge 30 minutes; to Victoria 24 minutes; to Blackfriars 34 minutes. Wallington Zone 5. Average journey time to London Bridge 34 minutes; to Victoria 34 minutes* ● **BUSES** *Tend to link neighbouring suburbs or head towards the nearest large shopping centres of Kingston or Croydon rather than into town. Night buses running from Trafalgar Square include the N44 via St Helier, Carshalton, Carshalton Beeches, Wallington and Sutton* ● **TRAFFIC TROUBLESPOTS** *Cheam: The area is criss-crossed by busy main roads including the A24 and the A217 carrying fast traffic to Surrey, the M25, Gatwick airport and the south coast. Sutton: The centre of the town has been pedestrianised (a good thing) pushing all the traffic into surrounding roads (a bad thing). Roads round Cheam and Carshalton Roads and St Nicholas Way tend to get clogged up with long queues at traffic lights. Carshalton Village: The constant stream of traffic queuing at the lights around Pound Street and the High Street detracts substantially from the pleasure of walking round the ponds and gardens of The Grove. Shopping in the pretty Victorian High Street is also spoilt by traffic* ● **PARKING** *Not too bad in most parts of the borough because space is plentiful. Even parking near the shops in Cheam and Carshalton isn't impossible and there's a good supply of car parks in Sutton. There's one controlled parking zone, in Sutton town centre with three zones. Cost of annual resident's permit: £25.*

LEISURE FACILITIES***

THEATRES & CONCERT HALLS *Two theatres. The Harry Secombe (named after the comedian, a long-time resident) in Sutton has ballet, opera, modern and classical music, plays, musicals and pantomimes, with lots of amateur dramatics and performances by local groups. The Charles Cryer theatre in Carshalton has more off-the-wall and innovative plays, dance and music, and is the centre of the borough's arts education programme* ● **CINEMA** *Only one, the six screen UCI in Sutton, showing mainstream films* ● **MUSEUMS & GALLERIES** *A small but interesting number of historic houses open to the public, reminders that Sutton was once a popular country stamping ground for the aristocracy and royalty (Henry VIII's palace at Nonsuch is just over the borough border in Epsom and Ewell). The 15th century Carew Manor behind imposing wrought iron gates overlooking Beddington Park is now a school but the medieval Great Hall and other parts of the house are open to the public. Carshalton House, a Queen Anne mansion, almost invisible behind high brick walls, is also a school but open to the public occasionally, as is the elaborate 18th century water tower overlooking the road. Honeywood, an attractive white stucco Victorian house overlooking Carshalton ponds, houses a well-presented local history museum with some fascinating archive photographs and a completely preserved panelled Edwardian billiard room. Whitehall, a white boarded Tudor house in Cheam village has an art gallery and exhibitions explaining the house's construction and history* ● **SPORTS FACILITIES** *Two leisure centres at Carshalton and North Cheam, both with pools, fitness centres and indoor sports facilities. All-weather athletics track at Sutton. Golf and squash at Oaks Park in the south of the borough. Tennis, athletics and other outdoor sports in*

parks across the borough. Leisure discount card scheme in operation
• **LIBRARIES** Well used, especially Sutton central library on three floors with coffee shop and one-stop leisure shop. Branch libraries are friendly but less well-resourced. Sutton claims to have pioneered the practice of offering a full range of services on Sunday (at Sutton central, Sunday afternoons only) but makes up for it by closing all libraries across the borough on Monday. 8.6 library visits per head. Position in library-use league table: 6th out of 32 (where 1 is best and 32 worst).

OPEN SPACES * * * *

Other boroughs would dispute Sutton's claim that it has more trees than anywhere else in London. But who's counting? Like neighbouring Croydon, Sutton's south edge abuts the North Downs and the borough is scattered with green space. Other open space within the borough tends to the flat and formal rather than wild and rural and there are no woods or heaths to speak of. Spaces popular with local residents like Nonsuch Park and Banstead Downs are just outside the borough boundary (but easily accessible).

RIVER WALKS One of the two sources of the Wandle (the other is near Croydon) begins just west of The Grove at Carshalton. Here the river begins its nine mile journey to the Thames at Wandsworth, flowing peacefully through the grounds of this lovely little park. The recently created Wandle trail is an excellent walk, combining seclusion with historical and industrial interest • **WIDE OPEN SPACES** Cheam Park (which continues into Nonsuch Park) with mature trees, manicured lawns and views over Surrey. Beddington Park is the largest space in the borough with boating lake and Carew Manor at its south-western edge.

SHOPS * * *

CHEAM & NORTH CHEAM Streets of pleasant individual shops in Cheam Village straggling out around the crossroads of Ewell Road, High Street, The Broadway and Station Way. A clutch of pretty half-timbered buildings housing real shops including antique and furniture shops. Budgens in The Broadway. A mixture of chain stores and local shops fronting onto busy main roads at North Cheam • **SUTTON** Has had to struggle to keep residents from decamping to nearby Croydon and is fighting back with two large shopping centres. The older of the two, St Nicholas, has just had a £3 million revamp and there are proposals for new shops and a leisure centre in the other shopping complex, Times Square. Most of the High Street is pedestrianised, encouraging the spread of pavement cafés and linking in well with the two indoor shopping centres. Few startlingly original shops (and some full of disturbingly tasteless knick-knacks and ornaments) but good branches of most chain stores and an Allders department store. Safeway in Cheam Road. Tesco in St Nicholas Way. Open-air market on Tuesday and Saturday
• **CARSHALTON** A small Victorian shopping street next to The Grove with up-market local shops including furniture and antique shops and a bakery. Unfortunately you take your life in your hands unless you cross at the crossing • **WALLINGTON** Mostly chain stores in roads around the station and in the pedestrianised Wallington Square alongside a handful of individual local shops. Recently arrived Sainsbury's in an aggressively modern building is fuelling fears that Wallington's local shops are dying. Traffic carves through the middle of the shopping centre on the main A237.

RESTAURANTS * *

Not a culinary hotspot. Some winebars, bistros and pubs serving good food in Carshalton and Cheam. Sutton has pasta and pizza chains including Pizza Express and a choice of local restaurants and pubs. Across the borough you'll find the usual scattering of Indian and Chinese take-aways and burger bars.

CRIME RATES * * * * *

Position in Metropolitan Police league table: 30th out of 32 (where 1 is worst and 32 best).

THE COUNCIL * * * *

POLITICAL AFFILIATION *Liberal Democrat* • **MINUS POINTS** *Low level of state nursery provision. Expensive for property searches* • **PLUS POINTS** *Recycles more waste than any other London borough. Enthusiastically environmental, with a number of recycling and sustainability initiatives. It is experimenting with a dual system of wheelie bins to separate rubbish and recyclables. The third most efficient rubbish collections in outer London. Excellent schools* • **PROPERTY SEARCHES CARRIED OUT IN 10 WORKING DAYS** *96.9%* • **STANDARD SEARCH FEE** *£125.60* • **COUNCIL TAX COLLECTED** 98%. • **COUNCIL TAX 2000-2001**

BAND	PROPERTY VALUE	CHARGE	BAND	PROPERTY VALUE	CHARGE
A	up to £40,000	£530	E	£88,001-£120,000	£972
B	£40,001-£52,000	£619	F	£120,001-£160,000	£1,149
C	£52,001-£68,000	£707	G	£160,001-£320,000	£1,326
D	£68,001-£88,000	£796	H	over £320,000	£1,591

TOWER HAMLETS

Tower Hamlets has changed physically and socially more than any other part of London in the last 15 years. At the beginning of the 1980s, the docks in the south of the borough which had provided most of its employment and community focus lay derelict after the death of the industries which had sustained them. Now the docks have re-emerged as Docklands, London's trendy new City in the East. Warehouses have been converted into luxury riverside apartments and there are new transport links. Gleaming office blocks including Europe's tallest skyscraper to date, Canary Wharf, house today's most money-spinning industries – financial services and technology. Geographically, Canary Wharf is part of the East End. Socially, it's part of the wealthy international City.

After huge teething problems (an unreliable and overcrowded Docklands Light Railway, a lack of coherent planning which deprived new residents of even basic shops and amenities, resentment from long-term residents in one of the poorest boroughs at being over-run with yuppies and a long recession which nearly destroyed the whole area), Docklands has taken off. Now it's bringing other parts of Tower Hamlets with it, as City workers move into Victorian terraces and workers' cottages a tube stop or two from the office.

Docklands is the most visible and well-documented part of Tower Hamlets, stretching from just east of Tower Bridge along the river via Wapping and Limehouse down to the Isle of Dogs, which hangs like an appendix across the river from Greenwich. Docklands also includes parts of Bermondsey and Rotherhithe (see Southwark).

Further north, the borough of Tower Hamlets takes in the East End proper, in which generations of refugees have settled, from French Huguenots to Jews and most recently Bangladeshis. Nearest the City are Spitalfields and Whitechapel, still a centre for the wholesale clothing industry. To the east are the council flats and cottages of Stepney and the newly trendy areas of Bethnal Green and Bow. Bromley and Poplar just above the Isle of Dogs have some of the most alienating council blocks ever built. Much of the borough was blown to bits by the Luftwaffe and council planners did their worst in the 1950s and 1960s to obliterate traditional street plans, so it's a common sight to see Victorian or Georgian streets cowering in the lee of council estates and rare to get large tracts of period properties. Not surprisingly the grids of Victorian streets which have survived are much sought after.

It's no longer daring to live in the East End. Even lawyers and bankers do, albeit safely locked behind the iron gates of their new homes with 24-hour security in Docklands. Bow and Bethnal Green have their middle-class colonies. The warehouses of Spitalfields and Whitechapel are being turned into loft developments and artists' studios. But the borough is still dominated by council estates. It's the sixth most deprived in the UK and it has more people out of work, at 12.7%, than any other borough in London. Its large Bangladeshi community, which accounts for nearly a quarter of the population, contributes hugely to the area's rich cosmopolitanism but is also traditionally one of the poorest of all ethnic communities.

The building of Docklands was an early experiment in generating private as well as public funds for regeneration schemes. Ironically for an area with such a Thatcherite pedigree, it needed the expensive publicly funded Jubilee Line to make it work and attract the big multinational finance and banking houses which are its lifeblood. Now more public and private money is pouring into schemes elsewhere in Tower Hamlets to improve jobs, education and the environment, and to create a new cultural quarter in Spitalfields.

PROPERTY AND ARCHITECTURE

SPITALFIELDS & WHITECHAPEL

Still very commercial areas with lots of wholesale shops and small factories but also lively and cosmopolitan places to live. Some wonderful and rarely on-the-market four-storey Georgian townhouses in streets off Brick Lane, the heart of Asian Spitalfields. New developments of offices and warehouses converted into luxury apartments and lofts in both Spitalfields and Whitechapel. Large houses are rare but you can occasionally still buy huge converted warehouse 'shells'. Lots of ex-council flats if you're looking for a centrally located bargain. Modern houses are cheaper than period ones.

ATTRACTS *Creative types; single people; young professionals*
● **CONSERVATION AREAS** *Artillery Passage; Fournier Street; Elder Street; Wentworth Street; Whitechapel Market* ● **AVERAGE PRICES** *Flats: studio £100,000+; 1-bed £110,000+; 2-bed £150,000+ Houses: 3-bed £200,000+; 4-bed £400,000+* ● **AVERAGE RENTS (WEEKLY)** *Flats: studio £200+; 1-bed £250+; 2-bed £270-£325.*

WAPPING & LIMEHOUSE

Warehouses in Wapping were among the first to get the conversion to luxury flats treatment in the late 1980s. Rooms in these flats can be a bit cramped and critics argue (with some justification) that it's a yuppie ghetto but it's one of the most central and popular parts of Docklands and most of the major building is finished. Wapping is still more expensive than Limehouse because it's nearer the City, but Limehouse is catching up fast as Canary Wharf takes off. Blocks of new apartments all around Limehouse Basin (great if you've got a boat which needs mooring) and more building going on along the river. The Basin is still a bit of a building site but hopefully not for much longer. Enclaves of handsome Georgian houses (some now flats) on the river at Wapping Pier Head and at Narrow Street in Limehouse, and streets of small Georgian terraces tucked away behind the noisy Commercial Road at Limehouse. Lots of council blocks round every corner.

ATTRACTS *City workers; well-paid professionals; creative types; people wanting pieds-à-terre; investors* ● **CONSERVATION AREAS** *Wapping Pier Head; Wapping Wall; St George's Town Hall; St Paul's Church Shadwell; Commercial Road; York Square; Albert Gardens & Arbour Square; Lowell Street; Narrow Street; St Anne's Limehouse* ● **AVERAGE PRICES** *Flats: studio £90,000-£100,000; 1-bed £135,000-£150,000+; 2-bed £175,000+ Houses: 2-bed £200,000+; 3-bed £250,000+; 4-bed £300,000+*
● **AVERAGE RENTS (WEEKLY)** *Flats: studio £180+; 1-bed £200+; 2-bed £250+ Houses: 2-bed £250+; 3-bed £300+; 4-bed £350+.*

BETHNAL GREEN

Getting very trendy as people with money realise it's only one stop from Liverpool Street. Its closeness to the City means it's a bit pricier than Bow further east. Pockets of former workers' cottages, once probably little more than slums and now cleaned up to provide small (and expensive) two- and three-bedroom houses in streets between Hackney Road and Columbia Road. Some streets of Victorian terraces around Bethnal Green Road. The main disadvantage (visually if nothing else) is that there are rarely more than a couple of streets before you turn the corner to yet another ugly council estate or tower block. But there are some bargains to be had with former council flats and houses on the better estates. Stepney to the south is almost all council property.

ATTRACTS *City workers; young professionals; first-time buyers; investors; parents buying property for student children* ● **CONSERVATION AREAS** *Globe Road; Jesus Hospital Estate; Boundary Estate; Carlton Road* ● **AVERAGE PRICES** *Flats: studio £55,000-£90,000; 1-bed £85,000-£160,000; 2-bed £95,000-£230,000 Houses: 2-bed £160,000-£300,000; 3-bed*

£180,000-£400,000; 4-bed £190,000-£600,000 • **AVERAGE RENTS (WEEKLY)** *Flats: studio £100-£160; 1-bed £160-£240; 2-bed £180-£300 Houses: 2-bed £250-£300; 3-bed £270-£360; 4-bed £370-£450.*

BOW

One of the best parts of Tower Hamlets. There are council blocks but there are also streets of attractive two- and three-storey Victorian terraces in roads north of Bow Road as well as Tredegar Square, a wonderful, almost complete square of Georgian brick and white stucco terraces. Roads around Tredegar Square have smaller Georgian terraces. Towards Victoria Park and the Hertford Union Canal there are streets of Georgian and Victorian terrace off Roman Road. Roman Road itself has a couple of popular estates with cheap ex-council flats.

ATTRACTS *First-time buyers; professionals; families; investors; people who can't afford Islington* • **CONSERVATION AREAS** *Victoria Park; Driffield Road; Roman Road market; Medway; Tredegar Square; Tower Hamlets Cemetery; Tomlins Grove* • **AVERAGE PRICES** *Flats: studio £60,000-£120,000; 1-bed £75,000-£150,000; 2-bed £90,000+ Houses: 2-bed £150,000-£245,000; 3-bed £150,000-£250,000+; 4-bed £175,000-£250,000+* • **AVERAGE RENTS (WEEKLY)** *Flats: studio £100-£160; 1-bed £160-£240; 2-bed £180-£300 Houses: 2-bed £250-£300; 3-bed £270-£350+; 4-bed £370-£450.*

ISLE OF DOGS

Known locally as The Island. Almost all the properties here were built within the last 15 years or converted from old warehouses, with more to come. Property is a mixture of swish apartments with all the trappings of river views, porterage, underground car parks and security, alongside modern townhouses, a scattering of dockers' cottages and Victorian terraces. Some ex-council bargains. Developers swear the demand for yet more new 'luxury' apartments is there, although some agents have their doubts and argue the area is being over-run with speculative building, which could make it vulnerable in a market downturn. The Isle of Dogs became much more established as a residential area in the late 1990s but it's an acquired taste and can be a rather soulless environment. Your neighbours will probably be people like yourself, only there during the week because it's a pied-à-terre or short term tenants because the owner has bought it as a rental investment. There's still a bit of Them and Us feeling between longstanding residents and wealthier newcomers.

ATTRACTS *Young single people; workers in the City and Canary Wharf; people wanting pieds-à-terre; investors* • **CONSERVATION AREAS** *Island Gardens; Coldharbour; Chapel House* • **AVERAGE PRICES** *Flats: studio £75,000; 1-bed £95,000-£115,000+; 2-bed £125,000+ Houses: 2-bed £145,000-£230,000; 3-bed £185,000+* • **AVERAGE RENTS (WEEKLY)** *Flats: studio £140-£150+; 1-bed £170+; 2-bed £220+ Houses: 2-bed £220+; 3-bed £250-£400.*

BEST POSTCODES

Every area is so mixed that postcodes are an unreliable indicator of relative social standing. Bow E3 and Docklands E14 are generally considered good areas but E14 includes the council estates of Poplar alongside the luxury apartments of Docklands. Proximity to a tube is often the decider, particularly in Bow, where otherwise attractive terraces around

Victoria Park are cheaper than property further south because it's a brisk walk to the tube station.

AMENITIES

SCHOOLS**

Tower Hamlets was the target of a scathing Ofsted report three years ago which found that the borough spent more money than any other local education authority for less tangible result. Next time round Ofsted found much more to praise in a borough with high levels of poverty and deprivation. But it still languishes near the bottom of the league tables both at primary and secondary level. It partly redeems itself by having the second most generous state provision for under-fives in London. One Islamic girls' secondary school.

PRE-SCHOOL PROVISION *7 state nursery schools; 49 nursery classes in state primary and church schools; 54 private and voluntary day nurseries and playgroups. Proportion of under-fives in state nursery schools: 83%* • **STATE PRIMARY SCHOOLS** *Overall league table position: 125th out of 150. Top scorers: St John the Baptist RC, Bethnal Green; St Saviour's C of E (with nursery unit), Poplar; English Martyrs' RC (with nursery unit), Whitechapel* • **STATE SECONDARY SCHOOLS** *Overall league table position: 137th out of 149. Top scorers: Mulberry School for Girls, Wapping; Bishop Challoner RC (girls), Stepney; Stepney Green (boys), Stepney* • **PRIVATE SECONDARY SCHOOL** *Madni Girls, Tower Hamlets.*

TRANSPORT****

Excellent in the west of the borough and dramatically improved in the Isle of Dogs now that the Jubilee Line has opened, giving quick access to the South Bank at Waterloo and the West End. Plans to extend the East London Line north through Hackney to Highbury and Islington and south to Croydon and Wimbledon would bring useful extra links to Wapping and Whitechapel.

TUBES *Whitechapel (District, Hammersmith & City, East London) Zone 1. Cost of annual season ticket £636. Wapping (East London) Zone 1. Bethnal Green (Central) Zone 2. Cost of annual season ticket £756. Average journey time to Oxford Circus 17 minutes. Bow Road (District) Zone 2. Average journey time to Victoria 22 minutes. Canary Wharf (Jubilee) Zone 2. Average journey time to Westminster 14 minutes* • **DOCKLANDS LIGHT RAILWAY** *Bow Church Zone 2. Average journey time to Stratford 6 minutes. Canary Wharf Zone 2. Average journey time to Bank 11 minutes* • **BUSES** *Fine in the north of the borough with plenty of services to the City and West End. Less frequent in Wapping and the Isle of Dogs where you can find yourself stranded late in the evening. Services include the 15 via Limehouse and Tower Hill to Paddington and the 25 via Bow, Mile End, Stepney and Whitechapel to Oxford Circus* • **TRAFFIC TROUBLESPOTS** *The Highway, Wapping: Carries lots of the traffic coming into East London including container lorries from Tilbury and newsprint lorries to the various newspaper companies in Docklands. The Aldgate Roundabout & Commercial Road, Whitechapel. A horrible junction of several main roads, always jammed with drivers trying to manoueuvre themselves into the right lane (see also City of London). The Limehouse Link and Rotherhithe Tunnel approaches at Commercial Road: The Limehouse*

Link is supposed to be the most expensive stretch of road ever built but it hasn't solved the area's traffic problems. Heavy traffic also pours out of the Rotherhithe tunnel onto Commercial Road • **PARKING** The borough is one big controlled parking zone so expect to pay for the privilege of parking your car outside your front door. There are parking zones in Bethnal Green, Bow & Poplar, Stepney & Wapping and the Isle of Dogs. Permits valid only in the zone for which they're issued. Cost of annual resident's permit: £35.

LEISURE FACILITIES * * *

THEATRES & CONCERT HALLS Half Moon Youth Theatre in Limehouse has workshops and plays by and about young people. Touring theatre companies and local productions at the Emery Theatre, Poplar and the Brady Arts and Community Centre in Whitechapel. Brick Lane Music Hall is a small surviving part of a tradition of East End music hall and pub theatre. Classical concerts at Christ Church, Spitalfields. Stand-up comedy at Jongleurs, Bow Wharf (see shops below) and Cabot Hall, Canary Wharf. Rock concerts at the Docklands Arena and variety of live music at Cabot Hall • **CINEMAS** Two multiplexes, in Stepney and the Isle of Dogs, both showing mostly mainstream films. Films at the Space Arts Centre, Canary Wharf • **MUSEUMS & GALLERIES** The Whitechapel Art Gallery with art nouveau exterior specialises in exhibitions of the work of living artists rather than housing permanent exhibitions. Local artists across the borough also open their studios and sell their work to the public. The Tower of London, one of London's most visited sights, is the borough's best known attraction. The Ragged School Museum on the Regent's Canal at Mile End housed in a former ragged school building has a mock-up of a Victorian classroom complete with slates and strict teacher (children love this) as well as exhibitions about the lives of the children who attended the school. Staffed by volunteers so opening hours are erratic • **SPORTS FACILITIES** Leisure centres in Wapping, Whitechapel, Bethnal Green, Poplar and Mile End. Athletics track and football pitches at Mile End. Watersports and sailing at Millwall Docks • **LIBRARIES** Poorly used and housed in old fashioned buildings. All this is set to change with the arrival of seven new 'Ideas Stores', whizzy new buildings with libraries, Internet access, courses, workshops and cafés. This ambitious plan will cost £20 million and the first two stores in Whitechapel and Bow could be open by next year. Meanwhile, the existing service continues, with patchy opening hours and everything closed on Wednesdays. 3.1 library visits per head. Position in library-use league table: 30th out of 32 (where 1 is best and 32 worst).

OPEN SPACES * * *

Generally badly off for green space. Tower Hamlets is a densely populated and built-up borough and the developers' drive to build profitably in Docklands didn't leave much scope for leaving large tracts of open space. One of the borough's biggest stretches of open space, Mile End Park, is getting a £25 million facelift. Otherwise, what greenery there is tends to be flat and municipal. But to compensate, it has the water resources of rivers, canals and docks.

CEMETERIES Tower Hamlets Cemetery. Satisfyingly overgrown and Victorian, a worthy competitor to Abney Park (Stoke Newington) or Nunhead • **CANALS** The Regent's Canal from Victoria Park to Limehouse Basin. The best way to walk through some of Tower Hamlets' less salubrious areas. At Victoria Park, the Hertford Union Canal splits off from the Regents' Canal, joining the River Lea from where you can walk through the Lea Valley Park (see Haringey and Enfield) or through to the tangle of rivers, old warehouses and locks at Bow Back Rivers (see Newham) • **RIVER WALKS** You can walk the whole way along the Thames Path from Tower Bridge to the Isle of Dogs opposite the Dome. A great way of keeping abreast of London's changing river • **PARKS** Victoria Park. Surrounded by canals with large boating pond and lush sloping lawns. (see also Hackney).

SHOPS * * *

Shops are generally a bit tatty. If glitzy shopping malls are your thing, this isn't the place to be. But Tower Hamlets excels in lively street markets. Get there early for the best bargains.

SPITALFIELDS & WHITECHAPEL The craft shops, small restaurants and organic wholefood shops in the covered former fruit and vegetable market at Spitalfields have been in an almost permanent state of flux for years as City developers manoeuvre to build on Spitalfields' juiciest sites. A bit dead in the week (except at lunchtime), much better on Sundays. Asian shops line Brick Lane, with clothes wholesalers (lots of leather jackets), sweet shops and bookshops. Sunday market in Brick Lane. Daily clothes and household goods market at Petticoat Lane, Aldgate on the fringes of the City (see City of London). The Whitechapel end of Commercial Road is almost all Asian clothes wholesalers. Local shops and general daily market in Whitechapel Road • **WAPPING & LIMEHOUSE** Wapping's supposedly premier shopping centre, Tobacco Dock, is all but dead after years of constant changes of ownership and indecision. The tobacco warehouse converted to two storeys of shops in the 1980s boom now has only one or two shops still open, with the rest empty. Plans to change it into a factory outlet never materialised. Mostly local shops along Commercial Road by Limehouse • **BETHNAL GREEN** Trafficky Bethnal Green Road has cheap clothes and electrical goods shops, second-hand furniture and cafés alongside chains. Large Tesco Metro. Alright for everyday shopping. Popular Sunday flower market at Columbia Road which also has an eclectic collection of permanent shops including garden design and Indian sweetshops • **BOW** Roman Road has a well-established clothes market with cheap fashions. The western end has some fascinating shops including designer clothes, expensive knick-knacks and antiques. Bow Wharf, with shops and restaurants, is taking shape just to the west of Roman Road, although only a few brave souls have taken shop space so far. Not quite Camden Lock but Bow Wharf's part of the regeneration project to improve Mile End Park and the canal-side • **ISLE OF DOGS** Fiercely criticised for its lack of shops when workers and daring residents first moved there. Canary Wharf is now much improved if you like your shopping predictable, with a striking four-storey shopping centre underneath the tower. Big Tesco Metro, a selection of up-market chains and a choice of City-style sandwich bars. Asda at Crossharbour. Nothing much elsewhere on the Island, with lots of boarded-up shops and dingy general stores, for desperate purchases only. Residents on the south end of the Island can now pop on the DLR extension to Greenwich for more shopping choice.

RESTAURANTS***

SPITALFIELDS & WHITECHAPEL *A good bagel bakery and a couple of recommended Indian restaurants among the huge choice along Brick Lane (you can smell the curry as soon as you turn into the street) and in Whitechapel, as well as pie and mash* • **WAPPING & LIMEHOUSE** *Good riverside pubs serving food include the Prospect of Whitby in Wapping and the Grapes in Limehouse. Otherwise, Pizza Express, Babe Ruth's American theme restaurant, a couple of smartish Chinese places and a recent addition, a smart restaurant in the former Wapping Hydraulic Pumping Station near the Prospect of Whitby* • **BETHNAL GREEN** *A couple of Thai restaurants. Vegetarian and Spanish among a lot of take-away dross. Not much going on in the evening* • **BOW** *Not much, despite a growing middle-class population. A pie and mash and a café or two overlooking Mile End Park but it's a bit dead in the evening, even in the pubs, according to locals* • **ISLE OF DOGS** *Considering the number of expense accounts around here, the offerings are limited. Café Rouge and a few other restaurant chains, winebars and cafés and American grill bars where City boys drink tasteless American beer from bottles.*

CRIME RATES*

Position in Metropolitan Police league table: 6th out of 32 (where 1 is worst and 32 best).

THE COUNCIL**

POLITICAL AFFILIATION *Labour* • **MINUS POINTS** *Still trying to extricate itself from a legacy of loony leftism and a distrastrous attempt at decentralisation during the previous Lib Dem adminstration. Schools are still poor if not quite as dire as they used to be. Poor street-sweeping. Disgracefully slow at turning round property searches. Poorly resourced libraries* • **PLUS POINTS** *Appears to be making more strenuous efforts to improve its education provision* • **PROPERTY SEARCHES CARRIED OUT IN 10 WORKING DAYS** *2.4%* • **STANDARD SEARCH FEE** £85.60 • **COUNCIL TAX COLLECTED** *88.1%* • **COUNCIL TAX 2000-2001**

BAND	PROPERTY VALUE	CHARGE	BAND	PROPERTY VALUE	CHARGE
A	up to £40,000	£484	E	£88,001-£120,000	£888
B	£40,001-£52,000	£565	F	£120,001-£160,000	£1,049
C	£52,001-£68,000	£646	G	£160,001-£320,000	£1,211
D	£68,001-£88,000	£727	H	over £320,000	£1,453

WALTHAM FOREST

Waltham Forest marks the beginning of outer east London, or inner Essex, whichever way you like to look at it. Sandwiched between the industrial Lea Valley to the west and Epping Forest bursting out between the built up suburban roads to the east, it's a favoured location for East Enders made good – or at least richer (see also Redbridge). Like Redbridge, Waltham Forest has never been top of the list for the fashion-conscious and has suffered from the same west London snobbery as other parts of east London which are more suburban than trendy.

The Victorian working class railway suburbs of Leyton and Leytonstone cover the bottom quarter of Waltham Forest, giving way to Walthamstow, a pleasanter railway suburb and the borough's main administrative and retail centre. To the north is salubrious Highams Park, with large detached and semi-detached villas on the edge of Epping Forest. At South Chingford next to the Lea Valley 1930s suburbia takes over where Victorian suburbia leaves off. At the northern tip of the borough, surrounded by Epping Forest on one side and the reservoirs of the Lea Valley on the other, are the large Edwardian and inter-war houses of North Chingford.

This isn't middle class commuter belt suburbia, although it's one of the most convenient parts of outer London for the City and a lot cheaper than more traditionally favoured areas. Unemployment is among the highest in outer London at 5.7% and it's the 22nd most deprived area in England. It has an inner city-style multiracial population, with more than a quarter of the population from an ethnic minority and large Afro-Caribbean and Pakistani communities.

Leytonstone, a previously obscure area of east London, hit the headlines dramatically a few years ago when protesters against the building of a road linking the M11 to the east cross route in Hackney held out for more than a year against the demolition of houses and trees in roads along the route. Shots of protesters in makeshift towers and partially demolished Victorian terraces painted in day-glo hippy colours remain many people's main image of Leytonstone. All the protesters' efforts were fruitless, because the motorway has been built. The only reminders of the homes which once stood in its way are the occasional partly demolished wall behind forgotten hoardings or a fruit tree in the middle of what was once a garden. Leytonstone has been brutally severed by the new road, signalled by bright new brick walls at the end of suburban roads, but there are signs that the road is removing some of the traffic from residential roads and Leytonstone High Road.

Part of Leytonstone High Road is being pedestrianised and various traffic calming measures introduced. But this is small beer compared with ambitious proposals being discussed for Walthamstow. A total of £56 million of public and private money will be invested in regenerating Walthamstow town centre over the next six years. There are plans to create a new town square and gardens in the shopping centre, improve the bus station, and build an arts centre and multiscreen cinema.

PROPERTY AND ARCHITECTURE

LEYTON & LEYTONSTONE

Leyton has speculatively-thrown-up grids of Victorian terraces built in the last twenty years of the nineteenth century after the Great Eastern Railway started offering cheap working men's fares, bringing commuting within the reach of humble clerks. Here and there are dashes of later building and, more visibly, a cluster of council tower blocks and estates near the centre of Leyton. Leytonstone is slightly more expensive than Leyton, with the best properties bordering Epping Forest at Bush Wood.

ATTRACTS *First-time buyers; young professionals and couples; people who can't afford Islington or Hackney* • **CONSERVATION AREAS** *Browning Road; Thornhill Road; Whipps Cross Road & Forest Glade* • **AVERAGE PRICES** *Flats: studio £60,000; 1-bed £75,000+; 2-bed £95,000-£110,000 Houses: 2-bed £130,000; 3-bed £170,000; 4-bed £200,000+* • **AVERAGE RENTS (WEEKLY)** *Flats: studio £115; 1-bed £125-£140; 2-bed £150-£170 Houses: 2-bed £180+; 3-bed £200+; 4-bed £210+.*

WALTHAMSTOW

Described in the last century by its most famous inhabitant, the designer William Morris, as 'a suburban village on the edge of Epping and once a pleasant enough place but now terribly cockneyfied and choked up by the gerry builder.' But now increasingly favoured by young professionals who want more space for their money and easy access to the efficient Victoria line. Mostly Victorian terraces again around the south of Walthamstow but quite spacious and set back from the road. North of the main Forest Road round Lloyd Park is a clutch of red brick working men's terraces and 19th century purpose-built flats with small wrought iron balconies, their line broken occasionally by an arch or gable. A refreshing change from the usual terrace, the terraces are known as Warners, after their builder. A good choice of conversion flats. Larger Victorian semis in Upper Walthamstow to the east and attractive old cottages in Walthamstow Village.

ATTRACTS *Young professionals; people who can't afford Islington or Hackney; commuters; first-time buyers* • **CONSERVATION AREAS** *Walthamstow Village; Leucha Road; Orford Road, Eden Road & Grosvenor Road; Forest School* • **AVERAGE PRICES** *Flats: studio £60,000+; 1-bed £75,000+; 2-bed £80,000+ Houses: 2-bed £110,000+; 3-bed £150,000+; 4-bed £180,000+* • **AVERAGE RENTS (WEEKLY)** *Flats: studio £110; 1-bed £120-£150; 2-bed £150-£180 Houses: 2-bed £160-£200; 3-bed £180+; 4-bed £205+.*

HIGHAMS PARK

More suburban and salubrious than Walthamstow with large Victorian and Edwardian semi-detached and detached houses in big gardens. Many have all their original features intact, the streets are wide and Epping Forest is there as a backdrop. Mostly up-market 1930s houses further south towards the north circular.

ATTRACTS *Families* • **CONSERVATION AREAS** *Ropers Avenue & Inks Green* • **AVERAGE PRICES** *Flats: 1-bed £60,000-£75,000; 2-bed £100,000*

Houses: 2-bed £115,000+; 3-bed £130,000+; 4-bed £170,000+ •
AVERAGE RENTS (WEEKLY) *Flats: studio £100-£110; 1-bed £120+; 2-bed*
£140+; Houses: 2-bed £165+; 3-bed £175+; 4-bed £235+.

CHINGFORD

Synonymous in many people's minds with the bruiser reputation of its
former MP Norman Tebbit. But North Chingford, at least, is much smarter
and more attractive than its public image would suggest. Epping Forest
opens out at the end of the main Station Road, and large half-timbered
Edwardian houses with flurries of turrets, carved wooden balconies,
porches and stained glass line the streets between the Forest and the
station. South Chingford is cheaper, partly because the houses are smaller
(more Victorian terraces mixed with some 1930s) and partly because it's a
long way from trains and tubes.

ATTRACTS *Families* • **CONSERVATION AREA** *Chingford Green* • **AVERAGE**
PRICES *Flats: 1-bed £60,000-£75,000 2-bed £80,000 Houses: 3-bed*
£125,000+; 4-bed £210,000+ • **AVERAGE RENTS (WEEKLY)** *Flats: studio*
£100+; 1-bed £120-£125; 2-bed £140+ Houses: 2-bed £165; 3-bed
£175+; 4-bed £235+

BEST POSTCODES

All in the London postcode area apart from a small section of Highams
Park. Chingford E4 is the smartest. Leytonstone E11 and Walthamstow E17
are better than Leyton E10. But factors like proximity to transport links have
the most significant effect on prices.

AMENITIES

SCHOOLS**

Uninspired overall league table performance from both primary and
secondary schools. Secondary schools do slightly better than primary
schools. At the age of five some schools operate a system of linked infant
and junior schools while others are primary schools taking children from
five onwards. A handful of private schools. Average numbers of pre-school
children in state nursery schools.

PRE-SCHOOL PROVISION *4 state nursery schools; 40 nursery classes in state*
primary and church schools; 69 private day nurseries and playgroups.
Proportion of under-fives in state nursery school places: 58% • **STATE**
PRIMARY SCHOOLS *Overall league table position: 138th out of 150. Top*
scorers: Handsworth (with nursery unit), Chingford; St Mary's RC,
Chingford; St Patrick's RC, Walthamstow • **STATE SECONDARY SCHOOLS**
Overall league table position: 111th out of 149. Top scorers: Chingford
Foundation (mixed), Chingford; Highams Park (mixed), Highams Park;
Walthamstow School for Girls, Walthamstow • **PRIVATE PREP SCHOOLS**
Forest Prep (mixed), Walthamstow • **PRIVATE SECONDARY SCHOOLS** *Forest*
(boys), Walthamstow; Forest (girls), Walthamstow; Normanhurst (mixed,
from 2) Chingford.

TRANSPORT***

Walthamstow's very well connnected, thanks mainly to the Victoria line
(generally efficient despite some problems with signalling occasionally).

Trains as well as tubes from a choice of different stations. Central line at Leyton and Leytonstone (improving). The north of the borough relies on trains.

TRAINS *Highams Park Zone 4. Cost of annual season ticket £1104; average journey time to Liverpool Street 22 minutes. Chingford Zone 5. Cost of annual season ticket £1332; average journey time to Liverpool Street 25 minutes* • **TUBES** *Leyton Zone 3. Cost of annual season ticket £896; average journey time to Liverpool Street 13 minutes. Walthamstow Central Zone 3. Average journey time to Victoria 25 minutes* • **BUSES** *Quite a good choice to the centre of town, with the necessary proviso that any long bus journey usually means sitting in traffic. Services include the 48 from London Bridge to Walthamstow Central via Leyton, the 55 from Oxford Circus to Leyton and the 56 from St Pauls to Leyton. Otherwise local services to neighbouring suburbs and shopping centres* • **TRAFFIC TROUBLESPOTS** *Leyton & Leytonstone: High roads in both areas are often clogged with traffic, although Leytonstone in particular is improving thanks to the motorway. Walthamstow: Forest Road, the main through-road across Walthamstow, is trafficky, particularly at junctions with roads linking to the North Circular. Quicker to walk on a Saturday. Chingford: Constant flow of traffic and buses along Station Road, the main shopping street, and long queues can build up around the Green at the end of the road by the library* • **PARKING** *Currently six controlled parking zones in the borough: Waltham Central East, Walthamstow Central West, Blackhorse Lane, Walthamstow Stadium (nights), Chingford (voucher parking) and Hoe Street, Walthamstow. Cost of annual resident's permit: £25. Further zones are being considered for Leytonstone, Leyton, North Chingford, Highams Park and Wood Street, Walthamstow.*

LEISURE FACILITIES * * *

THEATRES & CONCERT HALLS *The Waltham Forest theatre is set in attractive formal grounds by the lake in Lloyd Park, Walthamstow (although the building itself is unremarkable) and has a choice of mainstream plays, live music, community and children's shows. More choice of entertainment at Walthamstow Assembly Hall next to the Town Hall. Both can be hired, as can halls in Chingford, Leyton and elsewhere in the borough* • **CINEMAS** *Just one, the Walthamstow ABC, strictly mainstream* • **MUSEUMS & GALLERIES** *Interesting collection. The William Morris Gallery is housed in the designer's old home, a handsome Georgian mansion in Lloyd Park, once the grounds of the house. The museum is devoted to Morris's designs with rooms full of rich dark wallpapers, tapestries and stained glass put into context with explanation boards and photographs. Little on his social vision though. In Walthamstow village (worth a visit in itself for its ancient houses and picturesque church), the local history Vestry museum occupies what was once a workhouse. Mock-ups of the kitchens and living rooms of Walthamstow's first Victorian residents, exhibition of toys and games and temporary exhibitions. Art exhibitions, photography and show-cases for local artists at the Changing Room gallery, Lloyd Park and the William Morris Gallery* • **SPORTS FACILITIES** *Four leisure centres at Leytonstone (new Millennium fitness centre), Leyton, and Walthamstow (two, both with new or extended gym facilities). Pools in Leytonstone, Leyton, and Walthamstow. Golf in Chingford, greyhound racing at Walthamstow and tennis, football and other outdoor sports in parks and open spaces throughout the borough. Discount leisure scheme in operation* • **LIBRARIES** *Small cramped buildings even at Walthamstow Central, although this last* *is being refurbished and expanded. But libraries as a whole are some of the best used in London. Reasonable opening hours although Wednesday is a bad day. 8.99 library visits per head. Position in library-use league table: 4th out of 32 (where 1 is best and 32 worst).*

OPEN SPACES * * * *

Waltham Forest claims, along with almost every other outer London borough, to be one of the greenest in London. But does the pecking order matter with all having something striking to offer? Some beautiful open space here with the northern reaches giving way suddenly to gently undulating Essex countryside.

FOREST *Epping Forest. Runs down the whole of the borough's eastern border with Redbridge before taking over totally at Chingford. Owned by the Corporation of London and run by the Epping Forest and Open Spaces Committee. A mixture of mature woodland and open grassland, and a haven for riders, cyclists and walkers, the forest pops up all over the place, behind suburban homes and next to council flats* • **PARKS** *Lloyd Park. A green lung in an otherwise built-up area, with formal flower beds (overlooked by the William Morris Gallery) and lake with hungry ducks. Turns flat and featureless the further away you go from the gallery.*

SHOPS * * *

LEYTON & LEYTONSTONE *Busy, trafficky high roads with necessary but dull chains and the usual clutch of take-aways, chemists, charity shops and cash converters. Unexciting shopping. Tesco in Leyton. Proposed Tesco in Leytonstone* • **WALTHAMSTOW** *Much more colourful, with a 400 stall, mile-long street market, supposedly the longest daily street market in Europe, down most of the length of the High Street. Clothes, food, household goods and anything else energetically promoted by stallholders. Selbourne Walk, the indoor shopping mall opening off the High Street, is more functional than glitzy, with down-market chains but there's a good bookshop in the High Street. Sainsbury's* • **HIGHAMS PARK & CHINGFORD** *Unspectacular but useful shopping streets around Highams Park station. Chingford itself has tidy local shops in an Edwardian shopping street with a real butcher and grocer among other shops. Everyday shopping at Chingford Mount, with Sainsbury's.*

RESTAURANTS * *

A handful of recommended restaurants and eating experiences, including Spanish in Leytonstone. Pizzas, pie and mash, and trackside dining at Walthamstow dog racing track. Pizza Express in Chingford. Otherwise, it's the local Indian, Chinese or kebab house.

CRIME RATES * * *

Position in Metropolitan Police league table: 19th out of 32 (where 1 is worst and 32 best).

THE COUNCIL * * *

POLITICAL AFFILIATION *Labour* • **MINUS POINTS** *Not always as efficient at collecting street litter as it should be. Has had trouble with missed rubbish collections but appears to be improving* • **PLUS POINTS** *Cheap and efficient for property searches. Door-to-door recycling now covers nearly half the* *borough's homes with another 22,000 homes to be included next year. Well used libraries* • **PROPERTY SEARCHES CARRIED OUT IN 10 WORKING DAYS** *100%* • **STANDARD SEARCH FEE** *£85* • **COUNCIL TAX COLLECTED** *88%* • **COUNCIL TAX 2000-2001**

BAND	PROPERTY VALUE	CHARGE	BAND	PROPERTY VALUE	CHARGE
A	up to £40,000	£585	E	£88,001-£120,000	£1,073
B	£40,001-£52,000	£683	F	£120,001-£160,000	£1,286
C	£52,001-£68,000	£780	G	£160,001-£320,000	£1,463
D	£68,001-£88,000	£878	H	over £320,000	£1,755

WANDSWORTH

Wandsworth has spent the past 10 years becoming more and more middle class. The process started quietly but rose to a crescendo as the press started writing glowingly about its wonderful family houses, green space and excellent state schools. The council, a Thatcherite flagship, helped things along by setting the lowest council tax of any London borough (underpinned by some nifty central government grants) and energetically selling off council property to upwardly-mobile tenants. Now gentrification has spread to all four corners of the borough, with even formerly working-class Battersea now an unofficial annexe of Chelsea.

Like other south London boroughs, Wandsworth is big. At its northern edge along the river it sprawls along the river from Battersea to Wandsworth with a mix of Victorian terraces, council blocks and glitzy riverfront apartments and onto the riverfront mansion blocks, large Victorian terraces and detached Edwardian grandeur of Putney in the west. Further south, detached houses and smart modern blocks in Southfields give way to smaller Edwardian terraces in Earlsfield and detached houses between Wandsworth Common and Clapham Common. Victorian and Edwardian terraces and semi-detached houses of varying size and smartness take over again at Balham and around Tooting's two commons.

Parts of Wandsworth are very affluent and the influx of middle-class residents has kept its overall unemployment rate low. At 3.9%, it has the second lowest unemployment rate of any inner London borough, bested only by the City of London where many Wandsworth residents work. But the borough is also the 30th most deprived district in England, with much of the deprivation focused on the former industrial areas along the river at Battersea and Wandsworth. Millions of pounds have been pouring into Battersea to provide jobs and training and a massive £152 million is being spent on revamping Wandsworth's town centre and riverside. Meanwhile the long running saga of the proposed £500 million redevelopment of the derelict Battersea Power Station powers on. Plans for the site include hotels, leisure facilities, exhibition space, apartments and a shuttle rail service to Victoria.

Developers have been busier in Wandsworth than almost

anywhere else except Docklands, working to transform derelict buildings and abandoned industrial river sites into luxury homes, shops, hotels and restaurants, sometimes running into fierce opposition from residents. The attraction for developers of course is that Wandsworth is now more than acceptable to the middle classes, especially now the Jubilee Line extension at Waterloo makes a journey from Battersea to offices at Canary Wharf so much quicker. One problem for developers and residents alike, however, is that efforts to persuade successive governments to extend the tube network to Wandsworth have so far failed. The arrival of public transport enthusiast Ken Livingstone as London's first mayor could mean that plans for a £1 billion new line from Hackney to Chelsea extending to Wandsworth Town and/or Battersea may finally get off the drawing board. But the line will need expensive tunnelling and campaigners are now calling for a south London line to be built on existing track, linking Clapham junction with Brixton and the east London line at New Cross.

This lack of east/west links doesn't help the traffic congestion which is one of the borough's biggest problems. Wandsworth Town Centre itself is the junction of three major roads, including the notorious south circular and the main A3 to Portsmouth which also goes through Putney. More traffic pours out to Brighton via Tooting and across Wandsworth Bridge under one of the most brutal 1960s underpasses in London.

PROPERTY AND ARCHITECTURE

BATTERSEA

Once a mostly working-class district with a distinctly dodgy reputation but colonised by economic refugees from Chelsea and beyond since it was 'discovered' in the late 1980s. Small well-cared-for Victorian terraces and cottages predominate and around the yuppie spiritual centre of Battersea Square, mixed with new riverside developments and council blocks of all descriptions. Smart mansion blocks overlooking Battersea Park. Between a tangle of railway tracks and the area's main restaurant drag on Lavender Hill there are pretty streets of small Victorian cottages with deep porches on the Shaftesbury Park Estate. Larger Victorian terraces in roads off Lavender Hill and Northcote Road towards Wandsworth Common are dubbed 'nappy valley' by some locals because it has such a high proportion of young families.

ATTRACTS *Young professionals, both single and with families; people who can't afford Chelsea or Fulham* • **CONSERVATION AREAS** *Battersea Park; Battersea Square; Latchmere Estate; Parktown Estate; Shaftesbury Park Estate; Clapham Junction* • **AVERAGE PRICES** *Flats: studio £100,000+; 1-bed £140,000-£200,000; 2-bed £180,000+; Houses: 2-bed £270,000-£300,000; 3-bed £350,000+; 4-bed £350,000* • **AVERAGE RENTS (WEEKLY)** *Flats: 1-bed £240-£300; 2-bed £300-£360 Houses: 2-bed £380-£400; 3-bed £400+; 4-bed £500-£600.*

WANDSWORTH

Several distinct parts, all sought after. Small well-looked-after terraces in the sloping roads known collectively as The Tonsleys, centring on Tonsley Hill near Wandsworth Town railway station. Larger Victorian and Edwardian terraces, some converted, others still houses, in roads off East Hill. A mix of large Victorian terraces and semi-detached and detached Edwardian houses with large gardens, in the roads between Wandsworth Common and Clapham Common, an area known as between the commons or sometimes cloyingly as 'twixt the Commons'. On the other side of Wandsworth Common is a grid of roads of large Edwardian and Victorian houses known as The Toastrack because of its shape on the map, where it's not unusual for houses to change hands for over £1 million.

ATTRACTS *Families looking for green space and good schools (catchment areas are very important); people who can't afford the space they want in Clapham or Fulham* • **CONSERVATION AREAS** *Clapham Common; Wandsworth Common; Nightingale Lane; Wandsworth Town; St John's Hillgrove* • **AVERAGE PRICES** *Flats: 1-bed £150,000+; 2-bed £190,000+ Houses: 2-bed £250,000-£300,000; 3-bed £380,000-£400,000; 4-bed £450,000+* • **AVERAGE RENTS (WEEKLY)** *Flats: 1-bed £120-£150; 2-bed £150-£200 Houses: 2-bed £260-£280; 3-bed £350-£450; 4-bed £450-£550.*

BALHAM & TOOTING

Balham used to be a bit of a joke, not helped by Peter Sellers' mocking description of it as Gateway to the South. It had a bit of an identity crisis, with people claiming to live in Wandsworth or Tooting or Clapham – anywhere but Balham. But now the area is up-and-coming, particularly around Tooting and Wandsworth Commons. Mostly Victorian and Edwardian terraces, with handsome Edwardian double-fronted houses, some flats, on the Heaver Estate off Tooting Common. More Edwardiana in cheaper Tooting, with large semi-detached houses around Tooting Graveney Common. Cottage-style terraces in roads off Franciscan Road at Totterdown Fields in Tooting Bec, an early council estate.

ATTRACTS *Professionals, who praise the area's good community atmosphere; families who value good schools; people who can't afford Clapham or Earlsfield; members of the Asian community* • **CONSERVATION AREAS** *Heaver Estate; Totterdown Fields; Streatham Park; Dinsmore Road; Old Devonshire Road* • **AVERAGE PRICES** *Flats: 1-bed £80,000-£170,000; 2-bed £140,000-£250,000 Houses: 3-bed £190,000-£330,000; 4-bed £220,000-£450,000* • **AVERAGE RENTS (WEEKLY)** *Flats: 1-bed £150-£200; 2-bed £180-£320 Houses: 3-bed £230-£450; 4-bed £340-£500.*

SOUTHFIELDS & EARLSFIELD

Dull, straight, flat roads in Earlsfield and the east of Southfields lined with square-bayed Edwardian terraces and semis. But increasingly popular with couples who like getting relatively large amounts of space for their money and who can't afford Battersea or Wimbledon. West Southfields is more expensive and residents make a mint during Wimbledon fortnight renting out drives or whole houses. Large detached Edwardian and 1930s houses mixed with modern blocks on hills up towards Putney.

ATTRACTS *Families (Southfields); young professional couples (Earlsfield)* • **CONSERVATION AREAS** *West Hill Road; Wimbledon Park Road; Victoria Drive; Sutherland Grove* • **AVERAGE PRICES** *Flats: studio £85,000-*

*£100,000; 1-bed £125,000-£160,000; 2-bed £150,000-£230,000
Houses: 2-bed £240,000-£270,000; 3-bed £270,000-£350,000; 4-bed
£350,000+ • **AVERAGE RENTS (WEEKLY)** Flats: 1-bed £170-£195; 2-bed
£210-£250 Houses: 2-bed £270-£300; 3-bed £320-£390; 4-bed £400-
£500.*

PUTNEY & ROEHAMPTON

Putney has always been a good solid residential area but it has livened up
considerably over the past few years as more younger people have moved
in. As elsewhere, the draws are schools, green space and good transport.
A mixture of everything from large detached Edwardian houses in West
Putney (the grandest part) to cottages and Victorian houses and terraces of
all sizes in roads off Putney High Street and Lower Richmond Road. Some
conversions and clusters of modern blocks of flats, particularly at the top of
Putney Hill and large family houses around Putney Heath. Mansion blocks
by the river. Cheaper Roehampton has some large houses but a lot of it is
ex-council and the area is dogged by a lack of shops and good transport
links.

ATTRACTS *Young families; single professionals; affluent first-time buyers;
mature families* • **CONSERVATION AREAS** *East Putney; Rushholme Road;
Putney Heath; Roehampton Village; Westmead; Dover House Estate; West
Putney; Coalecroft Road; Charlwood Road; Lifford Street; Oxford Road;
Deodar Road; Putney Embankment; Putney Lower Common* • **AVERAGE
PRICES** *Flats: studio £70,000-£80,000; 1-bed £140,000+; 2-bed
£170,000-£240,000 Houses: 2-bed £300,000+; 3-bed £350,000-
£400,000; 4-bed £450,000+* • **AVERAGE RENTS (WEEKLY)** *Flats: studio
£150-£175; 1-bed £220; 2-bed £250-£260 Houses: 2-bed £260+; 3-bed
£350-£450 4-bed £495+.*

BEST POSTCODES

Not a big deal because postcode areas cross and recross the boundaries
of the various residential areas. Putney SW15, Wandsworth SW18 and
Battersea SW11 are all very acceptable. No big price differences. The
dividing line that matters is the borough boundary between Wandsworth
and Lambeth, with cheap and efficient Wandsworth the side everyone
wants to be on.

AMENITIES

SCHOOLS * * *

Widely praised by parents, although state schools generally don't do as
well in league tables as you might expect. Strict catchment areas operate
for many primary schools at the top of the tables. Several Wandsworth
secondary schools are partially selective although parental pressure and
the government's admissions adjudicator are forcing the borough to reduce
the proportions of selective pupils. Schools operate a common test. A good
selection of private schools at all levels and generous pre-school provision,
both state and private.

PRE-SCHOOL PROVISION *3 state nursery schools; 49 nursery classes in state
primary and church schools; 133 private or voluntary nurseries and
playgroups. Proportion of under-fives in state nurseries: 62%* • **STATE
PRIMARY SCHOOLS** *Overall place in league table: 112th out of 150. Top*

scorers: St Anselm's RC, Tooting; All Saints C of E, Putney; Our Lady of Victories RC, Putney. Tight catchment areas at other high scorers including: Beatrix Potter, Wandsworth; Franciscan, Furzedown, Penwortham and Sellincourt Schools, Tooting ● **STATE SECONDARY SCHOOLS** Overall place in league table: 98th out of 149. Top scorers: ADT City Technology College (mixed), Putney; Graveney (mixed), Tooting; Burntwood (girls), Tooting ● **PRIVATE PREP SCHOOLS** Finton House (mixed), Wandsworth; Thomas's Prep (mixed), Battersea; Prospect House (mixed), Putney; Putney Park (mixed to 11), Putney; Northcote Lodge (mixed), Wandsworth; Broomwood Hall (mixed), Balham; Ibstock Place (mixed), Roehampton ● **PRIVATE SECONDARY SCHOOLS** Putney High (girls), Putney; Ibstock Place (mixed), Roehampton; Emanuel School (mixed), Battersea; Putney Park (girls), Putney.

TRANSPORT***

Good tube services to the west and south of the borough but the east relies on trains and buses, although it boasts Britain's busiest railway station, Clapham Junction.

TRAINS Battersea (Queenstown Road) Zone 2. Cost of annual season ticket £756. Average journey time to Waterloo 6-10 minutes. Clapham Junction Zone 2. Average journey time to Waterloo 6-11 minutes. Wandsworth Town Zone 2. Average journey time to Waterloo 12-15 minutes. Balham Zone 3. Cost of annual season ticket £896. Average journey time to Victoria 13 minutes. Putney Zones 2/3. Average journey time to Waterlooo 14-17 minutes ● **TUBES** East Putney (District) Zones 2/3. Average journey time to Victoria 18 minutes. Balham (Northern) Zone 3. Average journey time to London Bridge 17 minutes. **BUSES** ● A good range of bus routes, particularly around Putney, Wandsworth and Clapham Junction in the north of the borough. Scarcer in the south, with mostly suburban services. Some useful cross-borough routes. Buses to town include the 14 from Putney to Tottenham Court Road, the 19 from Battersea Bridge to Piccadilly, the 22 from Putney to Piccadilly and the 77 from Tooting via Wandsworth Common, Clapham and Battersea to Waterloo ● **TRAFFIC TROUBLESPOTS** Wandsworth: Town Centre. Where several main roads (including the A205 south circular and the A3) meet and cross. Often bad traffic jams round the Arndale shopping centre. Roads around the common (Bellevue Road and Bolingbroke Grove especially) often jammed. Putney: The High Street. Too narrow for the amount of traffic it carries. Blockages are common where traffic has to move into one lane after coming over Putney Bridge. Problems with parked delivery vans. Battersea: Long tail-backs at traffic lights around Battersea Square. Small streets too narrow for the traffic they attract. Balham & Tooting: Always lots of traffic near the main shopping areas of Balham High Road and Upper Tooting Road. This succession of shopping streets doubles as a main road to Gatwick airport, among other places ● **PARKING** Parking is getting trickier as more car owners move in and commuters create their own unofficial park-and-ride schemes. Most of the borough, including Battersea, Clapham, Tooting, Balham and Putney, now has controlled parking. Permits issued for one zone aren't valid in any other zone. Cost of annual resident's permit: £43.25.

LEISURE FACILITIES***

THEATRES & CONCERT HALLS *Battersea Arts Centre (BAC) in the former Battersea Town Hall building (worth going to see just for its wonderful painted ceilings, marble staircase and mosaic floors). A variety of fringe shows and comedy as well as more mainstream theatre. The Wandsworth Symphony Orchestra puts on concerts at local venues* ● **CINEMAS** *Not a huge choice. Currently only one, the Putney ABC, which shows mostly mainstream films. Plans for a new 18-screen cinema in the Arndale Centre, now known as the Wandsworth Shopping Centre, as part of the area's revamp* ● **MUSEUMS & GALLERIES** *Not the best place for culture vultures. The Wandsworth Museum has interesting local history displays. Changing exhibitions of artworks in the Pumphouse Gallery Battersea Park* ● **SPORTS FACILITIES** *Well provided for. Leisure centres at Putney, Battersea, Balham, Tooting, Roehampton and Wandsworth. Popular outdoor Lido at Tooting Bec. Athletics track at Battersea Park. Rowing at Putney. Tennis and football at Tooting Bec Common and King George's Park by Putney Bridge* ● **LIBRARIES** *Well-resourced and some of the best anywhere in London. Sunday afternoon opening at four libraries: Balham, Tooting, Battersea and Putney (now in a swish new modern building). Good evening opening hours but almost all lending libraries closed either Wednesday or Thursday. Reference libraries at Battersea and Wandsworth. 10.79 library visits per head. Position in library-use league table: 2nd out of 32 (where 1 is best and 32 worst).*

OPEN SPACES***

Good supply of open space, although Wandsworth and Tooting Commons are blighted by busy roads and criss-crossed by railway lines. Close to beautiful Richmond Park and Wimbledon Common although technically these are in neighbouring boroughs (Richmond-upon-Thames and Merton respectively). Much of the borough's best open space is private, in the large gardens of many family houses.

URBAN WILDERNESS *The overgrown parts of Putney Heath and the wooded parts of Wandsworth Common are good for getting away from the traffic* ● **PARKS** *Battersea Park. Good views from the riverside frontage next to the striking peace pagoda and plenty of lush space and trees in an otherwise densely populated area. A popular venue for circuses and fireworks.*
● **INDUSTRIAL RIVERSIDE** *Paths have recently been opened up all the way down the length of the River Wandle from Wandsworth town to Carshalton (see Sutton) which makes a fascinating walk through the industrial heritage of the boroughs of Wandsworth, Merton and Sutton.*

SHOPS****

BATTERSEA & CLAPHAM JUNCTION *Estate agents have colonised almost anything in Lavender Hill that isn't a restaurant. This and the up-market furniture shops are a sure sign of a significant yuppie presence. Big choice of shops (mostly chains) around Clapham Junction and along St John's Road where there are plans to improve the street environment and cut traffic. Arding and Hobbs, the long-established local department store, is on the corner of St John's Road. Large Asda on Lavender Hill and Lidl discount food store. Smaller shops including a clutch of antique shops in Battersea Park Road. Kwiksave* ● **WANDSWORTH** *The Arndale Centre in Wandsworth Town Centre is an appalling 1960s concrete bunker, known locally as 'the morgue'. But after ten years of inaction, £50 million is finally* being promised to refurbish the shopping centre with cinemas, health clubs, bars and restaurants. It's already been renamed the Wandsworth Shopping Centre in a bid to perk up its image but no-one will be fooled until the revamp starts. Smart shops opposite Wandsworth Common in Bellevue Road which along with Northcote Road Battersea together provide bookshops, antiques, cosy cafés and other individual shops for the in crowd. You can usually count on meeting someone you know. Sainsbury's at Garrett Lane • **TOOTING & BALHAM** Wide range of shops in the confluence of roads around Tooting Broadway and Tooting Bec stations (although heavy traffic doesn't improve the experience and the streets themselves are architecturally dull). Chains including M&S and Boots but also ethnic supermarkets and some individual clothes shops. Tooting Market, an indoor market selling English and Afro-Caribbean fruit and vegetables, clothes and furniture. Appreciated by residents for its cheapness. Sainsbury's in Balham High Road • **PUTNEY** Radical improvements here over the past 20 years with the arrival of the Putney Exchange shopping centre in the High Street, a large Waitrose to supplement the rather cramped Sainsbury's and a host of new shops to cater for the influx of younger residents. All the usual chains plus antique and reproduction furniture, jewellers and designer clothes. Heavy traffic damps enthusiasm but residents and planners are thrashing out plans to ease some of the worst of it.

RESTAURANTS★★★★

BATTERSEA & CLAPHAM Bewildering choice in Lavender Hill with everything from Indian to Afro-Caribbean alongside brasseries, cafés and bars with pavement seating. Active in the evening. More pavement cafés around the small enclave of Battersea Square with awnings managing to replicate an authentic continental atmosphere • **WANDSWORTH** A good selection of brasseries, pubs and restaurants in Old York Road just down from The Tonsleys. Tables overlooking Wandsworth Common at pubs and restaurants in Bellevue Road and further options in Northcote Road • **TOOTING** A group of well-regarded Indian restaurants in Upper Tooting Road and Tooting High Street • **PUTNEY** A good buzz in the evening, even on weekdays. Everything from pubs to Thai, Indian and Italian. A cluster of interesting restaurants in roads down towards the river including the stunning glass bus-shelter-style Putney Bridge restaurant with river views.

CRIME RATES★★★

Position in Metropolitan Police league table: 16th out of 32 (where 1 is worst and 32 best).

THE COUNCIL★★★★

POLITICAL AFFILIATION Conservative • **MINUS POINTS** Enthusiastic espousal of Tory policies like selling off council property and operating selective schools are not to everyone's taste • **PLUS POINTS** The second lowest band D council tax in London after Westminster. Makes an effort to listen to residents through 1,000-strong panel and got the thumbs up for general performance. Active moves to cut down on crime with use of CCTV, neighbourhood watch schemes and council-hired Parks Police. Weekly door-to-door recycling collection of paper, glass and cans across the borough. Praised by residents for efficient street care and good schools • **PROPERTY SEARCHES CARRIED OUT IN 10 WORKING DAYS** 99.2%

● **STANDARD SEARCH FEE** £132.50 ● **COUNCIL TAX COLLECTED** 91.4%
● **COUNCIL TAX 2000-2001**

BAND	PROPERTY VALUE	CHARGE	BAND	PROPERTY VALUE	CHARGE
A	up to £40,000	£267	E	£88,001-£120,000	£459
B	£40,001-£52,000	£312	F	£120,001-£160,000	£579
C	£52,001-£68,000	£333	G	£160,001-£320,000	£669
D	£68,001-£88,000	£375	H	over £320,000	£802

WESTMINSTER

If you know London only as a tourist you will almost certainly have spent most of your time in Westminster (unless you're very enterprising). The City of Westminster, to give it its proper name, is home to most of the top sights on the tourist itinerary including the Houses of Parliament, Buckingham Palace, the Changing of the Guard and Madame Tussaud's. It contains London's most famous shopping streets including Oxford Street and Regent Street as well as many of London's poshest addresses.

But there's a lot of Westminster the tourists don't see and not all of it is attractive and/or expensive. In the top north-west corner lies West Kilburn, streets of small Victorian terraces, large stucco houses that have seen better days and the sprawling Mozart council estate. South of Kilburn, Paddington is a mess of hotels, railway tracks and council estates with some bravely gleaming roads of white stucco houses, particularly around Bayswater. But it should be all change over the next few years for the former industrial areas at Paddington Basin around the canal by the station and St Mary's Hospital. A total of £500 million is being injected into the area to create what developers hope will be a trendy new canalside quarter, with waterside cafés, restaurants, offices, homes and hotels around the basin. There are also plans to revamp the shabby, litter covered streets around Paddington Station. All this coupled with the successful (if expensive) Heathrow Express to Paddington will bring new impetus to a previously overlooked area.

Things get much posher to the east with the wide streets and canal-side homes of Maida Vale and Little Venice, with the smart villas of St John's Wood just to the north. Next to Regents Park is Marylebone, once dismissed as not much more than a traffic-clogged main road but now increasingly fashionable. Between Hyde Park and Green Park are the grand Georgian townhouses and terracotta mansion blocks of Mayfair, in complete contrast to the sex shops and trendy apartments of neighbouring Soho. South of Green Park are the stucco mansions and mews of Belgravia. Westminster and Pimlico are attracting new interest as developers move in.

The rich parts of Westminster to the east and south are among the richest in London. It has the fourth lowest unemployment rate of any inner London borough at 5.2%. It's also one of the most cosmopolitan, with nearly a quarter of its population from an ethnic minority and large Afro-Caribbean, Middle Eastern and Jewish communities. But the homes-for-votes scandal a few years ago in which a Conservative-run Westminster Council was accused of carrying out a policy of gerrymandering to move Labour-voting council tenants out of marginal wards drew attention to the sharp contrast between the rich and the poor in the borough.

The downside of living in central London is that it means fighting a constant battle against litter, traffic and crowds. Residents in Soho are demanding action to clamp down on late night noise and clean up the area which they say has become a magnet for drug dealers. The upside is that you're at or near the centre of one of the most exciting cities in the world.

PROPERTIES AND ARCHITECTURE

BELGRAVIA & KNIGHTSBRIDGE

Where the very best (or at least the very richest) live. Almost the whole of Belgravia is owned by the Grosvenor Estate, one of London's biggest landowners. Massive stucco terraces with elaborate columns in Eaton Square. Smaller scale (but still large) stucco houses in Chester Square, choice of Baroness Thatcher among others. Some of the most attractive mews houses in London, many reached through archways, tucked behind the grand houses. No property here is cheap but the shorter the lease, generally the cheaper the property. Embassies have taken over many of the large houses in Belgrave Square. You either love Belgravia for its elegance or hate it for its coldness. A mixture of red brick gabled mansion blocks, early Victorian flat-fronted terraces and mews cottages in equally smart Knightsbridge.

ATTRACTS *The wealthy of all nations, especially Europeans; bankers, stockbrokers; successful entrepeneurs; glitterati* ● **CONSERVATION AREAS** *Belgravia; Grosvenor Gardens; Albert Gate; Royal Parks* ● **AVERAGE PRICES** *Flats: studio £130,000+; 1-bed £300,000+; 2-bed £350,000+ Houses: 2-bed £450,000+; 3-bed £700,000+; 4-bed £1.5million+* ● **AVERAGE RENTS (WEEKLY)** *Flats: studio £240+; 1-bed £350+; 2-bed £450+; 3-bed £800+ Houses: 2-bed £600+; 3-bed £950+; 4 bed £1500+.*

PIMLICO & WESTMINSTER

Not as grand as neighbouring Belgravia. Pimlico used to be run down, its stucco houses divided into bedsits and short let flats. Now much improved as more properties are converted and the developers move in. Mostly flats and much more mixed than Belgravia with council blocks occupying prime river frontage next to Dolphin Square, the soulless but popular modern block where the Princess Royal once had a flat. Westminster and Victoria used to be for working in not living in (most government departments are here as well as a good number of corporate HQs). But developers are busy converting any building they can lay their hands on into luxury apartments. Some beautiful Georgian houses in streets behind Westminster

Abbey and period properties around Vincent Square. Mostly flats in Pimlico.

ATTRACTS *MPs wanting pieds-à-terre; well-off professionals* ● **CONSERVATION AREAS** *Whitehall; Westminster Abbey and Parliament Square; Smith Square; Vincent Square; Medway Street; Dolphin Square; Regency Street; Lillington Gardens* ● **AVERAGE PRICES** *Flats: studio £130,000+; 1-bed £170,000+; 2-bed £210,000+ Houses: 2-bed £385,000; 3-bed £600,000+; 4-bed £850,000+* ● **AVERAGE RENTS (WEEKLY)** *Flats: studio £160-£250; 1-bed £250-£400; 2-bed £350+ Houses: 2-bed £350+; 3-bed £550+; 4-bed £750+.*

MAYFAIR

Internationally known and sought-after area, particularly popular with Americans (the US embassy is here) and previously with oil-rich Arabs. Part-owned by the Grosvenor Estate. Architecturally a complete contrast to Belgravia, with lots of ornate terracotta mansion blocks and red brick mews houses in the area around the Grosvenor Chapel as well as anonymous and expensive apartment blocks. Cottages and smaller houses around the winding villagey streets of Shepherds Market in the south and some attractive mews streets are a relief from the grandeur. Mostly grand and anonymous apartment blocks in St James's. Again, short leases mean cheaper property.

ATTRACTS *UK and international captains of industry, bankers and lawyers; foreign royalty and aristocracy; well-off Americans and Europeans* ● **CONSERVATION AREAS** *Mayfair; Regent Street; Stratford Place; St James's* ● **AVERAGE PRICES** *Flats: studio £100,000+; 1-bed £180,000+; 2-bed £275,000+ Houses: 2-bed £450,000+; 3-bed £600,000+; 4-bed £900,000+* ● **AVERAGE RENTS (WEEKLY)** *Flats: studio £300+; 1-bed £400+; 2-bed £550+ Houses: 2-bed £600+; 3-bed £650+.*

SOHO & COVENT GARDEN

Now becoming seriously trendy places to live, particularly Soho, a favourite haunt of film-makers, designers and artists as well as London's gay and Chinese communities. Some new developments, many from converted office blocks and converted flats in Georgian houses above shops in narrow streets. Houses are rare. Sex shops in Soho are becoming less of a problem than drug-pushers. Slightly more expensive Covent Garden is now well on the tourist beat which takes the edge off it a bit but it is still a lively and attractive place to be. Mainly flats.

ATTRACTS *Affluent young singles; creative types; professionals working in the City or West End wanting pieds-à-terre; Europeans; members of the Asian community; members of the Chinese community* ● **CONSERVATION AREAS** *Soho; Leicester Square; Haymarket* ● **AVERAGE PRICES** *Flats: studio £175,000+; 1-bed £200,000+; 2-bed £250,000+* ● **AVERAGE RENTS (WEEKLY)** *Flats: studio £225+; 1-bed £275+; 2-bed £375-£600.*

MARYLEBONE

Rapidly becoming fashionable after years in the doldrums being dismissed as boring and trafficky. A mixture of red brick mansion blocks, 1930s buildings and modern blocks around Baker Street. Terracotta blocks and tasteful Georgian houses in the 'medical quarter' around Harley Street with mews houses tucked away behind. The most lively part is around Marylebone Village centring on Marylebone High Street. North of the

Marylebone Road is less grand than south, with a large council estate by the Regents Canal. Much of the area is owned by the Howard de Walden and Portman Estates. Prices depend on length of lease.

ATTRACTS *Professionals (lawyers, doctors); people who want to be central; people looking for second homes* • **CONSERVATION AREAS** *Portman Estate; Dorset Square; Regents Park; East Marylebone; Lisson Grove; Cleveland Street* • **AVERAGE PRICES** *Flats: studio £175,000; 1-bed £200,000+; 2-bed £250,000-£300,000 Houses: 2-bed £350,000; 3-bed: £500,000+; 4-bed £750,000* • **AVERAGE RENTS (WEEKLY)** *Flats: studio £275+; 1-bed £450+; 2-bed £450+ Houses: 2-bed £550+; 3-bed £650-£850; 4-bed £850+.*

PADDINGTON & BAYSWATER

Bayswater has traditionally been the poor relation to Kensington, with a slightly scruffy bedsit-land image. Now receiving more attention from people unable to afford Kensington or Notting Hill Gate. Architecturally similar to Kensington with lots of white stucco and grand porches around garden squares contrasting with streets of cottagey mews houses. Paddington also boasts streets of white stucco, some crumbling while others gleam, mixed in among council estates. Lots of the large houses are hotels. Mostly flats with some houses on the Hyde Park estate in Bayswater between Hyde Park and Edgware Road.

ATTRACTS *Middle Eastern buyers (Bayswater); young professionals who want to buy into a regenerating area (Paddington); people who can't afford Kensington or Notting Hill Gate* • **CONSERVATION AREAS** *Bayswater; Westbourne; Aldridge Road and Leamington Villas* • **AVERAGE PRICES** *Flats: studio £120,000+; 1-bed £200,000+; 2-bed £300,000+ Houses: 3-bed £550,000+; 4-bed £800,000+* • **AVERAGE RENTS (WEEKLY)** *Flats: studio £185+; 1-bed £275+; 2-bed £400+ Houses: 2-bed £450+; 3-bed £650-£1200; 4-bed £850+.*

ST JOHN'S WOOD

One of the first villa suburbs in London, it still maintains some of its original *rus in urbe* quality. Roads of large villas with elaborate pointed roofs and crenellated walls to give that lord-of-the-manor feel, enhanced by elaborate gates and CCTV security cameras. Pretty multicoloured three-storey Victorian houses in St John's Wood Terrace and large blocks of luxury apartments around Wellington Road. A wealthy, settled area – some would say smug.

ATTRACTS *Families; well-off professionals; city people wanting an easy journey on the Jubilee Line to Canary Wharf; Americans wanting to be near the American school; members of the Jewish community; members of the Asian community* • **CONSERVATION AREAS** *St John's Wood* • **AVERAGE PRICES** *Flats: studio £145,000+; 1-bed £175,000+; 2-bed £220,000+; 3-bed £350,000+ Houses: 3-bed £500,000+; 4-bed £800,000+* • **AVERAGE RENTS (WEEKLY)** *Flats: studio £200+; 1-bed £265-£400; 2-bed £350; 3-bed £450+ Houses: 3-bed £800+; 4-bed £1200+.*

MAIDA VALE

Always a sought-after area. Some of the best streets overlook the Regents Canal and its houseboat community at Little Venice in the south. Large, early Victorian white stucco houses with canal views in Blomfield Road. Further north, wide streets of red brick Victorian houses, many now converted into flats in roads off Warwick and Sutherland Avenues, where Maida Vale merges into Kilburn. Cheaper and less family-oriented than St John's Wood. Family houses are rare. Lots of large mansion block flats. **ATTRACTS** *Well-off professionals; international buyers* • **CONSERVATION AREAS** *Maida Vale; Paddington Green* • **AVERAGE PRICES** *Flats: studio £145,000+; 1-bed £175,000; 2-bed £220,000+; 3-bed £325,000 Houses: 3-bed £450,000+; 4-bed £500,000+* • **AVERAGE RENTS (WEEKLY)** *Flats: studio £200+; 1-bed £235+; 2-bed £280+; 3-bed £375+.*

WEST KILBURN

Once an area few would have considered but now starting to improve. Still markedly more shabby and run-down than neighbouring Maida Vale, with large crumbling stucco houses reminiscent of Notting Hill in the 1960s. Some pretty two-bed, two-storey Victorian cottages with deep brick porches in roads round Third Avenue in the Queens Park Estate opposite the Mozart council estate. Otherwise long, straight roads of four-storey Victorian terraces in roads off the Harrow Road, many converted into flats. **ATTRACTS** *Members of the Afro-Caribbean community; people who can't afford Maida Vale or North Kensington; workers from the BBC at nearby White City and from nearby hospitals* • **CONSERVATION AREAS** *Queen's Park Estate* • **AVERAGE PRICES** *Flats: studios £95,000; 1-bed £120,000-£130,000; 2-bed £175,000-£200,000 Houses: 2-bed £200,000+; 3-bed £230,000+* • **AVERAGE RENTS (WEEKLY)** *Flats: studio £150+; 1-bed £190+; 2-bed £240+ Houses: 2-bed £275+; 3-bed £300+.*

BEST POSTCODES

No significant postcode differentials – most of Westminster is in one desirable postcode district or another. Overall, SW1 has the edge over neighbouring W1; W9 is better than W10.

AMENITIES

SCHOOLS***

Unspectacular at secondary level where Westminster schools are nearer the bottom than the top of national league tables. Well-off residents don't tend to send their children to Westminster schools. Primary schools do much better. State school performance is partially redeemed by some good private schools. Below-average number of three- and four-year-olds at state-run nurseries although the borough is trying to increase numbers of places and offer free nursery education for all four-year-olds. **PRE-SCHOOL PROVISION** *3 state nurseries; 28 nursery classes in state primary or church schools; 85 private or voluntary nurseries and playgroups. Proportion of under-fives in state nurseries: 42%* • **STATE PRIMARY SCHOOLS** *Overall league table position: 22nd out of 150. Top scorers: St Peter's Eaton Square CE (with nursery unit), Belgravia; St Joseph's RC (with nursery unit), Maida Vale; St Luke's C of E, West Kilburn* • **STATE SECONDARY SCHOOLS** *Overall league table position: 122nd out of 149. Top scorers: St Marylebone (girls), Marylebone; Grey Coat Hospital (girls), Westminster; Westminster City (boys), Westminster* • **PRIVATE PREP SCHOOLS** *Pembridge Hall (girls), Bayswater; Westminster Abbey choir school (boys), Westminster; Westminster Cathedral choir school (boys), Westminster; Westminster Under School (boys), Westminster* • **PRIVATE**

SECONDARY SCHOOLS *Francis Holland (girls), Regents Park; Westminster School (boys, girls in sixth), Westminster.*

TRANSPORT*****

Excellent transport to all parts of the borough, particularly in the south. Some of the most efficient tube lines including the Jubilee and re-vamped Bakerloo run through its residential areas. Also includes four main line stations: Charing Cross, Victoria, Marylebone and Paddington.

TUBES *Central areas tubes all Zone 1. Cost of annual season ticket £636. Belgravia: Victoria (Circle, District, Victoria). Westminster & Pimlico: Westminster (Circle, District, Jubilee); Embankment (Circle, District, Bakerloo, Northern); Pimlico (Victoria). Mayfair: Oxford Circus (Central, Bakerloo and Victoria); Bond Street (Jubilee and Central); Marble Arch (Central); Piccadilly Circus (Piccadilly, Bakerloo). Covent Garden & Soho: Piccadilly Circus; Leicester Square (Piccadilly, Northern); Covent Garden (Piccadilly). Marylebone: Marylebone (Bakerloo); Baker Street (Circle, Metropolitan, Bakerloo and Jubilee). Paddington & Bayswater: Paddington (Circle, District, Hammersmith and City, Bakerloo); Bayswater (Circle and District)* ● **OTHER AREAS** *St John's Wood (Jubilee) Zone 2. Cost of annual season ticket £756. Average journey time to Westminster 8 minutes. Maida Vale (Bakerloo) Zone 2. Average journey time to Oxford Circus 14 minutes. Kilburn Park (Bakerloo) Zone 2. Average journey time to Oxford Circus 18 minutes* ● **BUSES** *Huge choice around the central area. Further out, buses to town include the 36 from Queen's Park to Victoria via Paddington; the 16 via Maida Vale to Victoria; the 13 and the 113 via St John's Wood and Marylebone to Oxford Circus and Charing Cross* ● **TRAFFIC TROUBLESPOTS** *One of the most trafficky boroughs. Knightsbridge: The junction by Knightsbridge tube station where four roads join is usually jammed with traffic and taxis setting people down at Harrods. Also often appalling jams down Park Lane waiting to get on to the Hyde Park Corner roundabout. Westminster: Still slow down the Strand despite extensive traffic smoothing measures. Frequent blocks around Trafalgar Square as traffic attempts to cross lanes. Slow on the confluence of roads around Victoria Station, particularly on Buckingham Palace Road. Marylebone: All along the Marylebone Road as traffic comes off the Westway towards central London* ● **PARKING** *Tricky. Westminster issues 35,973 permits but has only 27,946 parking spaces so be prepared for some frustrating drives around neighbouring roads, although the council is planning an extra 1400 parking bays over the next year. Seven parking zones in Belgravia, either side of the Westway in West Marylebone and Paddington, Maida Vale and St John's Wood, Westminster, Mayfair, East Marylebone and Soho and Covent Garden. There's now residents' parking across 98% of the City of Westminster. Cost of annual resident's permit: £90, only valid for the zone for which it is issued. Season ticket discounts of 90% available for residents in the borough's 21 car parks.*

LEISURE FACILITIES*****

THEATRES & CONCERTS *Theatreland, in the heart of Westminster, has 42 theatres showing everything from musicals to new plays but there are some complaints that the choice of plays is aimed mainly at American tourists. For concerts and music, there's the landmark Royal Albert Hall, home to the Proms among other musical events, the Wigmore Hall, Marylebone, the recently renovated Royal Opera House and English National Opera, as* well as regular concerts in various churches • **CINEMAS** This is cinema heaven. Everything from film premieres in cinemas around Leicester Square to arty (sometimes unwatchable) films at the ICA in Pall Mall • **MUSEUMS & GALLERIES** An excellent variety to choose from. Galleries include the National Gallery, National Portrait Gallery, Tate Britain, Royal Academy and the Wallace Collection. Museums include the London Transport Museum, Madame Tussaud's, the Planetarium and the Museum of Mankind • **SPORTS FACILITIES** Five leisure centres at Victoria, Marylebone, Bayswater, Paddington and West Kilburn. All the centres except West Kilburn are managed by Cannons Health and Fitness. Outdoor sports at Westbourne Green, Paddington and Paddington Recreation Ground, Maida Vale, including well-used tennis courts and cricket pitches. Discount leisure scheme in operation • **LIBRARIES** The best used in London (because they're used by workers as well as residents). Well resourced. Reference libraries at Marylebone and Westminster, archives and local history at Westminster. Good long opening hours with Sunday opening at Charing Cross, Marylebone (adults), Paddington (adults), Pimlico and St John's Wood. 12.67 library visits per head. Place in library-use league table: 1st out of 32 (where 1 is best and 32 worst).

OPEN SPACES * * * *

Contains all or part of some of London's best-known parks including Kensington Gardens, Hyde Park, Green Park, St James's Park and Regent's Park. Green space is urban, formal and elegant rather than wooded or countrified.

PEACEFUL OASES St James's Park (with lakes, islands and views of the roofs of Westminster). Green Park (no flowers, deckchairs in summer) • **CANAL VIEWS** The towpath on the Regents Canal between Little Venice and Regents Park. Colourful houseboats moored at Little Venice and sylvan views of lawns and grand houses by Regents Park. If you're into industrial dereliction, visit Paddington Basin (sandwiched between Paddington Station and the Westway) before it's redeveloped.

SHOPS * * * * *

BELGRAVIA & KNIGHTSBRIDGE Harrods at Knightsbridge boasts it sells everything within reason (if you can face finding it) and is why some people live in the area. Surrounded by designer clothes shops and big Boots. Small smart shops in Elizabeth Street and Motcomb Street, Belgravia. Antique shops in Pimlico Road • **WESTMINSTER** Victoria Street. Mostly chain stores in a dull street of office blocks. Useful for popping out in the lunch hour. Pretty dead in the evening. Sainsbury's • **MAYFAIR** Oxford Street on northern boundary. Possibly the nastiest place in London on a hot summer Saturday afternoon. Crowds of people, exhausting, but the biggest branches of many clothes, record and bookshops are here. Neighbouring Regent Street has Liberty's and more elegant clothes shops. Hatchards (books) and Fortnum and Mason (up-market food) in Piccadilly. Antique shops in South Audley Street • **SOHO & COVENT GARDEN** Small individual shops in Soho including record exchanges, music shops as well as exotic foodshops and delicatessens. Daily fruit and vegetable market in Berwick Street. Chinese supermarkets and other shops in Chinatown. Indulgent rather than useful goods in shops and stalls in Covent Garden market (good for crafts and New Age). Cheap clothes market in Jubilee Hall opposite market. Books, clothes and art materials in Long Acre. Chain stores in the Strand. Tesco Metro in Covent Garden • **MARYLEBONE** Marylebone High Street is called 'villagey' by residents but this is more in spirit than in physical reality. Recently turned fashionable. Long-established bookshop specialising in travel, music shops catering for the nearby music colleges. Waitrose • **PADDINGTON & BAYSWATER** Arab banks, bureaux de change, Halal meat and Lebanese cafés in Edgware Road. Safeway. Paddington has local, transitory shops – luggage, bureaux de change and small sandwich bars. Bayswater has Whiteley's, the original department store, rescued from closure and revamped as a shopping centre with cinemas • **ST JOHN'S WOOD** Victorian High Street, highly prized by residents for designer clothes shops, patisseries and a cluster of pavement cafés which give it a faintly mid-European feel • **MAIDA VALE & WEST KILBURN** Shabby shops in Harrow Road, with lots of cheap second-hand furniture and electrical goods, Halal meat and Afro-Caribbean grocers.

RESTAURANTS * * * * *

BELGRAVIA, KNIGHTSBRIDGE & MAYFAIR Expensive restaurants, some in smart hotels. Some good French, Italian and Middle Eastern places • **SOHO & COVENT GARDEN** Soho's the place for Chinese food in and around China Town, as well as any other type of food you fancy. Attempts to pedestrianise parts of Soho were reversed after complaints from traders and motorists, unfortunately for those who enjoyed the shortlived sensation of eating al fresco without a side order of traffic fumes. Covent Garden has wine bars and brasseries, vegetarian food in Neal's Yard and a good choice of American restaurants • **MARYLEBONE** Lots of new restaurants have opened up, particularly around Marylebone High Street (including a Conran restaurant, sure sign of arrival) and Marylebone Lane. Everything from fish and chips at the Sea Shell (long queues) to Scandinavian • **MAIDA VALE & ST JOHNS WOOD** A good choice of bars, cafés and brasseries with Jewish and French restaurants in St John's Wood High Street.

CRIME RATES *

Position in Metropolitan Police league table: 1st out of 32 (where 1 is worst and 32 best). The figures are distorted by the daily influx of workers and tourists.

THE COUNCIL * * *

POLITICAL AFFILIATION Conservative • **MINUS POINTS** Variable success in tackling what is admittedly a huge litter collection and street-cleaning task • **PLUS POINTS** The lowest council tax in London. Good library service. One of the most energetic boroughs in London at tackling the capital's disgraceful empty property problem with a housing department determined to enforce complex compulsory purchase rules • **PROPERTY SEARCHES CARRIED OUT IN 10 WORKING DAYS** 100% • **STANDARD SEARCH FEE** £100 • **COUNCIL TAX COLLECTED** 93.8%

• **COUNCIL TAX 2000-2001**

BAND	PROPERTY VALUE	CHARGE	BAND	PROPERTY VALUE	CHARGE
A	up to £40,000	£250	E	£88,001-£120,000	£459
B	£40,001-£52,000	£292	F	£120,001-£160,000	£542
C	£52,001-£68,000	£333	G	£160,001-£320,000	£623
D	£68,001-£88,000	£375	H	over £320,000	£750

POSTCODE LIST

W POSTCODES

Oxford Street	W1
Paddington	W2
Acton	W3
Chiswick	W4
Ealing	W5
Hammersmith	W6
Hanwell	W7
Kensington	W8
Maida Vale	W9
North Kensington	W10
Notting Hill	W11
Shepherds Bush	W12
West Ealing	W13
West Kensington	W14

NW POSTCODES

Camden Town	NW1
Cricklewood	NW2
Hampstead	NW3
Hendon	NW4
Kentish Town	NW5
Kilburn	NW6
Mill Hill	NW7
St John's Wood	NW8
Hendon (The Hyde)	NW9
Willesden	NW10
Golders Green	NW11

N POSTCODES

Islington	N1
East Finchley	N2
Finchley (Church End)	N3
Finsbury Park	N4
Highbury	N5
Highgate	N6
Holloway	N7
Hornsey	N8
Lower Edmonton	N9
Muswell Hill	N10
New Southgate	N11
North Finchley	N12
Palmers Green	N13
Southgate	N14
South Tottenham	N15
Stoke Newington	N16
Tottenham	N17
Upper Edmonton	N18
Upper Holloway	N19
Whetstone	N20
Winchmore Hill	N21
Wood Green	N22

POSTCODES

Aldgate	E1
Bethnal Green	E2
Bow & Old Ford	E3
Chingford	E4
Clapton	E5
East Ham	E6
Forest Gate	E7
Hackney	E8
Homerton	E9
Leyton	E10
Leytonstone	E11
Manor Park	E12
Plaistow	E13
Poplar	E14
Stratford	E15

Victoria Docks & N Woolwich	E16
Walthamstow	E17
Woodford	E18

EC POSTCODES

Clerkenwell	EC1
Moorgate	EC2
Fenchurch	EC3
Queen Victoria Street	EC4

WC POSTCODES

Bloomsbury	WC1
Strand	WC2

SW POSTCODES

Victoria	SW1
Brixton	SW2
Chelsea	SW3
Clapham	SW4
Earls Court	SW5
Fulham	SW6
South Kensington	SW7
South Lambeth	SW8
Stockwell	SW9
West Brompton	SW10
Battersea	SW11
Balham	SW12
Barnes	SW13
Mortlake	SW14
Putney	SW15
Streatham	SW16
Tooting	SW17
Wandsworth	SW18
Wimbledon	SW19
West Wimbledon	SW20

SE POSTCODES

Southwark and Bermondsey	SE1
Abbey Wood	SE2
Blackheath	SE3
Brockley	SE4
Camberwell	SE5
Catford	SE6
Charlton	SE7
Deptford	SE8
Eltham	SE9
Greenwich	SE10
Kennington	SE11
Lee	SE12
Lewisham	SE13
New Cross	SE14
Peckham	SE15
Rotherhithe	SE16
Walworth	SE17
Woolwich	SE18
Norwood	SE19
Anerley & Penge	SE20
West Dulwich	SE21
East Dulwich	SE22
Forest Hill	SE23
Herne Hill	SE24
South Norwood	SE25
Sydenham	SE26
West Norwood	SE27
Thamesmead	SE28

USEFUL ADDRESSES

BARKING & DAGENHAM
www.barking-dagenham.gov.uk

CIVIC CENTRE
Dagenham,
Essex RM10 7BN
Tel: 020 8592 4500

BARNET
www.barnet.gov.uk

TOWN HALL
The Burroughs,
London NW4 4BG
Tel: 020 8359 2000

EDUCATIONAL SERVICES
The Old Town Hall,
Friern Barnet Lane,
London N11 3DL
Tel: 020 8359 3326

BEXLEY
www.bexley.gov.uk

BEXLEY CIVIC OFFICES
Broadway,
Bexleyheath
DA6 7LB
Tel: 020 8303 7777

DIRECTORATE OF EDUCATION
AND LEISURE SERVICES
Hill View,
Hill View Drive,
Welling DA16 3RY
Tel: 020 8303 7777

TOURIST INFORMATION
Central Library,
Townley Road,
Bexleyheath,
DA7 5RE
Tel: 020 8301 5151

BRENT
www.brent.gov.uk

BRENT TOWN HALL
Forty Lane,
Wembley,
Middx HA9 9HX
Tel: 020 8937 1234

EDUCATION DEPARTMENT
Chesterfield House,
9 Park Lane,
Wembley,
Middx HA9 7RW
Tel: 020 8937 3110

ONE STOP SHOPS (FOR COUNCIL
INFORMATION) at
Brent Town Hall and in: Wembley;
Harlesden; Kilburn; Willesden
Green and Kingsbury
Tel: 020 8937 1200 to contact any
of the above

BROMLEY
www.bromley.gov.uk

BROMLEY CIVIC CENTRE
Stockwell Close,
Bromley BR1 3UH
Tel: 020 8464 3333

DIRECTOR OF EDUCATION
Bromley Civic Centre,
Stockwell Close,
Bromley BR1 3UH
Tel: 020 8313 4058

CAMDEN
www.camden.gov.uk

TOWN HALL
Judd Street,
London WC1H 9JE
Tel: 020 7860 5974

EDUCATION DEPARTMENT
The Crowndale Centre,
218-220, Eversholt Street,
London NW1 1BD
Tel: 020 7974 1625

CITY OF LONDON
www.cityoflondon.gov.uk

GUILDHALL
London EC2
Tel: 020 7606 3030

CROYDON
www.croydon.gov.uk

LONDON BOROUGH OF
CROYDON
Taberner House,
Park Lane,
Croydon CR9 3JS
Tel: 020 8686 4433

EDUCATION DEPARTMENT,
Room 10/13,
Taberner House,
Park Lane,
Croydon CR9 1TP
Tel: 020 8760 5453

EALING
www.ealing.gov.uk

TOWN HALL
Perceval House,
14-16, Uxbridge Road,
London W5 2HL
Tel: 020 8579 2424

ENFIELD
www.enfield.gov.uk

CIVIC CENTRE
Silver Street,
Enfield,
Middlesex EN1 3XY
Tel: 020 8366 6565

SCHOOLS ADMISSION SERVICE
PO Box 56,
Civic Centre,
Silver Street,
Enfield,
Middlesex EN1 3XQ
Tel: 020 8379 3434

GREENWICH
www.greenwich.gov.uk

TOWN HALL
Wellington Street,
Woolwich,
London SE18 6PW
Tel: 020 8854 8888

SCHOOL ADMISSIONS
Riverside House,
2nd Floor,
Woolwich High Street,
Woolwich, SE18 6DF
Tel: 020 8854 8888

TOURIST INFORMATION CENTRE
Pepys House, Old Royal Naval
College,
Cutty Sark Gardens,
London SE10
Tel: 0870 608 2000

HACKNEY
www.hackney.gov.uk

TOWN HALL
Mare Street,
London E8 1EA
Tel: 020 8356 5000

FIRST STOP SHOP
Town Hall (as above)

SHOREDITCH FIRST STOP SHOP
Shoreditch Library,
Hoxton Street,
London N1
Tel: 020 8356 4350

EDUCATION
Edith Cavell Building,
Enfield Road,
London N1 5AZ
Tel: 020 8356 7401

HAMMERSMITH & FULHAM
www.lbhf.gov.uk

TOWN HALL
King Street,
London W6 9JU
Tel: 020 8748 3020

HAMMERSMITH INFORMATION
CENTRE
Town Hall Foyer,
King Street,
London W6 9JU
Tel: 020 8576 5000

FULHAM INFORMATION CENTRE
Cashiers Office,
Fulham Town Hall,
Fulham Broadway,
London SW6 1ZT
Tel: 020 8576 5218

EDUCATION DEPARTMENT
Cambridge House,
Cambridge Grove,
Hammersmith,
London W6 0LA
Tel: 020 8748 3020

HARINGEY
www.haringey.gov.uk

CIVIC CENTRE
High Road,
Wood Green
London N22 4LE
Tel: 020 8975 9700

EDUCATION OFFICES
48, Station Road,
Wood Green
London N22 4TY
Tel: 020 8862 3876

ONE STOP SHOPS

DUKE HOUSE
Crouch Hall Road,
Hornsey N8 8HE
Tel: 0208489 0000

APEX HOUSE
820, Seven Sisters Road
Tottenham N15 5PQ
Tel: 020 8489 0000

SAFEWAY SHOPPING ARCADE
Unit 2, Safeway Arcade
High Road N22 6BH
Tel: 020 8489 0000

HARROW
www.harrow.gov.uk

CIVIC CENTRE
Station Road,
Harrow,
Middlesex HA1 2UW
Tel: 020 8863 5611

DIRECTOR OF EDUCATION
PO Box 22,
Civic Centre,
Harrow,
Middlesex HA1 2UW
Tel: 020 8420 9614

HAVERING
www.havering.gov.uk

INFORMATION SERVICES
Town Hall
Main Road,
Romford RM1 3BC
Tel: 01708 434343

DIRECTORATE OF EDUCATION
AND COMMUNITY SERVICES
The Broxhill Centre,
Broxhill Road,
Harold Hill,
Romford RM4 1XN
Tel: 01708 434343

HILLINGDON
www.hillingdon.gov.uk

CIVIC CENTRE
High Street,
Uxbridge UB8 1UW
Tel: 01895 250111

HOUNSLOW
www.hounslow.gov.uk

THE CIVIC CENTRE
Lampton Road,
Hounslow TW3 4DN
Tel: 020 8583 2000

EDUCATION ADMISSIONS
DEPARTMENT
The Civic Centre,
Lampton Road,
Hounslow TW3 4DN
Tel: (primary) 020 8583 2653
     (secondary) 020 8583 2649

TOURIST INFORMATION
The Treaty Centre,
High Street,
Hounslow
Tel: 020 8572 8279

ISLINGTON
www.islington.gov.uk

ISLINGTON TOWN HALL
Upper Street,
London N1 2UD
Tel: 020 7527 2000

EDUCATION DEPARTMENT,
Laycock Street
London N1 1TH
Tel: 020 7527 5566

TOURIST INFORMATION
Visitor Information,
44, Duncan Street,
London N1 8BW
Tel: 020 7278 8787

KENSINGTON & CHELSEA
www.rbkc.gov.uk

TOWN HALL
Hornton Street,
London W8 7NX
Tel: 020 7937 5464

COUNCIL OFFICES
37, Pembroke Road,
London W8 6PW
Tel: 020 7937 5464

SCHOOLS ADMISSIONS
Schools Services,
Room GO8/6,
Town Hall,
Hornton Street,
London W8 7NX
Tel: 020 7361 2510

KINGSTON
www.kingston.gov.uk

ROYAL BOROUGH OF KINGSTON
Guildhall,
High Street,
Kingston upon Thames,
Surrey KT1 1EU
Tel: 020 8546 2121

EDUCATION AND LEISURE
SERVICES,
Guildhall,
Kingston upon Thames
Surrey KT1 1EU
Tel: 020 8547 4610

TOURIST INFORMATION CENTRE
Market House,
Market Place,
Kingston upon Thames,
Surrey KT1 1JS
Tel: 020 8547 5592

LAMBETH
www.lambeth.gov.uk

TOWN HALL
Brixton Hill,
London SW2 1RW
Tel: 020 7926 1000

EDUCATION DEPARTMENT,
International House,
Canterbury Crescent,
London SW9 7QE
Tel: 020 7926 9390

LEWISHAM
www.lewisham.gov.uk

LEWISHAM TOWN HALL
Catford Road,
London SE6 4RU
Tel: 020 8314 6000

SCHOOLS ADMISSIONS UNIT,
Laurence House,
1, Catford Road,
London SE6 4RU
Tel: 020 8314 8282

ACCESS POINT (FOR COUNCIL
INFORMATION)
Laurence House,
1, Catford Road,
London SE6 4RU
Tel: 020 8314 6000

BOROUGH INFORMATION
CENTRE
Lewisham Library,
199-201, Lewisham High Street,
London SE13 6LG
Tel: 020 314 6000

MERTON
www.merton.gov.uk

MERTON CIVIC CENTRE
London Road,
Morden,
Surrey SM4 5DX
Tel: 020 8543 2222

NEWHAM
www.newham.gov.uk

TOWN HALL
East Ham,
London E6 2RP
Tel: 020 8430 2000

EDUCATION DEPARTMENT,
Broadway House,
322, High Street,
Stratford,
London E15 1AJ
020 8555 5552

NEWHAM CHILDRENS'
INFORMATION SERVICE
(re nursery & pre-school provision)
Stratford Advice Centre,
107-109, The Grove
London E15 1HP
0800 074 1017

REDBRIDGE
www.redbridge.gov.uk

TOWN HALL,
High Road,
Ilford IG1 1DD
Tel: 020 8478 3020

EDUCATIONAL SERVICES
Lynton House,
255-259, High Road,
Ilford, Essex IG1 1NN
Tel: 020 8478 3020

RICHMOND
www.richmond.gov.uk

CIVIC CENTRE
York Street,
Twickenham TW1 3BZ
Tel: 020 8891 1411

EDUCATION
Regal House,
London Road,
Twickenham TW1 3QB
Tel: 020 8891 7514

CHILDREN'S INFORMATION
SERVICE
Regal House at above address
020 8831 6298

RICHMOND INFORMATION
CENTRE
Old Town Hall,
Whittaker Avenue,
Richmond TW9 1TP
Tel: 020 8940 9125

TWICKENHAM INFORMATION
CENTRE
The Atrium,
Civic Centre,
44, York Street,
Twickenham TW1 3BZ
Tel: 0181 891 7272

SOUTHWARK
www.southwark.gov.uk

TOWN HALL
Peckham Road,
London SE5 8UB
Tel: 020 7525 5000

EDUCATION AND LIFELONG
LEARNING,
John Smith House,
144-152, Walworth Road,
London SE17 1JL
Tel: 020 7525 5050/01

TOURIST INFORMATION CENTRE,
London Bridge,
020 7403 8299

SUTTON
www.sutton.gov.uk

CIVIC OFFICES
St Nicholas Way
Sutton,
Surrey SM1 1EA
Tel: 020 8770 5000

DIRECTOR OF EDUCATION,
The Grove
Carshalton,
Surrey SM5 3AL
Tel: 020 8770 6568

TOWER HAMLETS
www.towerhamlets.gov.uk

CENTRAL SWITCHBOARD
tel: 020 7364 5000

ONE STOP SHOPS

BETHNAL GREEN
255, Cambridge Heath Road,
London E2 0HQ
Tel: 020 7364 3504/23

BOW AND NORTH POPLAR
Gladstone Place,
Bow, E5 5ES
Tel: 020 7364 5970

STEPNEY AND WAPPING
Cheviot House,
227-233, Commercial Road,
London E1 2BU
Tel: 020 7364 2711/2

ISLE OF DOGS AND SOUTH
POPLAR
Jack Dash House,
2, Lawn House Close,
London E14 9YQ
Tel: 020 7364 6111

TOWER HAMLETS INFORMATION
CENTRE
18, Lamb Street,
Spitalfields Market,
London E1 6EA
Tel: 020 7364 4970/1

WALTHAM FOREST
www.lbwf.gov.uk

TOWN HALL
Forest Road,
Walthamstow E17
Tel: 020 8527 5544

EDUCATION DEPARTMENT
Municipal Offices,
High Road,
Leyton E10 5QJ
Tel: 020 8527 5544

CENTRAL LIBRARY INFORMATION
SERVICES,
High Street,
Walthamstow E17
Tel: 020 8520 3017

WALTHAM FOREST DIRECT
Tel: 020 8496 3000

WANDSWORTH
www.wandsworth.gov.uk

TOWN HALL
Wandsworth High Street,
London SW18 2PU
Tel: 020 8871 6000

PUPIL SERVICES SECTION
4th Floor
Town Hall,
Wandsworth High Street,
London SW18 2PU
Tel: 020 8871 7962

WESTMINSTER
www.westminster.gov.uk

WESTMINSTER CITY COUNCIL
City Hall,
64, Victoria Street,
London SW1E 6QP
Tel: 020 7641 6000

EDUCATION OFFICES,
PO Box 240,
Westminster City Hall,
64, Victoria Street,
London SW1E 6QP
Tel: 020 7798 1817

ONE STOP SERVICES,
City Hall,
Victoria Street,
London, SW1
Tel: 020 7641 7777

ONE STOP SERVICES,
91-93 Church Street,
London NW8
Tel: 020 7641 7777

ONE STOP SERVICES,
313 Harrow Road,
London W9
020 7641 7777

INDEX

INDEX

INDEX

INDEX